COMPREHENSIVE CHORAL MUSIC EDUCATION

John B. Hylton

University of Missouri–St. Louis

PRENTICE HALL ENGLEWOOD CLIFFS, NEW JERSEY 07632

Library of Congress Cataloging-in-Publication Data

Hylton, John Baker
Comprehensive choral music education / John Hylton. — 1st ed.
p. cm.
Includes bibliographical references and index.
ISBN 0-13-045287-4
1. Choral singing—Instruction and study. 2. Choral conducting.
I. Title.
MT875.H95 1995
782.5'07—dc20 94-29344
CIP
MN

Acquisitions editor: Bud Therien
Editorial/production supervision, page layout,
and interior design: Jenny Moss
Cover design: Marjory Dressler
Buyer: Robert Anderson
Editorial assistant: Lee Mamunes

Acknowledgments appear on pages 315–316,
which constitute a continuation of the copyright page.

Printed in the United States of America
10 9 8 7 6 5 4 3 2 1

ISBN 0-13-045287-4

Prentice-Hall International (UK) Limited, *London*
Prentice-Hall of Australia Pty. Limited, *Sydney*
Prentice-Hall Canada Inc., *Toronto*
Prentice-Hall Hispanoamericana, S.A., *Mexico*
Prentice-Hall of India Private Limited, *New Delhi*
Prentice-Hall of Japan, Inc., *Tokyo*
Simon & Schuster Asia Pte. Ltd., *Singapore*
Editora Prentice-Hall do Brasil, Ltda., *Rio de Janeiro*

Contents

Preface

There have been many fine books written dealing with choral music and music education. The intent of this particular volume is to provide thorough coverage of the topics typically contained in a choral methods class, and to present these topics in the context of a comprehensive approach to choral music education. It is intended for use by conductors of secondary school, college, church, and community choral ensembles, and by students preparing for a career in choral music.

Several debts of gratitude must be acknowledged. An author brings to the writing of a book the sum of all his or her previous experiences. In this case, the choral conductors under whom I have sung or studied must be recognized. In particular, Charles Matz, Parker Wagnild, and Douglas Miller each offered encouragement and expertise at various points in my career.

In addition, the members of choirs I have directed have all contributed to the experiences that formed the basis for this volume. In particular, my students at the University of Missouri–St. Louis made suggestions for improving the manuscript and provided a setting in which many of the principles and strategies contained in this book could be tested.

Aron Blanke, a student at the University of Missouri–St. Louis, provided technical assistance with some of the illustrations and musical examples. Aron Blanke and Cathy Miller posed for the photographs in Chapter 3, which were taken by Marie Elliott of the University Relations division of the University of Missouri–St. Louis. Special thanks also go to Doris Hylton, choral director at St. Charles (MO) West High School for permitting me to include some of the materials she has created for use in her exemplary choral program.

My appreciation is also expressed to the following publishers who granted permission for the use of musical excerpts and other illustrative materials: the American Choral Directors Association, Associated Music Publishers, Beckenhorst Press, C.P.P. Belwin Music, Boosey and Hawkes, E.C.S. Publishing, Carl Fischer, Inc., Hal Leonard Publishing Corporation, Lawson-Gould Music Publishers, the Music Educators National Conference, C.F. Peters Corporation, Plymouth Music Company, G. Schirmer, Inc., the University of South Florida, and the Wenger Corporation.

Professional colleagues who reviewed this book made many helpful suggestions. The editorial staff at Prentice Hall, in particular Jenny Moss and Anne Lesser, contributed greatly to the clarity, organization, and appearance of the book. Any errors of omission or commission are solely my responsibility.

Finally, I must acknowledge the ongoing encouragement, assistance, and patience of my wife, Doris, without which this book could not have been written.

Introduction

A CAREER IN CHORAL MUSIC EDUCATION

During the twentieth century, choral music education in American schools has grown from modest beginnings into an important part of the curriculum. American music education has developed with a heavy emphasis on performing ensembles. An important model for music education programs, both choral and instrumental, has been the professional ensemble. Thus performance classes are referred to as rehearsals, the teacher as the conductor, and in many other ways the professional conductor and ensemble are emulated. This has resulted in American school choral programs that perform at a level of technical excellence unequaled anywhere in the world.

The adoption of the model of the professional musician has been a mixed blessing, however. There has been a tendency to ignore the educational implications of our rehearsal activities, a sometimes unhealthy emphasis on competition, and a failure to understand the implications of the fact that choral music education occurs in schools, where programs live and die, or expand and contract, according to their educational implications. Choral music education in the schools must be exactly that—choral *music education*—in order to meet the needs of students and to be accepted as a valid component of the curriculum. Music programs in many school districts around the country are currently being considered for possible curtailment or elimination. A compelling educational rationale for music programs is necessary to combat any such threat to the education of children in choral music, as well as the other arts.

If you are reading these words, you are probably pursuing, or at least thinking about a career in choral music teaching. Before considering the prerequisite skills and understandings needed by a choral music educator, reflect on your motivations and goals in choosing this vocation. It would be a useful exercise to write down your personal reasons for considering a career in choral music education and to decide whether they justify the significant expenditure of time, money, and energy required.

Choral music education is exciting, uplifting, challenging, exhilarating, and rewarding. It is also tiring, frustrating, complex, and demanding. Whether or not you will be able to maintain your energy, enthusiasm, and dedication, and avoid burnout, will depend in part on your reasons for pursuing this career.

The most important prerequisite for a choral music educator is a desire to work with and for people. To make choral music, a group of individuals must be led to work together toward a common goal, and in the process brought to an understanding of music, themselves, and their peers. To accomplish this requires a teacher who finds fulfillment in seeing the participants in a choral program grow, personally and musically.

In addition, the prospective choral music educator must aspire to be a fine musician and to make music that is technically and aesthetically pleasing. Choral music education requires knowledge of the broad field of music, as well as more detailed expertise in choral literature, vocal techniques, and rehearsal procedures. Functional keyboard skill, conducting proficiency, and knowledge of music history and theory are other important qualifications.

A third important motivation for a successful choral music educator is a desire to understand how learning takes place and the way choral music experiences must be structured to maximize the musical growth of each participant. In addition, the development of leadership qualities, classroom management strategies, administrative abilities, and organizational skills are important prerequisites for effective and efficient choral work. In the current era of retrenchment and reevaluation in the schools, choral music educators must be solidly grounded in the philosophical bases for choral music education and be able to articulate these ideas in both written and oral communication.

✣ THE PURPOSE OF THIS BOOK ✣

The purpose of this book is to prepare the prospective music educator for a career as a secondary-level choral music teacher. It is also intended for the in-service choral music teacher who desires a review of the basic concepts of comprehensive choral music education.

Comprehensive choral music education is inclusive, in depth, and *educates* the participant through experiences in choral music. This education is not limited to the learning of pitches and rhythms, but occurs through the provision of aesthetic experiences, the refinement of critical thinking skills, and the development of a fuller understanding of self. Comprehensive choral music education is not limited to the teaching of three pieces for competition or twelve selections for the spring concert, but rather seeks to facilitate student development in the areas of music reading, languages, and the historical and stylistic context of music.

Effective comprehensive choral music educators bring a variety of musical and educational skills and understandings to the classroom. A mastery of the fundamentals of vocal technique, a broad understanding of the field of music, an in-depth knowledge of choral literature, a personal concept of choral tone (which should be flexible and vary with the music under consideration), and a repertoire of effective rehearsal techniques are all essential. Comprehensive choral music educators structure the choral curriculum so students develop a logical sequence of musical understandings as they study choral literature. In addition, successful choral music educators are effective administrators, capable of organizing the choral program and working skillfully with students, parents, and administrators.

Of course, reading a text or taking a choral methods course will not, in and of themselves, prepare you for a successful career in choral music education. That preparation is an ongoing, lifelong process. We bring to our first teaching position the sum of all of our previous experiences. All of the ensembles in which we have sung and played, all of the classroom music experiences we may have had, and all of the concerts, recordings, and other music we have listened to are part of our preparation. For successful choral music teachers, this educational process continues for the rest of our professional lives. Both formal and informal in-service education are critical to maintaining teaching competence. The Suggested Reading at the conclusion of each chapter will be a particularly helpful resource, enabling you to acquire additional information on many of the topics introduced in the text.

Continuing education will stimulate your continuous development and change, resulting in increasingly sophisticated musical, intellectual, and emotional development for your students and growth in the performance level of the ensembles you teach and conduct. It is a dynamic and fascinating process.

✣ THE ORGANIZATION OF THIS BOOK ✣

This text describes the skills and understandings necessary to begin a career in choral music education. It is organized into three large sections. Chapters 1, 2, and 3 describe areas critical to the development of a fine performance ensemble: fundamentals of vocal technique, rehearsal methods, and conducting skill. Chapters 4 through 8 discuss music selection, score analysis, style in choral singing, the administration of the choral program, and the organization of specialized ensembles and special events. Chapters 9 and 10 deal with choral music education, the development of comprehensive musicianship, aesthetic education through choral music, and a career in choral music education. The concluding chapter also includes a description of the choral scene in the United States on the verge of the twenty-first century and some ideas about future developments and trends in the field.

Woven throughout the text is the notion of the comprehensive nature of effective choral music education. The idea that choral music education exists to benefit the student participants and to facilitate their emotional, intellectual, and musical growth is particularly evident in our discussion of rehearsal planning, literature selection, and choral curriculum design, and it provides the philosophical foundation for every topic presented.

Comprehensive musicianship is discussed explicitly and in detail in Chapter 9. We present strategies for making a choral music education program comprehensive, and summarize and synthesize references to previous sections of the text.

Chapter One

Building Tone

❖ ❖ ❖

❖ INTRODUCTION ❖

A fundamental attribute of the comprehensive choral music education program is its concern with the individual participant's musical, intellectual, and personal development. A cornerstone of successful choral music education, therefore, is the development of good basic vocal technique in each student.

Thus the choral music educator must possess a clear understanding of the vocal mechanism and strategies that help singers produce a focused, resonant, and tension-free choral sound, capable of a full range of pitch and dynamics. If students learn the fundamental principles for maintaining vocal health through participation in the comprehensive choral music education program, they will benefit for the rest of their lives, whether or not they continue to participate in choral ensembles.

The only vocal instruction most choral students receive comes from their choral music teacher. This is most readily accomplished when the teacher's philosophy and rehearsal techniques emphasize individual vocal development. The building of beautiful ensemble tone begins with the individual. Each participant in the choir must be provided with the skills necessary to sing to the limit of his or her vocal potential, while the tone of each section, as well as the choir as a whole, must be unified, balanced, and blended. There are different schools of thought regarding the nature and relative importance of various attributes of choral tone. In fact, the tone quality of an ensemble *should* vary according to the type of repertoire being studied; however, certain basic ideas on the development of solid individual vocal technique are applicable in most situations.

The material here presents a basic outline of how to develop vocal technique. You are urged to investigate this important area further. The Suggested Reading at the end of the chapter includes several excellent references. The better you understand vocal technique, the better you will be able to musically educate the individuals you teach.

✣ THE VOCAL MECHANISM ✣

Choral classes differ from bands and orchestras in the obvious sense that sounds are produced by the human voice, rather than by instruments. This creates some advantages for the choral music educator. Choral instruction involves a single type of instrument possessed by everyone (which does not need to be purchased and which none of the students forget to bring to rehearsal). In other respects, the development of choral ensembles presents difficulties that are not found in instrumental music education. The vocal mechanism is hidden and closely connected with an individual's personality and self-image. Thus it is a complex task to analyze the technical problems in a person's voice and to suggest appropriate solutions. Of course, the notion of a dichotomy between choral and instrumental musicians is fundamentally false, since many of the basic techniques and principles are identical. Also, choral directors work with instrumentalists and instrumental conductors with singers, in combined works.

Since the objective of good vocal technique is to sing naturally and without undesirable tension, it is not necessary for students to devote an extended period of time to vocal study before having a satisfying choral experience (in contrast to the student who wishes to participate in band or orchestra). This does not mean students enter the choral program prepared to use their natural tension-free voices. The style of singing currently popular with teenagers and the misuse of the voice that often occurs in childhood and early adolescence have made natural, vocally healthful singing relatively uncommon today. Undesirable habits and unhealthy techniques should be eliminated as they are discerned by the choral music educator in the rehearsal.

It is necessary to understand the physical structures involved in vocal production in order to teach a group of individuals to sing with optimal technique. The entire body is the vocal instrument. For optimal performance, a singer should be well rested, appropriately nourished, and in good general health.

Any kind of physical ailment or condition detracts from an individual's vocal capabilities. Some popular adolescent activities, such as yelling or singing outdoors (as at a football game), are injurious to vocal health. Smoking, other use of tobacco, or the abuse of alcohol affects many aspects of an individual's health adversely, including the voice. Psychological concerns, such as anxiety or depression, also exert a negative influence on vocal production. Although certain specific physiological structures are directly involved in the technique of sound production, *any* physical or emotional problem must be corrected in order for one to sing with maximum freedom, flexibility, and secure intonation.

The physiological structures and processes directly involved in the act of singing relate to the vocal processes of phonation, resonation, and breathing. Vocal sound is produced by vibrations, which create sound waves that move through the air, disturbing the molecules in a regular back-and-forth motion. If the frequency of these sound waves is within the range of audibility, they are received and processed in the ear and then the brain of the listener. Vibrations can be produced by many different sources, but if the vibration is periodic, then musical sounds may occur.

When a person sings, the vocal folds and other adjacent small muscles located in the larynx vibrate, creating the sound. Figure 1.1 illustrates the vocal mechanism, including the larynx and the vocal folds.

As the vocal folds come together, sound *(phonation)* occurs. As a singing tone is sustained, the folds rapidly open and close. Changes in the length, tension, and thickness of the vocal folds have an impact on the pitch and timbre of a sound. Individual differences in the size and shape of the various physiological structures involved in singing create the unique timbre and range of each person's voice. In addition to the structures in the laryngeal area, which vibrate to create the vocal sound, the sound resonates in the mouth and throat (pharynx), and, to a lesser extent, in any of the bony structures and cavities of the head.

Within the vocal cavity, the roof of the mouth begins immediately behind the front teeth with the hard palate, which becomes the soft palate further back in the mouth and throat. When a singer is asked to place the tone "forward," it maximizes the resonance created by the hard palate and minimizes the swallowing of tone that can occur when it is muffled by the soft palate. The pharynx (throat) should be kept comfortably relaxed and open during singing, so as to allow maximum resonance. When the soft palate is raised (as it is during inhalation), the sound waves are allowed to resonate freely.

In addition to the *phonation* and *resonation* of vocal sounds, the choral director should be familiar with the breathing mechanism and process. We present some warm-up exercises later in the chapter that help develop correct breathing, but a brief introduction here of what is involved provides the necessary conceptual framework. The correct breathing for singing is the natural way a baby breathes. Sleeping babies do not move their shoulders or chest up and down with each breath. Rather, the belly moves up and down as each breath is taken. Anyone who has cared for infants realizes they have a very natural ability to project the sound of their voices for an extended period of time without fatigue. This is because they produce a sound that is resonant, free from tension, and well supported by air.

Similarly, the correct breathing for singing is referred to as *diaphragmatic-costal* breathing. The diaphragm is a sheet of muscle and cartilage that separates the upper chest and lungs from the abdomen. *Costal* refers to the ribs,

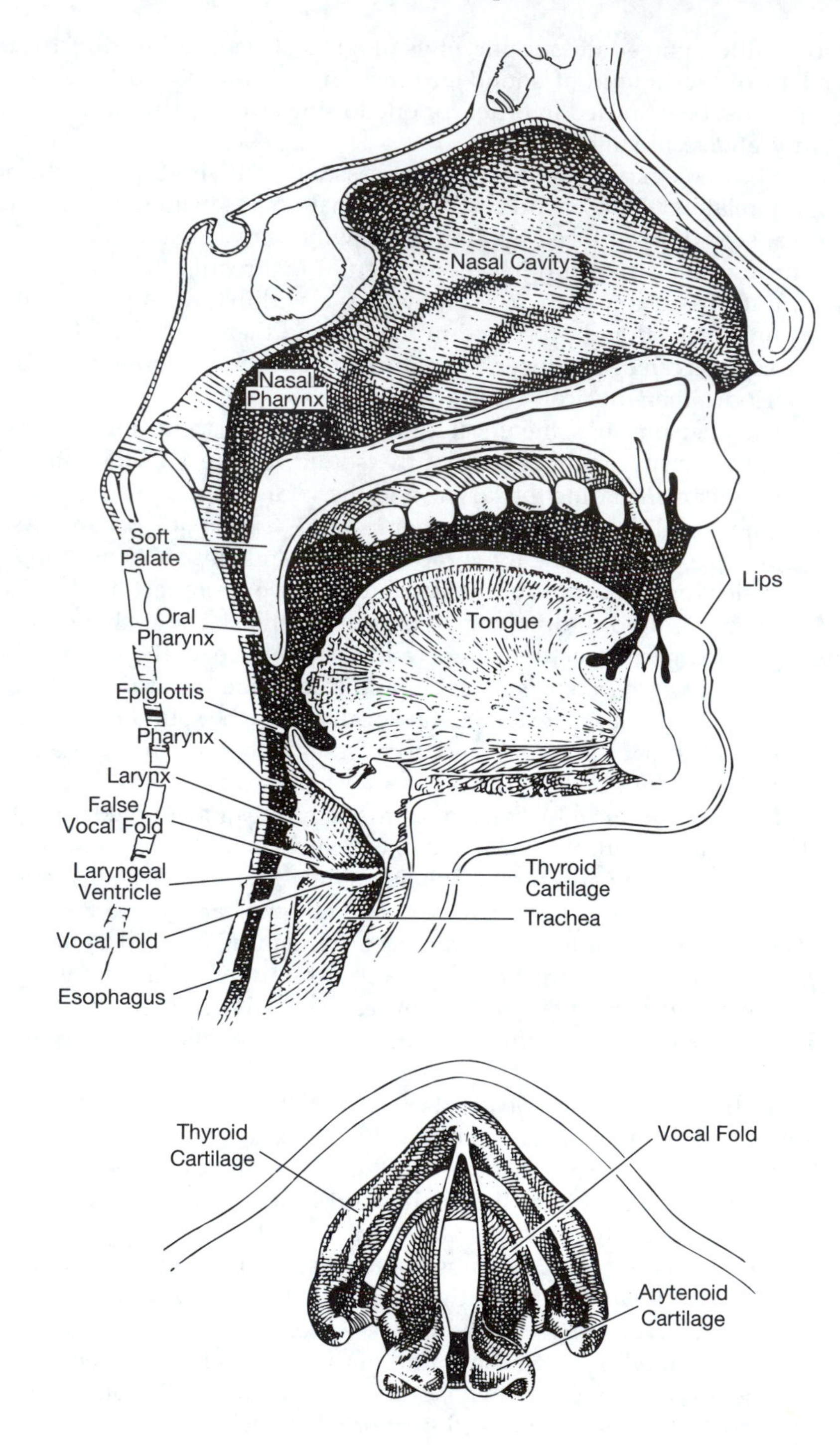

FIGURE 1.1 The Vocal Mechanism

(Adapted from "The Acoustics of the Singing Voice," by Johan Sundberg. Copyright © 1977 by Scientific American, Inc. All rights reserved.)

and in diaphragmatic-costal breathing, as the diaphragm moves downward to accommodate the intake of air, the ribs expand. When the air is taken in correctly and naturally, it moves the diaphragm down and out. This movement is involuntary. Therefore, try giving singers helpful images (e.g., filling a glass with a beverage, blowing up a balloon, panting like a dog to illustrate correct exhalation, etc.) to develop correct breathing before you give them a detailed explanation of the mechanisms involved. Devoting undue attention to the physiology of the process may actually be self-defeating because it focuses students' thinking on an involuntary action and may create unnecessary tension. Any attempt to push the diaphragm down by a voluntary act as part of the breathing process creates unwanted and unnatural vocal tension. The physiological structures involved in breathing are depicted in Figure 1.2.

There are many good texts available that focus on vocal production (see list at the end of the chapter). For a detailed discussion of the way musical sounds are produced and perceived by the listener, see Radocy and Boyle (1988). Miller (1986) contains an accurate and detailed discussion of all aspects of vocal physiology and technique.

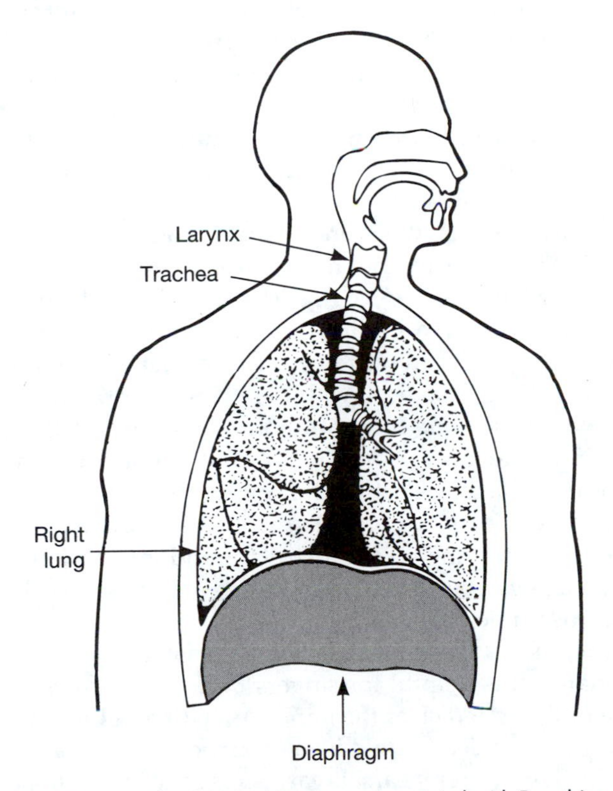

FIGURE 1.2 Physiological Structures Associated with Breathing

(Adapted from *Normal Aspects of Speech, Hearing, and Language,* Fred D. Minifie, Thomas J. Hixon, and Frederick Williams, eds. © 1973 by Prentice Hall. Used by permission.)

✣ WARM-UPS ✣

The place where vocal technique can be developed most readily is during the choral warm-up. Here principles can be demonstrated and potential problems in the music can be isolated and eliminated. Although warm-up exercises should be part of every choral rehearsal, they are particularly important at the beginning of the academic year as a way to instill in the choir the fundamentals of vocal technique.

When a clinician is brought in to conduct a festival or direct an all-state choir (a situation where time is scarce and rehearsals must be conducted efficiently), the majority of these choral experts devote an extended period of time to warm-up exercises. It is during these warm-up exercises that the observer can most readily discern the clinician's philosophy, concept of tone, and other information he or she wishes to convey to the students quickly and efficiently. If the choral expert with limited rehearsal available regards warm-ups as important enough to devote significant time to them, that is compelling support for taking time for warm-ups with your own groups, particularly at the beginning of the year.

Over the course of a semester, certain choral warm-up exercises should be repeated over a period of weeks or months so the choir members are absolutely secure and can focus on developing tone, without worrying about the pitches or rhythms in the exercise. Some warm-ups should be new, or may be related to specific problems in the music to be considered in that day's rehearsal. A specific troublesome passage may be excerpted from a piece and dealt with in warm-ups on a neutral syllable or at a different tempo. When it is encountered in context, students may already have mastered problems in the passage.

Choral warm-ups must be carefully monitored by the conductor. Provide appropriate feedback for the choir as well as questions that help singers evaluate how well they were singing (How did we do on that exercise, choir? Was the tone free and ringing or pinched and tight? What can we do to improve the situation? Did we think the pitch before we sang? Should we concentrate on getting a better breath before we start? Was the soft palate raised? Did we sustain our concentration to the end of the phrase? With some prompting, students are usually able to tell you what they need to do to correct vocal problems). This kind of questioning not only facilitates the development of students' vocal skills, it also stimulates critical thinking. Without careful monitoring by the instructor and interaction with students, warm-up exercises can become a period of meaningless, mechanistic repetition of limited usefulness.

Chorus members arrive at rehearsal in varying degrees of readiness for the work at hand. It is helpful for singers to do some physical exercises to warm up the muscles and clear the mind. As with any kind of choral warm-up, the exercises you select should have a purpose.

One objective of prerehearsal warm-ups is to unify the chorus by encouraging the singers to think as an ensemble. A variety of physical movements can be used to create this sense of unity. Lead the group in echo-clapping the rhythm of some of the music to be rehearsed. Carefully monitor their efforts to ensure they are clapping *as an ensemble.* As they sing a vocal warm-up exercise, ask the singers to walk in place to the steady beat—in the manner the music dictates. Discuss whether their steps should be light and springy or heavy and ponderous, as in the measured movements of a chain gang (appropriate to prepare for certain spirituals). With simple exercises like these, you not only create unity in the group, but also begin to develop a sensitivity to style on the part of the choral singers.

The seven basic areas for individual vocal development are listed here, along with suggested warm-up exercises and techniques to develop each of them.

Correct Standing and Sitting Posture

Singing is a physical phenomenon. Good singing requires a mental conception that precedes physical action, but the act of singing itself requires the coordinated use of a variety of muscles. Therefore, it is worthwhile, particularly in a school setting (where students may have rushed into class from a test, an argument with another student, or from lunch), to include in the choral warm-up some exercises that loosen, relax, and stretch the muscles and to describe (and insist on) good singing posture from the choir members.

Stretching, Loosening, and Relaxing Exercises

1. Raise the hands above the head; wiggle the fingers, the toes, clasp the hands and give the kind of victory sign a wrestler gives after a successful match; lower the hands to the sides and shake them out. Use the muscles of the face to express various emotions: surprise, anger, joy, sadness. Stretch like a cat. Yawn.
2. Roll the shoulders; reverse direction; rotate the head, first in one direction, then in the other.
3. Massage each other's back—use a variety of techniques including a kneading motion, light karate chops, or other ways of loosening up the muscles in the back and shoulders.

Assuming Correct Choral Posture. When standing, singers should place their feet comfortably apart. They should stand erect but not rigidly, chest held high, but without tension in the neck, shoulders, and chest. The chin should not project out and up but the head should be tilted slightly forward so that the chin is slightly tucked. A projecting chin is a good indicator of undesirable vocal tension. The body should be aligned in as straight a manner as possible from the head, through the shoulders, chest, waist, and legs. The top of the head should be as far from the ground as possible. From the shoulders up, the feeling is one of relaxation. The chest should be held high but without tension. If the singer visualizes a puppet suspended on a string attached to the rear of the top of the head, pulling the body erect, correct posture without unwanted tension will be facilitated. The singer should stand on the balls of the feet, with the weight of the body equally distributed. The knees should be flexed from time to time to be certain they are not locked.

Sitting posture involves maintaining the same position from the waist up while sitting in a chair. The chest should still be held high and the feeling of dynamic tension in the abdominal area maintained. Shoulders should be spread to the maximum and not allowed to collapse. Some choral teachers ask their classes to "stand down" rather than sit down, to communicate the idea that from the waist up standing and sitting posture should be identical.

Breath Support

Correct breathing and breath support are essential to good singing tone. Lack of breath support is often the reason for a poor beginning or ending of a phrase, where the sound lacks focus, intensity, and pitch, and for poor intonation generally. Correct breathing and breath support encourages the use of the entire body to support the tone, and discourages the phenomenon of singing "from the neck up" with a throaty, unanchored, unconnected quality.

As we noted, the technical term for the correct type of breathing is *diaphragmatic-costal*. Breathing for singing is a three-step process of inhalation, suspension, and exhalation. A mistake inexperienced singers and speakers sometimes make is to omit the second step and simply inhale and exhale as they speak or sing. This results in a rapid dissipation of the breath. To encourage correct breathing, have the choir inhale, suspend, and then exhale air, to a cadence counted off by the conductor. For example, inhale for four beats, hold the air in the lungs for four beats, and then exhale for sixteen beats. The number of beats used in each of the three steps may vary, but the exercise reminds singers that breathing does, indeed, involve three steps. The exercise should be done with correct standing posture and with the hands on the rib cage, so students get the feeling of expanding the ribs and filling the abdominal area with air. While doing this exercise, the conductor and singers should inhale the air with a sense of expansion as if they are sipping through a straw. As the air is inhaled, they should feel as if they are filling a glass; a glass is filled from the bottom to the top. Conceptualize the filling of the lungs with air this way to facilitate correct breathing. When the air is exhaled, it should be exhaled with an audible but unforced hiss, in a focused stream.

To encourage dynamic tension and breath support, have members of the choir pant like a dog on a hot day. They should feel the movement in the abdomen as each pant is expended. Have students raise their hands over their heads, inhale slowly, and exhale in short spurts, until the air in the lungs is exhausted. Bending forward at the waist and swinging the arms will similarly help to minimize undesirable raising and lowering of the shoulders and chest during breathing, and encourage the low abdominal breathing conducive to good singing.

Use of Falsetto and Head Voice

The cultivation of the falsetto voice for male choral singers is an important way to develop a light and buoyant tone throughout the range. The falsetto voice could be described to singers as the remaining "little boy's voice" possessed by every male singer after the voice change has occurred and for the rest of his life. Actually, the falsetto range is produced when the vocal folds vibrate and come in contact only at the ends. Point out to young male singers that the possession and control of the falsetto range is an advantage enjoyed solely by men and well worth developing. Some popular rock musicians use a well-developed falsetto range as an integral part of their style. This information should help dispel any negative feeling that work on developing the falsetto range is in any way sissy. The use of falsetto not only provides a means of extending range upward for men; it facilitates an even tone quality *throughout* the range.

Downward vocalization is the key to developing ease with the falsetto. The following exercise suggested by Herman (1985) for use with junior high singers is useful with male singers of all ages:

Move pattern downward by half steps.

EXAMPLE 1.1

Herman suggests using a diaphragmatic push on each word. As the pattern is repeated in descending half steps, instruct the men to make the shift from falsetto to full voice as subtly as possible, trying to conceal from the listener the point where the shift occurs. As the vocalization moves into the lower part of the range (C below middle C, etc.), change the syllable used from *ee* to *ah*, and caution the tenors to drop out when the range gets too low for them. Careful monitoring is particularly critical for this exercise, but when the men are reminded to retain the light quality from their falsetto production even as they descend into the lower range, it helps them unify the tone, lighten it, and keep it securely on pitch. When the men have developed a concept of falsetto singing, instruct the women in your ensemble to join them on this exercise, in unison, and to match the tone quality produced by the men. It may be helpful to replace the eighth notes separated by eighth rests with legato quarter notes. The sound that will result from the women approximates that of a boy soprano, and is particularly appropriate for the performance of sacred repertoire from the Renaissance. Both men and women have a tendency to shift gears at various points in their vocal range. One objective of the choral rehearsal should be to develop an automatic transmission, as it were, so the voice can move from the bottom to the top of the range and back again with a minimum of aurally perceptible shifting. Various terms have been applied to the kinds of shifts that occur in voices, including *registers, breaks,* the *lift* in the voice, and other descriptors. These divisions in the range do exist, but they should be negotiated as smoothly as possible.

Men and women both tend to have a point where the voice shifts gears as they move from the sensation of "head voice" to "chest voice." Of course, sound is actually produced by the movements of the vocal folds, but psychologically, the sound may be imagined as coming from various areas of the body. Encourage singers to use the image of the head voice, where the tone is light and free. Downward vocalization (see Example 1.1) that brings the head quality into the lower range will help develop an appropriately uniform quality.

One can observe the result of a failure to develop the head voice, particularly in certain female singers. A female vocalist who has sung tenor in an ensemble for a number of years or one who specializes in certain varieties of pop music will have developed the chest voice to the point where the upper range (which requires the use of head voice) disappears. For such a singer, it may be impossible to restore the lost upper range. Therefore, it is critical that as choir directors we limit the use of altos to supplement the tenor line to sections of music where the tenor line is in the upper part of the range. Also, a female singer should never be permanently assigned to a tenor part in the choir.

Here's another exercise to facilitate the development of uniformity of tone and maximum resonance throughout the range:

Move pattern up or down by half steps.

EXAMPLE 1.2

In this exercise the concept to keep in mind is that in negotiating the octave the jaw should be dropped, the sense of open throat, raised soft palate, and vertical space felt, and the connection between the relaxed vocal apparatus from the neck up to the dynamic tension of the abdomen should be maintained.

Maximum Resonance

Maximum resonance is achieved by having the students think of producing a "forward" tone, using the hard palate as a resonator. In reality, many physiological structures act as resonators, and vibration cannot be directed to any specific area of resonance. When the tone is produced correctly, it will naturally resonate in all available areas. For singers, however, as we already stated, the tone should be conceptualized as forward and projecting. One way to initiate this process is to have the chorus hum the following pattern and move it up in half steps:

Move pattern up or down by half steps.

EXAMPLE 1.3

As the students hum this exercise, have them keep the teeth slightly apart, behind their closed lips. Also, have them place one hand on the bridge of the nose as they hum, and indicate they should be able to feel the buzz of the resonance through the bridge of the nose.

An important point to remember is that a freely resonating and projecting tone will not feel as big to the singer as a tone that is stifled or swallowed, muffled by the soft palate. Such a swallowed tone may sound very big and impressive to the singer, but much less so to the audience. Point out to singers that when a tone is resonating freely and is being projected it will sound somewhat lighter and smaller internally.

The *see-ah* exercise (see Example 1.2) to facilitate evenness through the range can be helpful in this regard. The *ee* vowel promotes forward placement and the *ah* facilitates vertical space in the mouth. Another warm-up exercise that can help to make a tone more resonant is to alternate vowels:

Move pattern up or down by half steps.

EXAMPLE 1.4

The choir should be instructed to think the brighter quality in the *ee* sound and to bring that into the *ah* sound. Be certain that in singing the *ee* sound the choir does not spread the *ee* vowel. A bit of each vowel should be mixed with the other.

Relaxation with Dynamic Tension

The jaw, neck, and throat must feel relaxed, and the abdominal area should feel a sense of dynamic tension. This is an extremely important principle to instill in your vocalists for maximum tone. Each of the two parts of the statement are equally important. There must be a complete feeling of relaxation from the shoulders up in order for a singer to produce a freely ringing tone with secure intonation. At the same time, if the entire body is relaxed, the tone will be lacking in focus and energy. To encourage a feeling of relaxed jaw, neck, and throat, instruct the singers to sing the following pattern:

Move pattern downward in half steps.

EXAMPLE 1.5

As this pattern is sung, the singers should focus on relaxation and place their hands on their cheeks and necks and gently massage the face and throat in a circular pattern. The feeling inside the mouth should be one of total relaxation, yawning, and a completely slack jaw. In moving from note to note, the lower jaw should remain down. The front of the tongue remains anchored against the bottom teeth, while the back of the tongue flips up to produce the *y* sound. Direct students to turn their head from side to side as they vocalize. If they are locked into a position, then the sound will not be tension free.

To encourage the feeling of dynamic tension in the abdomen, singers could place a string, rope, or belt (real or imaginary) around their waists, and feel a sense of dynamic energy in that area. Or simply have students place their hands on their abdomens to feel the same sensation.

Flexibility

When a singer exhibits an inability to sing rapid scalewise or arpeggiated passages, this is usually an indication of some unwanted tension in the voice. Exercises to develop flexibility should be carefully monitored and performed at a rapid pace. A relaxed lower jaw and open throat will help matters. Flexibility is a particular problem as one moves through the changes in vocal register. The objective is to get the voice to operate smoothly, without apparent shifts in quality or production, throughout the range.

Some exercises for the development of flexibility could include the following:

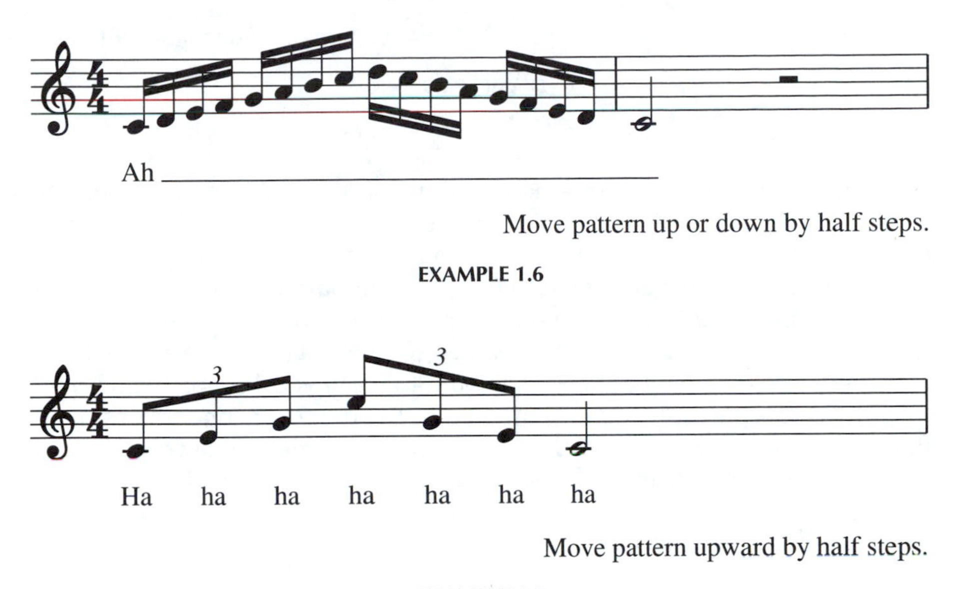

Move pattern up or down by half steps.

EXAMPLE 1.6

Move pattern upward by half steps.

EXAMPLE 1.7

Vowel Unification

Vowel unification and consonant clarity are important aspects of good basic vocal technique. Of course, this also gets into the area of diction, which we examine in more detail shortly. For the moment, we consider the sounds of vowels and consonants in relation to their impact on choral tone.

Vowel unification can be thought of in two senses. First, a singer's production of vowels should not be characterized by obnoxious or startling changes in color and production, and when a choral ensemble sings, there should be agreement on the vowel sound being sung. There are five basic vowel sounds for choral singing: *ee–eh–ah–oh–oo.* Have your choir sing these vowel sounds in succession, using the following patterns:

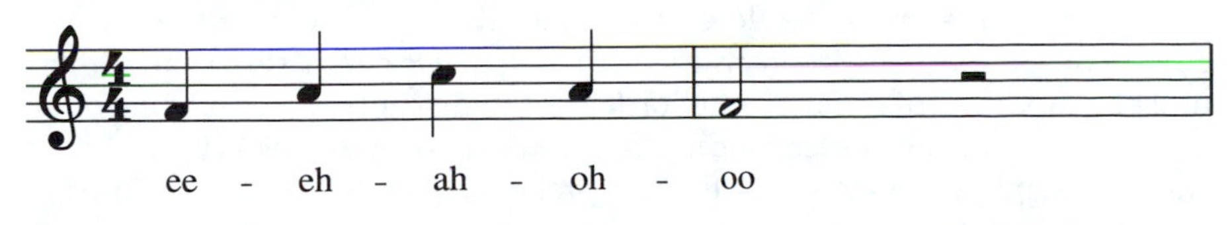

Move pattern up or down by half steps.

EXAMPLE 1.8

Move pattern up or down by half steps.

EXAMPLE 1.9

All of the sounds should be produced without spreading the sound and with a good sense of vertical space inside of the mouth. The lips should never be drawn back or spread. They should be thought of in an *oo* or *aw* position, no matter which vowel sound is produced. To summarize, warm-up exercises should be used to address certain basic aspects of good vocal technique. A few specific exercises have been presented to illustrate these various technical aspects. Warm-ups should be used both to teach vocal fundamentals and to address specific problems encountered in the repertoire under consideration. Warm-up exercises are useful not only at the beginning of rehearsal but they can be helpful during rehearsal to provide a break or to address a problem. The particular warm-up exercises used should be selected for the specific choir and rehearsal situation.

✤ DICTION ✤

In choral music, the text is almost always critically important to the expressive content and basic musical structure of the piece. Diction, in its simplest definition, refers to the correct and uniform pronunciation of the text of a song (or any other text, for that matter). For the meaning of the text to be accurately conveyed to the listener requires clear diction.

In addition to facilitating the understanding of text, diction is an essential component of good vocal production. After all, the choral tone is carried by the vowel sounds of the text. If the vowels are not pronounced correctly and are not shaped to produce a pleasing and uniform quality throughout the vocal range, the tone, intonation, expression, and every other aspect of good choral singing will be affected. Thus attention must be given to the vowel sounds, their relative brightness or darkness, and ways to make them uniform in quality.

Consonants break the flow of the choral tone carried by the vowels. Some consonants, in certain music, can help energize a selection. Others must be modified or minimized in order not to disrupt the vocal line. For all of these reasons, an understanding of diction and how it is achieved by a choral ensemble is essential for the comprehensive choral music educator.

Even when a single vocal line is performed, without polyphonic elaboration, the elongation of the vowel sounds can obscure the meaning of the text. Without clear diction, it is impossible for the listener to understand what the composer intends. If choirs were limited to singing monophonic music, such as Gregorian chant, the problem of diction would be greatly simplified. Although the singing of chant in an accurate style requires the utmost sensitivity to the rise and fall of textual accentuations, its primary purpose is to convey the beauty and mystery of the text; the musical setting is intended to facilitate that purpose.

The problem of good diction becomes more complex in dealing with polyphony. In polyphonic music, the interweaving of independent vocal lines tends to obscure the text. When different syllables or different words are pronounced simultaneously, the intelligibility of each line inevitably suffers. Consider the following excerpt from a Haydn *Missa Brevis:*

5
ten - tem, fa - cto - rem coe - li et ter - ræ,
fa - - - cta sunt, per quem o - mni a -
scen - dit de coe - lis. de -
lu - men de lu - mi - ne, De - im ve - rum de
7
vi - si - bi - li - um o - mni tum, et in vi - si - bi - li -
fa - - cta sunt, per quem o - mni - a fa - cta
scan - dit, de - scen - dit de coe - lis, de cœ - - -
De - - - - - o, de De - - -
9
um.
sunt.
lis.
o.

EXAMPLE 1.10

Four separate lines of text are set simultaneously. Even when the best diction is employed, the intelligibility of the words will be a problem.

Another challenge to good choral diction stems from the fact that choral music is written in a wide range of languages. Although English translations or transliterations may be available for many songs with texts in foreign languages, in a fine piece of choral music the text is closely wedded to the music and may suffer in the translation. If the intention is to perform the piece in a manner as close to the composer's intentions as possible, then the original language will probably be employed. Choral music educators and singers must learn the rules of diction in a variety of languages in order to more fully understand and communicate the meaning of a song.

In each language, there are regional differences in pronunciation, as well as varying rules of pronunciation (e.g., an American "southern drawl" or "midwestern twang" or "German" Latin versus "liturgical" Latin). No matter which language is sung, the aim is to pronounce words in a universally accepted manner, devoid of regional and colloquial mannerisms.

Our discussion is limited to some basic concerns regarding English and Latin diction. Several excellent sources for German, Italian, French, and Spanish diction are included in the Suggested Reading.

Vowels

As we mentioned earlier, vowels carry the sound of a choral piece. Therefore they must be pronounced uniformly in order for a choir to communicate expressively and to sing in tune. A problem with the standard English alphabet of twenty-six letters in terms of teaching pronunciation is that a given letter may imply several different sounds. For example, the letter *a* is pronounced differently in "bat," "base," "aloud," and "farm." An aid to the correct and uniform pronunciation of vowels is the International Phonetic Alphabet (IPA), developed in 1886 by the International Phonetic Association.

In a phonetic alphabet, a particular symbol represents a specific single sound. Thus a phonetic alphabet may be used to communicate the *sound* of a particular letter or combination of letters in any language, and is therefore helpful in communicating the sounds of words in languages unfamiliar to the choral music educator or singer.

The sounds of English vowels in the IPA are as follows:

IPA Symbol	*Letter*	*English Word*
[i]	e	s*ee*k
[I]	i	s*i*t
[ei]	a	pl*a*y
[ɛ]	e	g*e*t
[æ]	a	s*a*t
[a]	a	f*a*ther

[u]	oo	l*oo*t
[ʊ]	oo	t*oo*k
[o]	o	l*o*ad
[ɔ]	a	l*a*w
[a]	a	*a*h
[ʌ]	u	c*u*p
[ə] (schwa)	u	pizz*a*
[ɝ] (stressed, with r)	er	h*er*d
[ɚ] (unstressed, with r)	er	batt*er*

Diphthongs

[ei]	a	m*a*te
[ou]	o	c*oa*t
[ai]	i	k*i*te
[au]	ow	c*ou*ch
[ɔi]	oy	t*oy*
[ju]	u	f*u*se

Vowel sounds vary in their natural color from bright to dark:

Bright ————————————→ Dark

ee *eh* *ah* *oh* *oo*

In choral singing, the usual objective is to pronounce the vowels clearly, but to minimize changes in vocal production and color as a choir moves from one vowel to another within a particular vocal line. A few basic points concerning the position and placement of the five pure vowels are indicated here.

EE. Although the jaw is higher for the *ee* vowel than for any other, it is essential for the singer to keep as much vertical space as possible in the mouth when producing this vowel, without tensing or clenching the jaw. The lips should be relaxed, rounded, and the corners of the mouth should not be allowed to draw back and spread into the "mailbox mouth" position in which the *ee* vowel is produced with the corners of the mouth drawn back, with minimal vertical space, maximum horizontal spread, and an unattractively bright quality. It may be helpful to have students gently place their hands on their cheekbones and massage downward as they sing this vowel, to prevent tension in the jaw. The front of the tongue is against the back of the bottom front teeth, although the back of the tongue will tend to be slightly raised. The soft palate should be raised.

EH. The *eh* sound is easier to produce with a comfortably relaxed lower jaw than the *ee*. The most important problem for singers in producing a pure *eh* sound is to avoid producing a broad diphthong. The corners of the mouth may be somewhat more relaxed than in producing the *ee* sound. The front of the tongue remains against the back of the bottom front teeth, and the back of the tongue will naturally assume a somewhat lower position than when singing the *ee* vowel.

AH. The *ah* vowel is the easiest to produce in a relaxed and free manner. The lower jaw should be comfortably low, so as not to change the sound to *uh*. The tongue is low, and the lips are rounded and relaxed.

OH. The *oh* sound is relatively easy to produce correctly. In order to prevent the sound from becoming too dark or covered, ask the singer to think a little *ah* as the *oh* sound is produced. Although the lips should be rounded, the opening should be relatively large, and the lips should be forward, away from the teeth. The tip of the tongue remains anchored against the bottom front teeth, and the tone should be conceptualized as forward in the mouth.

OO. The *oo* sound is the darkest of the five basic vowels. To make the *oo* sound line up with the other vowels, instruct students to think an *ah* (as they did for the *oh* sound) and to simply form the lips in an *oo* position. As was the case with the *oh* sound, the lips should be forward, away from the teeth.

Although the five sounds mentioned here are of primary importance, there are two other pure vowel sounds that require special attention. The first is *uh*, as in "much" or "gun." There are instances where the letter *a* carries the *uh* sound, such as in "*a*lone" or "*a*wake." In these instances, it should not be modified to an *ah* sound. The production of the sound is almost identical, except the back of the tongue is slightly higher.

The other vowel sound that occurs frequently in English is *ih* as in "fit," or "still." The tongue is slightly higher than when pronouncing an *ee* sound but in other respects the production is quite similar. The *ih* sound should be employed in words that call for it, rather than modifying the vowel to an *ee*, which sounds affected and unnatural.

To attain uniformity of vowel sound, the choral music educator must listen carefully to the sounds that are actually being produced by the ensemble. Based on the relative brightness or darkness of the sound being produced, the director can then make suggestions for modifying the sound to attain uniformity and blend. As a choir sings a line, it is usually necessary to make some adjustments to the vowels being sung so that they move smoothly from one to the next, carrying forward rather than disrupting the flow of the phrase.

No matter what vowel is being produced, there should always be a sense of vertical space in the mouth. This is created by raising the soft palate, relaxing the lower jaw, and keeping the tongue low, with the front of the tongue resting against the back of the gum ridge beneath the lower front teeth.

The degree to which the mouth is opened for normal conversation is inadequate for singing. If a choir is asked to "open up the mouth" they will usually respond by pushing down the lower jaw and creating tension. Rather than asking them to open their mouths, a choir will respond better to a request for "more vertical space" or "a feeling of yawning" or "a dropped jaw."

It is revealing to ask an inexperienced choir to sing a vocalise, and then to observe the various degrees to which singers' mouths are open. Some individual's lips will hardly be parted, while others will attempt to push the lower jaw down, creating undesirable tension. Only after repeated exercises will the singer begin to understand the correct degree to which the mouth should be opened, the correct tongue position, and the raising of the soft palate.

Ah is the most natural vowel to sing with the correct mouth position. It may be helpful to ask the choir to take the breath in with an expression of surprise—*Ah*—which will have the effect of opening the mouth to the appropriate degree and raising the soft palate, without tension. After inhalation and suspension, have the choir sing the vowel *ah.*

In singing the other four pure vowels (*ee, eh, oh,* and *oo*), although there will necessarily be some slight shifting of the lower jaw's position, it should be kept as close as possible to the relaxed and low position it was in for the *ah.* As we mentioned previously, Examples 1.8 and 1.9 can help develop uniformity of vowel sounds.

The two pure sounds that are most problematic for choirs are *ee* and *eh.* The production of the *ee* sound requires the placement of the jaw in a somewhat higher position than for any other of the vowels; nevertheless, the choir should be asked to think of maximum vertical space inside the mouth in singing *ee,* with the corners of the mouth pulled in to avoid spreading the sound, and making it startlingly different in color than the other darker vowels.

The primary problem with the pure vowel *eh* is the tendency of inexperienced choirs to produce a bright diphthong—[*eh-ee*]—rather than the pure vowel. Diphthongs and triphthongs are vowel combinations and are discussed in the following section.

Any vowel can be modified and colored in a variety of ways. Young and inexperienced choirs may tend to sing with an unfocused, shallow tone. Older singers often tend to produce sounds that are overly dark and heavy. Adjusting a vowel to make it brighter or darker can improve intonation and tone quality. For example, adding some feeling of *ah* to an *ee* sound can darken and smooth a vowel that tends to be overly bright. Adding some feeling of *ah* to an *oh* sound can brighten it to an Italianate vowel, which is often desirable.

Choral music conveys emotion. Simply focusing the attention of singers on the particular emotion conveyed by a word will alter the color of the vowel. Words like "cold," "love," or "alone" can be made much more expressive through the modification of the color of the vowels.

Diphthongs and Triphthongs

A diphthong is a combination of two vowel sounds; a triphthong is a combination of three. For example, consider the word "might." Although the word contains only one vowel, it contains two sounds—*ah* and *ee*. In choral singing, the first sound should be sustained and the second added at the last instant before moving to the next word. Any disagreement in a choir about when to move from the first to the second sound in the diphthong or triphthong will result in a lack of intelligibility and poor blend. Even though the sound may technically be in tune, it will sound as if it is not.

In dealing with a triphthong, again the first vowel sound in the combination should be sustained and the second and third sounds added at the last instant. Triphthongs are considerably rarer than diphthongs. An example is the word "fire". The vowel combination consists of three separate pure vowels: *ah, ee,* and *uh*. The *ah* sound is sustained until the last instant, at which point the *ee* and *uh* are sung.

Consonants

Although vowels receive a greater proportion of the choral music educator's attention than consonants, the latter are also very important to good choral singing. There are four categories of consonants. The way in which consonants are sung depends on the category to which they belong and the type of articulation desired (detached or connected).

The four categories of consonants are as follows:

1. Pitched consonants: *m, l, n, ng, r, th* (as in "*th*ee"), *v, z*
2. Explosives: *b, d, g, k, p, t*
3. Sibilants: *f, s, sh, ch, th* (as in "wi*th*")
4. Aspirate: *h*

Consonants can help to energize choral singing, or in some cases they can completely disrupt a vocal line. The pitched consonants are sung on the same pitch as the vowel that precedes or follows them. They should generally be sung quickly, although occasionally the prolonging of a pitched consonant at the end of a word or phrase can produce an interesting special effect. The two pitched consonants that are the most potentially disruptive are *r* and *l*, when they occur at the end of a syllable or word, following a vowel. In this case they must be minimized or eliminated to preserve the line and to avoid a very unattractive and obnoxious sound. Consider the phrase, "Corn grew, where the corn was spilled." These are the opening words of "No Mark," a choral setting by Cecil Effinger of a poem by Thomas Hornsby Ferrill. An excerpt is found in Example 3.10 on page 117. The *r* sounds in "corn," "where," and the repetition of "corn" must be flipped or rolled to minimize the unattractive American voiced *r*. In the word "spilled" the vowel should be prolonged and the *l* sound should be attached to the final *d* and not voiced until the last moment: "spi - - - - lld." Consider the word "dearest." In singing this word, the *r* must be placed at the beginning of the second syllable, not the end of the first: "dea-rest," rather than "dear-est." The *r* should again be flipped or rolled to minimize the unattractive American voiced *r* sound.

In some cases an *r* or *l* may be attached to the next syllable or word. Consider the phrase "When peace like a river attendeth my way." The *r* at the beginning of the word "river" should be flipped or rolled; the one at the end should be attached to the following word, "attendeth."

Generally, to attain legato articulation, the final consonants of words may be attached to the following word, as long as the meaning of the text is not distorted. Some ludicrous-sounding phrases can result from attaching final consonants to the following word, in cases such as "cease not" or "the wondrous cross I'd bear."

The explosive consonants should be sounded prior to the beat at the beginnings of words, so the vowel, which carries the musical sound, occurs on the beat. This is a fairly difficult concept to instill in American singers, but when it is accomplished, the vocal line becomes wonderfully energized. When an explosive consonant is sounded on the beat, the ensemble sounds late on entrances, even when they are singing the consonant together.

The aspirate *h* sound is produced simply by expelling air from the lungs through the mouth. The *h* can be helpful in eliminating a glottal, pushed attack, when it is attached to the beginning of a phrase.

Latin Diction

Of all of the languages, Latin presents the least number of problems in terms of clear diction. Some basic rules for Latin diction are presented here. There are various systems of Latin pronunciation. The system described here is liturgical Latin.

In working with a choral ensemble in any language (including English), remind singers that uniform pronunciation is critical to successful singing. Therefore, singers must learn the pronunciation presented by the choral music educator, even if it differs from their recollection of some previous experience in the language. Unless everyone is pronouncing the text in the same manner, the music will never be blended, in tune, rhythmically alive, or intelligible. This means the music teacher must be secure in his or her knowledge of the correct diction. If the choir is singing the wrong pronunciations in perfect unity, the fault obviously lies with the director.

In Latin, there are only five vowel sounds:

Vowel	*Sound*	*IPA*
A	ah	(a)
E	eh	(ɛ)

I or Y	ee	(i)
O	oh	(ɔ)
U	ooh	(u)

A basic challenge of Latin vowels is that singers whose native language is English sound diphthongs where none exist. Inappropriate pronunciations derived from the English language occur in other instances as well. For example, the little word "in" occurs in Latin and in English, and students instinctively tend to give the English pronunciation ("ihn") in place of the Latin ("een"). Combinations of Latin vowels do not usually comprise diphthongs: *ae* and *oe* are pronounced *eh* (the first letter of the combination is silent and the second is pronounced). In the cases of *ei, eo, eu, ou,* and *ui,* each vowel is pronounced separately. The only Latin diphthongs are *au* and *ua* (as in the words "laudate" and "quam").

Unlike the vowel sounds, consonant sounds in Latin can change according to the context. Consonants that are not included in the following list are pronounced in the same manner as in English:

C: When it precedes *e, i, y, ae,* and *oe,* or when there is a double *c* (e.g., "ecce") it is pronounced as the *ch* in "much" (e.g., "coeli"). Otherwise, *c* is pronounced as a *k* (e.g., "fac").

G: When it precedes *e, i, y, ae,* or *oe,* it is pronounced as the *g* in "gem." In all other cases, except when followed by *n* it receives a hard *g* sound as in "go" (e.g., "gloria").

GN: In the middle of a word (e.g., "agnus") the *gn* combination is pronounced *ni,* like the English "reunion."

H: The *h* sound in Latin is silent, other than in words like "mihi" and "nihil," in which it has a *k* sound.

J: J is pronounced *y* as in "yellow" (e.g., "adjutorum").

R: The *r* should always be flipped or rolled.

SC: *Sc* is pronounced as the *sh* in the English word "ship," before *e, i, y, ae, oe,* and *eu* (e.g., "suscipe"). Otherwise, it is pronounced *sk* (e.g., "schola").

T: *T* is always pronounced as the *t* in "time," even when followed by *h* (e.b., "Sabaoth"), aside from the following exception.

TI: *Ti* is pronounced as *tsee* when followed by a vowel (e.g., "generationes"), and preceded by any letter other than *s, t,* or *x,* in which case it is pronounced as in English.

X: When preceded by an *e* and followed by a vowel, it is pronounced *egs* (e. g., "exultent"). Otherwise, it is pronounced *ek* (e.g., "excelsis").

Z: Z is always pronounced *dz* (e.g., "Lazaro").

✣ COLLECTIVE CHORAL TONE ✣

There have been many different schools of thought regarding the development of choral tone over the last century in the United States. Each had its own view of the relative importance of the various elements of good choral singing, resulting in a distinctive and readily recognizable sound associated with each school. Four such schools of choral singing are briefly described here. In Chapter 9, we present more details concerning the historical development of American choral music. The point to remember here is that the development of collective choral tone has been approached in a variety of ways. For a lengthier (and excellent) discussion of twentieth-century schools of choral singing, consult the chapter by Swan, in Decker and Herford (1988).

A distinctive choral sound results from the relative importance attached by a conductor to each of the various basic elements of music that influence choral tone, which include the following:

Balance and blend
Rhythmic integrity
Diction
Vocal freedom
Choice of choral literature

The first school of choral singing to exert a profound and widespread influence on American choral music education was the a cappella tradition of F. Melius Christiansen and the St. Olaf College Choir. The emphasis of the St. Olaf "a cappella" tradition was a perfectly blended, controlled, and balanced sound, with each individual submerging his or her individual voice into the collective sound.

Another important school of choral singing that grew out of the a cappella tradition in the 1920s was that of the Westminster College Choir, founded by John Finley Williamson. The ideal sound of the Westminster College Choir was a more soloistic and colorful tone than that of the St. Olaf model. The vocal development of each individual in the ensemble was an important emphasis of the Westminster Choir, resulting in a "choir of soloists." Clearly, the tonal ideal of Williamson was quite distinct from that of Christiansen.

Another important contributor to twentieth-century American choral music was Fred Waring and his Glee Club. As the name implies, Waring's ensemble performed popular music. Although he sought to convey a collegiate image with his group, it was a professional ensemble. Waring's emphasis was on diction and on detailed analysis of the vowels and consonants in each syllable of every word sung. Voiced consonants were often sustained in a distinctive style. Waring's emphasis on diction resulted in part from the fact that his ensemble performed regularly on the radio and was subject to the limitations of the sound transmission equipment in use at the time.

Robert Shaw was discovered by Fred Waring as a student at Pomona College and became the director of the Waring Glee Club. In the 1940s, Shaw created his own ensemble, the Robert Shaw Chorale. Shaw believes the sound of a particular piece of music should reflect the composer, style, and period in which it was composed. Thus for him there is no particular all-purpose sound. For Shaw, rhythmic integrity is critical to making music come alive, and each piece should sound as the composer intended it to sound.

The four men just mentioned provide examples of divergent viewpoints concerning choral tone. There have been many other important choral conductors in the twentieth century whose choirs have been significant influences on American choral singing.

Collective Choral Tone in Comprehensive Choral Music Education

Growing out of the individual choir member's vocal technique is the collective tone of the ensemble. Choral tone, in the collective sense, consists of the combination of various musical elements and the relative importance attached to each by the choral music educator.

Each choral music educator must determine his or her own individual concept of good choral tone and strive for the development of that tone in the choral ensemble. This tonal ideal should always be compatible with the *individual* concepts of good vocal technique instilled in the students as an ongoing aspect of rehearsal.

How do you develop a personal tonal concept? Your concept of excellent choral tone will evolve as you listen to a variety of choirs and think about the choirs in which you have sung or that you may have conducted. Your concept of choral tone will not be static, but will change as your experiences and insights in choral music broaden and deepen.

A well-educated choir's tone will vary according to the style of the music it performs. More will be said concerning this matter in Chapter 6, but the tone quality that is aesthetically desirable for a Renaissance motet will vary considerably from what is appropriate for a Brahms choral lied. Today, the notion of a unitary concept of choral tone (such as that of the St. Olaf or Westminster schools of fifty or sixty years ago) has been replaced by the idea of variability of tone quality according to the repertoire being performed.

✣ SUMMARY ✣

This chapter covered the development of individual vocal technique in the comprehensive choral rehearsal. The role of the choral director as voice instructor has not been universally accepted through the years, by studio voice teachers or by the choral directors themselves. Among the reasons for this has been the perception that choral conductors do not always hold the interests of the individual vocalist in high regard—that they will modify the individual singer's vocal technique in undesirable ways to attain their concept of collective choral tone. Also, choral conductors have not always possessed the necessary background to do a competent job of vocal teaching in the choral rehearsal. Finally, some choral conductors have simply felt the demands of rehearsing the repertoire under consideration are so large that there isn't time to devote to the development of individual vocal technique.

The central point of this text is that choral conductors are comprehensive music educators, and the objectives of choral music education are not limited to the polishing of the next performance or to the rote teaching of repertoire. When viewed in this context, it becomes clear that the encouragement of good individual vocal technique is essential to the development of the comprehensively educated choral ensemble.

The development of a pleasing tone quality, both individually and collectively, is one of the most important aspects of the choral music educator's task. To be an effective choral music educator, the teacher must have the knowledge and skills of a voice teacher and be able to apply them in the choral rehearsal setting. It also requires a preconceived concept of choral sound on the part of the choral music educator, providing a tonal objective for the rehearsal.

The development of good basic vocal technique in each student is a fundamental aspect of comprehensive choral music education. When each choir member understands his or her own vocal instrument, the development of fine ensemble tone is facilitated.

The physiological structures directly associated with singing are involved in the processes of phonation, resonation, and breathing. Posture, breathing and breath support, development of head voice and falsetto, the cultivation of maximum resonance, flexibility, and vowel unification are important aspects of vocal technique that should be developed in rehearsal. In addition, relaxation from the chest up with a feeling of dynamic tension around the abdomen aids the production of vital, focused, free sound. Vocal technique is developed most readily during warm-ups.

Clear diction, the correct and uniform pronunciation of the text, is an important attribute of fine choral singing. In addition to facilitating the understanding of a song's meaning, diction is an essential component of good vocal production.

As choral singing in the United States has developed during the twentieth century, various schools of thought regarding the nature of pleasing choral tone have influenced choral music educators. More recently, unitary concepts of choral tone have been replaced by the ideas of varying the tone quality of an ensemble depending on the repertoire being considered.

Questions

1. Why is individual student vocal development part of the choral music educator's responsibility, even in a group setting?

2. In what respects is it more difficult to develop the voice than it is to attain proficiency on a band or orchestral instrument?
3. What happens when phonation occurs?
4. What is diaphragmatic-costal breathing? Is the action of the diaphragm voluntary or involuntary? What is the significance of this for the choral music educator?
5. Name three images that would be helpful in teaching students to breathe correctly.
6. Reflect on your own experiences in choral singing. Were they helpful or problematic in your vocal development?
7. What are the basic areas of vocal technique that we seek to develop in our choral singers?
8. What are the three steps in the process of breathing for singing?
9. Should the falsetto range be developed or discouraged in adolescent males?
10. Create your own warm-up exercises related to each of the basic areas of vocal technique described in this chapter.

Suggested Reading

ALDERSON, RICHARD. *Complete Handbook of Voice Training.* West Nyack, NY: Parker, 1979.

APPELMAN, RALPH. *The Science of Vocal Pedagogy.* Bloomington: Indiana University Press, 1986.

ARMSTRONG, KERCHAL, AND DONALD HUSTAD. *Choral Musicianship and Voice Training: An Introduction.* Carol Stream, IL: Somerset Press, 1986.

BEATTY, CHRISTOPHER. *Vocal Performance.* Nashville: Star Song, 1992.

BERNAC, PIERRE. *The Interpretation of French Song.* New York: Praeger, 1970.

BOONE, DANIEL R. *The Voice and Voice Therapy* (3rd ed.). Englewood Cliffs, NJ: Prentice-Hall, 1983.

BRODNITZ, FRIEDRICH. *Keep Your Voice Healthy* (2nd ed.). Waltham, MA: College Hill Press, 1987.

BURGIN, JOHN CARROLL. *Teaching Singing.* Metuchen, NJ: Scarecrow Press, 1973.

CHRISTY, VAN A. *Expressive Singing.* Dubuque, IA: William C. Brown, 1961.

COLORNI, EVELYN. *Singers' Italian.* New York: Schirmer, 1970.

COX, RICHARD. *The Singer's Manual of German and French Diction.* New York: Schirmer, 1970.

CRAIG, DAVID. *On Singing Onstage.* New York: Schirmer, 1978.

DALBOR, JOHN B. *Spanish Pronunciation: Theory and Practice.* New York: Holt, Rinehart and Winston, 1980.

DECKER, HAROLD, AND JULIUS HERFORD. *Choral Conducting Symposium* (2nd ed.). Englewood Cliffs, NJ: Prentice Hall, 1988.

EHMANN, WILHELM, AND FRAUKE HAASEMANN. *Voice Building for Choirs.* Chapel Hill, NC: Hinshaw, 1982.

GRUBB, THOMAS. *Singing in French.* New York: Schirmer, 1979.

HALL, WILLIAM. *Latin Pronunciation According to Roman Usage.* Santa Ana, CA: National, 1971.

HAMMER, RUSSELL. *Singing: An Extension of Speech.* Metuchen, NJ: Scarecrow Press, 1978.

HENDERSON, LARRA BROWNING. *How to Train Singers* (2nd ed.). West Nyack, NY: Parker, 1991.

HERMAN, SALLY. *Building a Pyramid of Musicianship.* Minneapolis: Curtis, 1985.

HOGBEN, LANCELOT. *The Mother Tongue.* New York: Norton, 1965.

INTERNATIONAL PHONETIC ASSOCIATION. *The Principles of the International Phonetic Association.* London: University College, 1961.

JEFFERS, RON. *Translations and Annotations of Choral Repertoire.* Vol. I, *Sacred Latin Texts.* Corvallis, OR: Earthsongs, 1988.

KENNEY, JAMES. *Becoming a Singing Performer: A Text for Voice Class.* Dubuque, IA: William C. Brown, 1984.

KLEIN, JOSEPH. *Singing Technique: How to Avoid Trouble.* Princeton, NJ: D. Van Nostrand, 1967.

LINDSLEY, CHARLES E. *Fundamentals of Singing for Voice Classes.* Belmont, CA: Wadsworth, 1985.

MARSHALL, MADLEINE. *The Singer's Manual of English Diction.* New York: Schirmer, 1953.

MILLER, KENNETH E. *Principles of Singing.* Englewood Cliffs, NJ: Prentice-Hall, 1983.

MILLER, RICHARD. *The Structure of Singing.* New York: Schirmer, 1986.

MORIARTY, JOHN. *Diction.* Boston: E. C. Schirmer, 1975.

MOULTON, WILLIAM G. *The Sounds of German and English.* Chicago: University of Chicago Press, 1962.

ODOM, WILLIAM. *German for Singers.* New York: Schirmer, 1981.

RADOCY, RUDOLPH E., AND J. DAVID BOYLE, *Psychological Foundations of Musical Behavior* (2nd ed.). Springfield, IL: Charles C. Thomas, 1988.

REID, CORNELIUS. *The Free Voice: A Guide to Natural Singing.* New York: Colman-Ross, 1965.

———. *Voice: Psyche and Soma.* New York: Joseph Patelson Music House, 1975.

SCHMIDT, JAN. *Basics of Singing* (2nd ed.). New York: Schirmer, 1989.

SHEIL, RICHARD. *A Manual of Foreign Language Dictions for Singers.* Fredonia, NY: Edacra Press, 1986.

SHEWAN, ROBERT. *Voice Training for the High School Chorus.* West Nyack, NY: Parker, 1973.

STANTON, ROYAL. *Steps to Singing* (2nd ed.). Belmont, CA: Wadsworth, 1976.

TRUSLER, IVAN. *The Choral Director's Latin.* Lanham, MD: University Press of America, 1987.

TRUSLER, IVAN, AND WALTER EHRET. *Functional Lessons in Singing.* Englewood Cliffs, NJ: Prentice-Hall, 1960.

VENNARD, WILLIAM. *Developing Voices.* New York: Carl Fischer, 1973.

———. *Singing: The Mechanism and the Technic* (rev. ed.). New York: Carl Fischer, 1967.

WALL, JOAN. *The International Phonetic Alphabet for Singers.* Dallas: Pst, 1989.

WALL, JOAN, ROBERT CALDWELL, TRACY GAVILANES, AND SHEILA ALLEN. *Diction for Singers.* Dallas: Pst, 1990.

ZEMLIN, WILLARD. *Speech and Hearing Science.* Englewood Cliffs, NJ: Prentice-Hall, 1981.

Chapter Two

Rehearsal Planning and Techniques

✣ ✣ ✣

✣ INTRODUCTION ✣

A career in choral music education requires the development of a variety of skills and understandings. The setting in which you put most of these abilities into practice is the choral rehearsal. Public performance is a *part* of the choral music education process, but it is not the ultimate product. Thus effective rehearsal techniques are critical to successful choral music education. The ultimate product of this entire process is the musical education of your students.

In addition to reading the text and consulting the sources listed at the end of the chapter, we urge you to take advantage of every chance to *conduct* and *rehearse* an ensemble. If there is an opportunity to be observed and evaluated, so much the better. Utilize every experience you can in the choral music education program at your college or university. Create opportunities for rehearsal with fellow students. Volunteer to lead sectionals or to assist in other ways with ensembles in which you participate as a choral singer.

Opportunities are often available to lead a church choir, an excellent setting in which to develop and refine conducting technique and rehearsal skills. The preparation of fifty weekly musical selections in the course of a year develops rehearsal efficiency and clear conducting technique. It can also help eliminate any nervousness you may experience conducting a choir in public. Without the experience of actually working with singers, the concepts discussed in this chapter will not become a part of your personal repertoire of skills and understandings.

Take advantage of every opportunity to *listen* to choral ensembles. It is enlightening to listen to other conductors' choirs, to study the literature they have selected for performance, and to hear the choral tone they produce. Keep a file of all of the printed programs from concerts you attend. This will help you remember the musical selections you heard, and you will also have samples of printed programs for later reference.

Listen to all kinds of choirs. At professional meetings and festivals you can hear the very best ensembles, often selected by blind audition. It is also useful to observe choirs that are less than exemplary in some areas. A choir whose director sings along on every selection or that has difficulty walking on and off the stage with good decorum can illustrate the negative effects of such problems on performances.

As a choral participant, focus your attention on the techniques used by your conductors to get results. Viewing a rehearsal from the standpoint of a prospective conductor is different from simply participating as a singer. Try to figure out why the conductor uses certain techniques or selects certain portions of the music for consideration. Analyze how the conductor makes improvements in the music. Ask the conductor questions away from the pressures of rehearsal (your questions will be more thoughtfully answered if you avoid disrupting the flow of rehearsal). Resist the temptation to be overly judgemental if a conductor does things differently than you would. In short, begin to think as a conductor as well as a choral singer.

Improve your functional keyboard skill. Time invested in learning to play accompaniments, to accurately reproduce vocal lines singly and in combination, to give pitches in a musical fashion, and to use the keyboard effectively in rehearsal is well spent. Even if a competent accompanist is available, the more accomplished the conductor is at the keyboard, the easier it is to become an effective rehearsal technician.

✣ REHEARSAL PLANNING ✣

Auditions

The way you audition singers for the choral program has an important impact on the success of an ensemble. The purpose of an audition may vary according to the circumstances, but whenever possible, listen to each student individually, whether or not membership in the group is contingent on the performance. The audition gives you a chance to interact individually with singers and observe how they react to a high-pressure situation. Whether the purpose of the audition is to familiarize yourself with each student's voice or to determine the membership of the ensemble, or both, give each student your full attention. A friendly greeting will help allay fear and facilitate an accurate evaluation of the student's choral potential. Recall your own experience in auditions and empathize with the students as they experience the nervousness associated with the process.

Colds and other illnesses may strike auditioners when the appointed day arrives. Be kind and understanding, but generally ask the student to attempt the audition despite any physical limitation. You can then determine whether the student is indeed afflicted with a medical problem that adversely affects his or her voice.

After greeting the student, quickly determine whether he or she is capable of matching pitches (not all auditioners will be able to do so). Then direct the student to sing a familiar melody ("Happy Birthday," "America," or the like), and see whether he or she can produce the melody accurately. Remember that we live in a largely nonsinging society, and the singing students listen to on their cassettes, compact discs, and on the radio is of little help in preparing them for the audition. So be ready for anything. After establishing whether the student can match pitches, ask him or her to vocalize with some straightforward pattern of pitches from the bottom to the top of the range. Begin the vocalise in a comfortable part of the range and work up and then down. Be certain to vocalize the students to the extremes of their ranges. The objective is to find the outer limits of the student's usable range. Here are three exercises that may be used to check the range:

Move pattern upward by half steps.

EXAMPLE 2.1a

Move pattern upward by half steps.

EXAMPLE 2.1b

Move pattern downward by half steps.

EXAMPLE 2.1c

Prior to the audition, have students fill out an audition card where they indicate certain information about themselves prior to the actual audition appointment (see Figure 2.1).

There are actually several areas to evaluate in an audition if time permits. Check the student's range and timbre. Both are important in determining

(FRONT OF CARD—TO BE COMPLETED BY STUDENT)

NAME:

CLASS:

ADDRESS:

PHONE:

PARENT OR GUARDIAN:

PREVIOUS SINGING EXPERIENCE:

INSTRUMENTAL EXPERIENCE:

(BACK OF CARD—TO BE COMPLETED BY TEACHER)

RANGE:	TONAL MEMORY:
SIGHT-READING:	INTONATION:
VOICE PART:	

FIGURE 2.1 Audition Information Card

FIGURE 2.2 Ranges and Tessituras for High School Singers

a singer's appropriate placement in a section. Ranges and tessituras for high school singers are indicated in Figure 2.2.

Range is, of course, a helpful indicator of whether a young man is a tenor, a bass, or a baritone, or whether a young woman is a soprano or alto. It is not conclusive, however, and you will need more information to get a definitive answer (and even though definitive, it is not permanent, since adolescent voices are not fully settled). The individual's vocal timbre also comes into play. A student may be able to vocalize through a wide range of notes, enabling him or her to seemingly sing any part. This is where timbre becomes an important factor. Listen for the part of the student's range that sounds fullest and is produced with the most freedom. Ask the student which area of the range feels most comfortable. Determine what part they sang in their previous experience (which may yield a variety of interesting responses, including girls who have an exceptionally high range, but who have sung alto because they were good readers, or altos who have consistently sung tenor in their church choir or even in a school situation where there has been a shortage of male tenors; it might reveal a young man who started the previous year as an unchanged soprano but who is in the final stages of vocal change and is now ready for a baritone part. Nevertheless, it is interesting to ask!). Considering the two factors together (range and timbre), you can make a fairly accurate assignment of singers to appropriate voice parts. The singing voice during the adolescent years is constantly changing, so any determination is somewhat tentative. Urge students to monitor their voices and tell you when changes take place and reevaluation is necessary.

Probably the most revealing indicator of the probable success of your auditioners is their pitch retention, or tonal memory. To test this, play several sequences of pitches on the piano. After each sequence, ask the singer to reproduce it. Here is a sample group of sequences:

EXAMPLE 2.2a

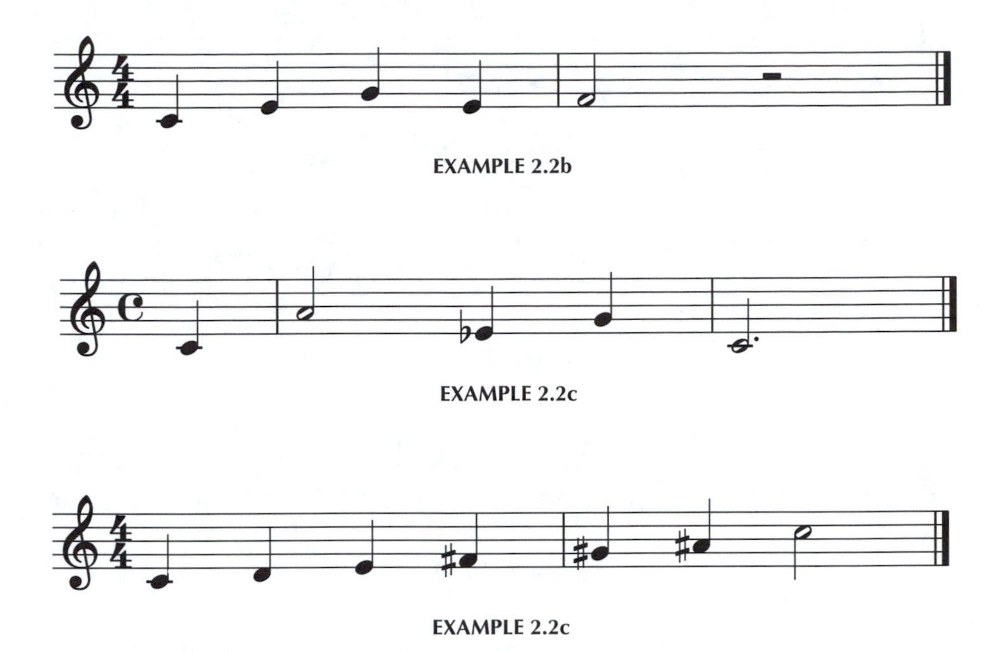

EXAMPLE 2.2b

EXAMPLE 2.2c

EXAMPLE 2.2c

Play each pattern only one time for auditioners. More repetitions may actually make the task more confusing. Stress to students at the outset that they will hear each pattern once, and they should immediately make their best effort to reproduce it. Pitch retention is much less dependent on previous singing experience (although, of course, it is not entirely uncorrelated with it) than sight-reading, which depends on a student's ability to read musical notation. The ability to retain pitches is particularly important when students are auditioned for membership in a small ensemble. In an ensemble of twelve singers, it is also important to determine whether a very large and bright voice can blend with the rest of the group. In auditioning people for a large ensemble, this issue becomes less important. A large and distinctive voice can much more readily be assimilated with twenty-five or thirty others in a section than with two or three.

You should also assess sight-reading ability in the audition. Both sight-reading and pitch retention exercises should cover a wide range of difficulty, progressing from very simple to more complex patterns. Here are some sample exercises:

EXAMPLE 2.3a

EXAMPLE 2.3b

EXAMPLE 2.3c

EXAMPLE 2.3d

Sight-reading skill is becoming an increasing scarce attribute in choral auditioners. Also, it is dramatically affected by the nervousness of the singer. Most importantly, sight-reading is a skill acquired through experience. Many excellent candidates for ensemble membership will be unable to sight-read well in an audition situation.

Prior to the audition, decide on its purpose (to determine membership in a select ensemble or to determine placement in the correct section of a non-select choir). Each audition should take less time than it takes to read the information presented here. If 100 to 200 singers are auditioning, it may not be possible to give each individual more than five minutes. Even at five minutes per person, eight hours will be necessary to listen to 100 singers. Auditions should be held outside of the regular rehearsal period, before or after school or during free periods.

Seating the Choir

The seating arrangement for a choir, like the tone quality you are striving for, is not static. Various arrangements can enhance music of differing styles. For example, homophonic music is often performed most effectively in a quartet arrangement, where the voice parts are intermingled. Renaissance polyphony is usually better served by a traditional sectional arrangement, in which the clarity of each line is enhanced by the distribution of the singers into discrete sections. When dealing with adolescent voices, you need to evaluate arrangement of sections, the assignment of singers to sections, and the distribution of individual voices within sections on an ongoing basis and make necessary adjustments as voices change and develop. Pay careful attention to the arrangement of the voices in the choir and assign seating carefully after listening to the voices in the ensemble, singly and in combination with others.

The present section describes some standard seating arrangements for SATB choirs and guidelines for the seating of singers within sections. We describe seating arrangements for specialized ensembles in Chapter 8 and suggestions for dealing with concerns of junior high/middle school ensembles are included later in this chapter.

Standard Seating Arrangements. A basic seating arrangement for a well-balanced SATB ensemble is illustrated in Figure 2.3. Note that in this arrangement, the outer and inner voices are adjacent. This is desirable so the sopranos and basses, and the altos and tenors can hear each other clearly, facilitating accurate intonation. When the choir is divided into eight parts, the arrangement illustrated in Figure 2.4 works well, again enabling the outer voices to hear each other easily and facilitating doubling between the altos and tenors.

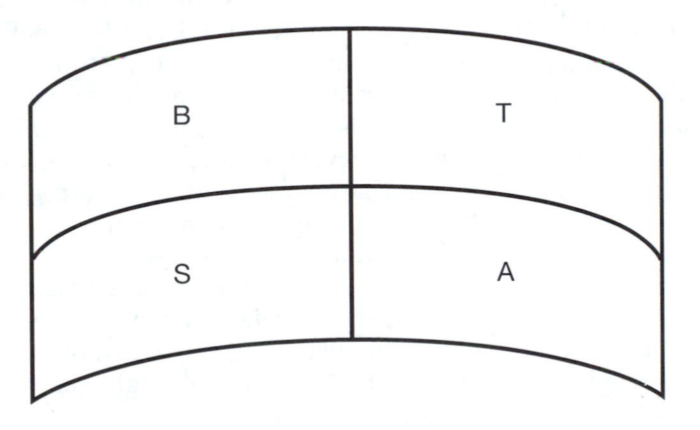

FIGURE 2.3 Basic Seating Arrangement for SATB Ensemble

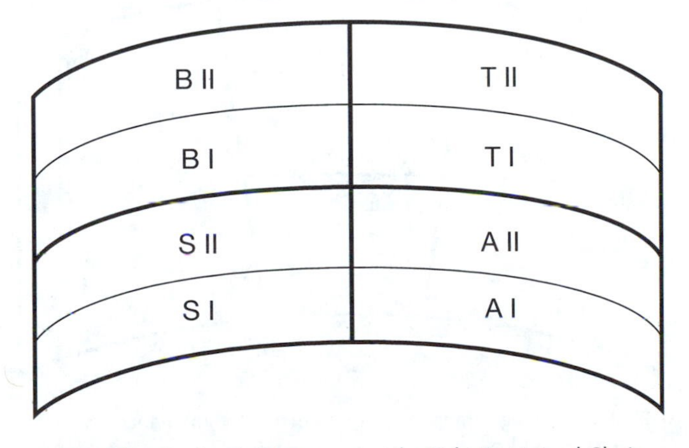

FIGURE 2.4 Seating Arrangement for Eight-Part Mixed Choir

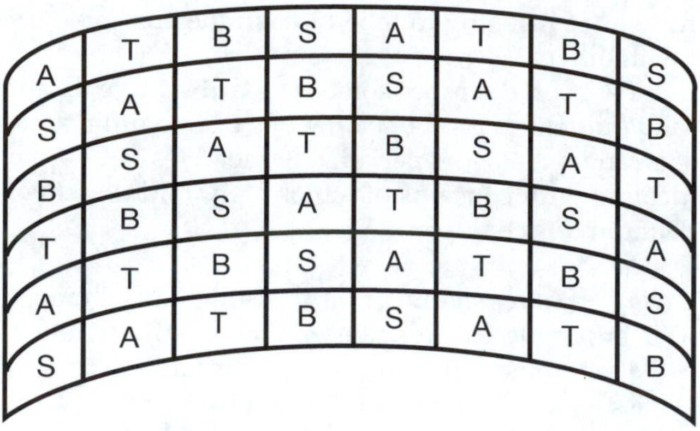

A T B S A T B S
S A T B S A T B
B S A T B S A T
T B S A T B S A
A T B S A T B S
S A T B S A T B

FIGURE 2.5 Scrambled Seating Arrangement

Sectional seating arrangements are well suited to polyphonic repertoire. For the performance of homophonic selections in which a more individualistic sound is desired and the integrity of separate lines of polyphony is not of primary importance (for example, many of the part songs of Brahms and Schubert, or certain twentieth-century repertoire), a scrambled, or quartet arrangement may be preferable (see Figure 2.5). Another advantage of this type of arrangement is that it develops independent musicianship on the part of each singer, which is an important objective of the comprehensive choral music educator. Inexperienced singers, however, may have difficulty with the demands of singing in a scrambled arrangement.

The choral music educator is often confronted with a situation in which the choir is numerically unbalanced. Typically, the women outnumber the men and the basses outnumber the tenors. In this situation, the arrangements illustrated in Figures 2.6 and 2.7 solidify the singing of the male sections and help balance the sound.

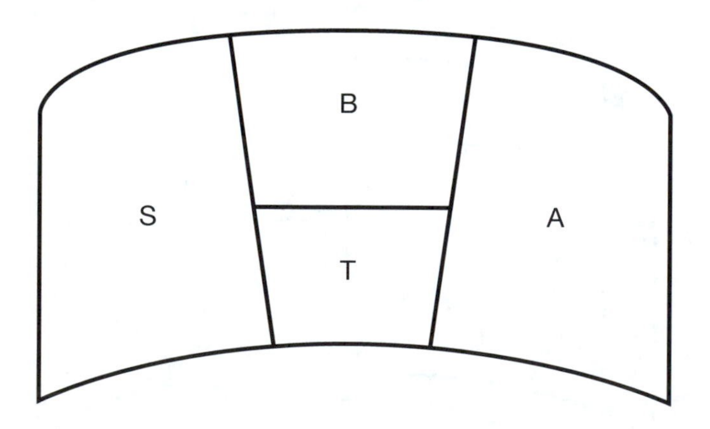

FIGURE 2.6 Seating Arrangement for Numerically Imbalanced Mixed Choir

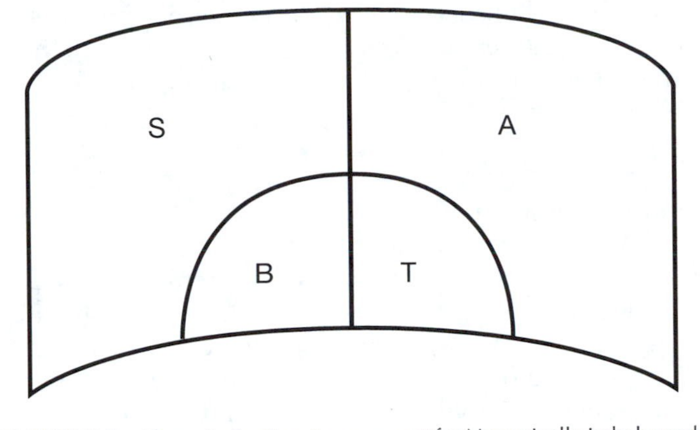

FIGURE 2.7 Alternate Seating Arrangement for Numerically Imbalanced Mixed Choir

Seating within Sections. In addition to arranging the sections of the choir in the most advantageous fashion, the seating of singers *within* each section has a profound influence on the sound of the ensemble. A few basic ideas about seating within sections are as follows:

1. *Sound.* Listen to the combinations of adjacent voices in the various choral sections. Some voices blend better than others. As a general rule, some directors prefer to place strong voices next to individuals with excellent reading skills. Others prefer to place the strongest voices in the center of the ensemble, creating a core of solid choral sound. Another approach is to place the stronger voices behind those that are less secure, enhancing both security and blend.
2. *Visual appeal.* Have the choir stand on the risers in their basic formation, and check to see how they look. How are the heights arranged? Singers can hear better and sound better when they stand next to someone of approximately the same height. Some choir directors even construct boxes for choir members to stand on that create a more uniform appearance. This is not nearly as awkward as it sounds. Singers carry their box (painted a discreet black) under their arm as they walk onto the risers. Are the singers with the most interesting and animated faces in prominent places? Determine whether all of the singers can see you easily. The appearance of a choir is critical to creating a positive impression on the part of the listener, before a sound is heard.
3. *Singer comfort.* Does each singer have enough room on the risers? Are the singers standing a uniform distance apart?
4. *Personalities.* Some singers will work well together; others may be overly talkative or clash. To the degree possible, save aggravation by recognizing and dealing with such situations in the choral seating/standing arrangement.

Some of these issues are of concern in preparing for performance rather than rehearsal. However, the seating arrangement of a choir for rehearsal has a significant impact on tone quality, balance, blend, and morale.

Preparing for Rehearsal

Establishing Positive Relationships. After completing student teaching, and following four or more years of study, it is tremendously satisfying and exciting to be offered a teaching position in the field of choral music education. However, at some point following the signing of the contract, anxiety about the upcoming school year may begin to replace your initial enthusiasm. An antidote to this feeling is to begin preparing for a successful year of teaching several weeks before school begins if possible.

You will almost certainly have had the opportunity to meet your principal during the hiring process. He or she will exert a tremendous influence on the development of your choral program, so be sure to cultivate a positive relationship. Determine the style of administrative leadership at your new school. *Listen* carefully, and be prepared to work in harmony with your principal. As a music educator, it may be necessary to educate (tactfully and gradually) administrators, guidance counselors, parents, colleagues, and the community concerning the value of choral music to the individual participants in choir and to the school as a whole. Administrators often view music programs as a way to foster good public relations for the school. Although this view misses some important basic philosophical and aesthetic justifications for music in the curriculum, it at least indicates that support for the program will, in all likelihood, be forthcoming.

Meet the guidance counselors and ascertain their attitudes toward music. Determine how the school schedule is constructed and by whom. Let the guidance staff know of your interest in each student, and indicate what your requirements are for those interested in participating in choral ensembles. Do the students need to audition before they are accepted into a choir? Are you willing to accept students who have presented behavioral or academic problems in other classes? Determine how many students have signed up for choral classes, the proportion of men and women, and encourage the counselors to inform students who are signing up for classes over the summer, and who may be new to the district, about the possibility of participating in a choral ensemble.

Take the opportunity to meet and get to know the custodial staff at your school. These people will have a profound effect on the success or failure of your choral program. Treat them with courtesy and respect. When an event is scheduled, it will be the custodial staff who will adjust the temperature in the auditorium, clean the room, and move equipment to the proper location, along with many other details. Insist that students treat the custodial staff with respect by keeping the choral rehearsal room in reasonably clean condition and by taking the time to thank them for any special work done to facilitate a rehearsal or concert.

Establish contact with the students who will be involved in the choral program. Get a list, if possible, of students who participated in chorus the previous year (perhaps from a concert program); determine how many have signed up for the coming year. Make some phone calls, and let students know you are interested in working with them to build the program. Determine who the student leaders are and make an effort to meet them.

Visit the practice sessions of athletic teams. Before classes begin, players and coaches will be working out, preparing for the season. Introduce yourself to the coaches, and let them know you are interested in getting players involved in music. If a few football players get involved in choir, this is an excellent start toward getting the school's student leadership to support the music program.

Make a conscious effort to be friendly and cooperative with colleagues in all disciplines, and particularly those in the music department. Choral work does not take place in isolation. One might think colleagues in a music department are all striving for closely related objectives and would naturally work in close harmony (indeed, this *is* an objective of comprehensive choral music education). Unfortunately, this often is not the case. When music colleagues *do* work closely together, there are a multitude of ways they can facilitate each other's efforts. Experienced colleagues can be of tremendous assistance to the beginning teacher. Observe them and learn what has helped them succeed. Many districts have developed formal mentoring programs in which experienced master teachers work closely with new faculty members on an ongoing basis.

The development of positive and fruitful relationships will have a very positive effect on the choral program. In fact, being a successful choral music educator initially involves more salesmanship than musicianship. A lack of musicianship will, in the long run, doom a choral music education program to mediocrity, but in getting things started the ability to relate to, inspire, and motivate people is more important than musicianship.

Planning the First Rehearsal. Your first meeting with your choirs will be very important in establishing patterns of rehearsal behaviors, procedures, and techniques. Therefore, it is critically important to carefully plan what will happen at the first rehearsal.

Prepare the rehearsal room. Be certain it is neat and clean, presenting a businesslike appearance. Put some displays on the bulletin boards. A visit to the local music store should yield some posters and other materials, perhaps humorous, that convey some basic principles of choral musicianship. Post announcements that may have been in your mailbox concerning upcoming community musical events, scholarship opportunities, or anything else that relates to music and to the interests of your students. This immediately conveys to the students your professionalism, knowledge of current events, and interest in them.

Spend some time familiarizing yourself with the choral library at the school. Look at programs from the previous year (if available) and see what the students have previously accomplished. Get a feel for the styles of literature the students are accustomed to singing and the levels of difficulty of the selections that have been performed recently.

Fill choral folders with music and establish a distribution procedure that enables students to get their folder of music quickly and efficiently. For the first rehearsal you might place the folders on the seats before the students enter. If a folder storage cabinet is available, you might wish to assign numbers as students enter the room so they may retrieve their own folders from the appropriate slots.

Check the present files for pieces to rehearse with the choir. There are some pitfalls to avoid in selecting music for the first rehearsal. It is crucial to be generally conservative in your initial selections. Schedule a piece to open rehearsal that includes a good amount of unison singing, providing an opportunity to emphasize the basic elements of good vocal technique and enabling students to succeed at their first musical endeavor of the semester. It should be of good musical quality, but technically approachable. Include two or three selections with contrasting tempo, texture, text, and tonality. All of the pieces the choir works on initially should be selected to facilitate the development of vocal technique. The selections that are placed in the folders (and all of the music to be rehearsed and performed) are tools for teaching students how to sing and for the development of comprehensive musicianship. Thus, in addition to the opening selection, you should also include a piece that will encourage the development of legato line through some sustained singing, along with music that will facilitate the development of rhythmic integrity.

Last but not least, include one piece that is more technically challenging, for use if the group is more advanced than you anticipate. This would be unusual. Even a very fine choir tends to lose its edge over the summer vacation due to the absence of a regular rehearsal routine, changes in personnel, and change in leadership.

The first rehearsal should emphasize enthusiasm, accomplishment, and excitement. Be available at the door of the room to greet students as they enter. Communicate a positive attitude. Convey to each student his or her importance to the group effort through eye contact, friendliness, and general enthusiasm. There should be a minimal amount of talking, particularly at the beginning of rehearsal. Get right into warm-ups and rehearsal of the music at hand.

Don't be too particular about seating at the first rehearsal. If there has not been an opportunity to meet with and audition the students in advance, indicate where the soprano, alto, tenor, and bass sections are located, and ask singers to sit in the appropriate place. If students are uncertain about which part they sing, seat them with their own sex and leave the fine adjustments of the seating arrangement for a later date. The opening piece should be rehearsed and the students led to a noticeable improvement in sound as vocal fundamentals are explained, demonstrated, and assimilated. Don't spend too long on one piece of music—just enough time to give students a feeling of accomplishment and satisfaction. They must buy into the product being offered: an excellent musical experience. Until this unity of purpose is achieved, rehearsals will not be productive. All of these ideas (greeting at the door, quick rehearsal pace, proper selection of music, quick attainment of rehearsal success) will facilitate the development of commitment to the group and high morale. One more thing should be mentioned: It is crucial to *be yourself*. It may be tempting to imitate a college or high school choir director, or some other person who influenced your musical development, but this will not prove successful in the long run. Each choral music educator possesses an individual and unique style of leadership and personality. Allow it to emerge in working with the ensemble. Certainly techniques that seem to work for others may be assimilated into each conductor's personal style, but an attempt to clone someone else's approach will not work.

Long-Term Rehearsal Planning

The long-term planning process may be the area that most clearly differentiates the comprehensive choral music educator from other choral conductors. Long-term planning includes consideration of the educational implications of the music being selected for study, as well as characteristics of the students who will be studying it.

We deal with the technical aspects of selecting music in detail in Chapter 5. However, music selection is an important and primary aspect of long-range rehearsal planning. The starting point for long-term planning is selecting repertoire. Choose music that provides the students with a representative sampling of choral literature and includes a variety of styles, composers, and periods. Musical learnings resulting from student interaction with the music should be anticipated and planned for. Thus, for each musical selection programmed, compile a list of musical concepts that you will emphasize, and structure rehearsals so the concepts are developed as the music is rehearsed. We present more detail on developing student musicianship and the educational implications of the choral music experience in Chapter 9. For the moment, however, consider two excerpts from "Every Valley" by John Ness Beck (Beckenhorst Press, SATB, no. BP1040, 1976). This is a relatively simple piece, beautifully melodic and requiring a smooth legato line. In planning to rehearse this selection, the following questions could provide a framework for the development of some appropriate musical concepts (a complete score is necessary to answer all of the questions):

Every Valley

For SATB chorus and organ or piano

For Charles Gleason, Walter Cory and all my friends at Cass Technical High Scool, Detroit, Michigan

John Ness Beck
A.S.C.A.P.

Isaiah 40:4, 5

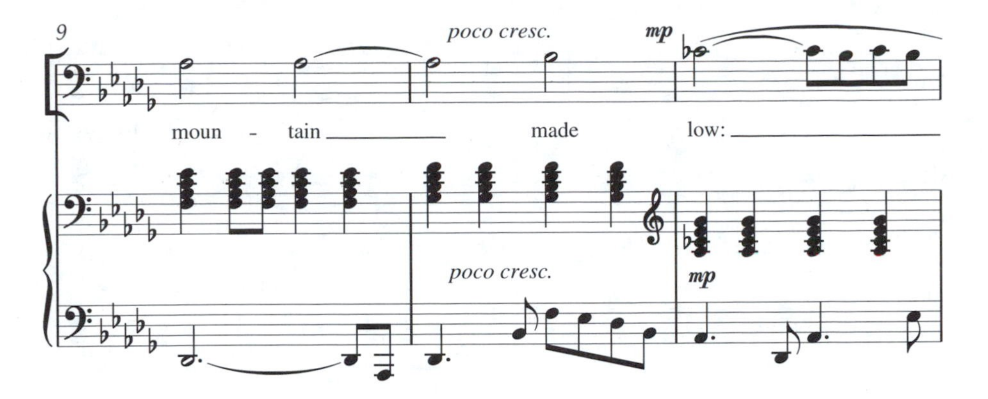
9
poco cresc.
mp
moun - tain made low:
poco cresc.
mp

12

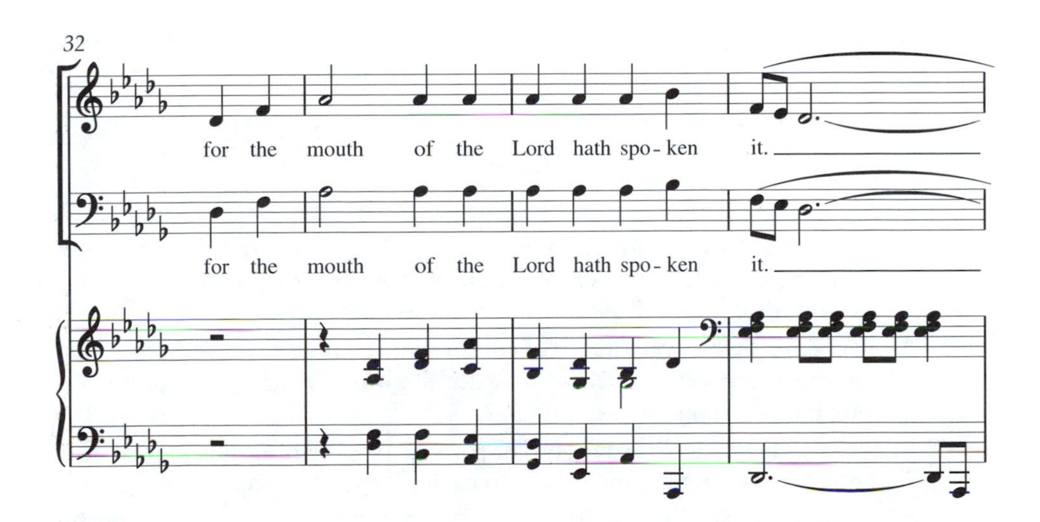
32
for the mouth of the Lord hath spo-ken it.
for the mouth of the Lord hath spo-ken it.

EXAMPLE 2.4

1. *Text:* Where did the text come from? What is its significance? How does the text affect the accentuation of the music? How shall we unify the sound of the sustained vowel combinations?
2. *Harmony:* Is this song major or minor? Why? Why does Beck include a key change at measure 37? Why does the music change from unison to four-part harmony at measure 37?
3. *Melody:* Is this melody smooth or rough? Are the intervals in it large or small? How does the melody help express the meaning of the words?
4. *Form:* Where is the repetition and contrast in this piece? How does the use of these two elements create unity, yet keep the selection interesting? What are the major sections of the piece?

5. *Expression:* What happens to the dynamic level of the song from the beginning to the end? Why? How do the dynamic changes relate to the harmonic changes?

These issues can be brought up and discussed as the song is rehearsed and interwoven into the ongoing flow of rehearsal. In fact, this is the most effective way to help students develop musical concepts. They should be an integral part of the rehearsal process. Notice that the concepts to be discussed are in the form of questions. This is a most effective way to help students develop conceptual, critical thinking.

Performances should be planned so students have goals to work toward and opportunities to present their music in public. Music should then be allocated to the various performances, with consideration given to the audiences for whom it will be presented (the selections for the local service club luncheon will probably differ from those performed at the state music teachers' meeting). The key point to keep in mind is that planning programs for specific performances is secondary in importance to determining the educational implications of the music. Nevertheless, as a practical matter, the objective is also to educate and entertain the audiences for whom we perform, and they deserve consideration in the planning process.

Consider the nature of the ensemble that will be studying the music in your long-range planning. If it is your first year with a particular group and the ensemble has been accustomed to a steady diet of contemporary pop music selections, they will need to be gradually moved from that lopsided approach toward a more balanced program. Of course, the selections you choose for a madrigal ensemble or show choir will be different from those you select for a concert choir, but there should still be a balance of styles and composers. Check the calendar and calculate the number of rehearsals prior to each performance. Then decide roughly when each piece will be introduced and when it will be brought to performance level. Consider the level of difficulty of each piece and the difficulty of sections within the music. Without this kind of planning, it is easy to focus on particular pieces or sections of pieces and neglect others, creating a pressure-filled situation as the performance approaches and certain aspects of the music have not been rehearsed adequately (for more detail on preconcert rehearsals, see Chapter 4).

The kind of long-range planning we have described to this point provides the basis for an academic year of comprehensive choral work. It should be placed into the context of a three-, four-, or five-year plan for your choirs. A guidance counselor or parent will probably ask you , "Why should a student be in choir for more than one year?" How do the experiences you provide differ from one year to the next? This is a particular concern for students who are academically gifted (the very students you wish to attract to the choir). The choral curriculum should include a variety of literature aimed at developing a diverse repertoire of musical concepts, so that each year of participation in choir builds on and extends learning from the previous one. This approach is educationally sound and justifies membership in the choir over several years. Of course, there are many musical selections that merit repeated use in the choral classroom. If such selections are placed in a cycle, based on the number of years students may participate in the choral program, it assures that a given student will be exposed to a wide variety of choral repertoire, helping provide a solid educational rationale for participation in the ensemble for several years.

Coordinate planning with choral teachers at the junior high and elementary levels. The most successful choral programs are those that include careful vertical articulation, that is, open communication and participation by music teachers at all levels to determine the kinds of experiences to be provided for students at each level. In this way, choral music experiences can be appropriately sequenced from one level to another, as well as within levels. For example, you might decide that by the time students have completed junior high school, they will have sung pieces in English and Latin. The high school director could be confident that incoming students had certain common musical experiences on which to build.

A key point to remember about planning for choral experiences is that the choral music educator must be flexible. Plans should constantly be evaluated to be sure they effectively reflect your educational philosophy and facilitate students' musical growth. As changes are needed, adaptations should be made. Long-term planning is critical to the success of the choral program. Without the establishment of long-range goals in terms of repertoire, musical concept development, and sequencing, you will not be a successful comprehensive choral music educator. Once you have made long-term plans, providing a conceptual and musical framework, you can plan individual rehearsals.

Short-Term Rehearsal Planning

Planning for each choral rehearsal should incorporate the same kinds of objectives included in the long-term plan. They need to be worked into the flow of each class. Ideally, each rehearsal should represent a microcosm of the long-term plan (although there will necessarily be occasional exceptions). Give students a variety of literature presented in such a way that it is efficiently learned, providing a vehicle for musical growth.

Within the progression of every rehearsal is a tempo and a rhythm. This changes as the rehearsal progresses. First, through warm-up exercises and initial encounter with the repertoire under consideration, the choir's attention must be focused on the task at hand. Following this opening period of focusing is the most potentially productive portion of rehearsal, during which the most detailed and difficult work may be accomplished expediently. This period of maximum productivity will not last until the end of rehearsal. Be sensitive to the waning of student attention and subtly shift gears to a less demanding rehearsal agenda—perhaps a review of material previously studied or the introduction of some simpler material to be considered in more detail at the next rehearsal.

Assuming a one-hour rehearsal, the following scheme might work well:

Warm-up	10 minutes
Introduction of new repertoire	10 minutes
Detailed rehearsal	20 minutes
Less intensive rehearsal	20 minutes

These times are approximate and obviously should be adjusted according to the length of rehearsal. Keeping in mind this curve of rehearsal efficiency, formulate a written plan for each rehearsal, indicating what repertoire will be covered and what will be accomplished with each selection. This is particularly important for those of you in the early stages of your career.

Here is the outline presented in more detail, with specific repertoire inserted:

Warm-ups (see Chapter 1):

1. Stretching.
2. Breathing exercise.
3. Vowel-shaping exercise.
4. Resonance-creating exercise.

"O Come Let Us Sing unto the Lord," Emma Lou Diemer, Carl Fischer, no. CM7903 (first reading)

1. Read through from beginning to end.
2. Point out large sections of piece (mm. 1–48, mm. 49–65, mm. 96–111, mm. 112–135, mm. 135–167).
3. Work on choral tone in opening unison section.
4. Discuss style of piece: biblical text, contemporary American composer, dramatic accompaniment.

"Every Valley," John Ness Beck, Beckenhorst Press, no. BP1040 (detailed rehearsal)

1. Work for dynamic contrasts: pianissimo men, piano women, using dynamics to shape phrases in mm. 4–36. Full, sustained sound, mm. 36–end, building from mezzo forte to fortissimo.
2. Diction—vowel unification throughout, ending consonants—exalted (m. 7), straight (M. 16), Lord (m. 24), and so on.
3. Discuss relation of texture and dynamics to text—expressive aspects of the piece.

"Now I Walk in Beauty," arr. Gregg Smith, G. Shirmer, no. 12374 (review previous work)

1. Sing from beginning to end.
2. Sing the melody together (mm. 1–8)—review shaping of phrase.
3. Work toward maintenance of phrasing when split into four-part canon (mm. 9–end).
4. Discuss the Native American origin of the melody and its modal character.

Just as long-term planning provided the framework for a year of effective choral music education, the short-term plan provides a similar framework for each rehearsal. As the school year progresses, the way in which the rehearsal is organized will change.

At the beginning of the year, the warm-ups that begin each rehearsal will be critically important in establishing the correct vocal techniques, unity, and rehearsal discipline for the singers. As the semester progresses, rehearsals should be devoted increasingly to the singing of larger sections of pieces, and then to entire selections and groups of selections, so the singers get a feel for pieces done in their entirety and understand the progression of the program from one selection to the next.

✣ REHEARSAL COMMUNICATION ✣

After the process of selecting music and planning for rehearsal is completed comes the most exciting and challenging part of choral conducting: taking the music and teaching it to the chorus in the most effective way possible in order to accomplish your plans and bring the music to performance level. Here we are talking about effective rehearsal interaction with your choral ensemble. For the purposes of this discussion we divide effective communication into two parts:

1. Communicating the specific musical ideas you have determined through your score analysis to your singers.
2. Listening perceptively to the ensemble and providing insightful and practical feedback that will ultimately lead to the musical learnings desired and the refinement of the choir's choral artistry.

As we stated earlier, rehearsal is the place where choral music education most clearly occurs. Rehearsal interactions should enable singers to grow musically. To accomplish the presentation of musical ideas and the refinement of the choir's singing through aural analysis and effective feedback assumes you have followed the process we outlined earlier—carefully selecting music of artistic merit, analyzing the music for potential problems, and determining the musical outcomes that will be accomplished as the ensemble lives with the music for a period of weeks or months.

As the conductor, you must have a mental conception of the sound the choir is working toward. Drawing together all of your past experiences (listening to choirs and recordings of choirs, singing in choirs, conducting, contemplating), you must have a preconceived notion of your personal ideal sound. This sound should vary according to the literature being studied, but there must be a tonal target you are aiming for in order for effective rehearsal to occur.

Following the determination of musical objectives based on analysis of the score, consideration of students' musical needs, and the ideal sound you are striving for, the next step is to determine strategies and techniques that facilitate communication of your objectives to the singers.

Feedback to the choir should be based on the characteristics of good choral singing:

good choral tone
blend and balance
rhythmic integrity
appropriate style and expression
secure intonation
diction

As the choir seeks to produce the sound you ask for, they will initially produce only an approximation. Also, it is not possible to present a list of thirty items to accomplish with a particular piece and have the choir assimilate them simultaneously. Therefore, as the piece is rehearsed we could compare the choir director to a sculptor: As the sound is shaped, a rough outline emerges. With continued work, the individual lines and phrases and the overarching design of the musical selection become more and more clear. Ideally, when the piece is brought to performance level, the imperfections have been smoothed away, the pitches and rhythms are sung with accuracy, the intonation has been made secure, and an accurate impression of the musical image intended by the composer and the conductor has been created.

One of the understandings you cultivate as you work with a choir is to know the speed at which a selection may be improved. As we noted earlier, it is not usually possible or desirable to attempt to take a choir from total unfamiliarity with a piece to performance level in one rehearsal. Conversely, it does not work to hope for the best and simply sing a selection through many times over the course of several weeks of rehearsal, without correcting mistakes. It is a matter of striking a balance. Although simple repetition, in and of itself, will tend to correct some musical problems as the singers become more conversant with the music, it will also tend to perpetuate certain errors. Choral problems must be brought to the attention of the choir in a timely fashion, along with suggested solutions.

Communication with choral singers begins before the first notes are sounded. A few points concerning preparing the room for the first rehearsal bear repeating here because they are applicable to every choral rehearsal. The appearance of the rehearsal room and the demeanor of the conductor as the chorus enters sets the tone for the first rehearsal, just as the first rehearsal sets the tone for the rest of the year.

To the degree possible, make the rehearsal room inviting and comfortable. Ventilation should be adequate and the temperature adjusted to remain reasonably cool, even when the room is filled with the singers. Attention to the matter of ventilation and climate control will forestall some problems in terms of intonation and concentration. Get rid of outdated announcements, and convey through the appearance of the room that important work is being done. All of these things will communicate to the singers your seriousness of purpose and concern for them.

The objective, which will carry over into the beginning of rehearsal, is to harness the motivation of the students in your chorus and direct it toward objectives you choose. You are attempting to get the students to buy into your plans. Until this occurs, nothing will be accomplished. After it occurs, the possibilities are exciting.

In rehearsal three basic modes of communication are available to the conductor: verbalization, demonstration, and conducting gestures. At various stages in the rehearsal process, different communicational modes may prove to be most effective. Initially, verbalization may be the best way to communicate. As the choir reads through a selection for the first time, they won't be able to closely observe your conducting while following the written score. Therefore, verbalization (even shouted over the singing of the group, occasionally) may be the most effective means of communication at that point. Often a demonstration of the correct approach (either vocally or at the keyboard) will effectively communicate. If a particular adjustment in tone quality or a correction of a rhythmic problem is desired, a demonstration can be worth a thousand words. As the chorus becomes more familiar with the music, and can begin to attend more closely to conducting gestures, the quickest means of communicating will be through clear conducting technique. If your conducting technique is not clear, you will need to devote an excessive amount of time to verbalizing the nuances of phrasing and dynamics, which could be very effectively conveyed by varying the size of your conducting pattern, some other appropriate gesture, or a change in facial expression. Effective conducting technique is critical, for the ensemble will tend to sing with whatever amount of sensitivity is conveyed to them through gestures, no matter how skillfully you verbalize your desires to them. As an experiment, select a piece of music that requires a soft, delicate tone to present to the chorus. Clearly explain exactly what dynamic level and tone quality you desire (for the purpose of this experiment, soft and delicate). Then, as the group begins, conduct the music with large sweeping gestures. If the group is watching you, they will ignore your verbal directive and respond almost instinctively to your conducting gestures. It is frustrating for singers to deal with a conductor who presents mixed signals (particularly when he or she becomes irate at the singers for failing to detect which signal is the appropriate one).

As you begin to rehearse, you will find the pace of rehearsal is critical to its success. The pace should be varied. In fact, every aspect of your rehearsal technique should be varied at one time or another. A conductor who utilizes the same method for rehearsing every piece of music soon loses the attention of the chorus. For example, some conductors almost invariably employ the following steps:

1. All sing their line.
2. Sopranos sing their line. Corrections are made.
3. Altos sing their line. Corrections are made.
4. Tenors sing their line. Corrections are made.
5. Basses sing their line. Corrections are made.
6. All sing their line together. Corrections are made.

Aside from its predictability, the method just described leaves 75 percent of the choir idle 80 percent of the time, and fails to take into account the relative difficulty of the various vocal lines. Perhaps the sopranos (or one of the other parts) don't need to have their line reviewed separately. Perhaps the sopranos and tenors or the altos and basses are singing parallel lines that should be rehearsed together. Each piece should be approached in a way that is most efficient and likely to lead to success, based on your analysis of the score. If the selection includes some unison singing, perhaps you should deal with that section first, to build the choir's confidence and enable you to develop appropriate choral tone. If the piece contains some tricky rhythmic passages, perhaps you could isolate the rhythms first using a neutral syllable or without pitch before they are approached in their musical context.

Generally, it is desirable to let the choir attempt to sing a piece (or a section of a longer work) through from start to finish initially. Unless they completely collapse, this will give them a sense of the totality of the piece before it is broken into segments and rehearsed in detail. If you know the piece has a particular trouble spot or two, rehearse those places first, so the choir can negotiate them and be successful singing through the selection. Once the choir has gained a sense of the whole piece, isolate and work on specific trouble spots. From prerehearsal analysis of the selection, it should be clear where most of the trouble spots are located. Do not devote valuable rehearsal time to unnecessary repetitions of sections that have already come together. Instead, focus on the specific pages, sections, phrases, or notes that need work. Then, put the corrected passage back into the appropriate musical context.

This general learning principle is the idea of synthesis, analysis, synthesis. There should be an opportunity to view the forest before looking at the individual trees. In approaching a piece of music in rehearsal, immediately begin to develop in your students an expressive feeling for the selection (synthesis). Do not simply begin with the learning of pitches and rhythms, devoid of expression and feeling. Select various musical elements to emphasize as you bring the piece to performance level. If the rhythm is complex and it is desirable to remove the text and the pitches to focus in on the rhythm pattern (analysis), try to put the words, pitches, and rhythms back together before the end of rehearsal (synthesis). If you are rehearsing an extended work, particularly a piece with multiple movements, be sure to take time at the beginning of the semester to calculate how many rehearsals are available and how many pages of music must be accomplished in the course of the semester. Then divide the piece into manageable sections and begin to rehearse. Formulate a plan assuring that every section of the piece will receive the necessary amount of rehearsal time. In approaching an extended work, analyze the piece to determine which sections are most approachable and which will need extensive explanation and careful work from the choir to make them accessible. Begin with the easiest section and save your prime rehearsal time for the more difficult portions of the work. Focus your prime rehearsal time on aspects of the piece that require the most intensive work.

Three elements that facilitate effective rehearsal communication are humor, honesty, and a positive attitude.

Humor. The use of humor in rehearsal lightens the atmosphere and can literally improve the quality of singing taking place. Two important points with regard to humor in rehearsal:

1. It should be natural.
2. Humor should not be at the expense of a person's feelings.

The most effective use of humor in the choral rehearsal is derived from seeing the funny side of the things that happen every day as you work together on the music. Most of us are not natural comics, and the prospective director should not feel pressured to create a half-dozen funny lines for every rehearsal. Simply be on the alert for humorous things happening around you, and you will find yourself very easily and naturally working humor into the fabric of your choral approach.

The other important point about humor is that it should not be a putdown of a student or a colleague. Participation in music should afford individuals an opportunity to improve their perception of themselves, which is not facilitated by negative comments from the director or from fellow students, even if the comments are intended to be joking. As the choral conductor, one of your most important responsibilities is to protect the self-esteem of the students who are working with you and nurture their sense of self-worth. Choral music can only flourish in an atmosphere of mutual respect and trust.

Honesty. Secondary school students are extremely adept at recognizing a fake. Therefore, it is important to be honest. For example, if you make an error or other miscue, immediately accept the responsibility and move on, perhaps making a light self-deprecating comment (e.g., "This is amazing. This is the first error I've made since 1971," or something similar). Do not try to bluff your way through such a situation, for the deception will be obvious to your choral singers. Another area where honesty is important is in the feedback provided for the choir. Look for opportunities to provide honest positive feedback, but if the director habitually tells the choir, "That was great" or "Wonderful job," the members of the ensemble will quickly learn to disregard the comments. Make the comments suit the circumstances.

Positive Approach. A positive approach to your work will be appreciated by your singers. Much of our rehearsal time is spent in listening carefully to the sounds the singers make and then giving them feedback about how they can improve their singing. The manner in which you give this feedback will have an impact on its effect.

Some examples of positive comments, which provide the necessary feedback, might include the following: "Good reading, sopranos. Let's sing your line again, and see if we can center on each pitch—our tone was a little flat the last time through"; or "Nice job remembering the accentuation of that phrase, choir; Let's work on our Latin diction today to make the vowel sounds uniform." These statements are both honest and positive. They provide both praise of something specific that was commendable, and they also provide valid suggestions of areas that need improvement.

Use of Imagery versus Musical Terminology

In your rehearsal verbalizations, there are two primary ways to communicate to the ensemble how to correct a problem: imagery or technical terminology. It is best to use a combination of both types of verbalization in working with a choir.

Consider the following musical line:

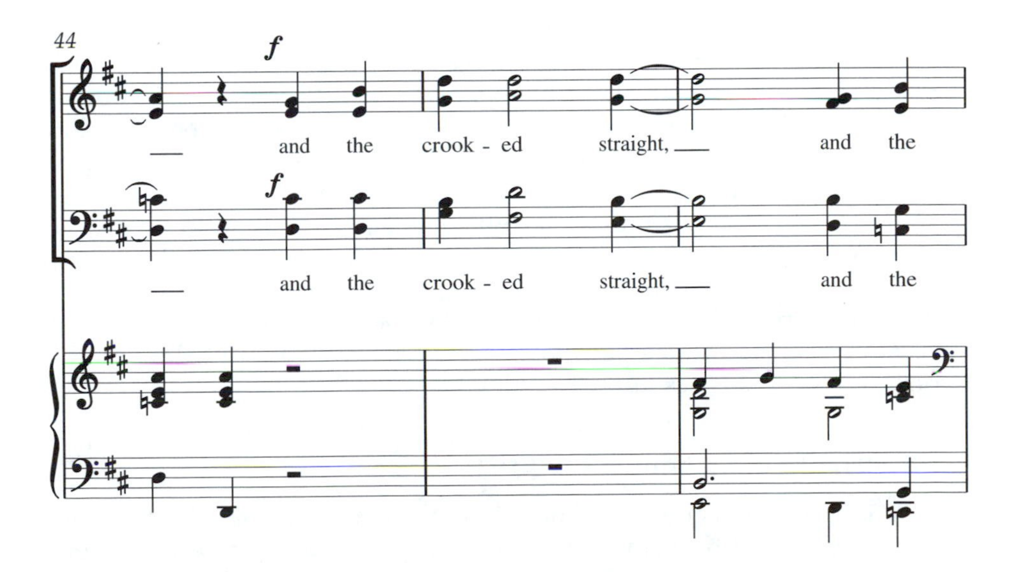

EXAMPLE 2.5 Excerpt from "Every Valley" by John Ness Beck

You could tell the choir this line is accented and syncopated and define syncopation, providing the singers with a bit of musical terminology and a concrete example to illustrate it. You could tell the students to write an accent mark on their score over the first syllable of the word "crooked," and discuss the concept of accent and the notational symbol for it. Another approach could be to relate the syncopation to the expressive import of the text—the pattern of accentuation is "crooked" to illustrate the word "crooked" from the text. Have the students focus on the emotion being conveyed in the text. Tell them to think of a situation with a boyfriend or girlfriend that became crooked or confused and how good it felt to get it straightened out. Probably a combination of technical terminology and imagery is most effective in communicating with a choir. The kind of imagery noted here is inherent in the music. Such musical devices as tone painting also exemplify imagery that is created by the composer. Tone painting should be highlighted for students (e.g., when the text states "et ascendit in coelum" and the musical line ascends). Another type of imagery is not inherent in the music, but is presented to the choir to elicit a musical response. The use of simile and metaphor can be very effective (e.g., "this line should be as steady and graceful as the Queen Mary coming into dock," or "glide through the phrase—like you've ridden your bicycle over a hill and you can coast for a while without pedaling," or "we need to ice skate through this phrase rather than hack through a thicket").

Importance of Rhythmic Integrity

Rhythmic integrity is an important attribute of artistic choral singing. The development of rhythmic integrity has positive implications for other aspects of choral singing, notably intonation and vitality, and it is closely related to diction and phrasing. Accurate rhythm and the feel for the underlying pulse in a piece of music have been cornerstones of Robert Shaw's choral technique.

Pieces of music with fairly fast, exciting rhythms are usually easier to bring to performance level than those that are slow and sustained. Certain pieces almost seem to "sing themselves," and are popular with students when they possess this characteristic. It is a more difficult challenge to take slower, more sustained music and to develop the same kind of vital and exciting choral tone that almost seems to develop effortlessly in faster pieces. An example of this contrast can be found in the Vivaldi *Gloria*. Most of this music is rhythmic, dancelike, and harmonically straightforward, like the opening chorus, for example. The most difficult section of the entire piece is the "Et in Terra Pax," which is slow, sustained, and more harmonically complex.

Rhythmic vitality can be developed in a variety of ways. For example, subdivide the notes in a phrase into eighth notes, remove the text, and sing the phrase on a neutral syllable or on numbers. To illustrate, consider the opening of the "Lacrymosa" section of the Mozart *Requiem*:

3
p
La - - cry-mo - sa di - - es il - la.
p
La - - cry-mo - sa di - - es il - la.
p
La - - cry-mo - sa di - - es il - la.
p
La - - cry-mo - sa di - - es il - la.
5
qua re - sur - get ex fa - vil - la
qua re - sur - get ex fa - vil - la
qua re - sur - get ex fa - vil - la
qua re - sur - get ex fa - vil - la

EXAMPLE 2.6

This is an example of singing that must be soft and sustained, yet exciting and rhythmically alive. It is tempting for choirs to sing these measures too heavily and to lag behind the orchestra (or keyboard instrument). In this case, the drama and pathos of the text, when approached in the wrong way vocally, can impede the development of an exciting soft choral sound by causing the singers to wallow in the notes.

A way to overcome this is to ask the choir to remove the text temporarily and to sing eighth notes, either on a neutral syllable or perhaps putting numbers with the notes and *thinking* the numbers on the rests. Example 2.7 includes all of the audible numbers above the musical line:

No. 7 Lacrymosa

5
1 4 7 10 1 4 7 10
qua re - sur - get ex fa - vil - la
qua re - sur - get ex fa - vil - la
qua re - sur - get ex fa - vil - la
qua re - sur - get ex fa - vil - la
1 2 3 4 5 6 7 8 9 10 11 12 1 2 3 4 5 6 7 8 9 10
7
cresc.
f
ju - di - can - dus ho - mo re - us.
cresc.
f
ju - di - can - dus ho - mo re - us.
cresc.
f
ju - di - can - dus ho - mo re - us.
cresc.
f
ju - di - can - dus ho - mo re - us.
cresc.
f

EXAMPLE 2.7

This approach immediately clears up several potential problems in the singing. The tone lightens up and has a sense of direction. The tendency to hang over into the two eighth rests at the ends of measures 3, 4, and 8 ceases. The pulse of the eighth-note pattern in the orchestral part is integrated into the choral sound and energizes it. It is a simple matter to then reassemble the line, adding the text, but retaining the feel of the underlying pulse of the phrase, letting it propel the line forward, energizing it.

Subdividing a long phrase and looking at it mathematically to see how the meter works and to locate the rhythmic pulse helps energize the piece. Simply removing the text temporarily and singing the phrase on a neutral syllable beginning with a hard consonant such as *d* or *t* often adds the necessary vitality.

The slower the rhythm, the more pronounced is the tendency of ensembles to wallow in the sound. Avoid this by subdividing the beat into smaller rhythmic units to highlight the underlying pulse of the piece.

Using Recordings

The use of audiotapes, videotapes, records, and compact discs as aids in teaching a choral ensemble is worthy of discussion. Such audio and visual aids are potentially very useful to the choir, but can present some problems.

It is very helpful to give your choirs the opportunity to hear examples of fine choral singing. This is particularly important today, where there are few acceptable models of good choral singing heard in society at large. Accumulate a library of recordings of fine choral ensembles, provide opportunities for the choir to listen to them, and discuss the characteristics of each ensemble's singing tone and choral artistry. At many conventions of the American Choral Directors Association and the Music Educators National Conference, audio and video recordings of the concerts and interest sessions are routinely made available (even to members who do not attend the event), and can be a valuable teaching tool.

Various opinions have been expressed concerning the value of playing recorded examples of other ensembles singing pieces currently being prepared by your ensemble as a way to motivate them and illustrate choral concepts you wish to develop. Some experts believe it stifles the choir's own efforts to try to emulate another group's approach. On the other hand, it may be helpful for the ensemble to hear a demonstration by a fine choral ensemble of the concept you are trying to develop (e.g., phrasing, rhythmic energy, evenness of crescendo).

Another way you can use the tape deck or videocassette recorder to enhance choral rehearsal is to tape rehearsals and watch or listen to them that evening or the following weekend to evaluate your own rehearsal pace, the sound of the group, the quality of the evaluative feedback provided, and all aspects of the rehearsal. Excerpts of the tape that illustrate areas for improvement or things deserving commendation can be quite helpful. It is invaluable to be able to sit back and watch your own rehearsal from the vantage point of an observer rather than a participant. A videotape enables us to do this.

Videotapes or audiotapes of performances are enjoyable for you and your choir to watch together after a concert, and can provide the basis for constructive comments concerning areas for improvement. A choir's musicianship will grow substantially if they are asked to evaluate their own and other performances. For more detailed discussion of the use of videotape in self-evaluation by the choir, see Chapter 9.

In recent years, a number of excellent videotapes have been made available commercially. Some illustrate aspects of vocal technique, presented by noted authorities or ensembles; others illustrate conducting or rehearsal technique. A listing of some of these resources is included at the end of the chapter.

Using the Piano

The piano is an essential tool for choral rehearsal, but it must be utilized properly for maximum effectiveness. The piano affords a convenient way to give pitches, demonstrate vocal lines, and, of course, provide accompaniment for repertoire that calls for it. Nevertheless, note the following precautions concerning the use of the piano in choral rehearsal:

1. The piano is a percussive instrument, and at best does not provide a good model for choral singing. When played in a percussive manner, it is particularly inappropriate for developing a sense of singing line. Develop the ability to play vocal lines on the piano in as smooth and singing a manner as possible. Teach the accompanist to do the same.
2. Pianos are often out of tune and do not provide accurate representations of the pitches we wish our singers to produce.
3. It is all too easy for choirs to become dependent on keyboard support in their singing, unable to do an effective job of singing unaccompanied repertoire. One objective of choral rehearsal is to develop musical independence in our singers.

Ironically, choral conductors who are strong pianists are most at risk of using the instrument inappropriately in choral rehearsal. We strongly urge you to use competent accompanists in rehearsal and performance, even if you are a skilled pianist. It is very easy to fall into the habit of sitting at the keyboard, focusing your attention on the piano line and not hearing the problems encountered by the choir in singing their parts. The piano should be used as an unobtrusive and helpful reminder of pitches and rhythms for choral singers as needed and to provide the accompaniment line as appropriate. Choirs grow in musicianship when they rehearse and perform with minimal keyboard support of vocal lines.

For the choral music education major with little keyboard experience, it is critically important to develop functional keyboard skills to the maximum. Despite the precautions just listed, the piano can be a very useful tool in the choral rehearsal, and the more proficient you are at the piano, the more at ease you will be utilizing it effectively in front of the ensemble. Moreover, you will certainly encounter situations where you will need to lead a rehearsal from the keyboard, such as when the accompanist is unexpectedly late or absent.

The Accompanist

The accompanist is a very important factor in the success of the choral music education process. Consider these points:

1. Whenever possible, recruit student accompanists for your choral ensembles. This is a more difficult task than it once was, since fewer students seem to reach the secondary school level with sufficient keyboard skill to play accompaniment parts or vocal lines. Nevertheless, this is the best way to handle the accompanying responsibility if students possessing the necessary proficiency are available.
2. Use multiple student accompanists. Rather than relying on one person, select two, three, or four students, depending on the talent available, and assign pieces to them according to their skill level and the difficulty of the piano part. This establishes a system that will continuously develop student accompanying talent. It also provides an opportunity for the individuals who signed up for chorus, but who happen to possess the keyboard skill necessary to accompany, to sing rather than confining them exclusively to the piano bench.
3. When student accompanists are not available, determine whether a parent or other supporter of the choir may be available to help out, or whether funds may be designated for the hiring of an accompanist. Increasingly, high school choirs are utilizing paid accompanists, which is a worthwhile investment.
4. Meet with accompanists(s) in advance of rehearsal and discuss the tempos and other expressive aspects of the repertoire. Also indicate how you would like the accompanist to give pitches and other aspects of rehearsal pacing. Competent accompanying requires specific skills that are not usually developed in students' piano lessons.
5. Work with your accompanist on playing musical lines with a vocal concept of legato singing tone.

Using Movement in Rehearsal[1]

Physical movement adds life to choral music, both in rehearsal and in performance. Movement and music are closely related, and the relationship is symbiotic. It is natural to respond to an exciting, rhythmically alive choral selection with physical movement such as foot tapping, head nodding, or finger snapping. Just as music can elicit a physical response on the part of the listener, physical movement of the singer in rehearsal can help inject rhythmic life, a sense of phrasing, and dynamic variety into a choral selection.

When a baseball player prepares to take a turn at bat, he warms up while waiting on deck by taking practice swings, stretching muscles, and clearing the mind of distractions. The act of swinging at the baseball requires concentration and muscular coordination. Singing requires similar muscular coordination and control: The intake and outflow of air, the moment of suspension with the air held in the lungs, the vibration of the vocal cords, and the articulation of sounds all require dynamic motion. For suggested warm-ups involving movement, see Chapter 1. Movement can be used effectively during rehearsal to elicit desired musical responses and to illustrate musical ideas. Suppose you were teaching a composition in which an important motif is passed from voice to voice. It can be quite challenging for a choir to give the important musical material appropriate prominence, and to "get out of the way" when their particular musical line is of secondary importance. To stimulate the group's thinking as the motif is sung by the various voices, ask those singing that line to stand while those singing material of secondary importance remain seated. This provides a physical and visual reinforcement of the desired musical effect.

Another means of illustrating a musical idea through movement is to ask singers to conduct themselves. If a particular beat pattern is demonstrated for them, their response will be structured, creating a definite picture and feeling for the beats in each measure and their relative importance. If singers are told to conduct themselves in an unstructured, phrasal manner, a different kind of response will be prompted, in which the expressiveness and phrasing will be emphasized.

Snapping fingers, tapping feet, tapping the fingers of one hand lightly on the palm of the other, or even tapping the shoulder of a neighbor provide means of physically responding to the underlying pulse of a composition. Beyond establishing a basic pulse, if you demand that the tapping be done in a particular style, a new level of musical sensitivity may be achieved. Provide specific information for the singers on whether the tapping should be heavy, with a strong downward emphasis, or light, with an emphasis on the rebound.

Starting together, building phrases, and ending together can present choral problems, particularly for inexperienced singers. Even if agreement is reached on the precise moment of starting or stopping, the tone quality may suffer or the intonation may waver as the tone is initiated or ended. These problems may be remedied through the appropriate use of movement. Have the entire class hold one hand out, palm up, and tap the fingers of the other hand on it. Depending on the tempo of the selection, the basic unit or subdivisions of the unit could be tapped. The character of a choral entrance may be completely changed by altering the height from which the left hand hits the right, the force with which one hand strikes the other, and the amount of rebound. To attain a floating quality as well as a precise release, strike the open palm of the right hand a light glancing blow with the left, continuing upward with the left hand. If the release is effected at the moment of impact, it is difficult *not* to maintain a floating quality in the sound, rather than the "lunge" that sometimes occurs at the moment the tone ends.

The idea of using body movement to enhance musical understanding was propounded by Emile Jaques-Dalcroze in the early part of this century. *Eurhythmics* is the aspect of Dalcroze's method wherein movement is employed as a means of developing musical concepts. According to Dalcroze, rhythm *is* movement, and each of music's basic elements may be internalized by discovering physical movements that parallel musical events.

✣ DIAGNOSING CHORAL PROBLEMS ✣

Diagnosing and correcting choral problems is a critical ability for the choral music educator. It depends on previous experience, the establishment of a clear personal concept of tone that provides a goal to strive toward, and the ability to hear subtle differences in choral sound. A few choral problems are so common that we discuss them here in detail:

Poor intonation
Breathiness and lack of focus
Singing with tension in the throat
Lack of phrasing or sense of line

Poor Intonation

A chorus unable to sing in tune, either within itself or with the starting pitch, cannot be successful. Although there is disagreement among experts concerning the nature of good choral tone or matters of interpretation and expression, a choir is either in tune or it is not. Therefore, you must cultivate the ability to deal with problems of intonation effectively.

Poor intonation can be caused by a variety of factors. The following list is not exhaustive, but it includes some common reasons for out-of-tune singing:

1. Unfamiliar intervals in the individual vocal line
2. Range, tessitura, and dynamics
3. Lack of familiarity with the music
4. Poor fundamental vocal technique
5. Nerves

6. Fatigue
7. The temperature, humidity, and acoustical environment of the room.
8. Lack of attention to matters of intonation.

The intervals found in each vocal line may cause a particular part to experience intonation problems relative to the rest of the choir (usually flatting), or it might cause the choir as a whole to sing under pitch. Choirs need to be reminded that ascending intervals should be conceptualized as somewhat larger than they actually are, and descending intervals need to be thought of as smaller. Lines with many large intervals need to be sung with special emphasis on exactness in intervallic relationships. The third and seventh degrees of the key in which a song is written are particularly susceptible to flatting, and may need to be conceptualized as higher than they really are to be sung in tune.

Intonation problems often occur when songs move into the extremes of the vocal range or when they remain uncomfortably high or low in pitch for an extended period. Likewise, when a passage is extremely loud or soft, the intonation may be affected. To combat this, remind singers their basic vocal technique should remain unchanged as the dynamic level of the music changes. It may be helpful to remind them to always keep some volume in reserve and never to sing at the limit of their capacity. When singing softly, tell the choir to focus and compress the same amount of tone quality that they use at a louder dynamic level into the softer singing; soft singing must be supported, focused, vibrant, and alive to an even greater degree than a fortissimo passage. Loud singing must never turn into shouting, but should be carefully controlled. These suggestions should help singers maintain an evenness of tone as well as secure intonation.

When a choir begins to rehearse a piece of music, there may be a tendency to sing under the pitch. When this occurs, bring it to the choir's attention so singers are aware of the problem. As the choir members learn their individual lines more solidly, their ability to sing in tune will improve. As we noted previously, certain intervals are more troublesome than others to sing with good intonation.

When a choir experiences chronic intonation problems, either sharping or flatting, this is often an indication of poor basic vocal technique, or a lack of understanding and aural discrimination on the part of the director. Good posture, breathing, and vocal production greatly reduce intonation problems. Also, note that in auditioning your choir, those students with tonal memory problems are likely to experience difficulty singing in tune. The smaller the ensemble, the more obvious will be the effect on intonation if one or two singers have these kinds of problems.

Nerves and fatigue affect intonation differently, but they both have an adverse effect. Nerves, when the choir performs a selection publicly, or even as the time of performance grows near, may cause a tendency to sharp. This must be carefully monitored by the director. Work to calm the choir and to reassure them so nervousness is minimized. Fatigue has the opposite effect on a choir. It may be thought of in two senses: individual, general fatigue on the part of the choir members, which may have an adverse effect on all the choir's activities, and vocal fatigue, which is noticeable after the choir has been singing for a period of time. Choir members should be made aware of the importance of proper rest, exercise, and nutrition to combat individual fatigue. Vocal fatigue may be lessened by planning the order of music to be rehearsed so pieces with wide dynamic and pitch ranges are interspersed with less demanding selections, and by limiting the amount of continuous rehearsal time devoted to a strenuous piece of music. The order of selections to be rehearsed should be arranged to include a variety of keys and tempos.

The temperature, humidity, and acoustical environment of the rehearsal room or performance hall affect intonation significantly. A warm or humid room may cause flatting. The temperature and humidity should be cool and dry in order to rehearse most effectively. The acoustical environment is particularly noticeable when the choir changes locations, as usually happens in performance. If the choir performs in a hall that is less reverberant than their day-to-day rehearsal setting, it may be very disconcerting for singers. They will hear their own voice more clearly, and the voices around them will be less prominent. This can cause them either to push or to become overly tentative, and can create unwanted vocal tension. When changing environments, it is desirable to change from a drier, less resonant rehearsal room to a more alive and reverberant acoustical environment for the performance. Such a move will actually stimulate a feeling of enhanced security in the choir. The more reverberant the performance setting, the more attention will have to be given to matters of diction, in order for the texts to be intelligible to the audience.

The last reason for poor intonation is a lack of attention to the matter from the conductor. If the choir is allowed to sing with poor intonation without having it brought to their attention, the singers will gradually become accustomed to producing out-of-tune singing and will learn to accommodate the out-of-tune sounds. Even more regrettably, the same thing can happen to conductors who fail to correct intonation problems. It is the director's responsibility to make the choir aware of sharping or flatting problems and to present strategies for correcting them.

Correcting Other Vocal Problems

Breathiness and lack of focus in the tone are a particular problem for women in the adolescent years. They retain a concept of their "little girl's" tone, which is immature and unfocused. This sound must be altered in order for the mature woman's sound to emerge. Several strategies may help overcome this problem. Remind singers to open their mouths to sing—to think in terms of vertical space in the mouth and throat, rather than a horizontal, smiling concept of facial expression, which creates a spread tone. Tell them to focus their tone on some distant point, to aim at a spot on the front wall of the rehearsal room or the last row of the concert hall, and to project a focused sound to that point. Singers must also be cautioned not to sing "from the neck up." A sense of connection with the breathing mechanism must be maintained by conceptualizing the sound from the feet up, utilizing the entire body as the instrument. The sound of young singers at this stage must be constantly and carefully monitored and feedback provided so appropriate corrections may be made.

The current pop vocal sound of many female singers is not a desirable model for choral singing, since it is breathy, lacking in focus, and dependent on electronic amplification for projection. Many male pop singers also produce a sound that is an inappropriate model for most choral situations, although a positive point is their use of falsetto. The development of the falsetto voice is helpful in creating a solid male choral sound. A problem that seems to afflict young men more frequently than women is singing with tension in the throat. This problem is heard most often in the tenor section of the choir, although it also afflicts baritones and basses from time to time, when they move into the upper part of the range. The sound becomes pinched and often is flat. In addition to audible signs of tension, there are visible signs as well, such as a flushed complexion, a projecting chin, and visible tendons and blood vessels in the neck and throat. To combat this problem, urge young men to sing lightly and to develop their falsetto and head voice. The use of falsetto will not only extend the usable range of each of your male singers, but when the falsetto quality is blended into the voice as it moves into the middle and lower range, it will lighten the sound and make it more even throughout. Encourage singers to use this falsetto concept in the high part of the range and to shift subtly to full voice whenever it is comfortable. This is much preferred to the painful, tense sound of a young man straining to sing a G or an A above middle C full voice and not quite making it. Young men should be reminded to sing with their chin tucked and with the same sense of vertical space recommended for the women to combat breathiness.

A final common problem of choirs is a lack of phrasing or inability to sing with a pleasing vocal line. This problem may be due to poor fundamental vocal technique, which makes it impossible for the singers to produce a sustained line. It may, however, be caused by other factors. Phrasing and vocal line is always related to the accentuation and meaning of the text being sung. The first step in studying almost any choral score is to look at the text and pronounce it and see how the scheme of textual accentuation fits into the metrical framework of the song. In teaching music to the choir, make it clear that not all quarter notes (or any note value, for that matter) are created equal. The emphasis given to any note depends on its location in the metrical framework of the song and the text it carries. After locating where the primary and secondary accents occur in a phrase, determine the length of the phrases, the starting and stopping points within a piece of music. Teach the choir to maintain the flow of the music between the pauses. This flowing sound, including various accentuations depending on the text pronunciation and meaning, makes for expressive and correctly phrased music.

✣ TEACHING MUSIC READING ✣

The development of musical literacy is a vital aspect of comprehensive choral music education. The ability to comprehend musical notation and to reproduce accurately the sounds represented by musical symbols is an essential component of each student's musical development. In addition to its importance for each student's individual musical growth, the development of sight-reading skill in a choral ensemble facilitates its collective development and increases the efficiency with which it can assimilate new music. Finally, many music competitions require the sight-reading skill of participating choirs to be rated and included in the ensemble's score.

We are really speaking of two somewhat different areas when we speak of musical literacy and sight-singing skill. In the broad sense, an individual who is musically literate *understands* musical notation and the meanings of and relationships among various musical signs and symbols. A person who is musically literate is able to determine a great deal about the structure and organization of a musical selection from examining a written or printed score.

Sight-reading refers to the ability of an individual or an ensemble to take an unfamiliar piece of music and reproduce accurately the pitches, rhythms, and expressive markings contained in the score at sight, without the aid of a piano or other external prompting. There are individuals who are musically literate, understanding a great deal about musical notation, who are not particularly proficient sight readers.

Note that the ability to read music is not an all-or-nothing proposition. For example, virtually any choral singer develops the understanding very quickly that a note's position on the staff indicates its relative highness or lowness. Likewise, as singing experience is gained, the sensation of where a particular pitch lies and how it feels in one's own voice can be helpful in reading music. This kind of rudimentary understanding is close to one end of a continuum that extends to a fine musician who can sing or play an unfamiliar passage at sight, complete with expression and style.

As comprehensive choral music educators, part of our overriding objective is developing musically literate singers. Through a comprehensive approach to rehearsal, the use of questioning techniques, the pointing out of important aspects of the music being performed, and the involvement of students in musical decision making, musical literacy becomes a natural and inevitable product of rehearsal.

Sight-reading skill must be intentionally focused on in order for a choir to develop it efficiently. As a starting point, be certain to provide opportunities for a choir to actually sight-read the repertoire to be rehearsed. It is easy to get into the habit of simply having the accompanist play the parts and then having the choir imitate the keyboard. Instead, ask the choir to examine a new piece for a minute or two, noting the meter, key signature, tempo, and the voice leading of each section's own part. Then have the accompanist give the starting pitches, set the tempo, and let the ensemble read through the selection. Once the choir has read through a composition, the director has made comments, and the pianist has played through a particularly difficult passage, the choir is no longer sight-reading; they are rehearsing the music.

A variety of published materials can facilitate the development of sight-reading skill (see list at the end of the chapter). Various approaches to sight-singing have been used successfully by choral conductors. Numbers, solfège, Kodály hand signs, and neutral syllables are examples of some aids to sight-singing. A key element of success in teaching sight-reading is to select a method and materials with which you are comfortable and proficient and to use them consistently at each rehearsal.

The teaching of sight-reading skill is an area where good communication among music teachers at all levels within a district can facilitate students' efforts. If the same approach is used from kindergarten through high school, excellent sight-reading skills can be developed.

As we mentioned earlier, sight-reading is an aspect of many choral contests and competitions today. The preparation of a choir for contest sight-reading is important if the ensemble is to compete successfully (see Chapter 8 for information on preparing for other aspects of competition).

To the extent possible, sight-reading should be practiced for several weeks prior to the competition under contest conditions. Some states have begun recently to make available copies of outdated contest sight-reading material. At the end of the chapter we list the publishers of such materials from Michigan and Missouri. The use of these kinds of exercises is excellent in preparing a choir for competition. Ascertain exactly how the sight-reading portion of the competition is administered. Determine what kind of information the conductor may give a choir before and during sight-reading. Encourage the choir to view sight-reading as an enjoyable challenge. Stress the idea that if individuals get lost along the way and have to drop out, they should reenter as soon as possible.

A comprehensive choral music educator draws students into the active consideration of every piece of music rehearsed. This kind of critical thinking and musical analysis inevitably results from comprehensive choral rehearsal. These same analytical techniques are employed as students examine a new musical selection and sight-read it. If you approach sight-reading regularly and consistently, a choir's skill in this area will develop naturally and easily.

✣ EVALUATING REHEARSAL TECHNIQUE ✣

Certain criteria provide valid bases for the evaluation of an individual's rehearsal technique. These can be useful for the purposes of self-evaluation or to gain maximum benefit from the observation of others.

Pacing

Pacing is critical to an effective rehearsal. A problem faced by many beginning choral conductors is an overly slow rehearsal pace. This can be the result of uncertainty on the part of the conductor as to what to do next, or it can stem from nervousness. There should be virtually no pauses in the flow of the rehearsal as the choir sings, as feedback is given by the conductor, and as the choir responds.

If you are inexperienced, you may find you simply do not know what to do next. Get into the habit of being prepared with something to say the moment the choir stops singing. It does not have to be the single best solution to the choral problems at hand. It should simply be a statement of something for the choir to do that will improve their singing. Have the statement ready to use when you stop the choir. As you gain confidence, you will be able to hear things that need to be corrected which will immediately be apparent as the choir sings in rehearsal. In this way, you will develop a quick but comfortable rehearsal pace.

Sometimes, as a result of nerves, or because of a desire to accomplish as much as possible in rehearsal, choral conductors employ too quick a pace. The singers need time to assimilate the information presented in rehearsal. This problem is much less common than that of an overly slow pace.

As you gain experience, you will link the pacing of rehearsal to the tempo and style of the music being rehearsed. A very natural progression from singing to verbalization from the conductor, to singing again to incorporate changes, and so on, will be closely tied to the music under consideration. Sometimes the link is subtle, but it will usually be present when rehearsal is going well. It is easy to observe when this natural effective pace is disrupted. This sometimes occurs when a director and accompanist are unfamiliar with each other, and there are many awkward pauses as the choir waits for pitches to be given or for the accompanist to find the correct spot to begin.

Error Diagnosis and Correction Skill

One of the most important abilities for a choir director is the ability to listen perceptively to a choir's singing and to hear what the specific problems are at any given moment. Then, once the problem is perceived by the conductor, it must be brought to the attention of the choir and a specific strategy suggested for its remediation.

In observing student conductors, perhaps the most challenging part of their task is to focus on specific problems audible in the choral sounds being made in rehearsal. For example, if a selection is being rehearsed and the altos are singing a C instead of a C#, this needs to be corrected before it becomes ingrained in the choir.

Recently, some instructional material has been created to assist music education students in developing error detection skills. Many of these have involved instrumental ensembles. However, a useful choral error detection program is "The Choral Score Reading Program" by Richard F. Grunow and Milford H. Fargo (see Suggested Reading).

Leadership

Leadership may seem a somewhat difficult criterion to describe and analyze. In front of a choral ensemble it is essential to take control. Act confidently, even if you do not necessarily feel that way. Speak with sufficient volume to be easily heard by everyone. Establish eye contact with the individuals in the ensemble and maintain periodic contact with each singer. Be certain singers are fully involved in the rehearsal process. Move about the room from time to time and listen to the singers in various sections. Provide quick feedback concerning their work.

Knowledge of the Score

It is impossible to rehearse efficiently or effectively unless you have studied the score well enough to recognize when there are discrepancies between the notation in the score and the singing being done by the chorus.

As you gain experience, the time necessary for thorough score study will decrease. During the early stages of a career in choral music education, thorough and detailed score study will require a relatively large expenditure of time. It both permits efficient and effective rehearsal and makes the inexperienced conductor feel more confident.

✣ JUNIOR HIGH REHEARSAL TECHNIQUES ✣

The basic principles of comprehensive choral music education apply equally to programs at all grade levels. However, some special areas of rehearsal planning and techniques relate specifically to junior high choral music education. For the sake of convenience, the term *junior high* is used here to describe choral music experiences for early adolescents. It refers to any designation for students in grades 6 through 9.

Choral music in the junior high school has received increased attention from music educators recently. For many years it was often a misunderstood and undervalued area. A misconception of the changing voice and the early adolescent personality and the notion that junior high choral teaching was less rewarding and important than senior high school contributed to the undervaluing. Moreover, junior high students have had a reputation for being difficult to motivate and to discipline. Of course, there have been many talented and effective junior high music teachers and a variety of excellent junior high choral programs over the years, but this long-standing lack of understanding and attention on the part of many choral music educators resulted in frustration for junior high teachers as they sought information concerning teaching strategies, literature selection, techniques for working with changing voices, and other areas of particular concern.

Several articles in choral periodicals as well as various convention interest sessions in the 1980s and 1990s have been devoted to middle school and junior high school choral music. A crisis in this area was identified, which particularly focused on early adolescent male singers who have tended to drop out of choral music activity during the junior high years. These individuals have been lost to choral programs for the rest of their lives. Various ideas for resolving the crisis have been discussed. Some helpful strategies for retaining young men in the choral program are suggested here.

Throughout adolescence, young people undergo a wide variety of changes. Physical, mental, and emotional transitions that occur during the teen years have an impact on the way students learn and the strategies that should be employed for effective teaching. An understanding of adolescents and their special needs and potentialities is critical to successful junior high choral music education.

One of the most important areas of concern in junior high teaching is the way we nurture the changing voice and facilitate the vocal transition that occurs during these years. The voices of both males and females undergo profound changes as individuals move from childhood through adolescence to adulthood. The more obvious change occurs in young men as they lose the treble quality of the unchanged male voice and make the transition to the mature male sound. Traditionally, some misunderstanding and disagreement has existed concerning the male changing voice. This section explains some of the current thinking concerning the changing voice and its implications for the teacher of junior high school choral music, and reviews the thinking of several influential experts on the topic.

The limitations and special needs of the changing voice, particularly when a number of individuals whose voices are at various stages of maturation are combined into a choral ensemble, make the selection of appropriate music a particularly acute problem for junior high choral music teachers. The music currently available for junior high ensembles includes a variety of voicings, styles, and quality.

The Place of the Junior High in the Comprehensive Choral Music Education Program

Although much of the present section is concerned with aspects of choral music education that are unique to the junior high school, or which merit particular emphasis in dealing with the early adolescent singer, remember that the junior high program is part of a continuum. A good comprehensive choral music program begins at the elementary level, continues through junior high, and culminates at the senior high school. The curriculum should be planned and implemented from kindergarten through senior high school in such a way that students receive the maximum opportunity for effective, sequential musical learning.

The junior high is critically important in this curriculum. The effects of an excellent elementary music program can be quickly negated when the junior high program is ineffective. Although a senior high school director of only marginal skill can have a relatively successful program when fed by a thriving junior high choir, it is very difficult for even a highly talented music educator to maintain a solid senior high choral program when the school(s) that feed into the high school do not provide effective, carefully planned choral music education experiences. Even more important than its impact on the rest of the curriculum is the fact that when junior high choral music education is ineffective, students at a particularly important time of their life are turned off to a musical experience that could enhance their adult lives.

There needs to be regular open communication between the teachers of music at all levels in a comprehensive choral music education program. You must create goals and objectives for the total program and plan the role of each level to fulfill your objectives. This process is described in greater detail in Chapter 9.

Teaching Adolescents

The junior high years are a time of many changes for young people, most of which are associated with the onset of puberty. Many physical changes accompany puberty in early adolescence. Hormonal changes initiate dramatic changes in sexual characteristics as well as height, weight, physical strength and coordination, and the emotions. Some of these changes relate directly to the vocal mechanism and are of particular interest to the choral music educator. They are described in greater detail later.

The level of maturity found among junior high students varies widely. The changes they experience begin at different ages and occur at different rates in each individual. Girls tend to mature earlier than boys, so there are marked differences in both the physical and emotional maturity of each student.

The emotions of junior high students are subject to wide variation. In a short space of time they can go from extreme disappointment and depression to happy exuberance. Since their emotions are subject to wide swings, students at this age appreciate orderliness and structure in the classroom and evenness and fairness from the instructor. Even though they may test the patience of the teacher, they expect an orderly and disciplined classroom. In such a setting, where a student's individual dignity and personality are protected and nurtured, adolescents are able to learn efficiently. Ironically, students who are most desirous of a structured learning environment may be the very individuals who test its limits (and the teacher's patience).

Junior high students are highly enthusiastic and motivated. The key is to channel their energy and direct their motivation toward the positive musical and educational goals you have planned. In reality, it is easier to recruit and to maintain the interest of junior high students than those in senior high school. Early adolescents are interested in exploring their strengths and weaknesses in a variety of areas, and they are not yet at a point where after-school employment, car ownership, and other interests compete for their attention.

Junior high students appreciate activities that require active involvement. A lengthy lecture concerning the stylistic characteristics of Brahms's "I'd Enter Your Garden" will not engage the interest of a typical junior high class. They need opportunities to *experience* things, rather than to be told about them. Present them with a variety of activities to hold their interest. The classroom should be carefully structured and consistent in format, but within that structure the activities provided on a day-to-day basis should be highly varied.

Although junior high students respond well to a hands-on approach to instruction, their intellect is making the transition from thinking in concrete terms to being able to deal with increasingly abstract ideas. Junior high students respond extremely well to choral pieces that deal with the emotional issues they are confronting, such as friendship, romance, and idealism. Avoid children's songs like the ones they sang in elementary school.

Junior high students appreciate a positive and enthusiastic approach. For example, the voice change is a phenomenon which, if approached positively, is an intriguing event in the life of an adolescent. A junior high male may experience a rapid growth spurt that suddenly gives him "two left feet," but it is exciting to become more adult in appearance. Junior high students respond to and appreciate an instructor who is positive about the events taking place in their lives and who takes an interest in each member of the choral music class.

Many of the attributes of junior high young people may seem paradoxical. Students at this level are rapidly developing individual personalities, learning styles, and attitudes, yet they are highly conformist. The right clothing labels, hairstyles, and activities are important to early adolescents even as their individuality and distinctive personalities emerge. Once junior high students see that choir is an activity their friends are involved with, positive peer pressure will make them eager to participate in the program. Since the early adolescent years are a transition from childhood to adulthood, there will be times when students act remarkably mature and sophisticated and other occasions when they revert back to childhood activities and attitudes.

A teacher of junior high students must possess all of the qualities of any fine choral music educator. However, two attributes are particularly important at this level of choral music education: enthusiasm and keyboard skill. A teacher of junior high students must be able to stimulate their interest through his or her own enthusiasm. If you are excited about the subject matter, the students will "catch" your enthusiasm. More than any other level of instruction, effective junior high level teaching requires solid functional keyboard skill. At the elementary level, children's expectations of the instructor in this area are minimal, and the music to be accompanied tends to be quite straightforward and relatively simple. At the senior high level, it becomes increasingly common for accompanists to be hired or for a student to possess accompanying ability. In the junior high, the accompaniments of many of the pieces are quite demanding, students expect the instructor will be able to realize them accurately, and it is unlikely a skilled accompanist will be available.

Dealing with the Changing Voice

Knowledge of the vocal changes that occur in the early adolescent years is critical to the junior high choral music educator. It holds important implications for repertoire selection, rehearsal strategies, seating arrangements, and other aspects of junior high school choral music education.

To begin with, note that everyone's voice is constantly in a state of transition, including people of all ages, and of both sexes, from birth to death. This transition is readily audible as individuals move through early adulthood, middle age, and the senior years. The fact that people's voices change constantly helps make choral music teaching an interesting and complex subject at any level. For teachers of junior high students, the dramatic vocal changes that occur in early adolescence, particularly in young men, have implications that cannot be ignored.

What Is the Changing Voice? Over the years, there have been a variety of theories, explanations, and descriptions of the changing voice. Before examining some of these theories, we present some basic information concerning the vocal change (or vocal mutation, as it is referred to by some).

As we noted previously, adolescence is a time of significant change for a young person as the transition is made from childhood to adulthood. As young men mature, the vocal quality changes from the characteristic treble sound of the boy's voice to the masculine quality of the adult male singer. This occurs as the vocal folds lengthen approximately one-sixth of an inch, thicken, and the larynx becomes larger. In addition to changes in the immediate area of the vocal folds, as a young man grows physically, other physiological structures grow and develop. Inasmuch as the entire body is involved in the act of singing, all of these changes contribute to the change in vocal quality.

Views of the Changing Voice. The vocal change begins at different times and occurs at various rates in each individual. These individual differences in the experience of the vocal change have prompted disagreement among experts on many aspects of the change as well as the most effective instructional strategies for dealing with it.

For many years, until the middle of the twentieth century, the most prevalent view concerning the changing voice held that the voice should be "rested" during the change. According to this line of thinking, when it became obvious a young man's voice was beginning to change, he was told to stop singing until the change was complete, at which point he could resume vocal activity.

A problem with this reasoning was that many young men lost interest in continuing their musical activity once they stopped singing during early adolescence. As a practical matter, it is difficult, if not impossible, for an adolescent male to rest the voice as he pursues his normal activities, including sports, play, and other areas where the voice is used in much more stressful ways than in chorus class. As a result of these and other problems with the notion of resting the voice during the change, some authorities espoused the view that gentle vocalization during the voice change was helpful in easing the transition.

During the mid-twentieth century, the changing voice began to attract the attention of some music educators who looked at the issue more rigorously and scientifically than had previously been attempted. Three men whose thinking greatly influenced American thinking regarding the changing voice in the middle of the twentieth century were Frederick Swanson, Duncan McKenzie, and Irvin Cooper. Each man viewed the vocal change somewhat differently, and each one's thinking has had a major impact on more recent research in the area. The information presented here briefly introduces the thinking of each expert concerning the voice change. For a full explanation of each theory, consult the writings of each man, found in the Suggested Readings.

Frederick Swanson, a music educator in Moline, Illinois, believed the vocal change was rapid, occurring over the space of a few weeks. According to his theory, at the time of vocal change, the voice often quickly drops an octave to the range shown in Figure 2.8.

Swanson labeled young men whose voices had recently changed "adolescent basses." Some other important facets of his thinking include the notion that when boys' voices change, for a time an "area of silence" can exist between the bass and treble voice (around middle C), wherein the young singer is unable to phonate. Another tenet of Swanson's thinking is that young men whose voices have changed (or who are in the midst of the change, which Swanson regards as brief) should receive vocal training apart from the young men with unchanged voices and the female singers.

A second theorist with important ideas concerning the changing voice was *Duncan McKenzie,* a music educator who began his career in Canada and later taught in the United States. Unlike Swanson, McKenzie claimed the voice change was gradual. Instead of the voice quickly dropping an octave and the change occurring over a few weeks, McKenzie believed that as the change occurred, an adolescent male singer began to lose notes in the

FIGURE 2.8 Swanson's Adolescent Bass Range

upper range and to add them on to the bottom, finally settling into the tenor or baritone range. During the transition process, there may be a period of time when a young man has a range of only four or five notes.

As a young man's voice begins to change, he moves down through the treble range and into an area with a distinctive sound, which is between the unchanged treble quality and the sound of a newly changed junior high baritone. McKenzie labeled the young man whose voice was at this point an "alto-tenor." After moving through the alto-tenor range the adolescent male voice becomes a junior high baritone, after which it settles into the tenor, baritone, or bass range. McKenzie's ranges for adolescent voices are shown in Figure 2.9.

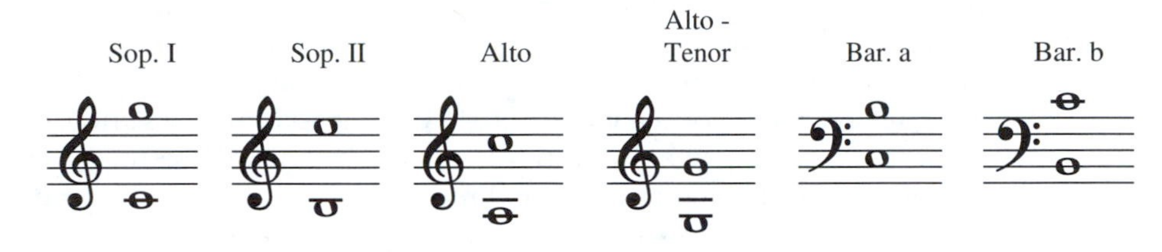

FIGURE 2.9 McKenzie's Ranges

A third mid-twentieth-century vocal change theorist was *Irvin Cooper*. Like McKenzie, Cooper taught in Canada and then came to the United States, spending two decades on the faculty at Florida State University. Cooper referred to the range of the changing voice as the *cambiata* range, and his method of dealing with the changing voice is known as the cambiata plan (see Figure 2.10). Cooper published several collections of songs arranged for ensembles with changing voices, including a cambiata vocal line suitable for use by young men whose voices were changing. Cooper's students and others have continued to write SACB music since his death in 1971.

As was the case with McKenzie, Cooper believed the voice change was gradual and should be monitored carefully so young men sing lines that are

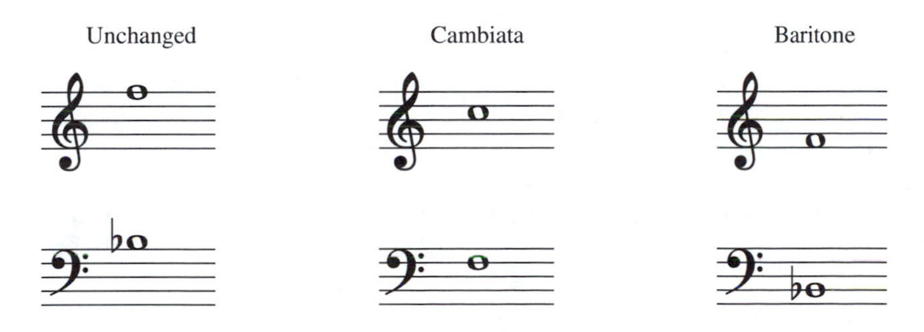

FIGURE 2.10 Cooper's Ranges

comfortable for them. Also, he believed that as young men moved from the characteristic treble quality of the unchanged voice into the changed quality, the voice moved initially into the baritone range before settling into the tenor or bass range of the completely changed voice.

Recently, the work of *John Cooksey* concerning the changing voice has received well-deserved attention. His "contemporary eclectic theory" of vocal mutation was first presented in a series of articles in the *Choral Journal* (see Suggested Reading) in the late 1970s. More recently he published a booklet (1992) updating his earlier writing and suggesting strategies for working with adolescent voices in the classroom. Cooksey's theory was based on and synthesized the work of Swanson, McKenzie, and Cooper, as well as Cooksey's personal research into the changing voice. Since its publication, further research by Cooksey as well as by other authorities have given it additional validity.

Cooksey describes a five-step process of vocal change (see Figure 2.11). He believes the process of vocal change takes from one to two years and that the age at which the change begins and the rate of change varies among individuals. Symptoms of the onset of vocal mutation in young men include changes in vocal range and tessitura, timbre, and in the quality of the speaking voice.

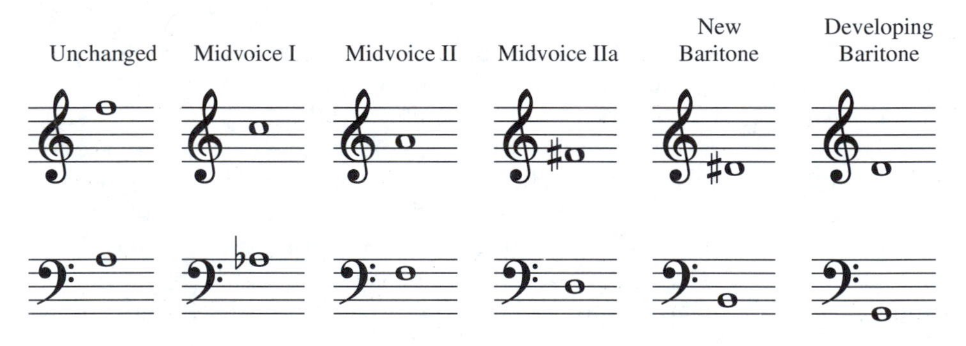

FIGURE 2.11 Cooksey's Ranges

The male vocal change has received much greater attention from choral experts than that experienced by females because of its more dramatic nature and its profound implications for choral music education at the junior high level. Adolescent female voices also undergo a transition, albeit less dramatic, as they move from the treble voice of childhood through adolescence to adulthood and vocal maturity. At both the junior high and senior high levels, female voices are rather uniform in range and quality. Adolescent young women should be given the opportunity to vocalize throughout their range and to try singing both alto and soprano lines before being assigned to one line or the other. As with the young men, they should be encouraged to constantly monitor their own voice and to communicate with the choral music teacher about any changes or other concerns.

In recent years, the work of *Lynne Gackle* concerning the female voice change has attracted national attention. She describes four stages in the vocal development of adolescent females (see Figure 2.12). A look at the ranges and tessituras of the four stages reveals that the changes occurring in the female voice are much more subtle than those in the male.
The labeling of the Stages IIA and IIB as pre- and postmenarcheal indicates the close association of the female voice change with the onset of menstruation. As the female voice changes, Gackle enumerates a variety of symptoms including pitch insecurity, breathiness or huskiness of tone, change in speaking voice, change in range capabilities, and the development of register breaks.

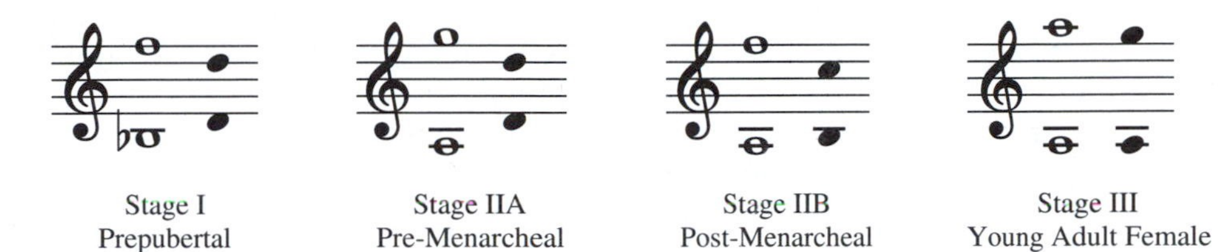

FIGURE 2.12 Gackle's Adolescent Female Ranges and Tessitura

Selecting Music

The selection of music for use with any ensemble is a critical concern. Where changing voices are involved, the selection process is even more complex and important. In recent years, publishers have done a much better job than previously of making available high-quality arrangements suitable for early adolescent voices. Nevertheless, the choral music educator must be discerning. Even a choral series with a title indicating it was created for young singers or for changing voices should be examined to determine whether it meets the needs of you and your singers in a particular semester or year.

Music in a variety of voicings is available for junior high choirs, including SATB, SAB, SSAA, SSA, unison, SACB or SSCB, as well as music with lines for midvoice range. Some music uses only numbers to label the various vocal lines, rather than assigning a name. Any of this music *could* be effective for a junior high choir, but it might just as easily be ineffective or even harmful. Therefore, criteria need to be developed for evaluating the appropriateness of music, whatever the voicing.

All of the criteria for selecting music for any choir, described in Chapter 5, are applicable to the junior high situation. Some of the criteria are of particular importance in dealing with junior high voices. These include range and tessitura, voice leading, and text.

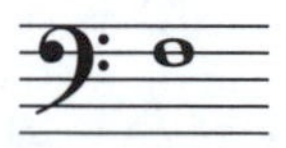

FIGURE 2.13 The Range of the Male Changing Voice

It should be obvious, based on the discussion concerning the changing voice, that range is an extremely important criterion in selecting music. Whatever label you apply to the male changing voice (cambiata, alto-tenor, or midvoice) it is clear that when the voice is changing it will fall somewhere into the range shown in Figure 2.13. At the height of the change, the range for a young man may be even smaller (see Figure 2.14). Therefore, you must carefully select music that suits your particular choir in a specific year, and be sure to check and recheck the ranges and timbres of the young men participating to be sure they are singing the correct part and their voice has not shifted since they were originally assigned a vocal line.

Unison music is usually inappropriate for a mixed choir of changing voices, since it is virtually impossible to find a range that accommodates all of the singers comfortably. Although it might seem simpler to have only one vocal line to deal with, the fact is that well-arranged six- or even eight-part music can be much more usable because lines may be written to accommodate individuals in various stages of vocal development.

In a lot of four-part (SATB) music, the soprano, alto, and tenor parts will often be too high for changing voices while the bass part is too low. Even if the soprano or alto part could be sung by the changing voices, it can have an unfortunate connotation for a junior high male to be assigned to a "girl's part."

Much three-part (SAB) music is written to be performed by adult choirs with too few male singers to perform four-part literature effectively. Such arrangements share the potential problems of SATB literature: None of the vocal lines are suitable for individuals with changing voices. An additional problem of many SAB arrangements is that the three-part texture results in unsatisfactory harmony and voice leading.

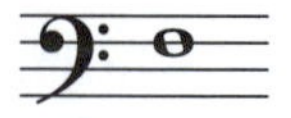

FIGURE 2.14 The Range of the Height of the Change

Some SSA or SSAA music might work for a mixed choir with changing voices, assuming some choir members sing their part down an octave, but the fact that young men would be singing girls' music would still be a problem. Some music is currently published with flexible voicing and each part is simply labeled with a number. Thus, when parts are assigned, the negative aspect of a male singing a girl's line is eliminated.

In addition to range, the second criterion for music selection that should be given particular weight is the matter of voice leading. When the voice is at the height of vocal mutation, it lacks flexibility. Examine music carefully to be sure the lines sung by those with changing voices are primarily stepwise in motion. Avoid pieces that contain lines with large leaps, particularly when they occur in quick succession.

Text is of primary importance in the evaluation of any choral piece, but for junior high choirs, the text must not only be interesting and carefully wedded to the musical line, but it must be appropriate for students at this grade level. Its emotional content must be understandable for early adolescents. It must not be childish, or else it will seem a throwback to elementary school, and no junior high student wants to do elementary school things. Current popular music must be evaluated in terms of its sexual references, language, and the ethic it teaches. Each school district and each choral music educator has a philosophy concerning what is appropriate for its students and what is not.

Working with Changing Voices

In working with changing voices, perhaps the first consideration is the seating arrangement for the choir. As we mentioned earlier, it is very important to monitor closely the voices of everyone in the choir. Since the voices will be shifting in range and timbre, there is little point in carefully placing students into a static arrangement. Be prepared to shift students around to accommodate the changes that occur in the course of a semester or a year.

The important point to remember in figuring out how to arrange the sections of a mixed chorus with changing voices is to set things up so all of the men are seated together. This means those young men whose voices are unchanged or changing will be seated along the edge of the men's section so they can sing with the young women whose voices are similar in range, yet remain a part of the men's section (see Figure 2.15).

The continuing development of good vocal technique will help ease the vocal transition. The exercises suggested in Chapter 1 are useful with adolescent singers in both junior and senior high. In vocalizing students whose voices are changing, be certain to insist on light singing; help students avoid oversinging by pointing it out whenever it occurs. Initiate vocalises in the most comfortable range for students and work outward from there. Avoid pushing the voice by demanding loud singing in the extremes of the range.

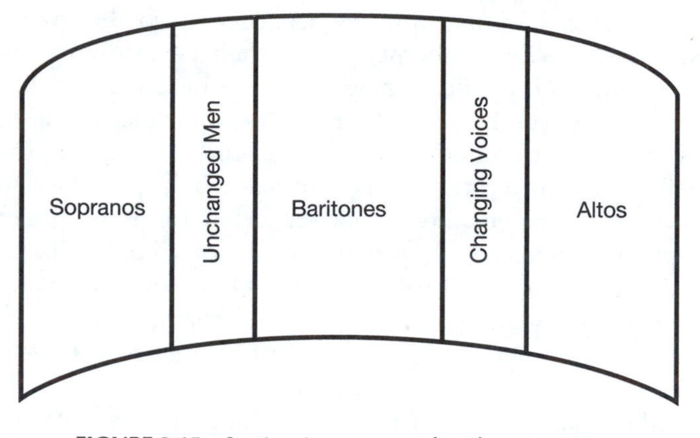

FIGURE 2.15 Seating Arrangement for Changing Voices

The exercising and development of the falsetto range and the extension of the light falsetto quality into the lower part of the range will help male singers keep the vocal quality light and will promote the use of head voice throughout the range.

Do not rehearse a piece of music for too long a period of time. Vocal fatigue can be avoided by using a variety of music and carefully monitoring the range demands of the music being rehearsed. Watch and listen for vocal stress—a pinched sound, intonation problems, red face, or bulging tendons in the neck are all indicators. Of course, a relaxed throat is a requirement for any singer, but it is particularly important when the voice is as vulnerable as it is during the early adolescent years.

Vocalises from Chapter 1 will help singers at the junior high level as well as older students to develop the solid basic vocal technique needed for successful choral singing.

✣ SUMMARY ✣

Effective choral rehearsal techniques are critical to the comprehensive choral music educator. This chapter focused on planning and implementing effective strategies for rehearsal. As we stated at the outset, the information contained in this chapter can only be assimilated by the prospective conductor by trying out the ideas presented here in front of a group of singers.

The discussion of rehearsal planning included information regarding auditions and seating arrangements, planning the first rehearsal, and short-term and long range rehearsal planning, including the development of musical literacy. In addition, techniques for rehearsal communication and the diagnosis of choral problems were presented. Issues pertinent to junior high choral music education were presented and strategies for dealing with junior high voices were discussed.

Perhaps the most important aspect of effective rehearsal technique is the ability to conduct clearly and expressively. Of all the modes of communicating with a choir, conducting gestures are the most effective and efficient. Chapter 3 is concerned with developing conducting skills.

Questions

1. What are some ways in which you can gain practical experience in choral conducting as an undergraduate student?
2. Among the various components of a choral audition, what is the best predictor of choral success?
3. What are some considerations in arranging the seating of an ensemble for rehearsal and performance?
4. What are some things to keep in mind in planning your first rehearsal with a new choral ensemble?
5. What differentiates comprehensive choral music education from other approaches in terms of rehearsal planning?
6. What are the three modes of rehearsal communication? How proficient are you in each mode? What can you do to strengthen your areas of weakness?
7. What are some problems to be avoided in the use of humor in the choral rehearsal?
8. What are some precautions to keep in mind concerning the use of piano in rehearsal?
9. Can you think of a way to use movement to teach a choir to sing expressively?
10. What are some factors that affect a choir's intonation?
11. Why is the junior high level so important to the comprehensive choral music education program?
12. In what respects do the special needs of the changing voice affect the selection of music for the junior high choir?
13. Why has there been disagreement concerning the nature of the changing voice?

Note

1. The material included in this section is drawn from John Hylton, "Keeping Your Choir on the Move," *Music Educators Journal, 74* (3) (November 1987), pp. 31–34.

Suggested Reading

BOYD, JACK. *Rehearsal Guide for the Choral Conductor.* West Nyack, NY: Parker, 1971.

COOKSEY, JOHN M. "The Development of a Contemporary, Eclectic Theory for the Training and Cultivation of the Junior High School Male Changing Voice." *The Choral Journal, 18* (2, 3, 4, 5) (October 1977–January 1978).

———. *Working with the Adolescent Voice.* St. Louis: Concordia, 1992.

COOPER, IRVIN. *Changing Voices in Junior High: Letters to Pat.* New York: Carl Fischer, 1953.

COOPER, IRVIN, and KARL O. KUERSTEINER. *Teaching Junior High School Music.* Boston: Allyn and Bacon, 1970.

DECKER, HAROLD A., and JULIUS HERFORD. *Choral Conducting Symposium* (2nd ed.). Englewood Cliffs, NJ: Prentice Hall, 1988.

DECKER, HAROLD A., and COLLEEN KIRK. *Choral Conducting: Focus on Communication.* Englewood Cliffs, NJ: Prentice Hall, 1988.

EHMANN, WILHELM. *Choral Directing.* Trans. George D. Wiebe. Minneapolis: Augsburg, 1968.

EHRET, WALTER. *The Choral Conductor's Handbook.* New York: Marks, 1959.

GACKLE, LYNNE. "The Adolescent Female Voice: Characteristics of Change and Stages of Development." *The Choral Journal, 31* (8) (March 1991), pp. 17–25.

GARRETSON, ROBERT L. *Conducting Choral Music* (7th ed.). Englewood Cliffs, NJ: Prentice Hall, 1993.

GRUNOW, RICHARD F. and MILFORD H. FARGO. *The Choral Score Reading Program.* Chicago: GIA, 1985. (Workbook and audio cassettes)

HEFFERNAN, CHARLES W. *Choral Music: Technique and Artistry.* Englewood Cliffs, NJ: Prentice-Hall, 1982.

HERMAN, SALLY. "Junior High Choirs: The Sky's the Limit." *The Choral Journal 25* (February 1985), pp. 17–21.

HILLIS, MARGARET. *At Rehearsal.* New York: American Choral Foundation, 1969.

HOWERTON, GEORGE. *Technique and Style in Choral Singing.* New York: Carl Fischer, 1957.

HYLTON, JOHN. "The Junior High Vocal Music Program," in Kenneth E. Miller, *Vocal Music Education* (pp. 75–117). Englewood Cliffs, NJ: Prentice Hall, 1988.

KOHUT, DANIEL L., and JOE W. GRANT. *Learning to Conduct and Rehearse.* Englewood Cliffs, NJ: Prentice Hall, 1990.

LAMB, GORDON H. *Choral Techniques* (5th ed.). Dubuque, IA: William C. Brown, 1988.

LONG, R. GERRY. *The Conductor's Workshop, Part I.* Dubuque, IA: William C. Brown, 1977.

MOE, DANIEL. *Basic Choral Concepts.* Minneapolis: Augsburg, 1972.

MCKENZIE, DUNCAN. *Training the Boy's Changing Voice.* London: Bradford and Dickens, Drayton House, 1956.

NEIDIG, KENNETH, and JOHN JENNINGS. *Choral Conductor's Guide.* West Nyack, NY: Parker, 1967.

PFAUTSCH, LLOYD. *Mental Warmups for the Choral Conductor.* New York: Lawson-Gould, 1969.

ROBINSON, RAY, and ALLEN WINOLD. *The Choral Experience.* New York: Harper's College Press, 1976.

ROE, PAUL F. *Choral Music Education.* Englewood Cliffs, NJ: Prentice-Hall, 1970.

SWANSON, FREDERICK J. *Music Teaching in the Junior High and Middle School.* New York: Appleton-Century-Crofts, 1973.

VAN CAMP, LEONARD. *Warmups for Minds, Ears, and Voices.* New York: Lawson-Gould, 1973.

WILSON, HARRY R. *Artistic Choral Singing.* New York: Schirmer, 1959.

Sight-Reading Methods and Materials

ANDERSON, TOM. *Sing Choral Music at Sight.* Vienna, VA: Music Educators National Conference, 1992.

ARKIS, STANLEY, and HERMAN SCHUCKMAN. *The Choral Sight Singer.* New York: Carl Fischer, 1970.

BAUGHESS, DAVID. *The Jenson Sight Singing Course.* New Berlin, WI: Jenson, 1984.

DRUMMOND, R. PAUL. *Never Love Unless.* Columbia: Missouri State High School Activities Association, 1993.

———. *Praise Ye the Lord.* Columbia: Missouri State High School Activities Association, 1993.

———. *Shall I Wasting in Despair.* Columbia: Missouri State High School Activities Association, 1993.

EHRET, WALTER. *See and Sing.* Miami: Belwin Mills, 1957.

LEACH, MARY BELLE, JOHN HEMMENWAY, and MARY NAN WEHRUNG. *The Key to Sight Reading Success.* Houston: AMC Music, 1977.

LEONARD, JAMES. *M.S.V.A. Sight Reading Materials (1972).* Champaign, IL: Mark Foster Music, 1972.

———. *M.S.V.A. Sight Reading Materials (1973).* Champaign, IL: Mark Foster Music, 1973.

———. *M.S.V.A. Sight Reading Materials (1974).* Champaign, IL: Mark Foster Music, 1974.

SNYDER, AUDREY. *The Sight Singer.* Miami: CPP/Belwin, 1993.

VANDRE, CARL W. *Three-Part Sight Reading Fun.* Miami: Belwin Mills, 1940.

———. *Sight Reading Fun for Changed Voices.* Miami: Belwin Mills, 1942.

Conducting/Rehearsal Technique Videotapes

ADAMS, CHARLOTTE. *Daily Workout for a Beautiful Voice.* Santa Barbara: Santa Barbara Music, SBMP21, 1992.

EHLY, EPH. *Excellence in Conducting.* Milwaukee: Hal Leonard, 1988.

———. *Positive Motivation for the Choral Rehearsal.* Milwaukee: Hal Leonard, 1988.

———. *Tuning the Choir.* Milwaukee: Hal Leonard, 1988.

HAASEMANN, FRAAKE, and JAMES M. JORDAN. *Group Vocal Techniques.* Chapel Hill, NC: Hinshaw Music, 1990.

LAWRENCE, DOUGLAS. *101 Things to Say to Your Choir.* Vol. 1, *Verbal Imagery.* Vol. 2, *Choral Development*. Anderson, IN: Thomas House, 1993.

PFAUTSCH, LLOYD. *Coming Alive: Choral Conducting.* Minneapolis: Augsburg Fortress, 1989.

Chapter Three

Developing Conducting Skill

❖ ❖ ❖

❖ INTRODUCTION ❖

As we discussed in Chapter 2, comprehensive choral music education occurs most clearly in the context of the rehearsal. Clear and expressive conducting is one of the most important attributes of effective rehearsal technique. It is a mode of rehearsal communication. Along with verbalization and demonstration, it has the potential to communicate quickly and efficiently what is desired from the choir. Chapter 1 stressed the importance of developing a personal concept of choral tone. Unless you have in mind a clear tonal objective for the choir, your conducting technique will be ineffective.

Clarity and expressiveness are the two critical attributes of effective conducting. If conducting gestures do not communicate clearly what the conductor intends, then they are ineffective and should be modified or discarded. In addition, conducting gestures must convey the expressive nuances of the music. Once the fundamentals of starting and stopping the choir and maintaining a clear and steady beat pattern are established, the conducting student can begin to work on communicating the expressive content of the music. In teaching conducting, it is critical to allow sufficient time for students to master the basic psychomotor skills required for a clear preparatory beat and basic beat patterns before concentrating on expression.

As with so many of the topics presented here, a cautionary note is necessary. This chapter includes some important basic ideas concerning conducting technique and applies them to examples of choral repertoire. Numerous excellent texts dealing specifically with conducting techniques are listed at the end of the chapter. This discussion introduces some of the basic issues in developing conducting skills because clear and expressive conducting is an important aspect of comprehensive choral music education.

Teaching Conducting

With the continuing development of high-quality, relatively inexpensive videotaping equipment, it is essential to provide regular videotaped feedback to conducting students. When teaching conducting, I begin at the first or second class meeting to develop a cumulative video record of each student's progress. Each student conductor brings a videotape to class for this purpose. Have a monitor available for immediate playback to students if time is available and class size permits. Otherwise, provide written or verbal comments concerning each students' work immediately, to be considered by the students as they view their own videotape privately at their convenience.

From the very beginning of the semester, get the students up, out of their seats, and conducting. In addition to facilitating the development of solid technique, this immediate involvement breaks down any inhibitions or reluctance on the part of inexperienced conductors to get up in front of a group of people, wave their arms, and rehearse a group of singers.

Initially, an extended period of time—several weeks—should be devoted to getting students acclimated to the various basic beat patterns. Monitor each student's progress carefully, and aim for clarity and simplicity of gesture. Only after this basic clarity of gesture has been established is it fruitful to work for more expressive conducting. Too often, students are rushed through the basic gestures and on to concepts of expression, style, and other sophisticated concerns. The result can be insecurity, a tendency to lose the beat, and the presence of idiosyncratic, unproductive mannerisms in the individual's conducting technique. The teaching of conducting is primarily a matter of individual coaching, encouragement, and feedback, particularly as students move beyond the concerns of clarity and work to develop an expressive conducting style.

A student who is completely lacking in previous experience may require significantly more work on basic beat patterns. Another individual who perhaps has had previous experience directing a choir could have an immediate grasp of the basic patterns, but will need to eliminate some bad habits in order to establish conducting clarity. In conducting, as in singing, much of your work as the teacher must be devoted to eliminating bad habits to make the student's technique natural, simple, and clear. Some students are reticent by nature and will need encouragement to make their basic beat pattern larger when the music calls for it; others will be more flamboyant and will need to concentrate on reducing the size of their gestures when the music requires it.

In the conducting class, as in the choir, it is important to provide feedback to students in a positive manner. Like singing, conducting is a physical phenomenon, requiring the student's total involvement. It requires physical, mental, and emotional discipline. A student's personality is closely connected with his or her conducting style, requiring careful nurturing and sensitivity to each conductor's unique strengths and weaknesses.

The next section focuses on the development of clarity of conducting gestures. Without a clear beat pattern, preparatory beat, and starting and ending gestures, it is impossible to communicate ideas regarding dynamics, articulation, textual accentuation, and other components of style and expression.

The second part of the chapter concerns the communication of expression through conducting gestures. Once the basic elements of clarity have been mastered, the conductor may then work to establish the expressive aspects of conducting technique, including the conveying of dynamic indications, textual accentuation, and mood.

Clear and expressive conducting technique is a potent communications tool, both in rehearsal and performance. Ultimately, the objective for the conductor is to present a visual image of the music, enabling the choral ensemble to understand the musical events taking place and to communicate that understanding to an audience.

✣ DEVELOPING CLEAR CONDUCTING GESTURES ✣

The correct basic posture for a choral conductor is identical to what we seek to develop in singers. Place the feet approximately 18 inches apart. Distribute your weight evenly on the balls of your feet. Stand comfortably erect and tall, chest held high, but without tension in the neck, shoulders, and chest area. Align your body in as straight a manner as possible from the head, through the shoulders, chest, waist, and legs. Let your arms hang loosely at the sides. The moment we stand in front of a choral ensemble, we must model correct singing posture. We should immediately convey an attitude of confidence and of relaxed intensity (see Figure 3.1).

The beat pattern is conducted with the right hand. Three joints are primarily involved in making the conducting gesture: the shoulder, the elbow, and the wrist. Conducting gestures should move primarily from the shoulder, less from the elbow, and even less from the wrist. Too much wrist movement may make the conductor feel more artistic or expressive, but it detracts from the strength and clarity of the gesture.

As an exercise, the instructor should demonstrate with a simple up-and-down motion of the arm, movement from the shoulder, the elbow, and the wrist, first individually and then in combination. Students should

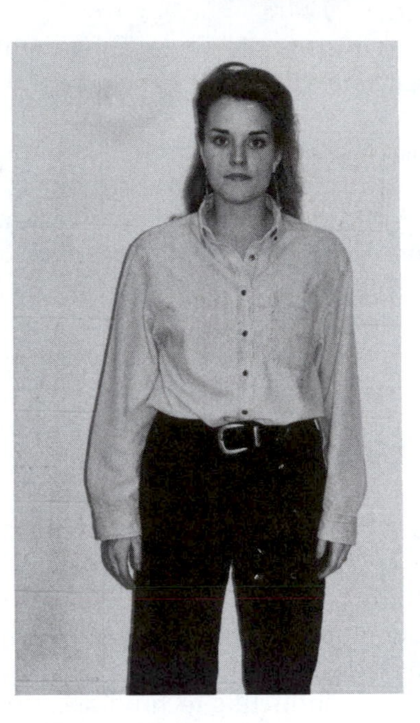

FIGURE 3.1 Correct Basic Posture

observe what communicates clearly and what does not. Ask the students to try it. When the arm is moved from the wrist, elbow, and shoulder equally, the beat is confused and unclear. When the movement is primarily from the shoulder it is clear and conveys strength and authority. Once this basic up-and-down beating pattern is mastered, the student is ready to tackle the basic patterns associated with various meters.

Beat Patterns

At this point feedback from the instructor and viewing yourself on videotape will assist in making the beat pattern as clear as possible. Initially, let the left hand continue to hang loosely at the side and become comfortable with making the pattern using the right hand. Ultimately, your left hand will be used for a variety of expressive purposes, but the habit of constantly mirroring the right hand with the left detracts from clarity and should be avoided. Keep the conducting gestures moving primarily from the shoulder with a minimum of tension in the arm.

The Four-Beat Pattern. The first of the basic beat patterns we consider is the four-beat pattern, which is the most commonly used (see Figure 3.2). Note that beat 1 is down, beat 2 to the left, 3 to the right, and 4 is up, to the left, returning to the position where beat 1 (and the whole pattern) started.

Each point in the pattern where a beat occurs is called an *ictus*. The ictus of beat 1 occurs at the lowest point in the pattern and is followed by a rebound that is virtually straight up (except in the case of an extremely

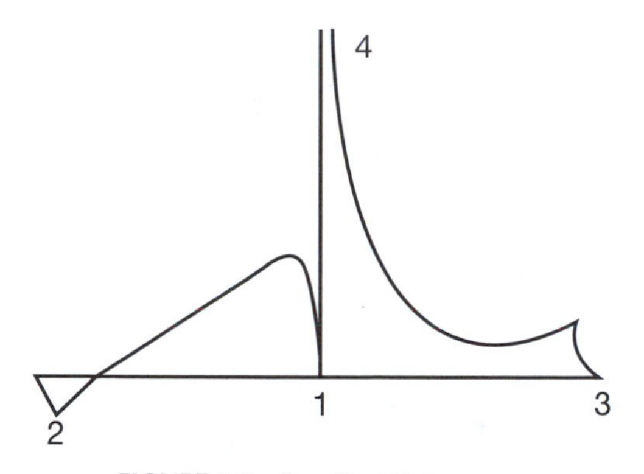

FIGURE 3.2 Four-Beat Pattern

marked articulation where the motion is stopped after each beat, which we discuss later in the chapter). This differentiates the downbeat from the rest of the pattern.

The area within which the beat pattern takes place extends approximately from the shoulders to the waist. The height of the plane of the beat pattern has an impact on the sound quality that is elicited from a choir. The higher the plane, the lighter the quality. The lower the plane, the heavier the quality. Occasionally, beat 4 may ascend slightly higher than shoulder level, but generally this should not be the case. Palms should remain down and fingers pointed toward the ensemble. Figures 3.3, 3.4, and 3.5 indicate two incorrect hand positions and the correct position.

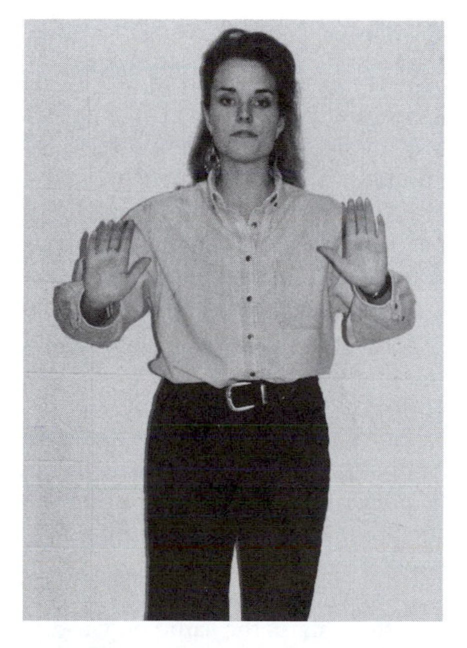

FIGURE 3.3 Student with Palms toward the Ensemble

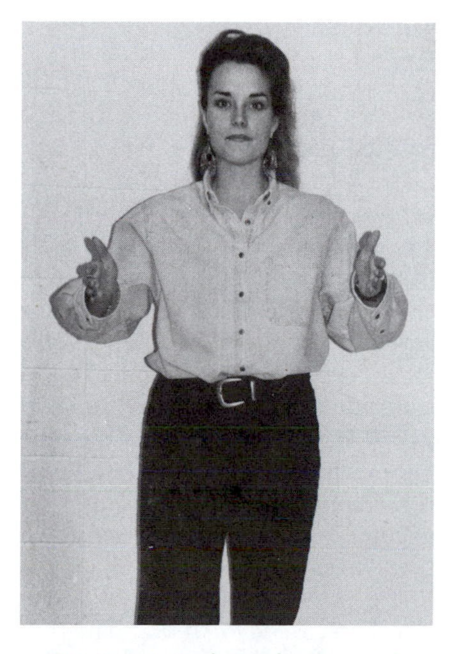

FIGURE 3.4 Student with Palm to Side

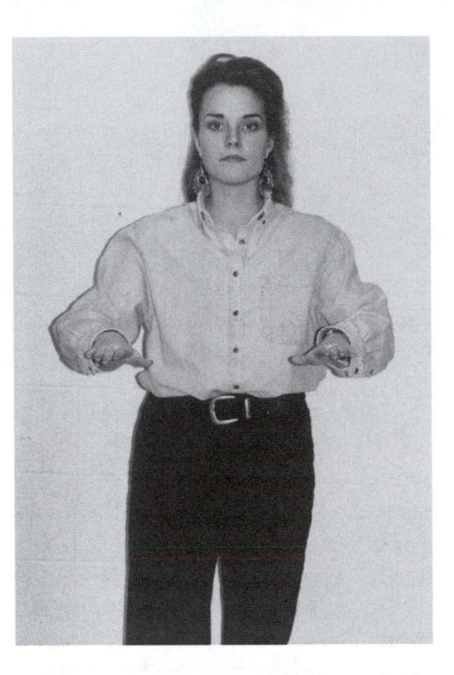

FIGURE 3.5 Student with Hands Correctly Placed

Make the beat pattern as clear and simple as possible. Initially, strive for a pattern that is neutral in expression. There should be no extra curls, loops, or other motions that detract from the absolute clarity of the four beats.

As you practice each basic pattern, observe the conducting technique of other students. Some individuals will naturally tend to have a rather marked pattern; others will be more legato in style. Some people tend toward a large beat pattern; others are smaller. At this stage, each person should work toward the establishment of a clear beat, which is "middle of the road" in terms of communicating dynamics and articulation. Once this baseline conducting technique is established, you can adjust it to reflect changes in the expressive qualities of a choral piece. In establishing this baseline technique, the intent is also to eliminate extraneous movements that are a consistent and unconscious part of each student's pattern and do not communicate anything but detract from clarity.

Diagrams for some of the other common beat patterns are presented in Figures 3.6 through 3.13. Ample time must be provided for students to become comfortable conducting a few basic patterns before adding other expectations to their conducting assignments. Some students may require several weeks to become comfortable; others will progress more quickly.

The Three Beat Pattern. The three-beat pattern starts the same way as the four-beat pattern, but beat 2 is eliminated, so the pattern moves down (beat 1), to the right (beat 2), and up (beat 3). Figure 3.6 illustrates a three-beat pattern.

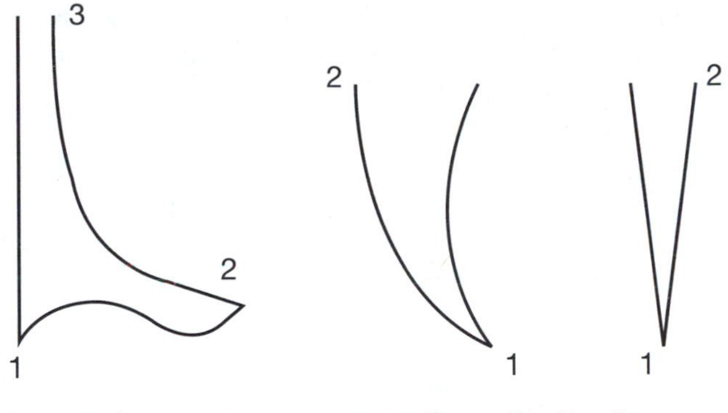

FIGURE 3.6 Three-Beat Pattern

FIGURE 3.7 Two-Beat Patterns

The Two-Beat Pattern. The two-beat pattern has a somewhat different feel than four and three. The two different possibilities are illustrated in Figure 3.7. Figure 3.8 illustrates a one-beat pattern. Figures 3.9, 3.10, and 3.11 illustrate symmetrical patterns of 6, 9, and 12 beats per measure.

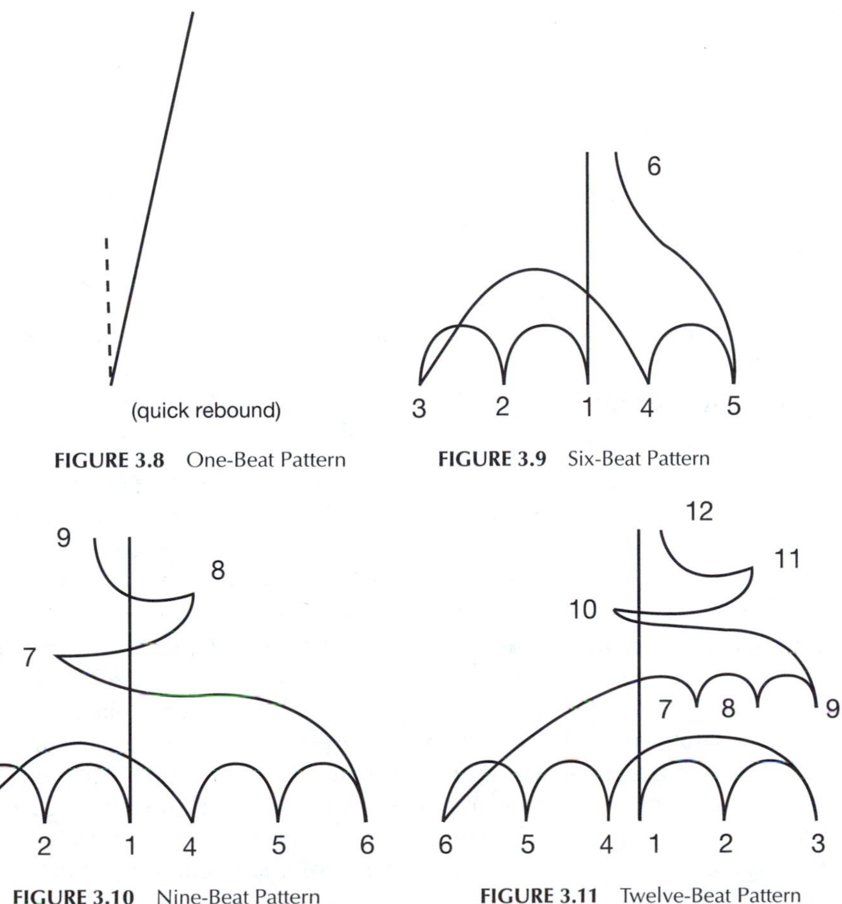

FIGURE 3.8 One-Beat Pattern

FIGURE 3.9 Six-Beat Pattern

FIGURE 3.10 Nine-Beat Pattern

FIGURE 3.11 Twelve-Beat Pattern

Asymmetrical Meters. Asymmetrical meters are irregular and often combine patterns we discussed previously. For example, a five-beat pattern typically breaks down into (3+2) or (2+3). The seven-beat pattern may be analyzed as (4+3) or (3+4).

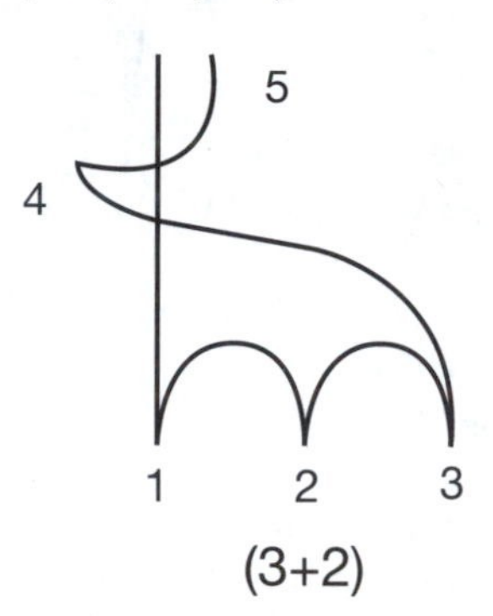

FIGURE 3.12a Five-Beat Pattern

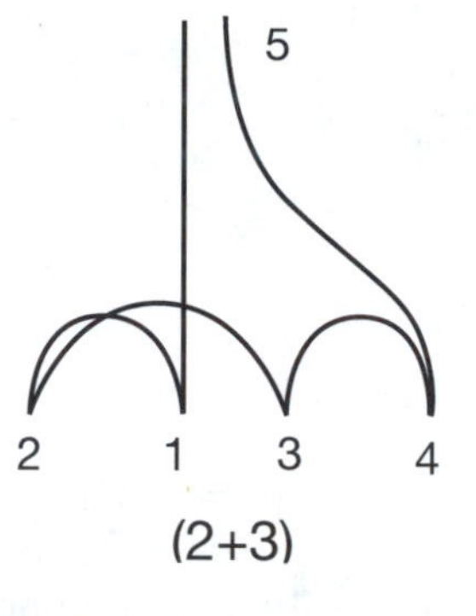

FIGURE 3.12b Five-Beat Pattern

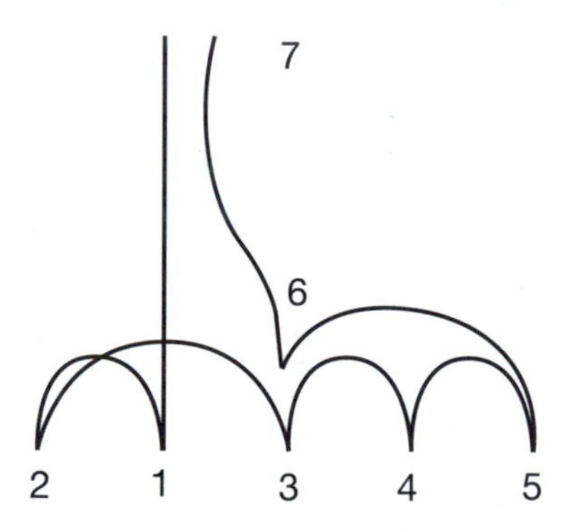

FIGURE 3.13a Seven-Beat Pattern

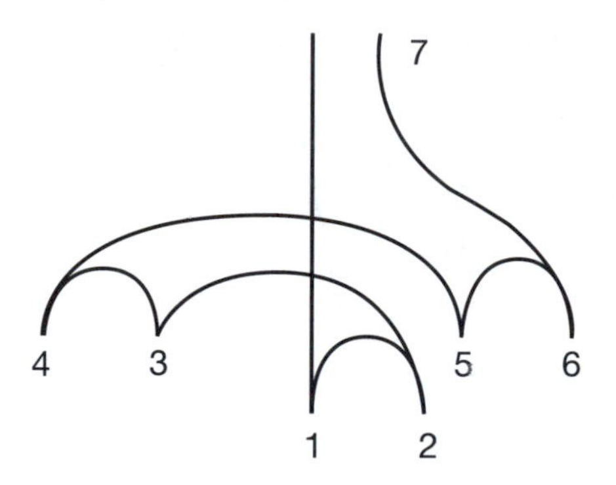

FIGURE 3.13b Alternative Seven-Beat Pattern

Subdivided Beats

The tempo of a piece of music will occasionally be slow enough that it is necessary to subdivide the beats. This happens when the tempo is so slow there is too much time and space in each beat of the standard pattern for clarity. As an experiment, establish a tempo of about 120 beats per minute. Tap the beat, with your right hand hitting the palm of the left. Gradually slow the tempo. You will find that at around 60 beats per minute you will *mentally* begin to subdivide the beat in order to maintain a steady and accurate tempo. The same principle needs to be illustrated visually to the choir by conducting subdivided beat patterns. Subdividing means each beat in the standard pattern is made into two beats (or perhaps three, depending on the meter) so each beat or subdivision occurs more quickly and clearly, enabling the conductor to more easily maintain energy and phrasing through the vocal line (see Figure 3.14). The following example of an appropriate place to use a subdivided beat occurs in a portion of the Credo from Beethoven's *Mass in C Major:*

EXAMPLE 3.1 Excerpt from "Credo" from Beethoven's *Mass in C Major*

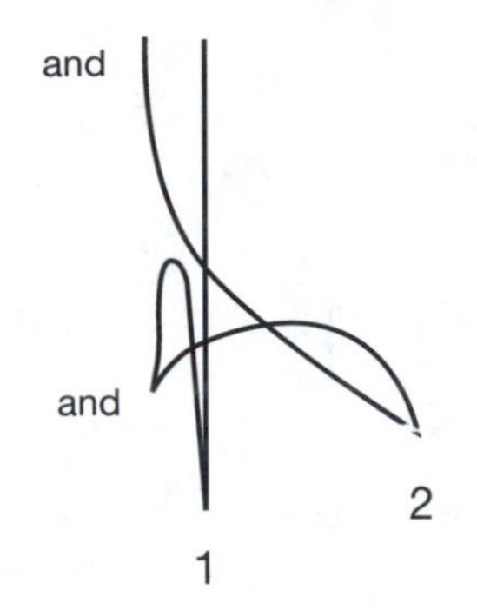

FIGURE 3.14 Subdivided Pattern

Subdividing the beat allows the conductor to communicate more sustained energy and intensity in the music. Similarly, in a piece of music quite different in style, subdividing beats 2, 3, and 4 enables the conductor to be precise in indicating the ritard to the accompanist (see Figure 3.15). Look at the following example:

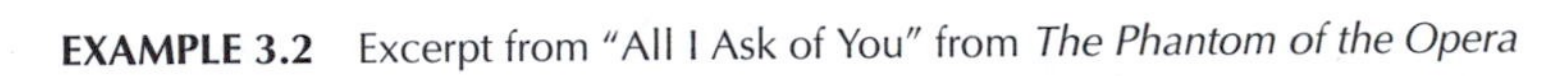
EXAMPLE 3.2 Excerpt from "All I Ask of You" from *The Phantom of the Opera*

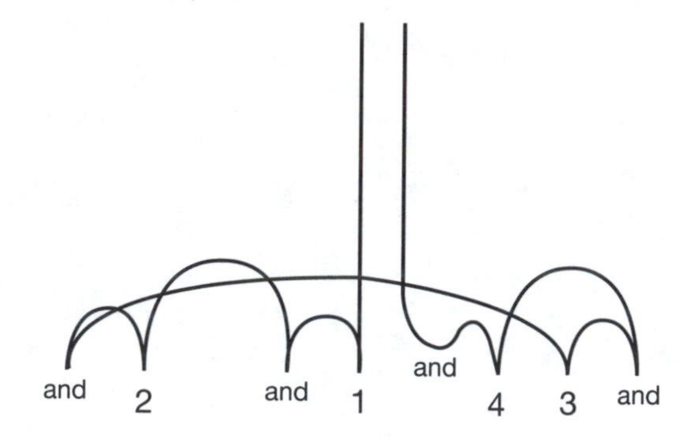

FIGURE 3.15 Subdivided Four-Beat Pattern

It is up to the discretion of the conductor when to subdivide the beat for most effective rehearsal communication. If you subdivide the beat when the tempo is not sufficiently slow, the music will be labored. If you do not subdivide when the tempo is slow enough to require it, it will lack energy and sustained drive through the phrases.

Starting and Ending

Starting. Once the basic patterns are assimilated, it is time to consider the matter of beginning a piece of music. The word that has traditionally used for the beginning of a piece or a section is *attack.* In my opinion, it is preferable to use some other word, such as *beginning.* The connotations of the word *attack* in terms of a choral entrance can yield some unfortunate results. In choral music, the desired beginning is smooth, without the lunge, glottal stroke, or other problems that can occur when we "attack" a piece of music.

The *preparatory beat* is the gesture that prepares for and immediately precedes choral sound. It occurs at the beginning of a musical selection and follows any pause in the music, such as a new section or after a fermata that ends in a pause. Starting with the correct basic posture described earlier, bring the arms up in front of the body. The elbows should be away from the body.

Note that in Figure 3.16, the elbows are drawn in, hugging the ribs. This position does not allow the freedom of movement necessary for a clear and expressive beat pattern. In Figure 3.17, the elbows are raised excessively high, with the same undesirable effect. Figure 3.18 illustrates the correct position. The elbows are raised comfortably but not excessively. The arms are somewhat extended in front of the body. The hand position illustrated may be attained by visualizing holding an invisible beach ball. Once you have raised your hands and are holding the ball, turn the palms downward. This will result in a good basic position from which to initiate a preparatory beat signaling the beginning of the choral sound.

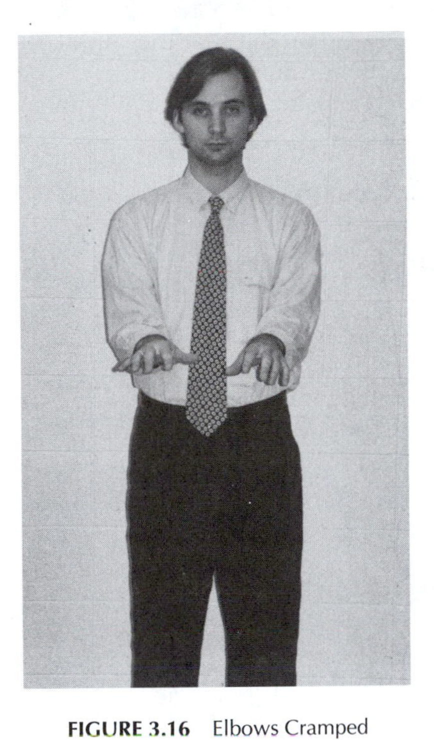

FIGURE 3.16 Elbows Cramped

FIGURE 3.17 Elbows too High

FIGURE 3.18 Correct Basic Conducting Position

The exact position of your hands will depend on the beat the choral selection begins on. The preparatory beat uses the gesture for the beat in the pattern immediately preceding the entrance. Consider these opening measures from a Bach chorale:

Jesus, I Will Ponder Now
(Jesu, Deine Passion)

Sigmund von Birken (Betulius), 1653
Translated by August Crull, 1890

Melody by Melchior Vulpius, 1609
Arranged by Johann Sebastian Bach

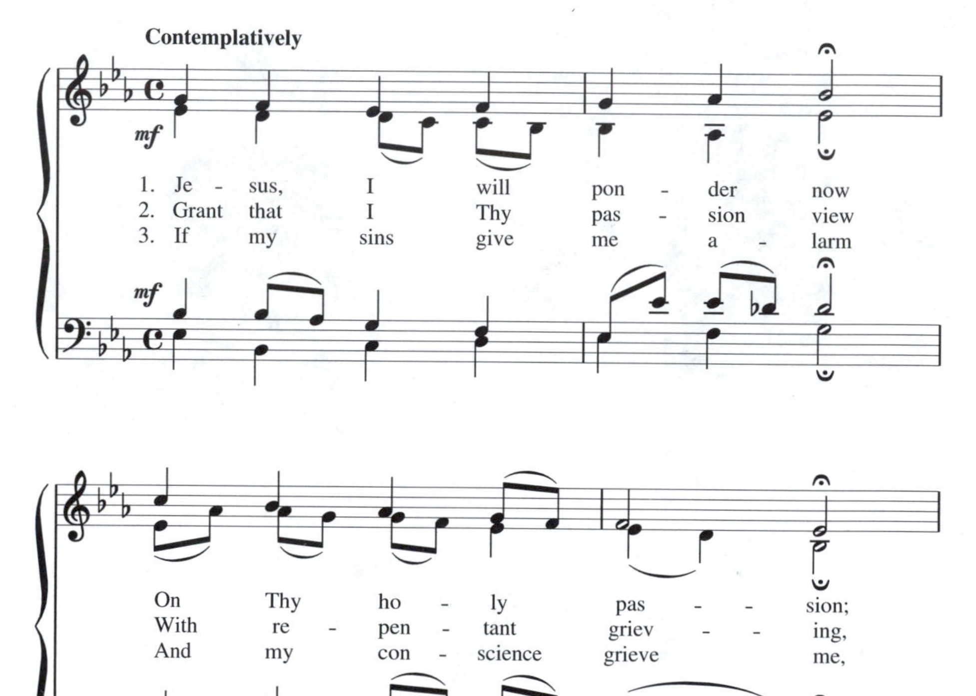

EXAMPLE 3.3

The chorale begins on beat 1, so the preparatory beat is beat 4. Therefore the right hand must be raised to the point in the pattern where the ictus of beat 3 occurs. The preparatory beat will be beat 4, initiating the choral sound on beat 1 (see Figure 3.19).

The steps in the process are as follows:

1. Assume the correct posture for conducting.
2. Raise the right hand to the position for beginning the preparatory beat.
3. Stop all motion.
4. Make the preparatory gesture.
5. The choral sound begins on the next beat.

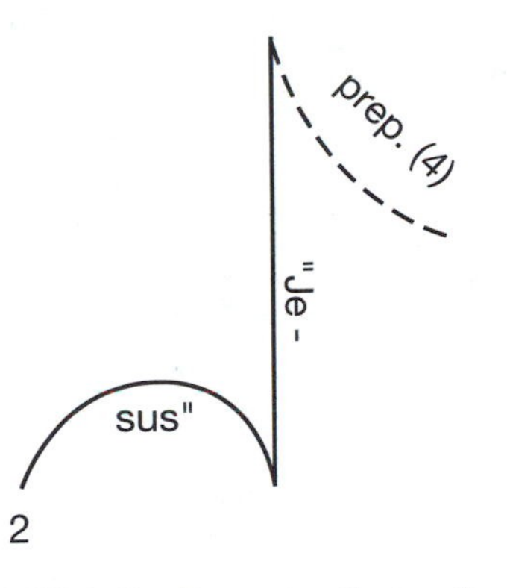

FIGURE 3.19 Preparatory Beat on Four

The preparatory beat must be in the style and tempo of the music. Therefore, the conductor should have a clear idea of style and tempo *before initiating the preparatory beat*. Take a few moments when you stand before the ensemble and mentally establish the tempo and style before making any overt gestures to the singers. A problem for beginning conductors is that in their nervousness they step before the group and immediately raise their hands. *Then* they think about the tempo and style and begin to move prior to giving the preparatory beat. This results in confusion and lack of clarity. Once you raise your hands, they must remain absolutely still until you begin the preparatory beat. Your preparatory beat must then be decisive and authoritative.

Of course, choral selections do not always begin on beat 1. Consider the following example:

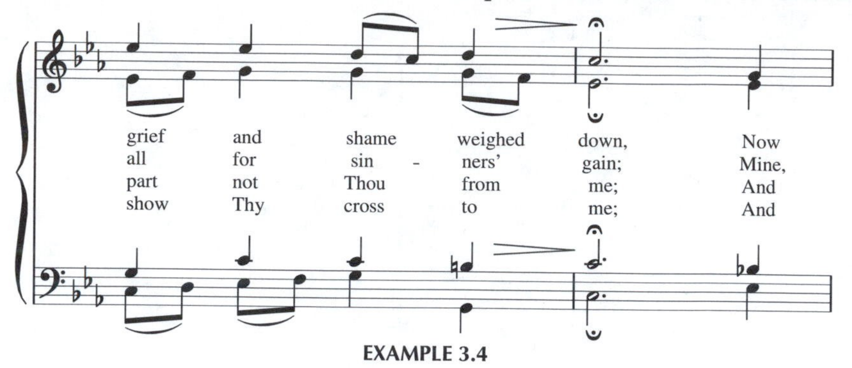

EXAMPLE 3.4

Because the music begins on beat 4, the preparatory beat will be beat 3 (see Figure 3.20).

In the following example the music begins on beat 2:

Four Chorales from "Saint Paul"

For Four-Part Chorus of Mixed Voices
with Organ or Piano Accompaniment

EXAMPLE 3.5

Since the music begins on beat 2, the preparatory beat is beat 1 (see Figure 3.21).

Preparatory beats are fairly straightforward when the music begins simultaneously with the beat. When the music begins on an upbeat, the situation becomes a bit more complicated. For maximum clarity, the preparatory beat should include one full beat plus the fraction of a beat preceding the entrance. Here is an example of this kind of entrance:

Zigeunerleben
(A Gypsy's Life)

For Four-Part Chorus of Mixed Voices
with Piano Accompaniment

(Triangle and Tambourine ad lib.)

Emanuel Geibel
English translation by Peggy Simon

Robert Schumann, Op. 29, No. 3
Edited by Abraham Kaplan

EXAMPLE 3.6

The preparatory beat is diagrammed in Figure 3.22.

It is occasionally advantageous to give two or more preparatory beats, even when the music begins on a beat. This situation could arise if the tempo is quick or if you are working with a group of singers and/or instrumentalists with limited rehearsal time (for example, a one-day workshop). Whatever is decided regarding the preparatory beat, it should be done consistently, so the singers are confident as they begin a musical selection.

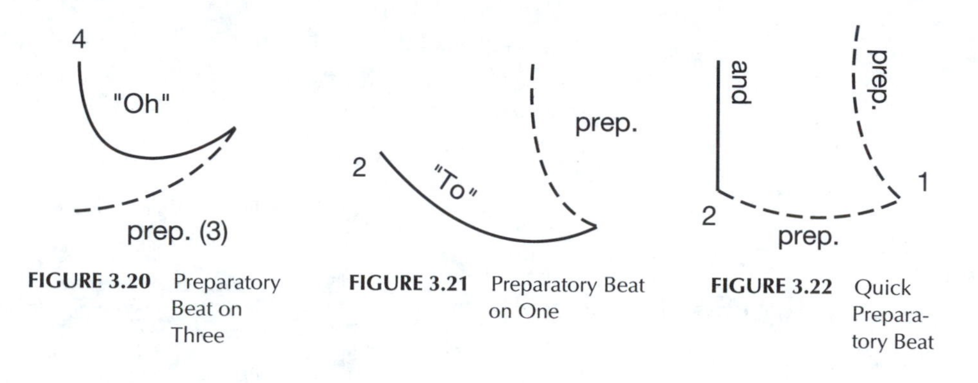

FIGURE 3.20 Preparatory Beat on Three

FIGURE 3.21 Preparatory Beat on One

FIGURE 3.22 Quick Preparatory Beat

Ending. Just as *attack* is a term with unfortunate connotations for choral musicians, another problematic word is *cutoff.* At the end of a phrase there should not be any change in the breath support, conceptualization of style, or any other aspect of the sound (unless desired by the conductor, of course). When a choral singer is asked to cut off the sound, it may have harmful consequences. Ask choral singers to end or release the sound, rather than cutting it off.

Two conducting gestures can be used to end a choral piece or section. The first is illustrated in Figure 3.23 and simply consists of bringing the hand down and changing direction when the sound is to end. The other option is a circular motion, illustrated in Figure 3.24.

The motion illustrated in Figure 3.23 is preferable. It is the clearer of the two. In a circular ending gesture, there is a question as to exactly where the sound is to end. No matter which gesture you use, there should be an upward rebound at the end and a sense of lift and floating breath support.

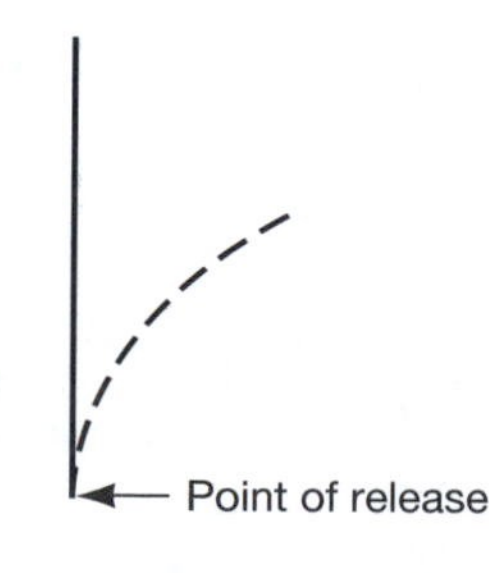

FUGURE 3.23 Preferred Ending Gesture

FIGURE 3.24 Circular Ending Gesture

Conducting Fermatas

The *fermata* represents a pause in a choral piece in which the meter is temporarily suspended. This suspension of the steady beat pattern and its resumption following the fermata require clear conducting gestures.

Consider Example 6.7, an excerpt from a Bach chorale.

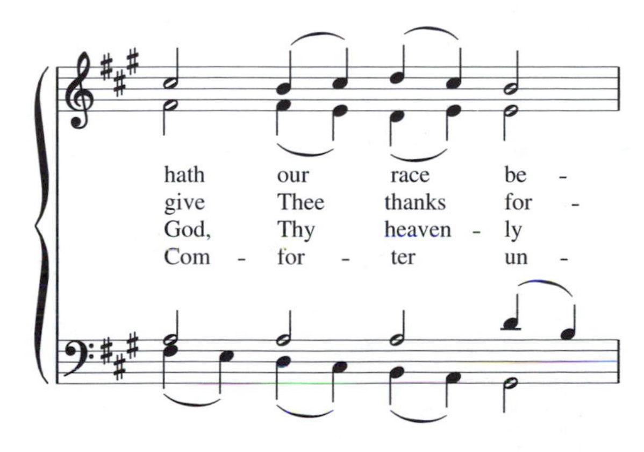

EXAMPLE 3.7

The fermata may be handled in two different ways. In the first, the fermata is followed by a complete break in the sound (see Figure 3.25). In the second, the fermata does not interrupt the sound, which continues after the fermata with no break (see Figure 3.26).

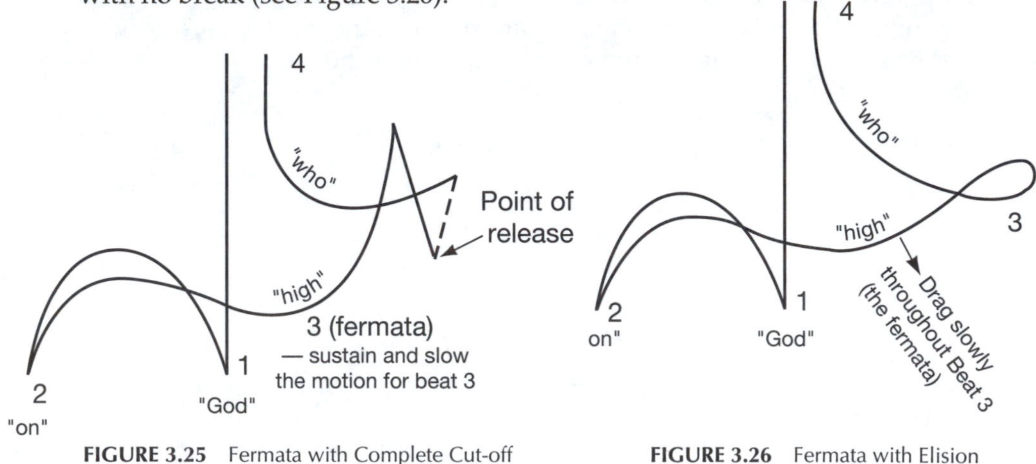

FIGURE 3.25 Fermata with Complete Cut-off

FIGURE 3.26 Fermata with Elision

An even more complex situation exists in the following excerpt, where the upper voice continues in the meter and the lower voice sustains a fermata. One hand may be assigned the fermata (preferably the left hand), so the right hand can continue its customary role of indicating the beat pattern until the fermata occurs in that voice, at which point the right hand cues the fermata in the accompaniment and then joins the left in the suspension of the beat pattern and the indication of the fermata:

Crawdad Hole

American Folk Song

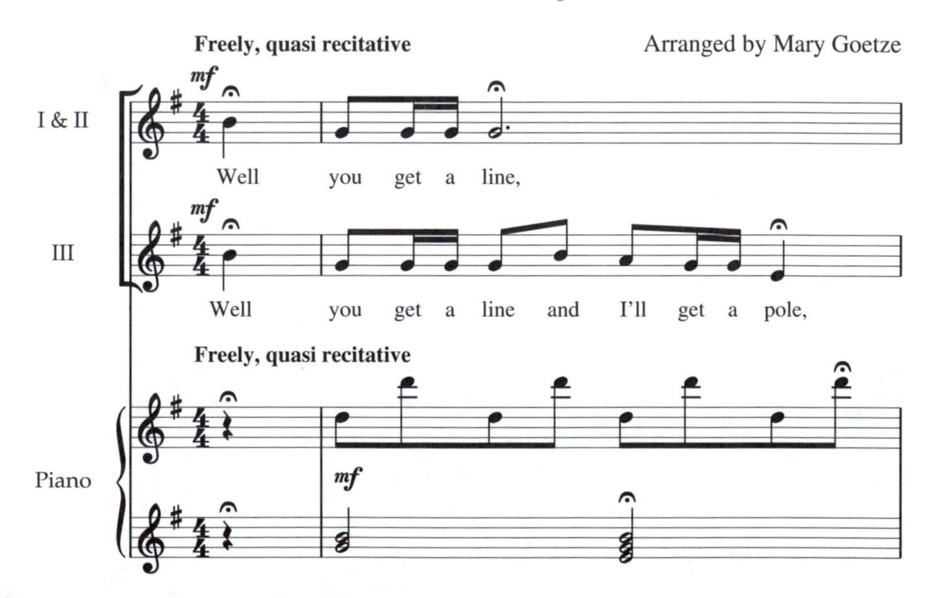

EXAMPLE 3.8

Using the Left Hand

The fermata illustrated in Example 3.8 called for the use of the left hand to indicate something independent of the right. Up to this point, we have said nothing concerning the left hand. In practicing the basic patterns and beginnings and ending, your left hand may initially simply hang loosely at your side or on your hip. After you are comfortable with the repertoire of gestures and conducting issues discussed to this point, it's time to practice using the left hand.

The left hand should function independently of the right. Occasionally, mirroring the right hand with the left can be an effective means of adding emphasis, but as with any other gesture, if you fall into the habit of constantly mirroring the right hand with the left, it will lose its ability to communicate effectively and will instead detract from the clarity of conducting gestures.

How should you use the left hand?

1. It may occasionally mirror the right hand to add emphasis to the beginning or ending of a phrase or section of music.
2. It can indicate dynamics. Raising the left hand, palm toward the choir, can be an effective way to indicate a low dynamic level.
3. It is used to cue an entrance.
4. It is used to cue a release (cutoff).
5. It can help to indicate phrasing and the expressive qualities of the music.

✣ EXPRESSIVE CONDUCTING ✣

Once you master the basic mechanics of conducting, you may begin to develop more advanced, sophisticated, and subtle ways to communicate via conducting gestures. In a very real sense, the conductor must depict the music being rehearsed and performed. This is a much more complex idea than simply starting, keeping the group together, and ending cleanly. At this point conducting moves beyond a basic skill to an art.

You should study and practice the basic beat patterns depicted in the previous section until you are comfortable with each of them. It should be noted that although the diagram of each pattern correctly indicates the position of the beats, it is necessarily a compromise. The amount of the rebound from each beat, the size of the field of beating, the height of the pattern, and the manner in which you move from one beat to the next (e.g., smooth and gliding versus marked and pulsing) varies with the expressive requirements of the repertoire.

To illustrate some ideas concerning expressive conducting, we present three brief excerpts from a variety of choral selections. Some of the expressive concerns associated with each are highlighted. Following the presentation and discussion of the excerpts, we make some generalizations concerning expressive conducting.

The beautiful, simple, and placid Austrian carol illustrated in Example 3.9 is in 4/4 meter at a slow tempo. Practice conducting the excerpt. Initially, your primary concern was a clear beat pattern and making sure the ensemble started and ended together. But there are many other things to communicate via conducting gestures, even in a short excerpt like this.

Still, Still, Still

S.A.T.B.

Austrian Carol

Lyrics by Marilyn Keith and Alan Bergman — Arranged by Norman Luboff

Still, still,
mp
Still, still,
mp
Still, still,
mp
Still, still,
mp
6
still one can hear the fall - ing snow. For
still one can hear the fall - ing snow. For
still one can hear the fall - ing snow. For
still one can hear the fall - ing snow. For

EXAMPLE 3.9

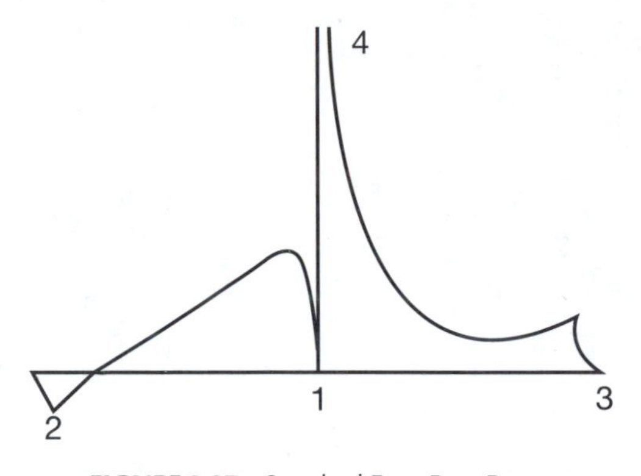

FIGURE 3.27 Standard Four-Beat Pattern

Before beginning the preparatory beat, think about all of the expressive aspects of the phrase. Picture the falling snow, a quiet night, or whatever other images occur to you as you prepare the music. Consider the breath control necessary to sustain energy and intensity through the entire phrase. Let these images permeate your facial expression, your posture, and the character of your preparatory beat. *Breathe* with the choir as you give the preparatory beat. The pace of your intake of air should match the pace of your preparatory beat.

In light of the sustained and delicate nature of this piece, the gestures of the four-beat pattern should glide through the entire excerpt. At no point is the phrase broken. At each ictus, there should be no interruption of the motion, but simply a smooth change in direction, always with a sense of pulling the choir through the phrase.

In measures 1, 2, and 4 of the excerpt, beat 2 can be melded with beat 1. When a beat is melded, no ictus is given; the hand travels in the usual pattern, without delineating the point where the beat occurs. Compare the standard four-beat pattern illustrated in Figure 3.27 with Figure 3.28, a melded pattern.

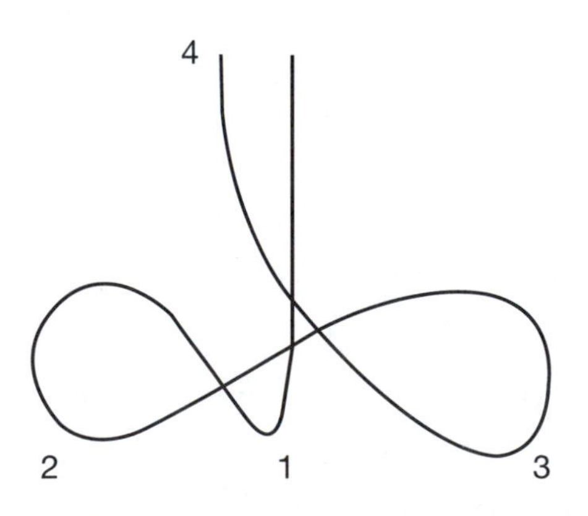

FIGURE 3.28 Melded Four-Beat Pattern

1. No Mark
From Four Pastorales

For Four-Part Chorus of Mixed Voices and Oboe, a cappella

EXAMPLE 3.10

This excerpt is an excellent example of an appropriate place for melded gestures. Melded gestures help convey a sense of movement through portions of the music where any interruption of the flow of the sound is undesirable; the negative aspect of melded gestures or any other deviation from the standard patterns is that they tend to obscure the beat. In this instance, the music is slow, homophonic, and highly expressive; obscuring the beat should not be detrimental and is offset by the increased sense of legato line and expression that will result.

"No Mark" is a highly dramatic and expressive piece, one of a set of *Four Pastorales* by contemporary American composer Cecil Effinger, with the text drawn from the poetry of Thomas Hornsby Ferrill. Conduct the excerpt. Although the tempo of "No Mark" is not much faster than that of "Still, Still, Still," the text, mood, style, and character are completely different. The text of the Effinger piece is concerned with violent death, which the style of the music reflects.

Rather than being sustained and tranquil, the words have an edge and a bite to them. The four-beat pattern should be marked. This is accomplished by actually stopping the beat pattern at the points where some of the beats occur.

The preparatory beat for "No Mark" should be given with a sense of urgency and drama and at the correct tempo. The phrase begins with a hard consonant: *c*orn. This consonant should be used to energize the beginning of the piece.

The question then arises, at what point in time should the consonant occur? The *c* sound should actually occur slightly ahead of the beat in this example. The portion of any word that carries the singing tone is the vowel (or perhaps a voiced consonant). In order for this music to have the appropriate sense of urgency and drama, the vowel should occur exactly on the beat.

Tell the choir that at the point where the ictus occurs, the vowel should be voiced. If this concept can be developed, the choir will have a much better chance of maintaining the tempo you desire. Some choirs typically sound as if they are behind the conductor's tempo. They may be getting to the vowel sounds late.

The choir should pronounce the text of this poem together, to determine where the accents should be placed: "Corn grew where the corn was spilled, in the wreck where Casey Jones was killed." The words that receive the primary accents are on the first beat of each measure and also on the word "Jones," beat 3 of measure 3.

"O Magnum Mysterium" by Victoria is a hauntingly beautiful example of a Renaissance motet. In this selection, the text is the key to determining where the accents should occur in each line (see Chapter 6 for an explanation of accentuation and other aspects of Renaissance style). The dynamic level should generally be soft and restrained. Consider the editorial dynamic markings in the overall framework of limited dynamic range. To convey this to the choir, keep the beat pattern small and use your left hand to indicate fine adjustments in dynamics and phrasing.

O Magnum Mysterium

For Four-Part Chorus of Mixed Voices

a cappella

EXAMPLE 3.11

The first note on the word "O" in the sopranos should have a floating buoyancy carrying energy into the more heavily accented word "*mag*num." Therefore, the beat pattern should be melded as indicated, with the accented syllable being emphasized by having the left hand mirror the right on that beat. On the second syllable of "magnum," which is unaccented, the energy recedes, and again the left hand might be used in a gesture with the palm toward the choir indicating a softer sound.

This pattern of accentuation and dynamic shading occurs in each voice as it enters. Cue each voice as it enters, and maintain the pattern of accentuation. Although the meter of the piece is 4/4 (a contemporary editorial addition), each vocal line should maintain independence and include the appropriate rise and fall of the phrasing within that line.

✣ EVALUATING CONDUCTING TECHNIQUE ✣

As a choral music educator it is important to be able to observe other conductors and to understand the positive and negative aspects of their technique. Use the following list of criteria to evaluate conducting technique.

1. *The beat pattern must be clear.* If the beat pattern is not clear to the singers, then all is lost. Before attempting to conduct the expressive aspects of choral music the beat pattern must be clear.
2. *The beginnings and endings in the music must be clear.* The preparatory beat at the beginning of a selection or section should be clear, as should the gesture used to end a particular phrase, section, or selection.
3. *The size of the beat pattern must reflect the dynamic level and expressive intent of the music.* Conductors have a natural tendency to conduct a particular size of beat pattern. An important characteristic of good conducting is that the size of the beat pattern changes to reflect the dynamic level of the music being performed.
4. *The left hand must function independently of the right, communicating entrances, dynamics, or other expressive elements.* A problem for some conductors is the proper use of the left hand. The left hand should not be used simply to mirror what the right hand is doing.
5. *Eye contact with the ensemble should be maintained and the expressive aspects of the music conveyed through facial expressions.* Eye contact is essential to good conducting and it is dependent on secure knowledge of the music being rehearsed. The face should be alive and communicative, rather than buried in the score.
6. *All of the individual elements of conducting should combine to create a picture of the music.* Once the basic conducting patterns are assimilated, the conductor should present a picture of the music under consideration. The conductor's facial expression, size of beat pattern, use of the left hand, and posture on the podium should all reflect the emotion being communicated through the music.

✣ SUMMARY ✣

Conducting is communication. In order to communicate effectively, conducting must be clear and expressive. A few basic ideas have been presented here concerning the conducting of choral music because through good conducting a variety of aesthetic and expressive aspects of choral music can be communicated to students without saying a word.

It is important to understand the standard conducting gestures and beat patterns and to employ them in order to be an effective choral music educator. As a conductor gains experience, a personal style of rehearsing and conducting will inevitably develop. This is a positive occurrence.

There have been and will continue to be choral conductors whose approach is highly individualistic. Some of them, with sufficient rehearsal time, produce choirs that sound well and sing with expression. Such conductors, however, tend to have a difficult time in situations where there is limited rehearsal time and ideas must be conveyed quickly and efficiently.

Comprehensive choral music education is focused on the musical and personal growth of every student in the program. Effective conducting technique is one way to guide students to a fuller understanding of the music they encounter in choral rehearsal.

Questions

1. What are the two most important attributes of effective conducting?
2. Why is it so important to become familiar with the standard conducting gestures, rather than developing your own?
3. Describe the basic conducting posture.
4. What is a melded gesture and when should it be employed?
5. What aspects of the choral score must the conductor have in mind before initiating the preparatory beat? Aside from the tempo, and the point at which to begin the sound, what information is conveyed by the conductor through the preparatory beat?
6. What is the problem with the terms *attack* and *cutoff* for the choral conductor?
7. In what ways is the left hand used by the effective choral conductor?
8. When is it appropriate and effective to subdivide the beat?

Suggested Reading

ADLER, SAMUEL. *Choral Conducting.* Chicago: Holt, Rinehart and Winston, 1971.

BUSCH, BRIAN R. *The Complete Choral Conductor: Gesture and Method.* New York: Schirmer, 1984.

DAVISON, ARCHIBALD T. *Choral Conducting.* Cambridge, MA: Harvard University Press, 1954.

DECKER, HAROLD A., and JULIUS HERFORD. *Choral Conducting: A Symposium* (2nd ed.). Englewood Cliffs, NJ: Prentice Hall, 1988.

DECKER, HAROLD A., and COLLEEN J. KIRK. *Conducting: Focus on Communication.* Englewood Cliffs, NJ: Prentice Hall, 1988.

EHMANN, WILHELM. *Choral Conducting.* Minneapolis: Augsburg, 1960.

EHRET, WALTER. *The Choral Conductor's Handbook.* New York: Edward B. Marks, 1959.

GREEN, ELIZABETH A.H. *The Modern Conductor* (4th ed.). Englewood Cliffs, NJ: Prentice Hall, 1987.

HEFFERNAN, CHARLES W. *Choral Music: Technique and Artistry.* Englewood Cliffs, NJ: Prentice-Hall, 1982.

HUNSBERGER, DONALD, and ROY ERNST. *The Art of Conducting.* New York: Knopf, 1982.

KAPLAN, ABRAHAM. *Choral Conducting.* New York: Norton, 1985.

KJELSON, LEE, and JAMES MCCRAY. *The Conductor's Manual of Choral Music Literature.* Miami: CPP Belwin, 1973.

KOHUT, DANIEL L., and JOE W. GRANT. *Learning to Conduct and Rehearse.* Englewood Cliffs, NJ: Prentice Hall, 1990.

KRONE, MAX T. *The Chorus and Its Conductor.* Park Ridge, IL: Neil A. Kjos, 1945.

MOE, DANIEL. *Problems in Conducting.* Minneapolis: Augsburg, 1968.

RUDOLF, MAX. *The Grammar of Conducting* (2nd ed.). New York: Schirmer, 1980.

SIMONS, HARRIET. *Choral Conducting: A Leadership Teaching Approach.* Champaign, IL: Mark Foster Music, 1983.

STANTON, ROYAL. *The Dynamic Choral Conductor.* Delaware Water Gap, PA: Shawnee Press, 1971.

THOMAS, KURT. *The Choral Conductor.* New York: Associated Music, 1971.

WILSON, HARRY ROBERT. *A Guide for Choral Conductors.* New York: Silver Burdett, 1950.

Conducting Videotapes

EHLY, EPH. *Excellence in Conducting.* Milwaukee: Hal Leonard, 1988.

PFAUTSCH, LLOYD. *Coming Alive: Choral Conducting.* Minneapolis: Augsburg Fortress, 1989.

Chapter Four

Performance

✣ ✣ ✣

✣ INTRODUCTION ✣

In this chapter we present ideas related to the planning and preparation required for public performance. Additionally, we discuss the proper role of public performance in the comprehensive choral music education program.

The public performance of choral music is an important component of the comprehensive choral music education program. It is not, however, the ultimate objective. The overriding concern of choral music education programs is educating singers, helping them grow personally, musically, and intellectually. Although high performance standards are an important component of the musical education of singers, they are a means to an end, a step in a process.

In fact, the pursuit of an excellent performance level, to the exclusion of other considerations, may actually hinder the musical education of choral participants. For example, if the highest possible level of performance is the *overriding* goal, then the tendency could be to focus on an inappropriately narrow range of literature. The notion of picking a few selections at the beginning of the year and working on them exclusively for several months may result in a highly polished performance, but in focusing the program so narrowly, the opportunity is lost for students to experience a wide range of composers and styles.

If rote learning supplants the development of musicianship, a student may learn the alto line to twelve pieces of music flawlessly, without any knowledge of the music's context, style, or salient characteristics. Preparing three selections for performance at a contest as the focus for the program from January through April is clearly unhealthy and educationally unsound.

Although it is important and necessary to accommodate various audiences with literature appropriate for the occasion (e.g., a somewhat different group of selections for the Rotary Club than for a convention of music educators), if the primary criterion for literature selection is the suitability of pieces for a particular year's performance obligations, then opportunities for music education through choral music will be lost.

The exploitation of students is to be avoided at all costs. Consider the following scenario: A high school show choir has become a popular representative of the school and is in demand for performances at a wide range of functions. Sometimes groups seeking to engage the group's services offer a fee and sometimes they do not, but the ensemble performs forty concerts in the course of an academic year. The school principal is pleased because the community has a positive image of the school. The choral director is pleased because he or she receives many compliments on the students, their performances, and on the wonderful experiences they are having. The show choir even makes a trip to Hawaii, after a massive fund-raising campaign.

But there is a negative side. The show choir is so popular that few students sign up for concert choir. Understandably, students feel the place to be is in the group that has the fun! Students must make a commitment to the show choir that includes many weekend engagements, including every weekend in December and April. With the pressure of such an intensive performance schedule, it requires all of the group's effort to prepare the pieces for the show, often selected from that year's "top 40." The fund-raising required to support the travel, the hiring of a professional choreographer, and the costumes is extensive, from the beginning of school in September until the doors close in June. Clearly, the situation described here does not represent exemplary comprehensive choral music education. The education of the students has been lost when an ensemble becomes primarily a public relations tool and entertainment medium.

Another issue to consider regarding the public performance of choral music is the ethical implications of performing in situations where professional musicians might otherwise be employed. The Music Educators National Conference, in cooperation with the Music Industry Council, has published "The Music Code of Ethics," which delineates the kinds of performances that are appropriate for school ensembles and those that are more appropriate for professional musicians (see Appendix A).

You can avoid the potential problems mentioned here by placing performance in the context of the rehearsal planning process we described in Chapter 2. The selection of literature and the scheduling of concerts is accomplished as part of the total choral music education program. Each choral music educator and each school situation is unique, and the number and nature of choral performances scheduled each year must be based on the educational implications for the students. There is no absolute number of choral performances that is best for every situation. They should be an outgrowth and extension of classroom experiences in choral music education.

In the context of the comprehensive choral music education program, public performance represents the culmination of a period of effort expended by students and teacher on a particular group of choral selections, and it provides a public showcase of some of the results of this effort. Therefore, careful planning for successful public performances is an important aspect of the choral music educator's responsibility.

✣ PRECONCERT REHEARSALS ✣

As a public appearance becomes imminent, the way rehearsals are conducted will change. Early in the semester you should emphasize the development of sound basic vocal technique, as described in Chapter 1. A synthesis, analysis, synthesis approach to rehearsal will predominate, in which music is considered in relatively small segments for most of the rehearsal period to correct errors and to teach the expressive details of individual notes, measures, and phrases. As the semester progresses, shift gradually from primarily analytical rehearsing to a more holistic approach, which provides students with an understanding of each selection as a whole and each group of selections comprising the program.

This shift in rehearsal emphasis toward the holistic culminates in the rehearsals immediately preceding the performance. During these last few rehearsals prior to performance (the number will vary according to the schedule of your particular ensemble) there will be a further change in approach. For the purposes of the present discussion, we assume the choir rehearses three times per week. You will need to adjust the numbers according to the rehearsal schedule of your particular ensemble.

Six rehearsals (approximately two weeks) prior to the performance, give the ensemble the opportunity to sing through the program without interruption. This is a particularly opportune time to record the group so the singing can be analyzed after rehearsal to identify specific areas in need of work. Singing through the entire program gives the choir an opportunity to gain a sense of the progression from one piece and one section of the program to the next.

During the next two rehearsals, focus on the trouble spots you have identified, reinserting the portions of music rehearsed in detail into the selection and program section where they fit, again giving the singers the opportunity to experience the progression and flow of the program. Depending on the length of the program and the length of the rehearsal period, continue to provide the opportunity to sing through sections of the program without interruption.

During this period of rehearsals immediately preceding the concert, it is essential to encourage a confident attitude on the part of the singers. Monitor closely the mental set of the group and plan interactions with the ensemble to create a positive attitude toward the upcoming performance. A balanced approach to this psychological preparation for performance is important. The choir may be apprehensive about singing in public, particularly if they are inexperienced. Thus, they will need encouragement. Conversely, if they become too excited about singing, they may forget some of the vocal techniques and expressive nuances they have learned in rehearsal. So you must maintain an attitude of calm confidence, encouraging the singers, but keeping their focus on what they have learned.

One common symptom of nerves that commonly occurs as a concert approaches is a tendency toward sharping. If this happens, point it out to the group. Encourage them to be as relaxed as possible in presenting the music. If the music is unaccompanied, rehearse it in a different key to combat intonation difficulties.

Three rehearsals away from the performance, again have the choir sing the entire program without stopping. At this point, if appropriate long- and short-range rehearsal planning was done, there should be a minimum of problems to correct. Many choral directors set up the choral risers to be used in performance in the rehearsal room so students become accustomed to singing in concert formation. If there are numerous problems still evident in the music, it is an indication of faulty rehearsal planning. If you find yourself in this position, determine which problems can be fixed and which will be left uncorrected. Don't try to correct too many problems in the rehearsals immediately prior to a public appearance. This will diminish the singers' confidence and have a negative impact on the performance. The level of performance is your responsibility. This is not the time for a temper tantrum or other contrived emotional outburst. Such behavior is inappropriate and counterproductive.

If possible, schedule the last two rehearsals prior to performance in the actual performance setting. There are numerous adjustments required on the part of the choir to adapt to singing in a new environment.

The acoustics of the performance hall will probably be somewhat different than those in the regular rehearsal space. It is advantageous if the performance space is more live than the rehearsal room. This will have a confidence-building effect on the choir and facilitate a solidly blended sound. If the performance hall is acoustically drier than the rehearsal room, explain to the singers that they will hear things differently than in rehearsal. Each singer's own voice may be more distinctly audible to him or her. Emphasize that singers should continue to sing in the same manner and at the same volume level they did in rehearsal even if it sounds different to the individual singer in the new environment. If each singer adjusts his or her tone quality and volume level based on individual perceptions of the ensemble sound, it will lead to problems like pushing, disrupted balance and blend, and poor intonation.

In addition to acoustical adjustments, a variety of other aspects of the performance will need to be sorted out during the last rehearsal or two. The arrangement of the choir on the stage and on the risers and transitions from one standing arrangement to another will need to be determined and rehearsed. If more than one choir is participating, you will need to plan the entrances and exits of each ensemble. Check the group when they are onstage to be certain the arrangement of singers is optimal both visually and aurally.

This is a time to stress the importance of a professional appearance and attitude from the choir. Even before they sing, choirs are judged by an audience. As they file on stage and wait for the opening downbeat, the audience is assessing their professionalism and discipline. These aspects of the performance need to be rehearsed until the choir is comfortable and confident regarding their appearance and movements on stage.

Be certain each choir member clearly understands all aspects of appropriate attire and stage deportment. The visual effect of thousands of dollars worth of choir robes, tuxes, gowns, or other apparel can be destroyed by an inappropriate pair of socks or shoes or a gaudy piece of jewelry.

Take the opportunity to listen to the choir from various locations in the performance hall to check the balance, blend, and visual impact. Pay particular attention to the balance between choir and accompanist. The height of the piano lid or the positioning of the instrument may need to be adjusted for proper balance and audibility.

✥ LOGISTICAL CONCERNS ✥

The most important aspect of effective concert planning is preparing the musical program. Beyond this basic requirement, however, a variety of other concerns must be considered in preparing for a public presentation, including the following:

1. Scheduling
2. Tickets
3. Publicity
4. Program
5. Ushers
6. Recording the concert
7. Stage and auditorium setup; lighting

Even a choral program that is in a rebuilding stage musically can be professional in the nonmusical aspects of concert preparation and presentation. All of the nonmusical concerns related to concert presentations are excellent possibilities for delegation to others. An interested parent could take charge of any of the areas, with the possible exceptions of scheduling and auditorium setup, relieving the choral music educator of a responsibility that does not require musical expertise.

Scheduling

As early as possible, consider the scheduling of choral concerts. This should happen late in the spring or possibly more often, depending on the rehearsal schedule, goals, and objectives. Determine when you will present concerts during the next year, and then check the school schedule and add the choral events to it. Avoid conflicts with other school functions. The earlier this scheduling is completed, the fewer conflicts there will be. Once the schedule has been determined, consider distributing a copy to the administration and faculty. This will help prevent conflicts as other departments plan their special events. A particularly common conflict to avoid is with athletic events. The maintenance of open communication with the athletic director and coaches will help resolve any difficulties.

It is perhaps inevitable that from time to time there will be scheduling conflicts. Even when plans are carefully made and scheduling procedures followed, problems can occur. An example might be when an athletic team advances to tournament play and games occur that were not originally in the schedule. A particularly attractive but unforeseen opportunity for students to enjoy a special musical event could create a potential conflict.

When such unforeseen conflicts arise, it is critically important to avoid placing students in the middle of a dispute and to try to resolve matters between the faculty members involved, or, when necessary, to have situations mediated by an administrator. Generally, the principle to follow should be that the first event scheduled has precedence. In fact, the observance of this principle will preclude most scheduling difficulties.

Tickets

When a concert is planned, decide whether it will be free or whether there will be an admission charge. If you are new to the school, check the records to determine the school policy and precedent concerning admission to school events. If the choir has traditionally charged an admission fee and by doing so raised money to support the program, then the practice probably should be continued. Conversely, if district policy or tradition has included free concerts, then it probably would be wise to continue that tradition, at least initially.

There are advantages and disadvantages to ticket sales. Even if the admission to a concert is free, it can be a promotional aid to have tickets printed and to distribute complimentary tickets to chorus members, parents, friends, and family members, as well as anyone else who should be made aware of the choir's activities.

The use of tickets, even when they are low priced or no cost, lends a prestigious note to a concert. A printed ticket also serves as a reminder of the date and time of the event. Last but not least, with reserved seating, the use of tickets facilitates the distribution and control of the crowd. Of course, when an admission fee is charged for a concert, the income derived from ticket sales can be used to help defray other expenses of the choral department.

On the negative side, the use of tickets requires careful supervision, record keeping, and the handling of money. If this task is delegated, it requires a person with good organizational and interpersonal skills. This particular responsibility should be assigned to an adult, not a student.

If at all possible, the choral director should not handle the responsibility for tickets because it is a nonmusical area, requiring a significant investment of supervisory time. Once the concert is scheduled, make a decision regarding admission charge and ticket sales. Early in the planning process, this responsibility should be carefully delegated and closely monitored. Part of this responsibility includes supervision of a box office (or table) on the evening of the concert and accountability for number of tickets sold and money collected.

Publicity

Publicity and public relations is discussed in Chapter 8. The publicity and promotion for each concert should be accomplished in the framework of the overall promotional strategies used in the choral program. A timetable must be worked out so that press releases and other materials publicizing the concert are created and disseminated at the most advantageous time.

If a parent or other booster of the choral program has a flair for public relations, it might be beneficial to make that person the publicity chair. He or she could then delegate responsibilities for particular events or take care of them personally, depending on the degree of interest and available time.

The Printed Program

The printed program for a concert should not be created until a few days ahead of the event. This will allow last-minute changes in musical selections and personnel to be accommodated, making the printed program as accurate as possible.

In the present era of desktop publishing, there is no reason not to have a professional-looking attractive program, with minimal expense. Assemble a file of programs from other concerts attended, and use them for ideas to make your own printed materials tasteful and appealing.

A class in desk-top publishing techniques would be helpful to the choral director who designs programs. Basic ideas, such as uniformity in type fonts, correct spacing, the use of art, and other matters, can help you take maximum advantage of the computer. In addition to the page layout of the program, pay careful attention to the weight, finish, and color of the paper used. All of these factors affect the impact of printed materials.

Be certain the program's information is as complete and accurate as possible. Make sure every participant's name is included, that it is spelled accurately, and in the form the participant desires (e.g., "Michael" versus "Mike," or "Beth" versus "Elizabeth"). In addition to choral participants, list the names of anyone who assisted in the presentation of the concert—the custodial staff, parents who helped with aspects of the preparation, the stage crew, and anyone else involved. Many choral music educators routinely include the names of school administrators in the printed program. To the extent that time and space permit, program notes can be very helpful to an audience's understanding and appreciation of a concert. Certainly, if a selection is performed in a foreign language, the English translation should be given.

While all of this attention to detail requires time and effort, the printed program will become a lasting memento of the event for many of the participants and parents, and will create an impression of the quality of the program (and the competence of the choral music educator) long after the sounds of the concert have faded from memory. Just as the appearance and professionalism of the singers will help to create a good impression of the choral program before a note is sung, the printed program also has an impact immediately before, during, and long after the event.

Print many more copies of the program than you think you will need. Provide a copy for each participant to use for reference during the performance and at least one copy as a memento. Start a portfolio of printed programs from events you have conducted and any other materials related to your professional accomplishments. This can provide an excellent supplement to your résumé, should you decide to investigate other professional positions.

Ushers

Remember to recruit ushers to distribute programs, assist people to their seats as needed, and generally to facilitate the entrance and exit of the crowd. Students make excellent ushers. They need to be instructed on how to greet members of the audience as they arrive, take them to their assigned seat, and any other tasks you wish to have them accomplish. Do not assume students (or parents) have an accurate preconceived notion of concert etiquette.

Ushers can often be recruited from musical groups at the school who are not participating in the concert. If there is a music honor society or other similar group, they may wish to provide ushers as a service project. This encourages students to hear their peers perform and promotes increased participation in the choral program.

Recording the Concert

It is highly desirable to maintain a library of recordings of all of the concerts presented by the school's choral ensembles. The audiovisual department can probably provide this recording service. Video recordings are more informative than audio cassettes, but either format provides an accurate permanent record of the choral ensemble's accomplishments. If the school does not provide this kind of service, consider borrowing the necessary equipment and assigning a student or parent to turn the recording device on and off as needed.

Such recordings can be used instructionally. After concerts, give the ensembles a chance to view their efforts. Oral or written comments evaluating the performance from every point of view—musical, visual, and organizational—should be elicited from students. From time to time, ask the students to evaluate recordings of other choirs. This can help them place their own performances into a broader context. Opportunities to listen critically help students become more perceptive musicians.

In addition to their instructional potential, recordings provide a permanent record of the accomplishments of the ensemble and the choral music educator. As was the case with the printed programs, a cassette of excerpts from concerts strengthens a résumé by providing aural evidence of the building of a choral program.

Stage and Auditorium Setup and Lighting

Advance planning is necessary to ready the auditorium for a concert. The custodial staff must be notified well in advance of the event of any special setup and cleaning requirements.

Does a piano need to be moved to a particular location? Does the instrument require tuning prior to the event? Students should be instructed prior to the first rehearsal in the auditorium concerning the importance of maintaining its cleanliness and orderliness.

Will the curtain need to be opened and closed at various points during the concert? If so, a person will need to be assigned to the task. What kind of lighting will be required for the concert? At a minimum, the houselights will need to be turned on as the audience enters the auditorium, dimmed when the concert begins, and adjusted appropriately at the end of sections and end of the concert. In addition, there may be choral selections that will benefit from special lighting effects. All of these matters need to be thought through well in advance of the concert date and delegated to individuals who can accomplish the work competently.

✣ PROGRAM BUILDING ✣

Assembling a concert program of music that is educationally valid, has integrity, and is both enlightening and entertaining for the audience is a challenging task. To be educationally valid, a program must fit into the planning framework of the total choral music education process. To have integrity, it must result from the best efforts of the choral conductor to find music that is interesting and of lasting value. To be enlightening and entertaining, the music must be selected to suit the audience for which it is performed.

Before the planning of any specific concert programs, the choral literature for the year or the semester should be selected according to the criteria indicated in Chapter 5. From this total list, the specific programs for each of the concerts to be presented may be chosen.

To illustrate, a sample list of repertoire for a mixed choir, a treble choir, and a men's choir is presented here. This repertoire constitutes a good variety of literature, representing various composers, styles, and periods. It could provide a solid basis for a year of comprehensive choral music education. This listing could represent the literature to be studied during a particular academic year. Sample programs appropriate for various occasions are then selected from this list.

MIXED CHORUS

"O Come Let Us Sing Unto the Lord"—Emma Lou Diemer. Carl Fischer, no. CM7903.

"Keep Your Lamps"—Andre Thomas. Hinshaw, no. HMC-577.

"O Sifune Mungu"—David Maddux. Word, no. 3010467168.

"Bach Again"—J.S. Bach, Edwin London, Rhonda Sandberg. Aberdeen Music, no. 1064.

"No Mark"—Cecil Effinger. G. Schirmer, no. 11059.

"Gentle Annie"—Stephen Foster, arr. Eliot. Beckenhorst Press, no. BP113.

"Kyrie"—Andrea Klouse, Hal Leonard, no. 08704233 (SAB).

"Coronation Anthem #4"—G.F. Handel. G. Schirmer, Ed. no. 2710.

"Magnificat"—G. Pergolesi. Walton, no. WM-102.

"Cantate Domino"—Giuseppe Pitoni, ed. Norman Greyson. Bourne, no. ES5.

"When Jesus Wept"—William Billings. Mercury Music, no. MP101.

"Six Folk Songs"—Brahms. Belwin Mills, no. MC9.

"Praise Him"—J.S. Bach, ed. Barrie. Lawson-Gould, no. 51472.

"Carol of the Bells"—Leontovich, arr. Wilhousky. Carl Fischer, no. CM4604.

"Christus Factus Est"—Anton Bruckner. G. Schirmer, no. 11395.

"Alexander's Ragtime Band"—Irving Berlin, arr. Simeone. Shawnee Press, no. A-638.

"Selections from *Phantom of the Opera*"—Andrew Lloyd Webber, arr. Lojeski. Hal Leonard, no. 08252941.

"Still Still Still"—Norman Luboff. Walton, no. W3003.

"Polly Wolly Doodle"—Gail Kubik. G. Schirmer, no. 9854.

"Meet Me in St. Louis, Louis"—Kerry Mills, arr. Carl Strommen. C.P.P. Belwin, no. 1405 MCIX.

"The Colors of My Life"—Cy Coleman, arr. John Leavitt. Studio P.R., no. SV8716.

"Ol' Dan Tucker"—arr. Gilbert Martin, Hinshaw Music, no. HMC-1093 (SAB).

"Walking on the Green Grass"—Michael Hennagin, Boosey and Hawkes, no. 5443.

"Neighbors Chorus"—Offenbach, Broude, no. 130.

"La Virgen Lava Panales"—arr. Robert DeCormier and Eddie Sauter. Lawson-Gould, no. 52227.

"There Shall a Star Come Out of Jacob"—Felix Mendelssohn, ed. Bev Henson. Jenson, no. 413-20014.

"O Magnum Mysterium"—T. L. Vittoria, ed. Shaw-Parker. G. Schirmer, no. 10193.

"Hodie Christus Natus Est"—Healey Willan. Carl Fischer, no. C.M. 469.

"Do You Hear What I Hear"—Noel Regney and Gloria Shayne, arr. Simeone. Shawnee Press, no. A-708.

"An Irving Berlin Christmas"—arr. Roger Emerson, Jenson, no. 403-09054.

WOMEN'S CHORUS

"Four Sacred Songs for the Night"— Houston Bright, Shawnee Press, no. B-190.

"Cantate Domino"—Hassler/Greyson. Bourne, no. B201863-354.

"May the Road Rise Up to Meet You"—Dale Grotenhuis. Jenson, no. 436-13023.

"Psalm 67"—Julie Knowles. Jenson, no. 417-16013.

"Laudamus Te"—Vivaldi. Heritage, no. HRD 185.

"Gloria"—Haydn/Suchoff. Walton, no. 5025.

"Agnus Dei"—John Leavitt. CPP Belwin, no. SV9008.

"Ave Maria"—Gabriel Faure. Broude, no. 45.

"Velvet Shoes"—Louise Evans. no. R-5003.

"Waters Ripple and Flow"—Deems Taylor. Belwin Mills, no. FEC5065.

"Sleigh Ride"—arr. Roger Emerson. Jenson, no. 403-19153.

"O Pastorelle, Addio"—Giordano. G. Schirmer, no. 11602.

"My True Love Has My Heart"—Eugene Butler. Hinshaw, no. HMC-621.

"Ma, He's Makin' Eyes at Me"—arr. Lojeski. Hal Leonard, no. 08238843.

"Let It Snow! Let It Snow! Let it Snow!"—arr. Lojeski. Hal Leonard, no. 08720119.

"I Enjoy Being a Girl"—Rodgers and Hammerstein/arr. Warnick. Williamson, no. 220750-353.

"Beau Soir"—Claude Debussy, arr. Spevacek. Hal Leonard, no. 08756903.

"At Times My Thoughts Come Drifting"—Brahms/Harris. Lawson Gould, no. 52009.

"In the Woods"—Eugene Butler. Heritage, no. H6048.

"I Wandered Lonely as a Cloud"—Mary Lynn Lightfoot. Raymond A. Hoffman, no. H5012.

"Gelobet seist du, Jesu Christ"—Schein. Tetra/Continuo, no. TC 224.

MEN'S CHORUS

"The Christmas Song"—Mel Torme, arr. Ehret. Edwin H. Morris and Co., no. E9824a.

"Wait for the Wagon"—Buckley, arr. Shaw/Hunter. Lawson Gould, no. 541.

"Widerspruch"—Schubert, ed. Shaw/Parker. Lawson Gould, no. 513.

"Sweet Love Doth Now Invite"—Dowland/Greyson. Bourne, no. B212688-355.

"Stouthearted Men"—Romberg, arr. Scotson. Harms, no. 6-H5003.

"Shenandoah"—Newbury. G. Schirmer, no. 12306.

"Five German Folk Songs"—Brahms/Pfautsch. Lawson-Gould, no. 51235.

"Five Foot Two, Eyes of Blue"—Henderson, arr. Artman. Hal Leonard, no. 08583000.

"Down in the Valley"—Mead. Galaxy, no. 1.1716.

"Die Nacht"—Schubert. Roger Dean Publ., no. HRD 178.

"A Capital Ship"—arr. Richardson. Mark Foster, no. MF 1065.

"Bonnie Eloise"—arr. Hunter/Shaw. Lawson-Gould, no. 529.

"Blow the Candles Out"—arr. Richardson. Mark Foster, no. MF 1061.

"A-Roving"—Luboff. Walton, no. W1004.

"America—Our Heritage"—Steele, arr. Ades. Shawnee Press, no. C-133.

"You'd Better Run"—arr. Whalum, Lawson-Gould, no. 51749.

"Soon Ah Will Be Done"—Dawson. Tuskegee Choir Series, no. 101.

"Songs of the Masters"—arr. Grotenhuis. Jenson, no. 436-19011.

"Sing Unto the Lord"—Gower. Galleria Press, no. GP-300.

"O God of Love, O King of Peace"—Grotenhuis, Code no. 4321.

"God Rest You Merry, Gentlemen"—arr. Kern. Shawnee, no. C-268.

"Festival Piece on Sine Nomine"—Vaughan Williams, arr. Elrich. Harold Flammer, no. C-5069.

"Eternal Father, Strong to Save"—Dykes/Treharne. Williamson, no. 10394(2426).

Programming Concerts at the School

Full-length concerts presented at the school or elsewhere provide an opportunity to demonstrate the results of the choral music education process and to give an idea to the audience of the range of literature studied by choral participants. Most choral programs include two or three such concerts in the course of a school year.

These concert programs may be organized in a variety of ways. One standard format is to present literature in chronological order, beginning with a piece from the Renaissance and proceeding through the twentieth century. This is an excellent way to present a variety of composers, styles, and periods.

There are other ways to organize interesting and innovative concert programs. One approach is to pick a theme, or a particular text, and to examine how it was treated by a variety of composers. A concert program focusing on choral pieces dealing with love, or war, or patriotism are all possibilities. All-American (or French or British, for example) programs have been well received. Depending on the philosophy of your particular district, a concert with a holiday theme may be expected (or precluded) in December.

Whatever format is used, certain programming principles will help ensure a concert that is interesting and rewarding for the listener. Each of the formats just suggested (or any other organizational format) gives the program a structure or unifying element. Once that unifying element has been determined, there needs to be variety as well.

Variety can be added to a program in a number of different ways. Consider the tonality of each of the pieces in arranging the program order. A succession of pieces all in the key of F major tends to sound monotonous. The tempo, the texture, and other musical characteristics should all be taken into account.

Varying the forces involved in the selections also helps add interest to the program. Using soloists or small ensembles from within the larger group is a possibility. Try different accompanying instruments—using some unaccompanied literature, some with keyboard accompaniment, and some with combinations of instruments.

Think carefully about the length of any concert. It is far better to leave them wanting more than to present a concert that should have been shorter. The maximum length for an effective choral presentation should usually be no more than an hour and a half, including intermissions. When the concert is longer than that, it can become tedious for many listeners. The goal is to present the results of the students' efforts in choral music class in the most positive way possible. The length of the program should be planned to facilitate the accomplishment of that objective.

For some choral conductors, the notion of presenting an entertaining choral concert constitutes a cheapening of the choral art. This is a misconception. A well-planned choral concert *should* be enjoyable and entertaining for the audience, while it is at the same time educational and edifying. Particularly if you are starting a new position, it is advisable to present music in public that is not radically different in style from previous years. If parents have been accustomed to hearing programs consisting entirely of choral arrangements of current hits, a program entitled "The Renaissance Motet from Binchois to Schutz" will probably be poorly received. It is educationally sound to begin with the familiar and then to progress to the less familiar. This applies to audiences at concerts as well as to students.

A programming idea that has been successfully employed by a number of choral music educators is the demonstration concert, presented early in the school year. In such a concert, time is devoted not only to the formal presentation of choral pieces, but also to a demonstration of rehearsal techniques, warm-up exercises, characteristics of the adolescent voice, and the objectives of the choral music education program. This would be an excellent setting in which to have students who are comfortable speaking in public comment on the musical aspects of the pieces being presented, educating the audience and also demonstrating the educational value of the choral music education experience for participants. Another advantage of a demonstration concert is that it limits the amount of repertoire that must be mastered early in the year.

Programming Shorter Concerts

In addition to the full-length concerts that are part of the choral music education process, there are usually opportunities for brief appearances by the choir, or by subsets of the choir, for luncheons, club meetings, and other events in the community. (For information regarding choir travel, touring, exchange concerts, and other major choral projects occurring away from school, see Chapter 8). The number and nature of such events to be accepted by your choral ensemble should be carefully considered and communicated to students, parents, administrators, and other faculty members. As we mentioned previously, the *Music Code of Ethics* published by the Music Educators National Conference and the Music Industry Council addresses the ethics and appropriateness of various kinds of out-of-school performances by school ensembles.

The specific musical selections chosen for a particular public performance on a specific occasion will depend on several factors, including the length of the performance, its purpose, the nature of the audience, and the acoustical environment in which the performance will take place.

As we noted earlier, the selections you choose should vary depending on the audience. The program performed for the PTA will vary from that selected for the convalescent home.

Sample Programs

To illustrate the points concerning program planning, we use the repertoire for a year of choral work by a high school mixed choir listed earlier as the basis for program planning. The same process would then be used to plan the programs for each choral ensemble (treble choir, men's chorus, etc.). Remember that we selected the list of repertoire on the basis of its musical and educational value. After this process was completed, we chose the selections to be used for specific occasions from the list.

For the purposes of illustration, the following schedule of performances is assumed:

Major Concerts

Late October or early November: Fall Demonstration Concert
December: Holiday Concert
March: Joint Concert with Neighboring School
May: Spring Concert

Shorter Choral Appearances

October: PTA Meeting
November: Rotary Club Luncheon Meeting
December: Convalescent Home
February: Music Educators' meeting
March: Women's Club
April: School Board Association

Sample programs for the these performances are listed here. It is assumed the full-length programs at school are shared with the other choral ensembles, lessening the demands on each group.

Major Concerts

Fall Demonstration Concert

Cantate Domino
Praise Him
When Jesus Wept
Keep Your Lamps (with conga drum)
The Colors of My Life
Alexander's Ragtime Band

Holiday Concert

I.
Pergolesi *Magnificat* (with string ensemble)

II.
O Magnum Mysterium
La Virgen Lava Panales
There Shall a Star Come Out of Jacob

III.
An Irving Berlin Christmas
Carol of the Bells

Still Still Still
Do You Hear What I Hear

Joint Concert with Neighboring School

O Come Let Us Sing Unto the Lord
No Mark (with oboe)
Gentle Annie
Polly Wolly Doodle
Selections from *Phantom of the Opera*
Combined Selection: Haydn *Te Deum* (with orchestra)

Spring Concert

I.

Coronation Anthem no. 4 (with orchestra)

II.

Bach Again
Six Folk Songs
Christus Factus Est
Neighbors Chorus

III.

O Sifune Mungu
Hold On
Keep Your Lamps

IV.

Ol' Dan Tucker
Gentle Annie
Show Tune

Shorter Choir Appearances

October: PTA Meeting

Keep Your Lamps
Gentle Annie
Alexander's Ragtime Band

November: Rotary Club Luncheon Meeting

Keep Your Lamps
Gentle Annie
Alexander's Ragtime Band
Polly Wolly Doodle
Meet Me in St. Louis, Louis

December: Convalescent Home

Hodie Christus Natus Est
Carol of the Bells
Still, Still, Still
Do You Hear What I Hear
An Irving Berlin Christmas

February: Music Educators' meeting

O Magnum Mysterium
Coronation Anthem no. 4
Christus Factus Est
La Virgen Lava Panales
Bach Again
Neighbors Chorus

March: Women's Club

O Sifune Mungu
Keep Your Lamps
Six Folk Songs
Neighbors Chorus

April: School Board Association

O Sifune Mungu
Keep Your Lamps
Six Folk Songs
Neighbors Chorus

✣ SUMMARY ✣

This chapter discussed both the role of performance in the comprehensive choral music education program and the planning and preparation for successful concerts. Although public performances are an important component in the comprehensive choral music education program, they are a step in a process. There is no absolute number of performances that is best for every situation. Performance should be an outgrowth and extension of classroom experiences in choral music education.

As a performance becomes imminent, rehearsal planning shifts in emphasis from analytical rehearsing to a more holistic approach. In addition, such logistical concerns as scheduling, tickets, publicity, ushers, stage and auditorium set-up, printed programs, and recording must be addressed in an efficient and timely manner.

We have presented lists of repertoire and constructed sample concert programs drawn from the repertoire lists. Chapter 5 focuses on the selection of music and basic principles of score analysis.

Questions

1. Why is it important to view performance as something other than the final goal of the choral music education program? What *is* the final goal of the comprehensive choral music education program?
2. How is it possible to exploit students through an overemphasis on performance?
3. What principles should guide the scheduling of performances for your choral ensembles?
4. How does the choral music educator's rehearsal planning change as a performance becomes imminent?
5. What often happens to a choir's intonation immediately before a performance? What can be done to correct this problem?
6. List the advantages and disadvantages of having tickets for a choral concert.
7. What are some programming formats that add cohesiveness and interest to a concert?
8. Create your own concert program using choral selections with which you are familiar. Decide on a format and an organizational scheme.
9. Using a computer, create a printed program, incorporating the selections chosen for question 8. Use whatever software you are familiar with.

Suggested Reading

GARRETSON, ROBERT L. *Conducting Choral Music.* Englewood Cliffs, NJ: Prentice Hall, 1988.

LAMB, GORDON H. *Choral Techniques.* Dubuque, IA: William C. Brown, 1988.

MENC COMMITTEE ON STANDARDS. *Guidelines for Performances of School Groups: Expectations and Limitations.* Vienna, VA: Music Educators National Conference, 1986.

MILLER, KENNETH E. *Vocal Music Education.* Englewood Cliffs, NJ: Prentice Hall, 1988.

MUSIC EDUCATORS NATIONAL CONFERENCE and THE MUSIC INDUSTRY COUNCIL. *The Music Code of Ethics.* Vienna, VA: Music Educators National Conference, 1988.

ROE, PAUL F. *Choral Music Education.* Englewood Cliffs, NJ: Prentice-Hall, 1983.

Chapter Five

The Score

✣ ✣ ✣

✣ INTRODUCTION ✣

Comprehensive choral music education focuses on people and on music. The selection of the music to be rehearsed and performed by a choral ensemble profoundly influences the quality of the music education experiences provided to the singers. Once you select the music, study and prepare the score carefully to facilitate the most effective teaching of it. Only with intensive preparation will you be able to provide the highest quality musical experiences for student participants. In this chapter we focus on the selection of music and the study of the score.

✣ SELECTING MUSIC ✣

The choral music educator who knows how to select repertoire that is appropriate for an ensemble has set the stage for successful rehearsals and performances. For any choral conductor, the selection of music involves evaluating a score based on several criteria. For the comprehensive choral music educator, the educational implications of the music selected must be considered as well.

Range and Tessitura

The range of each vocal line should be within the capabilities of the students who will be singing it. (See Figure 2.2 on page 38 for ranges of high school voices.) More important, the *tessitura,* or the range in which most of the notes in a given part lie, should be comfortable for the singers. Secondary school singers can much more easily handle an occasional note in the extreme of their range than a line that lies consistently in the high part of the range. For basses, for example, a high E at the end of a selection will be easier to sing than a part that remains in the A (top line, bass clef) to middle C range for several measures.

Text

With a very few exceptions, the text of any choral piece is the most important aspect of it. The text usually provided the aesthetic inspiration for the composer and should be studied carefully. Where did it come from? Is it biblical? Did it originate with the composer? Is it excerpted from a poem? Speak the text. If the text is interesting and the music supports it well, the piece merits further consideration.

Consider the text in relation to the ensemble. For example, depending on the maturity level and vocal experience of the ensemble, the Renaissance madrigal "Rest Sweet Nymphs" may require some explanation of aesthetic and artistic ideals during that period in history for the select junior high choir. Many of the secular pieces from the Renaissance are filled with double entendres and references to love, nature, and other secular matters. Again, the maturity level of the performers will help determine the way you approach such texts.

Some publishers take a current popular hit and quickly arrange it for various combinations of voices to capitalize on the piece's (fleeting) popularity. Carefully examine the lyrics of such arrangements to determine whether they are appropriate for your ensemble. Some selections with explicit lyrics appear each year in voicings appropriate for junior high, middle school, or even elementary school choirs. Be certain your personal standards and those of the community in which you teach are not violated by the lyrics of the music you select.

Once you choose the music, the text supplies the basis for many interpretive and musical nuances. We provide more information on this topic in the discussion of score analysis, rehearsal techniques, and style.

Voice Leading

Voice leading refers to the horizontal organization of each vocal line as it moves from one pitch to the next. Determine whether the line is "singable." A singable yet interesting vocal line is a thing of beauty, and to find several of them successfully combined in a choral piece is a good indication the music is worthwhile. To be singable, the vocal line must present a logical progression of intervals.

One important facet of the genius of J.S. Bach was that he managed to make each vocal line interesting. Consider the following two vocal lines, both of which are excerpted from Bach chorale harmonizations:

EXAMPLE 5.1 J. S. Bach, "Break Forth O Beauteous Heavenly Light"

EXAMPLE 5.2 J. S. Bach, "O Sacred Head, Now Wounded"

Which would be more singable for a secondary school bass or tenor section? There would be many more challenges associated with Example 5.1 than Example 5.2. Why? Primarily because of the voice leading—the way in which Example 5.1 skips around the range and Example 5.2 is mostly smaller intervals. Both are interesting and worthwhile, however Example 5.1 would be virtually impossible for a men's section of a middle school or junior high choir with a large number of changing voices because of the vocal range and agility necessary to negotiate the vocal lines successfully.

Accompaniment

Consider the accompaniment of each selection you consider programming. Is it within the capability of the accompanist(s) who are available? Is the accompaniment appropriate for the text and for the choral setting?

If there is a skilled accompanist available, an interesting accompaniment part can greatly enhance a straightforward and relatively simple choral part. The music sounds much more complex than it really is because of the accompaniment line. Consider the following excerpt:

It Is Good to Give Thanks

for Unison Chorus with Piano or Organ

Psalm 92
Adapted by K. M.

Kirke Mechem
Op. 41, No. 3

Allegro con brio ♩ = *ca.* **144**

EXAMPLE 5.3

This music is quite interesting to listen to. The accompaniment is pulsating, complex, and drives the piece along. The changing meter adds another element of interest for the listener. This tends to obscure the fact that the selection is a relatively straightforward, though challenging unison piece, with a singable vocal line.

In selecting a program, there should be a variety of styles of accompaniment represented. A large proportion of the choral repertoire is intended to be performed without accompaniment, and singers should be given that experience. Unaccompanied singing also presents some musical challenges, particularly in terms of intonation and blend, which are not found when there is an accompanying instrument. Overcoming these challenges builds the musicianship of the singers.

Harmony

Examine the harmonic organization of the piece. Is it tonal? Is it major or minor? How much chromaticism is present? Is the piece consistent in its treatment of the harmony? Play through the selection, paying particular attention to the harmonic rhythm. Do the chord progressions make sense? Are they interesting or trite?

How the Piece Fits the Choir

Each choir is different. As personnel changes from year to year there will be various strengths and weaknesses in individuals and sections. The music you rehearse and perform in a given year should enhance the strengths of the ensemble and hide the weaknesses.

If there is a singer with a particularly pleasing voice, that voice could be featured as a soloist. Are the tenors outstanding? Then music can be programmed that shows off the tenor section and their capabilities. If you have a fine accompanist, music may be programmed that includes a technically demanding accompaniment part.

Conversely, it is desirable to hide the weaknesses of the choir when performing publicly. This is particularly important when preparing for contests or competition, but it also pertains to a lesser extent to all of the choir's performances. If the bass section is filled with young singers, don't schedule the piece that ends on a sustained low Db or demands agility to negotiate wide intervals in the line.

Finally, consider the nature of the choir and its musical tradition, amount of rehearsal time available, and the experience of the singers involved. The music for the advanced highly select chamber choir will naturally be different from what you choose for the nonselect chorus. Music for specialized ensembles reflects the specific area of interest (for example, jazz or madrigals).

Educational Implications

All of the criteria listed here relate to the educational impact of the pieces you select. For example, if a piece has a range that is not possible for a choir or a section or if the text is trite or inappropriate, students won't have a successful learning experience.

What are the musical and contextual characteristics of the selection that should be considered by the choir? What musical characteristics are predominant? Driving rhythm? Flowing legato line? Unusual harmonic treatment? When was it written? By whom? Is it typical of that composer's music or is it unusual? Is it innovative or conservative in style? How can the choir most effectively be led to discover the essence of the music? How can their progress be evaluated, aside from determining whether they are singing the pitches and rhythms of the piece correctly? Chapters 2 and 9 suggest some strategies to be used in this endeavor.

In order to lead students to understand and personalize the expressive essence of a piece of music, it goes without saying that you must first have a clear understanding yourself. This understanding is developed through extensive and intensive analysis of the musical score, which we discuss in a moment.

How the Piece Fits the Total Program

Once a piece has been evaluated in terms of its individual merits, you can decide to accept or reject it from further consideration. In this manner, you can identify a group of choral selections meriting further study.

Choose a variety of selections for rehearsal and performance. Variety in terms of style, composer, meter, key, text, and accompaniment adds interest to rehearsal and performance.

The next step is to determine how to combine the selections into an effective program (see Chapter 4 for details). An important point merits repeating: Each selection should be evaluated on its musical and educational merits *before* you construct the programs for the various public performances scheduled.

This process makes the comprehensive choral music education program distinctive from programs whose primary emphasis is on performance and the entertainment of the audience, although it may not be readily apparent to a casual observer. Nothing is taken away from the performance. The musical and technical quality of the program are not affected. Once you analyze the musical and educational criteria for music selection it is still important to construct appealing programs, but your first consideration should always be the musical education of the participants.

The student choral singers may not be able to articulate what it is that makes the program distinctive, but they will know when the primary emphasis is on their development. Experiences with choral music should be designed for the students rather than using students as a way to put on a good show for an audience or to boost the ego of the conductor.

Programming Sacred Music

The programming of sacred music has become a controversial issue in some school districts and in some areas of the country. But an effective and representative choral music program must include sacred music along with the secular. So much of the Western choral heritage has been associated with our Judeo-Christian traditions that to exclude the sacred portion of the repertoire would destroy any possibility for balanced programming. To address this issue, the Music Educators National Conference has produced a pamphlet entitled "Religious Music in the Schools" that presents the rationale for the inclusion of sacred music in public school choral programs, along with suggestions for music selection.

Here are a few guidelines to keep in mind when programming sacred choral selections:

1. Whether sacred or secular, select repertoire on the basis of its musical merits.
2. More than one religious orientation should be reflected in the music you program.

3. Make no attempt to convince students to accept any particular religious view. This does not, however, mean that students may not learn about the religious connotations of a choral text in order to facilitate a more effective and insightful performance.
4. Consider scheduling concerts in a way that makes clear the sacred repertoire has not been programmed to observe any particular religious holiday.

✣ ANALYZING THE CHORAL SCORE ✣

Score analysis, a fascinating and dynamic process, is at the very heart of comprehensive choral music education. Its importance is rooted in the interrelationship of the choral music educator, the composer, the choral singers, and the audience.

A choral composer *creates* a composition and the choral conductor seeks to *recreate* it. A choral score is a written outline of a composer's intentions. Usually, though not always, it utilizes a standardized and conventional set of signs and symbols designating pitch, duration, tonal and metrical organization, and perhaps some expressive aspects. Often, the editor acts as an intermediary between the choral music educator and the composer. You should determine which of the markings on the score are the composer's and which have been added by an editor. Chapter 6 provides some strategies to help you. In a good edition the editorial markings are clearly identified. You have a responsibility to the composer to develop an accurate understanding of his or her intentions as expressed in the score and elsewhere.

This understanding must then be communicated to the choral singers. The results of your study of the score and other references must be incorporated into both the rehearsal and performance of the music. Beyond this, assist the students in developing their own ability to evaluate, study, and understand the music. The development of musical understanding in students usually is a gradual, cumulative process, which builds during the time the students live with a choral selection in rehearsal and, ultimately, performance. It is multifaceted and may vary somewhat from one selection to the next, but it includes a secure knowledge of the technical aspects of the music (the accurate production of the pitches and rhythms), and also the expressive and aesthetic aspects of the piece, leading to an understanding of its essence. The technical and the expressive are closely interrelated and interdependent. Choral singers must be able to sing in tune and with rhythmic precision to effectively understand and communicate the expressive and the aesthetic essence of the music. Although singers can, in a relatively short period of time, present excellent performances by incorporating strategies and techniques *you* provide, it is only after many such experiences that they develop their own individual aesthetic and conceptual framework for *independent* musical thinking.

The intentions of the composer, conveyed to the singers by the conductor/teacher, is then transmitted to those who listen to the choir sing. The essence of the music is conveyed to the audience. When this happens, the listener is engaged intellectually and emotionally. The audience attending a concert presented by a comprehensively educated ensemble is educated as well as entertained. Lamb uses the analogy of a pyramid to describe the manner in which knowledge is conveyed from the choral director to the choir and finally to the audience.[1] At the broad base of the pyramid is the instructor's knowledge. As the pyramid narrows, it includes the knowledge conveyed to the singers and, finally, the audience.

Through score study each of you will arrive at your own specific understanding of a choral piece. This understanding may differ from that of other choral conductors in terms of the exact tempo or the appropriate text inflection, which is fine. Because the written score is only an outline of the composer's intentions, there is room for differences; this is what makes each concert distinctive and exciting. Your task is to make the best educated musical decisions possible based on thorough score study.

The process we have outlined is a lengthy one. A large responsibility rests on your shoulders. The idea of finding the aesthetic and expressive essence of a piece may seem a bit ethereal or impractical. In reality, it is central to your task. To accurately understand the essence of what a composer is conveying, to foster a similar understanding in choral singers, and to communicate that understanding to an audience is demanding. The process begins with skillful and accurate score analysis.

Thorough score analysis involves several steps. You must place the selection in context, consider its overall outline, and then examine it in detail, so you have a clear understanding of the significance of every symbol on the page and how that aspect of the music fits into the broad outline of the work and the historical and musical context in which it was created.

Context

Every piece of choral music was created in a particular context that includes consideration of the composer, the stylistic period, the historical and social period, and the performance setting.

What is known of the composer of the work? When did they live? Where? What else did he or she write? Where does this particular piece fit into the composer's total output? Was it innovative and progressive, or does it continue an established stylistic line? Do we know what the composer thought of the work—are there any writings that shed light on its performance? If the work is contemporary, is the composer available to answer questions related to the performance of the piece?

Examining the Broad Outline

Consider the selection in its entirety. Examine the key signature, the metrical and rhythmic layout of the music, and its overall form.

Count the measures in the piece. Where does the composition divide into sections? It is helpful to graphically lay out the selection in the form of a chart or time line. See how the text, the harmony, the melody, and all of the other elements relate to the form of the piece. Are there shifts in tonality? How do they relate to changes in the text? Does the texture change? How does it relate to the other elements? Answering these questions in relation to the total score helps illuminate the broad outline of the music and the points where significant musical events occur.

Detailed Analysis

After placing the piece in context and examining the broad outline of the musical events contained in it, consider every mark on the page. Be certain of the meaning of all expressive markings, words, and notes. Ascertain where the most challenging material is found. Make notes, and determine some appropriate strategies for mastering the complexities of the score.

Consideration of context, broad outline, and the specifics of all the notation will prepare you to provide a successful experience for the participants in the choral ensemble.

✤ SCORE STUDY APPLICATIONS ✤

Figures 5.1 and 5.2 present two examples of graphic analyses of choral pieces.

It Is Good to Give Thanks

Kirke Mechem
Carl Fischer cm 7896

108 measures
Tonality: D Major - E minor - D Major
Meter: $\frac{3}{4}\ \frac{4}{4}\ \frac{3}{4}\ \frac{4}{4}\ \frac{3}{4}$
Tempo: Allegro con brio

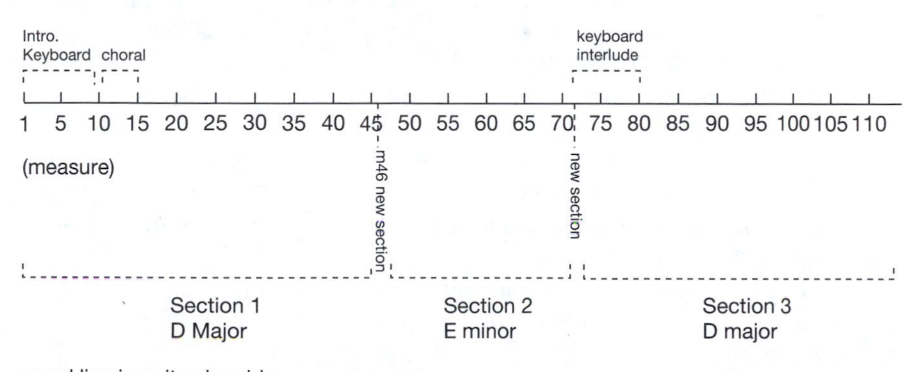

vocal line is quite singable
duet between driving, complex accompaniment
and unison vocal line.

FIGURE 5.1 Graph of "It Is Good to Give Thanks"

Keep Your Lamps

Andre Thomas
Hinshaw HMC 577

Chorus with congas
72 measures
Tonality: F minor
Meter: Cut time
Tempo: Moderato

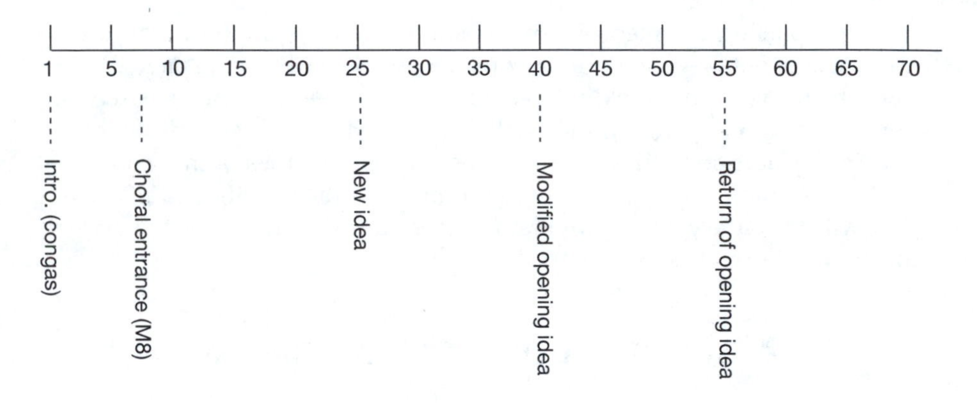

FIGURE 5.2 Graph of "Keep Your Lamps"

The graphic analyses above provide a framework for the choral music educator to use in considering the overall form, harmony, and other prominent characteristics of a choral piece. Such graphs should indicate in a linear fashion the measures in a choral selection and its general design, along with any other details helpful in analyzing potential rehearsal problems, strategies, and educational implications.

An extended work requires careful preparation and study not only of the individual movements and sections of the piece, but consideration of the way the movements tie together and comprise the whole. Examine the graphic representation of the design of the Fauré *Requiem* in Figure 5.3a–g.

Once you discern the design of a musical selection, it will guide every aspect of rehearsal. By determining how the selection breaks down into sections, you can lend coherence to rehearsal. In the case of an extended, multimovement work, such graphic analyses are even more helpful in the appropriate allocation of rehearsal time.

Without adequate advance study of the music, rehearsal can be haphazard and inefficient. The results of a score study form part of the basis for rehearsal planning.

✣ SUMMARY ✣

Score study is a lifelong process. The more choral music you examine, the more proficient you will become in its analysis. Each time you study a particular score of lasting worth, it will yield new insights. Adequate score analysis requires a significant investment of time, but it will make rehearsals and performances come alive for both the students and the audience as the nuances of the text are clearly communicated and the composer's intentions fully realized.

FIGURE 5.3 Graph of Overall Design of Fauré Requiem

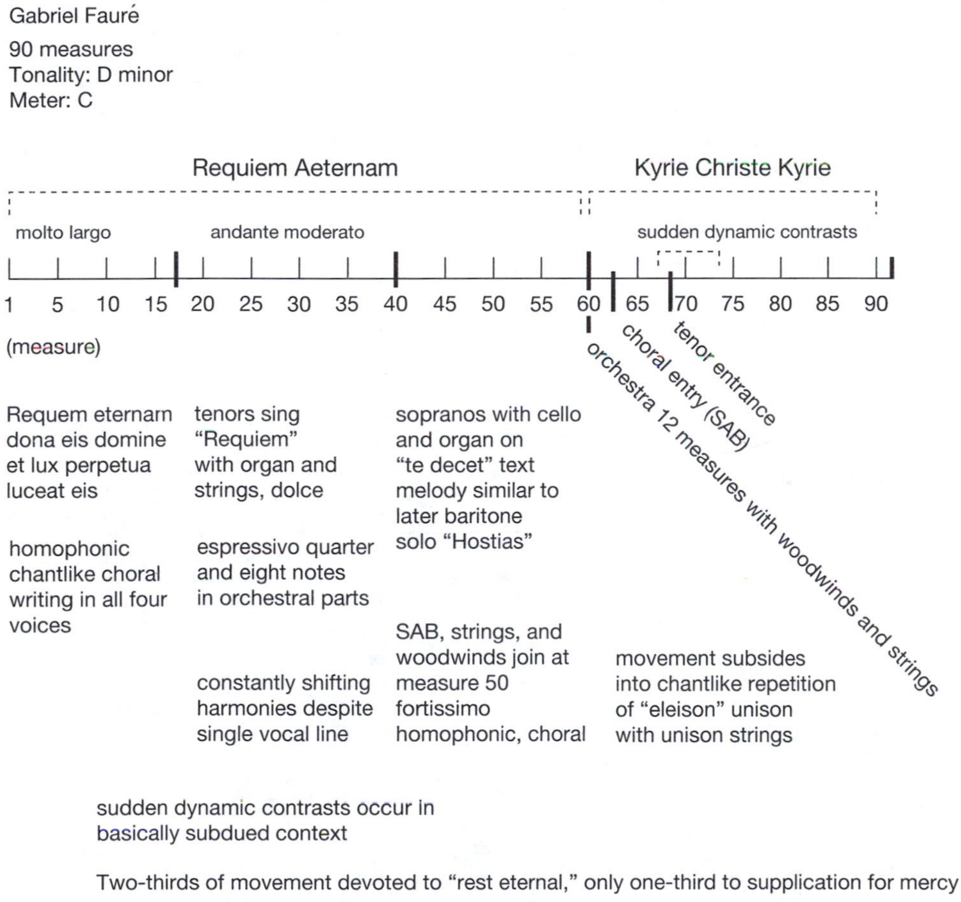

Gabriel Fauré
90 measures
Tonality: D minor
Meter: C

Requiem Aeternam
Kyrie Christe Kyrie
molto largo
andante moderato
sudden dynamic contrasts
1 5 10 15 20 25 30 35 40 45 50 55 60 65 70 75 80 85 90
(measure)
orchestra 12 measures with woodwinds and strings
choral entry (SAB)
tenor entrance

Requem eternarn dona eis domine et lux perpetua luceat eis

homophonic chantlike choral writing in all four voices

tenors sing "Requiem" with organ and strings, dolce

espressivo quarter and eight notes in orchestral parts

constantly shifting harmonies despite single vocal line

sopranos with cello and organ on "te decet" text melody similar to later baritone solo "Hostias"

SAB, strings, and woodwinds join at measure 50 fortissimo homophonic, choral

movement subsides into chantlike repetition of "eleison" unison with unison strings

sudden dynamic contrasts occur in basically subdued context

Two-thirds of movement devoted to "rest eternal," only one-third to supplication for mercy

FIGURE 5.3a

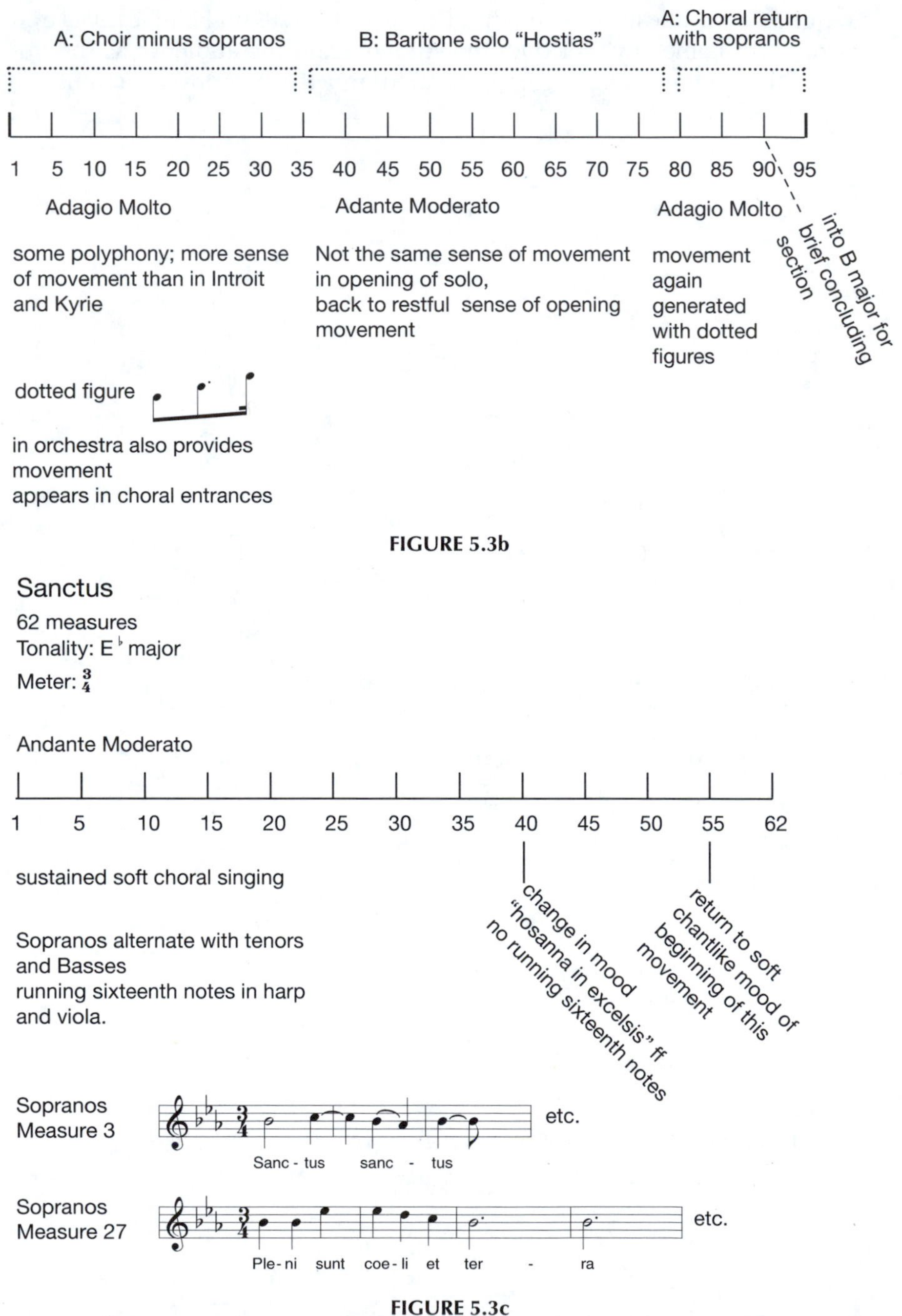

FIGURE 5.3b

FIGURE 5.3c

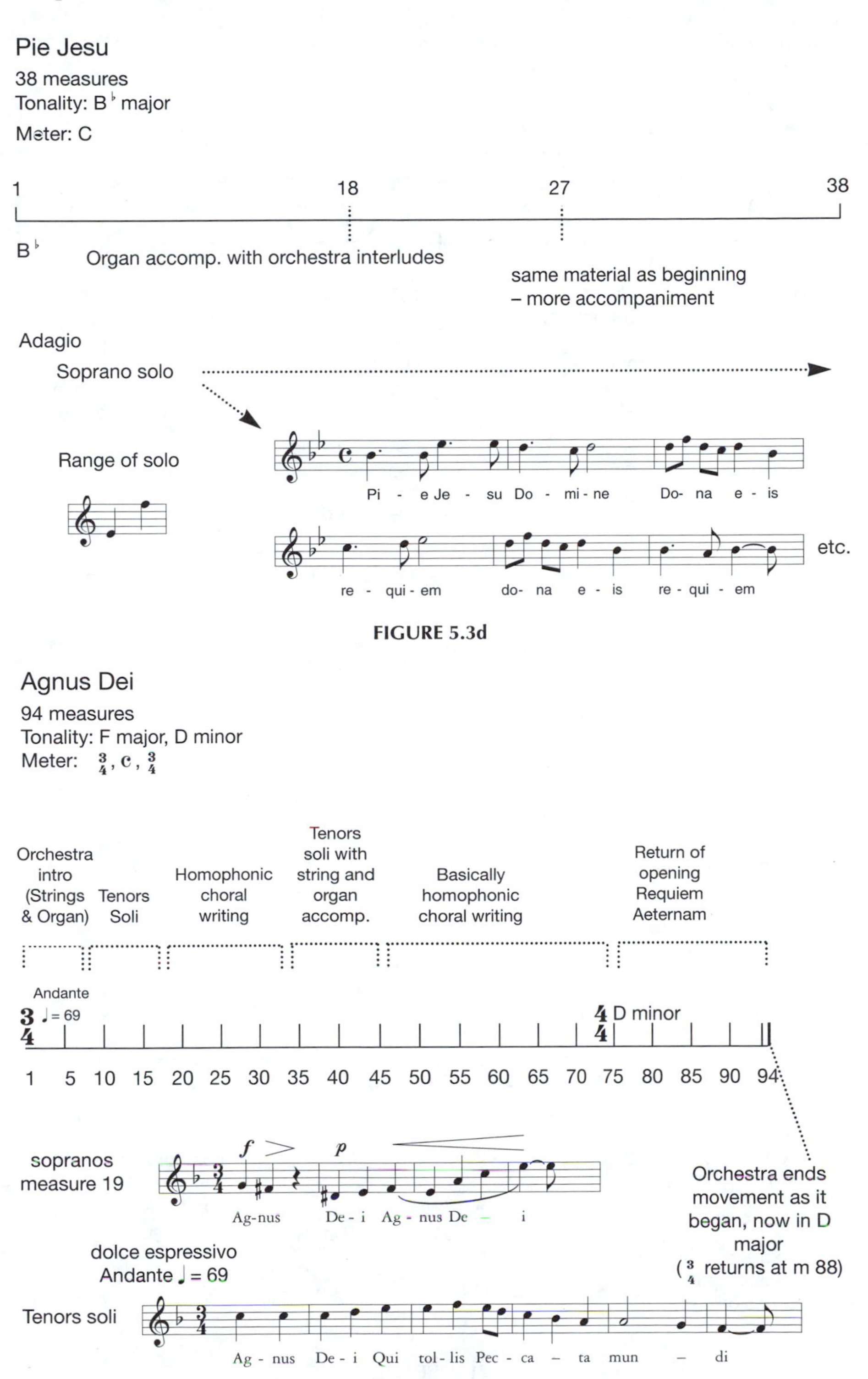

FIGURE 5.3d

FIGURE 5.3e

Libera Me

136 measures
Tonality: D minor
Meter: ¢, $\frac{6}{4}$, ¢,

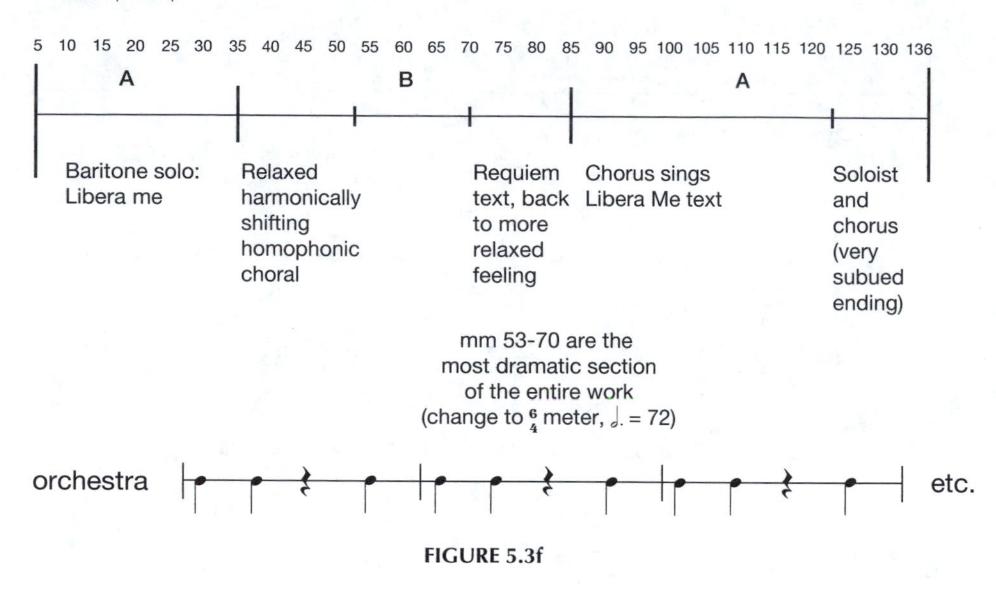

FIGURE 5.3f

In Paradisum

61 measures
Tonality: D major
Meter: $\frac{3}{4}$

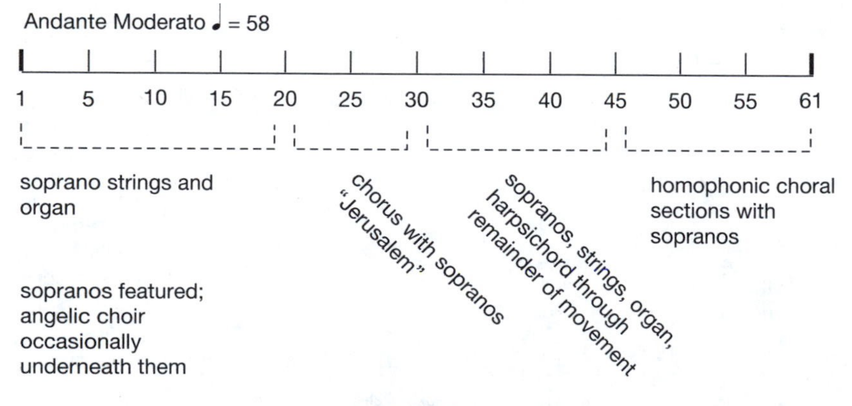

FIGURE 5.3g

Questions

1. Distinguish between range and tessitura.
2. What aspects of text must be considered in evaluating music for a secondary school choral ensemble?
3. What is meant by the educational implications of a piece of choral music? Isn't all good music educational by its very nature?
4. What factors must be considered in determining how a selection fits into the total program?
5. What elements are included in the context of a musical selection? Why is it important to consider the context on the piece in studying the score?
6. Construct a graph of a choral selection with which you are familiar. Include as much information as you feel will be helpful.

Note

1. Gordon H. Lamb, *Choral Techniques* (3rd ed.) (Dubuque, IA: William C. Brown, 1988, p. 90).

Suggested Reading

BERNSTEIN, MARTIN. *Score Reading.* New York: Witmark, 1947.

GREEN, ELIZABETH A.H., and NICOLAI MALKO. *The Conductor's Score.* Englewood Cliffs, NJ: Prentice-Hall, 1985.

GRUNOW, RICHARD F., and MILFORD H. FARGO. *The Choral Score Reading Program.* Chicago: G.I.A., 1985.

HEFFERNAN, CHARLES W. *Choral Music: Technique and Artistry.* Englewood Cliffs, NJ: Prentice-Hall, 1982.

HERFORD, JULIUS. "The Choral Conductor's Preparation of the Musical Score," in Harold A. Decker and Julius Herford (eds.), *Choral Conducting Symposium* (2nd ed.) (pp. 199–251). Englewood Cliffs, NJ: Prentice Hall, 1988.

HILLIS, MARGARET. *At Rehearsals.* New York: American Choral Foundation, 1969.

LAMB, GORDON H. *Choral Techniques* (3rd ed.). Dubuque, IA: William C. Brown, 1988.

MUSIC EDUCATORS NATIONAL CONFERENCE. *Religious Music in the Schools.* Vienna, VA: 1987.

ROBINSON, RAY, and ALLEN WINOLD. *The Choral Experience.* Prospect Heights, IL: Waveland Press, 1992.

Chapter Six

Style in Choral Singing

✣✣✣

✣ INTRODUCTION ✣

The following scenario happens all too frequently, usually sometime in the spring when choirs attend festivals and contests for the purposes of receiving evaluative comments or a competitive rating from a panel of adjudicators. The choir has spent a significant amount of time preparing three pieces for the competition, one from the Renaissance, one from the Baroque era, and one contemporary selection. The ensemble has learned the music very well. Every pitch and rhythm is secure.

When the choir's assigned performance time arrives, they file onto the stage and onto the risers in good order, creating an air of confident expectation on the part of the panel of adjudicators and others in the audience. The performance goes well, in the sense that the choir is able to present what they have learned with confidence.

When the rating sheets are received, however, the choir has received a rating of II, rather than the top rating of I on their performance. Why? Reading the comments of the adjudicators, it is clear that something was missing. Although the choir sang with good vocal technique and secure intonation, all of the music sounded alike. There was no difference in approach to the performance of the piece from the Renaissance, the one from the Baroque, and the contemporary composition. The adjudicators commented that there was a lack of appropriate *style* in the performance.

Every piece of choral music is a product of the environment and historical period in which it was created. It should be your objective to help students perform choral music in as authentic a manner as possible. In other words, the music should clearly represent the intentions of the composer and the performance practice of the time in which it was written. For example, a Palestrina motet should be performed with a relatively limited dynamic range, emotional objectivity, and a subtle accentuation, based on the rise and fall of the textual inflections. In contrast, certain Brahms choral songs may require the exploitation of the singers' full range of dynamics, pulsating metrical accentuation, and extremes of emotional expression.

Of course, an important step in learning about choral style is thorough score study (see Chapter 5). You should be familiar with and teach the singers about all of the markings on the printed page. Beyond this, however, there are other factors to consider in making a performance as authentic as possible, such as the number of singers per part, the desired tone quality, appropriate dynamics and tempo, ornamentation, and phrasing.

The older the music under consideration, the more complex the question of authenticity becomes. Twentieth-century composers usually indicate very specifically in the score how they wish to have the music performed. If there are aspects of the performance left to the discretion of the performer, that, also, is usually indicated. The notation used by the composer is standardized (the exception being certain avant garde compositions). It is often possible to contact a contemporary composer if questions arise concerning the interpretation of his or her music.

Conversely, performance editions of music written during the sixteenth century have been transcribed in modern notation by an editor, to make them accessible to contemporary performers. Keys, clefs, bar lines, note values, and meters have all been placed in the music editorially. Their appropriateness depends on the expertise of the person doing the editing. In order to make an informed decision concerning matters of performance practice and musical style, ask questions like these: In what sort of setting was the music originally performed? What was the nature of the performing group? What is an appropriate starting pitch? What is the correct tempo?

Teaching a choir to sing with a sense of appropriate musical style is a hallmark of the comprehensive choral music educator. To sing a choral piece in the correct style depends on the relative importance attached to various basic musical elements.

It has only been during the last thirty years that knowledge of style and performance practice have become recognized as indispensable elements of good choral singing (see Chapter 10). It is now widely accepted that a single, unitary concept of choral tone and style, to be employed no matter what the repertoire, is not musically valid. This idea has been replaced by the notion of a flexible approach to choral music, with the relative importance of the various musical elements dependent on the repertoire under consideration.

To begin to understand choral style, you need knowledge of the flow of choral music history from the Renaissance to the present day. Although an in-depth discussion of choral music history and style is beyond the scope of this book, the outline here will provide a framework for further investigation. Use the Suggested Reading for more intensive study.

Although there were important antecedents to the choral developments in the Renaissance period (1450–1600), choral music that continues as part of the standard performance repertoire was written during the fifteenth century and later. Therefore, our discussion begins with developments that occurred in the Renaissance, and then we describe each period in music history leading to the present day. The discussion of the Renaissance, Baroque, and Classic periods includes essential forms, important composers, and some basic stylistic guidelines for performance. Discussion of the Romantic period and the twentieth century where stylistic considerations are more straightforward concentrates on certain composers and styles and their relevance for choral music educators.

✣ THE RENAISSANCE (1450–1600) ✣

Renaissance means rebirth. During the fifteenth and sixteenth centuries, Europe experienced a new flowering of intellectual and artistic activity. Developments in literature and the visual arts, as well as in music, were stimulated by a new emphasis on the human spirit. Although this new spirit of humanism prompted momentous changes in the church, most notably the Protestant Reformation, initiated by Martin Luther (1483–1546), the church continued to provide the primary impetus for musical activity. In addition, the courts of various members of the nobility provided important support for musical activity, both sacred and secular. The invention of the printing press around 1450 facilitated the dissemination of printed materials of all kinds, including musical scores.

A variety of musical styles developed during the Renaissance, beginning with the music of Dufay (c. 1400–1474) and the Burgundian School. The Franco-Flemish tradition of sacred polyphony culminated in the music of di Lasso (1532–1594). At the same time, the conservative Catholic musical tradition most clearly exemplified by the Italian Palestrina (1525–1594) and the English secular and sacred musical tradition most clearly exemplified by Byrd (1543–1623), Tallis (1505–1585), and others embodied significant stylistic and formal changes. Finally, madrigal singing, an important tradition of secular music, with its roots in Italy, exerted an influence during the sixteenth century and was appropriated and adapted by the English during the reign of Elizabeth I, herself an ardent supporter of the arts and an amateur musician. The Venetian polychoral tradition led to the music of Monteverdi (1567–1643) and Schütz (1585–1672), whose compositions represent the transition from Renaissance practices to Baroque ideals.

Important Sacred Forms

Mass. The mass is a sequence of prayers and ceremonies commemorating the sacrifice of the body and blood of Christ. Along with the Offices, it constitutes the basic liturgy of the Roman Catholic church. The mass may be said or sung and consists of two parts: the proper and the ordinary. Those portions of the mass constituting the *proper* change throughout the year. The *ordinary* of the mass, however, consists of the invariable sections of the service. For musical purposes, the ordinary of mass is of the most interest, for it has inspired thousands of choral works. The ordinary of the mass consists of the Kyrie, Gloria, Credo, Sanctus and Benedictus, and the Agnus Dei (see Appendix B for a complete translation). When musicians speak of a mass, it is usually the ordinary of the mass they are referring to. Composers sometimes set individual sections of the mass to music (e.g., a "Kyrie" or an "Agnus Dei"), or they may compose a musical setting of the entire ordinary.

Requiem. The requiem is a mass for the dead, with the word itself from the Latin *requies*, which means "rest." In a requiem mass, certain sections of the proper become invariable and are added to the chants of the ordinary, and the joyful sections of the ordinary (the Gloria and Credo) are omitted, resulting in the following sequence of sections: Introit, Kyrie, Gradual, Sequence, Offertory, Sanctus and Benedictus, Agnus Dei, Communion. Settings of the requiem by various composers may omit certain of the sections just listed, reflecting the composer's attitude toward death; a desire to emphasize certain aspects of the text for musical, dramatic, or spiritual reasons; or the liturgical tradition for which it was written. The text of the Requiem also is found in Appendix B.

Motet. The term *motet* first arose in the thirteenth century and was applied to a type of composition that developed from the clausula, when a text was added to the previously unvoiced part of a two- or three-part composition based on chant. Originally intended to be sung by solo voices, by the middle of the fifteenth century, the motet was a sacred choral composition, using a text other than the ordinary of the mass.

Anthem. The anthem is a sacred choral composition, intended for use in the Anglican services of morning or evening prayer. Two types of anthems developed known as "full anthems" and "verse anthems." *Full anthems* were written entirely for choir; *verse anthems* featured alternating choral and solo passages.

Chorale. The chorale is a hymn tune of the Lutheran Church. Some of these tunes were adaptations of Latin hymns used in the Catholic church, some were adaptations of preexisting German hymns or secular songs, and some were newly composed. Chorales were often used as the basis for more extended choral works such as chorale motets, which became a highly significant part of the repertoire during the Baroque era.

Calvinist Psalm Setting. The Calvinist church opposed the singing of nonbiblical texts, and musical settings of Psalm texts were an important feature of the Calvinist service. These were based on both preexisting and newly composed melodies.

Important Secular Forms

Italian Madrigal. The Italian madrigal was the most important secular musical form of the Renaissance. The origins of the word may relate to the mother tongue *(matricale)* or a pastoral poem *(mandriale)*. The madrigal was preceded by the frottola, a love poem set in three or four parts, with the top part sung and the others played. The Italian madrigal went through three stages of development, beginning with the chordal style of Arcadelt and Festa continuing through the generation of composers that included Willaert, Di Lasso, and their contemporaries, and culminating in the chromatic, expressive works of Marenzio and Gesualdo. Monteverdi's madrigals demonstrate clearly the transition from Renaissance to Baroque musical style.

English Madrigal. Italian madrigals became highly popular in Elizabethan England. Initially, translations of the Italian music were often performed, and eventually, English compositions based on Italian models were numerous and well received. The English madrigal style was lighter and simpler than the Italian, both textually and musically.

Chanson. The chanson was the primary French secular form of the Renaissance. Renaissance chansons fall into three categories: contrapuntal, program, and Parisian. Contrapuntal chansons, best exemplified by those of Josquin, are primarily imitative in style, in five parts. The Parisian chanson consisted primarily of chordal writing in four parts. The program chansons included musical representations of bird songs, street vendors, battles, and other "programs."

Composers

During the Renaissance, the centers of musical influence in Europe shifted from one location to another. During the first half of the fifteenth century, the dukes of Burgundy, most notably Philip the Good, were important patrons of the arts, and the area in which they lived became an important musical center (the area presently comprised of Holland, Belgium, and northeastern France). Two important musical figures predominate in the Burgundian School: Dufay (1400–1474) and Binchois (1400–1460). Dufay wrote around twenty-five mass movements or pairs of movements, as well as eight complete masses, in addition to isorhythmic motets. Isorhythm was a unifying technique in which a particular pattern of long and short notes was used in successive divisions or repetitions of a melody. Binchois composed mass movements, motets, and chansons.

The Franco-Flemish choral tradition continued with the work of Johannes Ockeghem (c. 1430–1495) and Jacob Obrecht (c. 1450–1505). Ockeghem was a conservative composer, a student of Dufay, noted primarily for his sacred music. Obrecht, born in the year that is generally used to mark the beginning of the Renaissance, utilized imitative counterpoint and cantus firmus technique. In a cantus firmus mass, a preexisting melody (secular or sacred) provides the unifying basis for a composition. Obrecht was also noted for his parody masses, in which a preexisting section of polyphony (or an entire work) was modified and adapted.

The most important musical figure during the first half of the Renaissance was Josquin des Prez (1440–1521). Born in Flanders (present-day Belgium), Josquin worked in Italy and later in France. His compositions summarized and embodied all that had come before, just as Bach's would two centuries later. Josquin's compositions included masses, motets, and secular pieces, and exerted a strong influence on other composers of his day. Josquin's music displays not only northern European contrapuntal characteristics, but blends with them the influence of Italian secular solo singing, resulting from his years in Italy. His compositions thus constitute an unusually beautiful and expressive mixture of colors, styles, and techniques.

Other notable composers who were contemporaries of Josquin or were of the following generation included Nicolas Gombert (c. 1490–1556), Pierre de la Rue (c. 1460–1518), Heinrich Isaac (c. 1450–1517), and Jacobus Clemens (c. 1510–c. 1556) who was also known as Clemens non Papa.

The Franco-Flemish musical influence culminated in the work, a century later, of Orlando Di Lasso (1532–1594). Di Lasso was born in Mons, and was taken as a boy to Rome, where he was a choir boy and later choirmaster. He traveled to England and France, and in 1556 became a member of the chapel of the Duke of Bavaria in Munich. His large musical output includes hundreds of compositions, both sacred and secular. Di Lasso's compositions included masses, motets, madrigals, lieder, and chansons.

In the sixteenth century, the main center of musical influence shifted southward from the Franco-Flemish area to Italy. Even those composers who were natives of northern Europe often traveled to Rome for periods of time. Rome and Venice were both important musical centers. The Catholic church continued to provide strong impetus for musical composition. The Council of Trent, which met intermittently from 1545 to 1563, sought to preserve the integrity and purity of church music by setting forth strict rules concerning the use of polyphony and the use of secular melodies as the basis for sacred compositions. The sacred music of Giovanni Pierluigi da Palestrina (c. 1525–1594) embodies the reforms called for by the Council. It is characterized by strictly controlled melody, rhythm, and dissonance, creating a sense of unparalleled devotion and restraint. Palestrina's work includes over five hundred sacred compositions, as well as madrigals. Similarly, the music of Tomas Luis de Vittoria (c. 1548–1611), a Spaniard who studied in Rome with Palestrina, is also characterized by reverence and restraint.

In the latter part of the sixteenth century and the beginning of the seventeenth, an interesting choral tradition developed that was centered in Venice. The Venetian style foreshadowed Baroque innovations in its preoccupation with antiphonal singing and the juxtaposition of contrasting musical forces. The architecture of St. Mark's Cathedral encouraged the use of multiple choirs.

The Venetian style was begun by Adrian Willaert (c. 1490–1562) and continued by Cipriano de Rore (1516–1565), Claudio Merulo (1533–1604), and Andrea Gabrieli (c. 1520–1586), and culminated in the works of Giovanni Gabrieli (1557–1612), which were written for as many as four or five or more antiphonal choirs.

The Protestant Reformation, begun by Luther in 1517, resulted in some new directions for sacred music during the sixteenth century. In addition to the music being written for the Catholic church, the Anglican anthem, the Lutheran chorale and chorale motet, and Calvinist settings of Psalms have continued to be significant parts of the choral repertoire. William Byrd, probably the foremost English composer of the late sixteenth and early seventeenth centuries, wrote Latin motets and masses, as well as anthems and complete services for the Anglican church. Other important composers of anthems included Orlando Gibbons (1583–1625), Thomas Tompkins (1572–1656), Thomas Morley (1557–1602), Thomas Weelkes (c. 1575–1623), and John Wilbye (1574–1638). In addition to Martin Luther (1483–1546), chorales and chorale motets were written by Hans Leo Hassler (1564–1612) and Johann Eccard (1553–1611). The chorale motet reached its highest stage of development during the Baroque era. Claude Goudimel (c. 1505–1572) was the most important Renaissance composer of Calvinist Psalm settings, which were French translations and versifications of the Psalms intended for congregational singing.

Secular music composed during the Renaissance has also remained an important part of the choral repertoire. The secular music written during this period was vocal chamber music. It is therefore best suited to performance by a small ensemble, employing a light and subtle tone. The roots of the madrigal are in Italy. Three generations of sixteenth-century Italian madrigalists are recognized today. The first generation is represented by Jacob Arcadelt (c. 1505–1560), Philippe de Verdelot (d. 1550), and Costanza Festa (c. 1490–1545). The second generation and the next stage in the development of the form is represented by Willaert and Cipriano de Rore, each of whom has already been mentioned in connection with their sacred compositions in Venetian style, as well as Di Lasso, Giaches de Wert (1535–1596), and Philip de Monte (1521–1603). During this period, Giovanni Gastoldi (c. 1556–1622) was noted for a particular type of simple, dancelike madrigal known as a *balletto,* which featured a "fa-la-la" refrain.

The final stage in the development of the Italian madrigal is evident in the compositions of Luca Marenzio (1553–1599) and Carlo Gesualdo (c. 1560–1613). The madrigals of Marenzio are characterized by a variety of compositional techniques and by the use of chromaticism to bring out the expressive nuances of the text. Gesualdo's music carries to an extreme degree the emotionalism and the chromaticism found in the music of Marenzio.

During the last half of the sixteenth century, the madrigal became highly popular in Elizabethan England. Initially, translations of Italian madrigals were published and performed. This led to the composition of madrigals by English composers, using English texts (usually somewhat lighter and more popular in character than the Italian pieces). The Italian balletto was adapted and termed a *ballett*, using the same "fa-la-la" refrain. Major English madrigal composers include Morley, Weelkes, Wilbye, and Gibbons.

Renaissance Style

As we have seen, the Renaissance was a period with a wide variety of musical styles. An Italian madrigal should be performed differently than a mass by Palestrina or an anthem by Gibbons. Festive music from Venice requires a different approach than a Parisian chanson. The sound of music written for the cathedral should differ from that intended to be sung informally after dinner.

Text was of great importance to Renaissance composers. Text and music became totally integrated and mutually enhancing. New forms, styles, and compositional techniques, while they add to the complexity of the choral conductor's task, also added greatly to the richness of the repertoire from this period.

The original scores of Renaissance music contain less information than those from later periods in music history. What information there is may be written in notation that is unintelligible to most contemporary choral singers. Many musical decisions were routinely left to the performers, who often included the composer. For the present-day performer, this requires careful selection of the performance edition used. The problems of old notation, starting pitch, unwritten but necessary accidentals, and other esoteric questions will have been answered by the editor. The issue for the contemporary conductor is to be certain the score selected has been skillfully edited. In recent years, the level of scholarship in choral music has increased markedly, but there are still editions available containing inappropriate dynamic, tempo, and expressive markings.

How can you tell when a score is well edited? A well-edited score will clearly indicate what markings are from the composer and which have been added editorially. It often includes notes concerning the piece, the composer, and the style. A well-edited score from the Renaissance will *not* include numerous expressive and dynamic markings without indicating they are editorial.

Once a score has been selected, what are the important issues? The appropriate use of voices and instruments, interpretation of pitch, tempo, and rhythmic markings, and matters of expression are some basic areas of concern. Remember, however, that any performance of older music is necessarily a compromise because it is impossible to duplicate the conditions under which it was originally performed.

The tone quality desired for Renaissance music will vary according to the purpose of the composition. It is impossible to recreate the sound of a Renaissance cathedral choir with a twentieth-century school choir of mixed voices. The Renaissance ensemble utilized men and boys, with boys singing the soprano and alto parts. The male castrato sound that was characteristic of certain music of the Renaissance and Baroque does not exist today.

Although it is impossible to duplicate exactly the choral sounds heard in a Renaissance cathedral, it should be noted that much Renaissance sacred music is well suited to the adolescent voice. It does not make large demands in terms of range, and the light quality of the young singer is much better suited to it than to many other types and styles of literature. A perfectly straight, vibrato-less tone is not desirable for any music. Choirs should have the opportunity, however, to listen to performances or recordings by contemporary choirs of men and boys, to hear the tone quality. Then, within the bounds of good vocal production, that sound may be emulated.

The number of singers most appropriately employed for Renaissance sacred repertoire is relatively small. The papal choir in the sixteenth century reached a high of twenty-four singers, which was considered the ideal number for performances of sacred literature. Here again, it may be necessary to make a compromise if you want the concert choir of sixty voices to have the opportunity to perform some of this literature. Simply be aware of the compromise being made and alert the students to the necessity for light, controlled singing.

This kind of ethereal, carefully controlled choral sound had its roots in the Franco-Flemish polyphonic tradition. The southern Italian tradition of solo chamber singing requires a light, soloistic approach to the sound. Probably the majority of the madrigal repertoire was originally performed with one person per part. In emulating this kind of sound with a contemporary madrigal ensemble, each singer has the difficult task of singing lines that were probably intended for a single voice, but singing them with careful attention to blend and uniformity of approach to the nuances of textual accentuation.

The use of instruments can enhance the performance of Renaissance choral music. For young choirs, the inclusion of instrumental parts has the added benefit of providing additional support for the singers. The use of instruments in Renaissance music differs from current practice in some important respects.

The instruments of the period differed from our contemporary versions. The recorder, a predecessor of our current cross-blown flute, and the sackbut, a predecessor of the present-day trombone, were employed. The krummhorn, a double-reed instrument, was somewhat analogous to the current oboe. Krummhorns and recorders come in various sizes (soprano, alto, tenor, and bass being the most common). Viols of various sizes, similar to the modern cello, were prominently used. Small percussion instruments such as finger cymbals or tambourine may be used to reinforce pieces with a strongly rhythmic character. The lute, a forerunner of the guitar, provides a very beautiful and characteristically Renaissance sound, which can be used to good advantage. Currently, depending on the size of your community, you may find a surprising number of players of Renaissance period instruments. It is worth investigating whether such individuals or ensembles might be available to participate in a concert or to come to the school and demonstrate for students the instrumental sounds of the Renaissance. Recordings of authentic instruments also help students understand and appreciate the sounds of Renaissance instrumental music.

If authentic instruments are not readily available, you will need to make a decision about substituting modern instruments for their Renaissance counterparts. The contemporary flute can be substituted for the recorder, and a contemporary cello could replace a viol da gamba quite satisfactorily. Likewise, the guitar may be used in place of a lute. A brass quartet may be used to good effect in polychoral music of the Venetian school.

The piano was developed in the eighteenth century. Its tone quality is not appropriate for music of the Renaissance. Fortunately, the increasing availability and affordability of synthesizers and other digital keyboards as well as harpsichords of high quality make it possible to avoid the use of the piano for this repertoire.

The instruments were used in a different manner than they are today. They doubled and reinforced vocal lines rather than playing independent parts. That said, there are a variety of ways in which the colors of the instruments can be exploited to add richness and variety to Renaissance choral pieces. The Renaissance notion of leaving decisions to the performer means it is very much in keeping with the style of the period to experiment with instrumental colors in various roles in support of vocalists.

Here are some suggestions for the use of instruments:

1. Use a quartet of recorders, flutes, or krummhorns. Have the singers sing a selection through without instrumental support, then have the instrumental quartet play the selection through, and follow that with a combined vocal-instrumental rendition.
2. Simply have a cellist support the base line or a string quartet support the vocal lines in the manner described in number 1.
3. Use small percussion instruments to reinforce strong rhythms.
4. Use the lute or guitar to provide an accompaniment for madrigals or other secular songs.
5. A choir and a brass ensemble may provide a beautiful contrast in color in a polychoral festive piece of the Venetian school with the singers as choir I and the instrumentalists as choir II.

As we mentioned earlier, the interpretation of Renaissance notation is best left to the editor of the performance edition used. However, even with a well-edited modern edition of a Renaissance choral work, some basic aspects of pitch, rhythm, and tempo require some discussion and explanation.

There was no standardized concert pitch during the Renaissance. It is difficult if not impossible to determine the exact starting pitch intended by the composer, although an examination of the ranges of the vocal parts provides a good basis for making a well-educated guess. Given the variability of pitch from country to country, city to city, and church to church up until the nineteenth century, the contemporary conductor should feel free to experiment with the tonal center for any piece of Renaissance music and to select the key that best suits the particular ensemble in terms of comfortable vocal ranges and secure intonation. It is often a help in rehearsal to try several different starting pitches.

When a Renaissance piece is transcribed in contemporary musical notation, the note values of the original score are usually shortened, while of course retaining the same relative lengths as in the original score. Bar lines are usually added as a convenience for modern performers. However, the metrical scheme implied by the barlines should not necessarily be adhered to. Consider the well-known Italian madrigal "O Occhi Manza Mia." The rhythm and meter of several twentieth-century performance editions is as follows:

EXAMPLE 6.1

Actually, the accentuation should be based on the text, as follows:

EXAMPLE 6.2

There are many similar examples. In recent years, some editors have produced editions in which each part is barred independently, based on the text of the particular line. In any case, allow the natural accentuation of the text and the rise and follow of the melody to dictate the accentuation. This is a difficult concept for inexperienced singers to incorporate into their performance. There is a tendency to all follow the same accentuation (usually that of the soprano line) rather than for each line to be independent of the others, with its own pattern of rising and falling accents. When moving from one section of a piece to the next, when there is a meter change from duple to triple or the converse, one measure of duple usually equals one measure of triple, rather than maintaining a constant beat.

Tempos in the Renaissance tended to be somewhat slower than today. A good indication of tempo is to check the text and mentally sing through a selection to see what tempo works best. It should be fast enough that the linear flow of each vocal part is not impeded, but not so fast that the integrity of the text and clarity of the polyphony is compromised in the quicker sections.

The dynamic range used in Renaissance music is smaller than that employed in later periods of music history. Nevertheless, the dynamics should also be judged according to the setting for which the music was written. Festival pieces utilizing singers and a brass ensemble naturally tend to be louder than those written for the drawing room.

The predominant determinant of appropriate dynamics should be the expression of the nuances of the text. The closely related interdependence of text and musical line in the Renaissance must always be considered.

Remember that any performance of music from the Renaissance will represent a compromise in terms of authentic performance practice. We must go back to the basic premise of thorough score study, the selection of a well-edited score, and a desire to bring out the musical and expressive nuances inherent in it. Also, note that much of the information currently in use concerning style and performance practice has only come to light in the last twenty-five years. Undoubtedly, the continuing efforts of musicologists and choral conductors will supply additional information that will replace some of what is currently accepted. Thus continuing study is critical to the effective musical education of students and the presentation of performances that are based on the most accurate information available.

✣ THE BAROQUE PERIOD (1600–1750) ✣

The transition from Renaissance to Baroque musical style began in the late sixteenth century. The polychoral motets of the Venetian school, with two or more independent choirs juxtaposed to exploit the resulting contrast in color, provided the seedbed for the Baroque notion of conflict. Composers of the Venetian school also employed large performing forces, including choirs of instrumentalists, in their music. This led to the development of concertato style, in which the playing of a soloist or small group of players was contrasted with that of the full ensemble. This style of composition led to the development of the concerto. The concerto, of course, is an instrumental form, and during the Baroque era, instrumental music assumed far greater prominence than previously.

An examination of the madrigals of Monteverdi, written over a fifty-year period, reveals many of the stylistic changes that signaled the transition from Renaissance to Baroque. Monteverdi's early madrigals (written 1587–1603) were composed in the style of the high Renaissance. Similar in character to the works of Marenzio in their use of chromaticism, they nevertheless begin a departure from the ideal of equality of voices and moved toward the Baroque notion of soprano-bass polarity. In contrast, his last four books of madrigals (written 1605–1638) include independent instrumental sections contrasted with choral interludes (concertato style) and increasing use of figured bass.

Several pairs of contrasting terms have been applied to the "old style" of Renaissance music versus the "new style" of the Baroque. *Stile antico* and *stile moderno* is one such pair. Another, used by Monteverdi, was *prima prattica* and *seconda prattica.* In the first half of the seventeenth century the two styles coexisted, with the earlier style employed most frequently in sacred music, while the new style was evident in secular music, most notably in the operas of the early Baroque.

Text was of extreme importance to composers of both the Renaissance and Baroque eras. However, the manner in which it was approached differed markedly. The Renaissance ideal was of several independent vocal lines, each with its own inflections and accentuation. In the early to mid-seventeenth century, the trend was away from this polyphonic ideal, toward soprano-bass polarity, in which a single melody was sung and a figured bass line was played by an accompanying instrument or instruments. By the late Baroque era, in the first half of the eighteenth century, polyphony had returned to popularity. The polyphony of the late Baroque differed from that of the Renaissance: It was rooted in tonal harmony and characterized by an energetic, metrically conceived, driving rhythm.

The tradition of requiring full participation by the performer in decisions concerning tempo, articulation, ornamentation, and other matters continued from the Renaissance into the Baroque era. Keyboard players presented with a figured bass line were expected to "realize" it, filling in chords, adding ornaments, and otherwise embellishing their playing. Singers, particularly soloists, were expected to improvise ornamentation and elaboration for a melody found in the score.

Although all of the stylistic changes mentioned here occurred over a period of decades, the year 1600 is widely accepted as a convenient if somewhat arbitrary date to mark the end of the Renaissance and the beginning of the Baroque. It should also be noted that many if not all of these changes were interrelated. For example, the move away from polyphonic texture toward an accompanied melody was closely related to the shift from modality toward the major-minor key system and the use of figured bass. The increasing significance of new instrumental forms grew out of the employment of independent instrumental parts, contrasted with choral sections. The total impact of all of these changes taken together propelled music forward into the new era.

Important Forms

In the Baroque period, some of the important choral forms, such as the mass and the motet, represented the continued development of Renaissance ideas. Others, such as the cantata and the oratorio, were newly created or assumed a new importance in terms of stylistic development. Some forms crossed the boundaries of sacred and secular. The cantatas of Bach, for example, include both classifications. For the purposes of this discussion, opera is not considered. A brief definition of each of the important Baroque choral forms is presented here.

Anthem. The anthem tradition begun in Elizabethan England by Gibbons, Byrd, Tallis and others continued in the Baroque, reaching its highest state in the anthems of Purcell and Handel. The Baroque anthem was more elaborate than that of the Renaissance, utilizing recitatives, instrumental accompaniments with continuo, independent instrumental sections and interludes, and elaborate solo passages.

Cantata. Derived from the Italian word *cantare* meaning "to sing," the cantata developed in the seventeenth century as an extended piece of accompanied secular music with recitatives and arias. In Germany, the Lutheran chorale formed the basis for extended treatment in the "chorale cantata," a sacred work written for soloists, chorus, and orchestra, and brought to its highest development by J.S. Bach.

Madrigal. In the Baroque era, the madrigal continued to be popular and came to embody the "new style" in the form of the continuo madrigal developed by Monteverdi, using figured bass, and incorporating sections for solo, duet, or trio with continuo and contrasting sections for instruments with those for choir.

Magnificat. A musical setting of the canticle of the Virgin Mary found in the first chapter of the Gospel of Luke. Polyphonic settings were written as early as the fourteenth century. The Magnificat is a part of the Catholic service of Vespers and the Anglican service of Evensong. Monteverdi, Hassler, Purcell, and most importantly Bach, wrote significant settings of this text.

Mass. During the early Baroque, the mass tended to be a conservative musical form, similar in style to the Franco-Flemish mass of the sixteenth century. As the seventeenth century progressed, masses began to incorporate concertato style and to have instrumental accompaniments. These developments led to the five masses of J.S. Bach, whose *B Minor Mass* is one of the towering monuments of Western music. Unlike his other masses, the *B Minor Mass* is two hours in length and divides the ordinary into twenty-five separate movements characterized by a wide range of expressive and musical devices.

Motet. The motets of the Venetian school were written in concertato style, exploiting the colors of contrasting choral and instrumental forces. Schutz, Monteverdi, and Lully wrote motets that included a wide variety of forces, textures, and emotions. This led to the multimovement motet of the late Baroque, exemplified by the works of Bach and Buxtehude.

Oratorio. The setting of a sacred or heroic text for chorus, soloists, and orchestra. The details of the story are conveyed through recitative. Similar in character to opera, an oratorio is not staged, nor are the singers costumed. The first important composer of oratorio was Carissimi. The Baroque oratorio reached its highest point in the works of Handel.

Passion. The passion is a musical setting of the events at the end of Christ's life, from the Last Supper to the Crucifixion. The story is carried in recitatives sung by the Evangelist. Other soloists perform recitatives and arias, and the role of the chorus varies from the singing of chorales, more complex contemplative choral sections, and *turba* sections in which the chorus assumes the identity of the crowd.

Te Deum. The opening words of this text, "Te deum laudamus," mean "We Praise Thee, God." It is sung at the Roman Catholic office of Matins, at Anglican Morning Prayer, and for other festive sacred and secular occasions. Purcell and Handel each wrote significant musical settings of the Te Deum.

Vespers. Evening worship in the Roman Catholic rite. Vespers includes a series of psalms, a hymn, and the Magnificat. Monteverdi's Vespers of 1610 utilized choir, instrumentalists, and was written in concertato style. It is the most important Baroque example of the form.

Composers

Two composers predominated in the first half of the Baroque period. Their music embodies many of the elements of the transition from Renaissance to Baroque style. These two composers were Claudio Monteverdi (1567–1643) and Heinrich Schütz (1585–1672).

Born in Cremona, Italy, Monteverdi composed eight books of madrigals, three masses, vespers, magnificats, and motets. He wrote at least twelve operas, three of which have been preserved. As mentioned earlier, Monteverdi's music illustrates the transition from the *prima prattica* to the *seconda prattica,* from Renaissance polyphony to Baroque homophony.

Schütz was the greatest German composer of the seventeenth century. Born in Saxony, he studied with Gabrieli in Venice. Schütz's music is diverse, reflecting his long life and the varied conditions under which he worked. His first published compositions were Italian madrigals. He was Lutheran, and his sacred compositions were written for the Lutheran church. Schütz wrote several highly varied collections of motets as well as oratorios and passions.

Other important composers of the early Baroque include Jean-Baptiste Lully (1632–1687), Jan Pieterszoon Sweelinck (1591–1652), Johann Hermann Schein (1586–1630), and Giacomo Carissimi (1605–1674). Carissimi's fifteen oratorios are of particular importance. They contain recitatives, arias, choral sections, and instrumental interludes, utilizing a variety of textures.

In the late Baroque period, the works of Bach and Handel predominated and constitute an important part of the choral repertoire performed today. Other major composers of this period include Dietrich Buxtehude (1637–1701), Marc-Antoine Charpentier (1634–1704), Henry Purcell (1659–1695), Georg Philip Telemann (1681–1767), and Antonio Vivaldi (1675–1741).

The music of Johann Sebastian Bach (1685–1750) represents the culmination of the two centuries of musical development that preceded it. Bach's choral, orchestral, and keyboard music display an amazing variety of expressive quality, technique, and organization. His choral output includes six motets, a magnificat, five masses, three hundred cantatas, and two complete passions.

While all of Bach's choral works constitute an important part of the repertoire, two works are choral monuments: the *B Minor Mass* and the *St. Matthew Passion.* In addition, the hundreds of Bach cantatas include a wide variety of difficulty levels, and some are performable by choirs with limited experience and resources. The relatively modest resources required for the performance of many Bach cantatas is understandable, since he wrote the majority of them for performance by his church choir in Leipzig and was limited by the available finances and personnel. Although his singers were regularly under his instruction, the instrumentalists who constituted the orchestra were recruited on an ad hoc basis and in fact were probably sight-reading the music in performance.

George Frideric Handel (1685–1759) was born in Halle, Germany. Handel was a cosmopolitan man, traveling to Italy for three years in 1707 and living in London from 1711 until his death. His choral output included twenty-one oratorios, three Te Deums, fourteen anthems, and two passions. His oratorios were designed for concert presentation rather than for use in the church. They were musical narratives of the lives of heroic figures from the Bible and mythology. Handel's best known oratorio, *Messiah,* is atypical of the rest in that it presents a series of meditations on the life of Christ and its significance rather than a dramatic narrative of a sequence of events.

Baroque Style

The performance of Baroque choral music requires life and energy. It is music that is full of emotion. In Baroque music there tends to be unity of emotion within a given section of a composition. This stems from the Baroque idea that an individual is controlled by a single affect or emotion at any given time. But this does not mean the music should be emotionless. More overt emotion may be displayed in a Baroque choral piece than in music from the Renaissance. Contrast in emotion must be achieved as one section ends and another begins in a new tempo and with new dynamics.

Terraced dynamics, wherein dynamic changes occur between sections of music (as opposed to long crescendos and decrescendos within sections) is a typically Baroque musical characteristic. Similarly, the tempo of a Baroque composition should be steady within each section of a work. Sharp contrasts in tempo occur *between* sections.

The tone to be used in a Baroque mass is bigger and more dramatic than what would be appropriate for a sixteenth-century setting of the same text. A freer approach to vibrato along with a wider dynamic range help distinguish the two styles.

The use of an orchestra to accompany Baroque choral music adds to the variety of color available and accentuates the need for choir members to sing with warmth and projection. As was the case in the Renaissance, it was quite common and accepted to double the vocal lines in a composition with instruments. In the Baroque period, in addition to the instrumental doubling, compositions also typically contained an independent orchestral accompaniment, often calling for strings, trumpets, oboes, and a keyboard instrument (harpsichord or organ) providing the continuo.

Some Baroque choral music tends to be "instrumental" in conception. Such music is characterized by driving dotted rhythms, and it must be infused with life, energy, and a sense of propulsion. Slower sections should be distinctly contrasting. Consider this excerpt from this first movement of the Vivaldi *Gloria* compared to the beginning of the second movement:

18
glo - ri- a,
glo - ry be,
glo - ri- a,
glo - ry be,
glo - ri- a,
glo - ry be,
glo - ri- a,
glo - ry be,
glo - ri- a,
glo - ry be,
glo - ri- a,
glo - ry be,
glo - ri- a,
glo - ry be,
glo - ri- a,
glo - ry be,
20
glo - ri- a
glo - ry be
glo - ri- a
glo - ry be
glo - ri- a
glo - ry be
glo - ri- a
glo - ry be

EXAMPLE 6.3

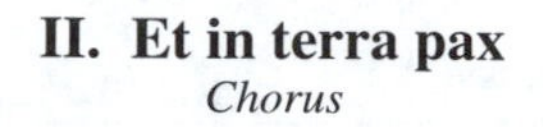

II. Et in terra pax

Chorus

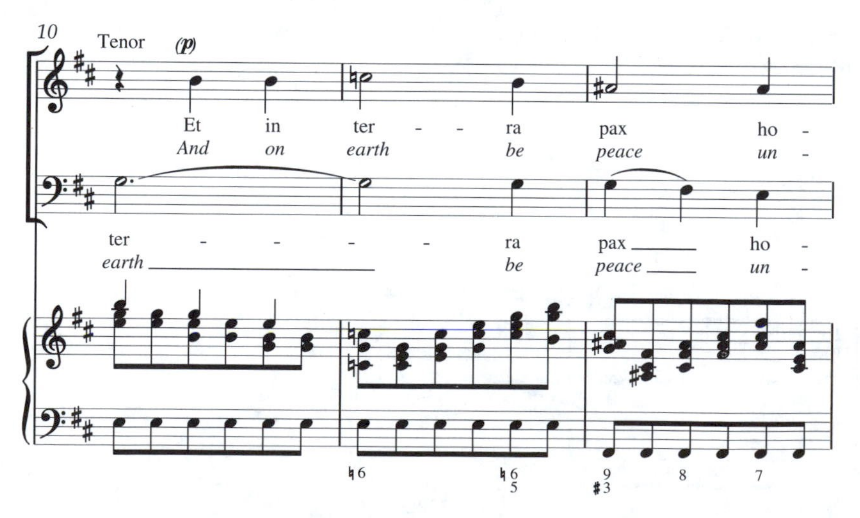

EXAMPLE 6.4

The contrast in text, tempo, rhythm, and affect should be fully exploited by the conductor and performer.

The performance of the dotted note in Baroque music requires a bit of explanation. Dotted notes are often performed as longer than written ("double dotted"). For example, the written rhythm illustrated here

EXAMPLE 6.5

should be performed as follows:

EXAMPLE 6.6

✣ THE CLASSICAL PERIOD (1775–1825) ✣

The Baroque period culminated in the masterpieces of J.S. Bach and G.F. Handel. In the middle of the eighteenth century, contemporaneous with the mature years of Bach and Handel, a new musical style developed that is known as Rococo or preclassical style. This style is most evident in keyboard and orchestral music, but it is mentioned here because it represented a transition from the Baroque to the Classical era, occurring between 1725 and 1770.

In the world of painting, Rococo style is characterized by delicate colors, many decorative details, and a graceful and intimate mood. Similarly, music in the Rococo style is homophonic and light in texture, melodic, and elaborately ornamented. In France, the term for this was *style galant* (gallant or elegant style) and in Germany *empfindsamer stil* (sensitive style). François Couperin (1668–1733), in France, and two of the sons of J. S. Bach, C. P. E. Bach (1714–1788) and Johann Christian Bach (1735–1782), in Germany, were important composers of music in the Rococo style.

In the second half of the eighteenth century, a reaction against Rococo style occurred. There were objections to its lack of depth and to the use of decoration and ornamentation for their own sake. This led to the development of Classical style.

The Classical period itself lasted from approximately 1775 to 1825. The name *classical* is applied to the period because in art and literature, there was keen interest in, admiration for, and emulation of the classical artistic and literary heritage of Greece and Rome.

Intellectually, this era has also been labeled the Age of Enlightenment. Philosophers such as Rousseau, Voltaire, and Montesquieu wrote of the value of the common person and the power of human reasoning in overcoming the problems of the world. This revolution in thinking inevitably led to conflict between the old order and new ideas. The French and American revolutions in the last quarter of the eighteenth century were stimulated by this new attitude.

The musical scene in the classical period reflected the changes occurring in the society in which the music was being written. This was the first era in music history in which public concerts became an important part of the musical scene. Music was still being composed for the church and the court, but the advent of public concerts reflected the new view that music should be written for the enjoyment and entertainment of the common person.

Unlike the Renaissance or Baroque eras, which included many important composers and trends, the choral music of the classical era was dominated by three composers: Franz Joseph Haydn (1732–1809), Wolfgang Amadeus Mozart (1756–1791), and Ludwig van Beethoven (1770–1827). For the first time, during the Classical period most of the important stylistic advances that occurred can be observed most clearly in the instrumental forms: the symphony, concerto, sonata, and in instrumental chamber music (e.g., the Beethoven string quartets). Church music tended to be more conservative than secular compositions, which also helps to explain why stylistic innovations were seen most clearly in instrumental music but were less prevalent in the choral music of the period.

Choral and instrumental forms overlapped during the Classical period to an unprecedented degree. Forms developed in the instrumental area were appropriated and used to good effect in choral music. Sonata allegro form, for example, often found in sonata or symphony movements, is also used in sections of classical masses. Beethoven included choral sections in two instrumental works, his *Choral Fantasia* and the *Ninth Symphony.*

This period in music history is sometimes referred to as "the Viennese Classic period," and it was centered in Vienna. Beethoven, Haydn, and Mozart, though none was a native Viennese, all worked in Vienna for significant periods in their careers. Although Vienna was the focal point for musical activity of the period, classical music is not parochial but universal in spirit and in style.

Important Forms

Important forms of choral music during the classical period included the following:

Mass. The mass continued to be an important form for each of the three primary Classical composers. During the Classical period, masses involved orchestra, soloists, and choir in a fully integrated work, utilizing organizational principles derived from instrumental forms.

Missa Brevis. This concise treatment of the mass text may consist of strictly delimited development, simultaneous setting of several lines of text, or the omission of certain sections of the mass.

Missa Solemnis. When choral musicians refer to the *Missa Solemnis* they are usually speaking of Beethoven's *Mass in D Major,* a milestone in the development of choral music. In a broader sense, however, the term refers to a more elaborate and extended musical treatment of the mass text than that employed in the Missa Brevis.

Oratorio. The Baroque oratorio tradition, begun by Carissimi and culminating in the works of Handel, was continued in the Classical period primarily by Haydn, who wrote two oratorios, *The Creation* and *The Seasons,* which have remained an important part of the choral repertoire.

Requiem. Although many musical settings of the Requiem were composed during the Renaissance and Baroque periods, the Classical period produced a setting by Mozart (completed by a student following Mozart's death) that has become a staple of the choral repertoire and two settings by Cherubini that are also often performed.

Vespers. Mozart wrote two settings of this service each of which includes psalms and the Magnificat, written for choir, quartet of soloists, and orchestra.

Choral Symphony. A symphony which includes sections written for choir and orchestra. The earliest and probably best known example of this is Beethoven's *Ninth Symphony,* incorporating choir and soloists in the fourth movement.

Composers

Haydn. Franz Joseph Haydn was born in the Rohrau, Austria, in 1732. At age eight he was accepted as a choirboy at St. Stephen's Cathedral in Vienna. When he left St. Stephen's in 1749, he became an assistant to Nicola Porpora. In 1759, he worked briefly as musical director for Count Morzin, and in 1761 was employed as assistant music director and then music director for the Esterhazy family, residing at their estate. He remained with the Esterhazys for nearly thirty years, until 1790.

During the last decade of the the eighteenth century, Haydn made two trips to London. He had been hired by Johann Peter Salomon to compose and conduct six symphonies for his first trip (1791–1792) and six for his second (1794–1795). Haydn's London appearances were highly successful.

Upon his return to Vienna in 1795, Haydn composed some of his most significant choral music. The six masses from this period, composed for Prince Nicholas Esterhazy (the son of Haydn's earlier employer), and his two oratorios, *The Creation* and *The Seasons,* are his most significant choral works. Haydn's total choral output included twelve masses, three oratorios, a passion, two Te Deums, a Stabat Mater, and a few other smaller works.

In his later years, Haydn was a celebrity whose works were widely recognized and appreciated, in contrast to the decades spent in the relative isolation of the Esterhazy estate. He died in 1809 in Vienna.

Mozart. Wolfgang Amadeus Mozart was born in Salzburg, Austria, in 1756. At the age of six, he could play the harpsichord and violin, compose, and performed in Munich and Vienna. Between the ages of six and fifteen, Mozart was taken on tours of Europe and England, organized by his father, Leopold Mozart, a Salzburg court composer. Although he was away from home more than half of the time, he produced a steady stream of compositions during this period.

In 1781, Mozart left Salzburg and moved to Vienna, teaching, concertizing, traveling, and continuing to compose constantly. In contrast to Haydn, who worked in the isolation and relative obscurity of the Esterhazy estate for many years and then became an international celebrity in his sixties, Mozart was thrust into international prominence as a child and encountered decreasing public acceptance of his music when he was an adult.

By 1791, Mozart's health was failing. He received a commission that resulted in the composition of *The Magic Flute.* He was also visited by a representative of a Count Walsegg, who commissioned a requiem. Mozart may have believed he was writing a requiem for himself. He died before completing the work, and it was finished by a pupil of Mozart's named Sussmayer, working from Mozart's sketches of the unfinished portion.

Mozart's choral output includes eighteen masses, the *Requiem,* two Vespers settings, and a variety of shorter choral pieces.

Beethoven. Ludwig van Beethoven was born in Bonn, Germany, in 1770. He came to Vienna in 1792, where he studied with Haydn and Albrechtsberger. His first public performances in Vienna as a pianist and composer came in 1795.

Beethoven protested against the patronage system that bound musicians to the service of an employer. Increasingly deaf, Beethoven eventually was forced to retire from public performance and to concentrate on composition. Unlike Mozart, who seemed to conceive of music in final form and who simply wrote down his conceptions, Beethoven's sketchbooks provide a record of his agonizing struggle to arrive at a composition he felt was satisfactory.

Beethoven was primarily a composer of instrumental music, and it is in his symphonies, piano music, and string quartets that the transition from Classic to Romantic style is most clearly discernible. Nevertheless, his choral music is an important part of the repertoire, and his *Mass in D Major*, the *Missa Solemnis,* is one of the monuments of Western musical tradition. Beethoven's choral output included two masses, an oratorio, two symphonic works with large choral sections, and a few smaller pieces.

Classical Style

Music from the Classical period is distinctive in style from what preceded and followed it. Some of the questions related to performance practice in Renaissance and Baroque music are less complex because at this point in music history we have much clearer and more explicit indications from the composer concerning the tempo, dynamics, and expressive qualities of the music under consideration.

Moreover, there have been public performances of this repertoire from the time of its composition to the present. This is both a help and a hindrance in light of the fact that through the last two centuries, certain Romantic conventions have become an accepted part of the performance of this music, and they are not always appropriate to authentic Classical style (this same problem of inappropriate performance conventions added during the Romantic period exists with Baroque repertoire and, to a lesser extent, music from the Renaissance).

Classical choral music tends to be more homophonic and lighter in texture than that of the Baroque. This lightness needs to pervade the choral lines. There is still rhythmic energy and drive, but without the weightiness of Baroque music.

The lighter quality of Classical music also is derived from its slower harmonic movement. Baroque music, with its emphasis on vertical structure and use of figured bass and basso continuo, is characterized by frequent harmonic changes, sometimes on every beat. Classical music changes chords much less frequently, giving it a more graceful sweep and lightness of phrasing than that created by the pulsating feel of a harpsichordist realizing a Baroque figured bass part, supporting the choral singing with rapidly changing embellished chords. During the Classic period, the keyboard player was no longer typically the composer/conductor, but instead was simply one of the players in the orchestra. The keyboard part should be much less obtrusive and less highly decorated than that of a Baroque work.

The choral music of the Classic period is generally conservative, and therefore often contains sections of free counterpoint, fugue, and use of continuo, reminiscent of the Baroque. This is particularly true in the music written in the early part of the period.

The Classical era was an era of formality. The music was characterized by careful attention to form and by elegance and restraint. The formal structure was based on the use of thematic development and harmonic structure.

The music of the Classical era is characterized by objectivity. While emotion is an important aspect of all music, in the Classical period, emotions were carefully controlled. This control is evident in the use of dynamics and expressive differences within sections or movements of a composition. The Baroque notion of terraced dynamics, coupled with the expression of a single emotion in a given section of a composition, was replaced by the classical trait of varying the emotional content of a given movement, section, or even a measure of a piece. Dynamically speaking, this was accomplished through the use of crescendo and decrescendo.

Consider a few measures from the beginning of the *Kyrie* of Beethoven's *Mass in C Major* (Example 6.7).

Within the space of a few bars we find a considerable range of dynamics and expression included. Note the words of Beethoven at the beginning of the section. He leaves no doubt as to exactly what gradations of tempo and expressive content he desired.

There is some debate concerning the use of tempo *rubato* in Classical music. *Rubato,* an Italian term, literally means to rob. In music, it refers to the speeding up and slowing down of the tempo for expressive reasons. In music of the Classical period, rubato should be used with restraint, but it is appropriate as a means of enhancing the expressive quality of the music.

The size of forces to be used depends on the nature of the music under consideration. For pieces of large scope, designed for festive occasions or for the concert hall, large choral and instrumental forces may be used, and the writings of the Classical composers concerning how their works should be performed support this idea. It is necessary for a performance of Beethoven's *Missa Solemnis,* for example, to have a large orchestra and chorus. The heroic proportions of the work call for large numbers of performers. Conversely, works of a more intimate nature designed for the chapel or the drawing room require fewer singers and instrumentalists.

By the Classical period, the orchestra consisted mostly of instruments still in use today. There have been changes in instrument design over the years with the result that a contemporary performance will have a somewhat different sound than one which occurred in the eighteenth century. Also, there are occasional uses of unusual instruments. The Mozart *Requiem,* for example, calls for the use of two basset horns, which are instruments not often heard today. They are usually replaced by clarinets in contemporary performances, which represents a modification of the sound intended by Mozart.

Mass
I. Kyrie

L. v. Beethoven, Op. 86

EXAMPLE 6.7

✣ THE ROMANTIC PERIOD (1825–1900) ✣

The Romantic period began with the second quarter of the nineteenth century. It should be noted, however, that throughout the history of music there has been a tension between the Classical and Romantic views of life and art. Objectivity versus subjectivity, form versus freedom, and individuality versus universality are issues that composers and other artists have confronted in every age. Romantic tendencies were evident in the music of all three of the preeminent Viennese classical composers (particularly Mozart and Beethoven), and by the end of Beethoven's career, the romantic spirit was firmly entrenched in Europe, remaining the dominant force in music until the beginning of the twentieth century.

There are some fundamental Romantic characteristics that should be noted to begin this discussion. Classicism and romanticism represent two opposing views of life and art. Whereas classicism is objective, romanticism is subjective. Control of harmonic tension, balance between dissonance and consonance, and the careful and complete exploitation of thematic development give Classical music a definite and distinct formal structure. Conversely, the Romantic spirit requires the loosening of formal constraints and the uninhibited expression of the individual composer's ideas and emotions.

One way in which the Romantic spirit was expressed in the nineteenth century was through nationalism. Whereas classical music tended to be universal in character, during the nineteenth century certain composers and compositions paid tribute to their country of origin through the use of folk melodies, dances, or instruments, or through the musical depiction of some locale in the homeland.

Just as nationalism reflected a preoccupation with the composer's own national heritage, exoticism was a Romantic fascination with music from other lands. An often cited example of this tendency was Rimsky-Korsakov's *Scheherazade*, depicting scenes from the Arabian Nights. In fact, anything mysterious or exotic appealed to the Romantic mind. The writing of Poe exemplifies this preoccupation with the mysterious or morbid.

Berlioz's *Symphonie Fantastique* tells of a young man's opium-induced visions of his beloved. Berlioz wrote a commentary, or program, describing the extramusical scenes depicted by each of the work's five movements. The idea of *program* music, intended by the composer to depict specific nonmusical ideas, was another important aspect of nineteenth-century Romantic style.

Although the forms of the Classic period continued to be used by Romantic composers, they took many more liberties with them, expanding and contracting them to suit their individual tastes. During the Romantic period, both miniature and heroic forms became popular. The lieder of Schubert exemplify the romantic spirit in a small and intimate form, just as Mahler's *Symphony of a Thousand* does so by involving two four-part choirs, a boys' choir, seven soloists, and a large orchestra in an undertaking so massive that it limits the opportunities to hear it performed.

During the Romantic period, the resources of tonality were completely exhausted, and chromaticism too was fully exploited. The highly chromatic works of Wagner and other late-nineteenth-century composers represented the final stage of this process, which led to a variety of alternative harmonic organizational structures that signaled the end of the Romantic era, around the beginning of the twentieth century.

Romantic composers were anxious to exploit to the fullest the potential of the orchestra in terms of tone color, as well as pitch and dynamic range, making unprecedented demands on players. The orchestra increased in size during the nineteenth century to the point where it sometimes numbered in the hundreds. By the late nineteenth century, dynamic markings such as *pppp* or *ffff* were common, and extensive use of crescendo and decrescendo added to the expressive resources available to composers.

Much of the writing for chorus from this period also seeks to fully exploit the possibilities of the human voice. Beethoven's *Missa Solemnis* makes great demands on the singers, and the performance of choral-orchestral masterworks composed later in the century also requires singers with solid vocal technique for a successful performance. This fascination with tone color and the use of augmented instrumental forces helps explain the dominance of instrumental music in this era. Without exception, the musical giants of the era were primarily composers of instrumental music. Most of the great choral masterworks of the period were choral/orchestral works.

Three hundred years earlier, during the Renaissance, choral music had been predominant, with instrumental parts added occasionally that reinforced (doubled) the choral lines. Through the ensuing centuries, the balance in importance between choral and instrumental music as the setting for stylistic change shifted steadily from choral to instrumental forms.

The Requiem in the Romantic Period

Because the choral forms of the Classical period continued into the Romantic era (although many were altered, expanded, and otherwise changed by the Romantic composers), they are not listed here and redefined. Instead, we discuss one form, the requiem, as an example of the way the Romantic composers put their own unique stamp on the forms with which they worked. The drama inherent in the requiem text made it particularly appealing to Romantic composers.

The Romantic style resulted in some choral masterworks that are monuments in our Western musical heritage. This style, however, with its exploitation of range, color, and harmony, the use of massive forces, thick sonorities, and extremes of dynamic range make some of the repertoire unsuitable for use by secondary school ensembles. It is presented here so you have a complete basic conceptual framework for an understanding of choral music style.

There have been some unfortunate attempts to get high school choirs to sing certain Romantic repertoire. Many of the choral masterpieces of the nineteenth century require mature (adult) voices in order to present the music effectively and avoid vocal damage to adolescent singers. Of the four requiem settings mentioned here, Fauré's is an excellent work for a well-prepared high school choir to study and perform. It is a choral masterpiece, yet it is within the vocal and expressive capabilities of young singers.

Some of the most significant and profound settings of the requiem text anywhere in the choral repertoire were composed by four Romantic composers. The requiem settings of Berlioz, Brahms, Verdi, and Fauré represent four distinctly different approaches to the music and the text, in keeping with the Romantic ideal of subjectivity and uniquely individual expression.

The Berlioz *Requiem,* composed in 1837 on a commission from the French Minister of the Interior, was first performed at a memorial service for

French soldiers fallen in Algeria. It was written for a large orchestra, augmented by four brass ensembles, tenor soloist, and a choir of sopranos, tenors, and basses, with altos employed for two brief sections. Although Berlioz used large choral and instrumental forces in this composition, they are used in a variety of ways, and the texture and tone of the work varies from delicate to massive. The pervasive tone of the piece is one of sadness, although the orchestral/choral writing is highly dramatic when Berlioz unleashes all of the forces at his disposal.

The Verdi *Requiem* was composed in 1873–1874 in memory of Alessandro Manzoni, an Italian novelist who was admired by Verdi. The work was written for a four-voice choir, quartet of soloists, and orchestra. Some of the writing, particularly the Dies Irae, is operatic in nature, and extremely exciting for performer and listener. The almost lurid musical rendering of the Day of Judgment is balanced by moments of sustained and restrained pianissimo singing. The overall tone of the work is reverent and often beautifully melodic. In the case of Verdi, as with Berlioz, the large forces involved are utilized beautifully to express the nuances of the text, ranging from comforting to majestic, from quiet acceptance to the terrors of the last judgment.

Brahms's setting of the requiem, *Ein Deutsches Requiem (A German Requiem)* is quite different from the settings of Berlioz and Verdi. First, as the name indicates, it was written in German, not Latin. Secondly, its seven movements are based on biblical texts selected from Luther's German Bible. While the requiems written up to this time had been settings of the Roman Catholic mass for the dead, this was a work written to comfort the living rather than to commemorate an individual who had died. The *German Requiem* was written in 1866 and 1867, for choir, baritone and soprano soloists, and orchestra. Although the forces called for by Brahms were more modest than those required by Berlioz and Verdi, he similarly varies the texture and tone to suit the expressive implications of the texts being set. The nature of the biblical quotations that comprise the text give the work a pervasive sense of comfort, hope, and acceptance.

The last of the four Romantic requiem settings to be discussed is also unique in style. The Fauré *Requiem* was composed in 1887, in memory of the composer's father. It requires a four-voice choir, soprano and baritone soloists, orchestra, and organ. An interesting aspect of Fauré's orchestration is the very limited use made of violins (none at all in the first movement) and no oboes. The result is a subdued tone and a transparent texture. This is an optimistic treatment of the traditional Roman Catholic text, and Fauré chooses to omit the more dramatic and terrifying sections of the sequence that figure so prominently in the settings of Berlioz and Verdi. Within the context of the limited palette of colors Fauré uses, a work of great depth, beauty, and harmonic ingenuity is created. The restraint that is evident in this work, in terms of the relatively limited forces involved and the reasonable demands placed on the singers in terms of pitch and dynamic range, make it the most accessible of the four requiem settings discussed, particularly for singers whose vocal technique is not yet settled and secure.

Romantic Composers and Style

Gioacchino Rossini (1792–1868), though noted primarily for his operas, wrote several choral works in his later years. The two most important works were his mass, which he called *Petite Messe Solenelle (Little Solemn Mass)*, and his setting of the *Stabat Mater.* Despite its title, the mass is a major work involving choir, quartet of soloists, and orchestra (originally, it was scored for two pianos and the orchestration was added later).

Franz Schubert (1797–1828) wrote six masses and several shorter choral works on both sacred and secular texts. Schubert's last two masses are considered his most important choral pieces, although it should be noted that his *Mass in G* and the shorter works (sacred settings and choral lieder) provide some excellent performance possibilities for school choral ensembles.

Felix Mendelssohn (1809–1847) wrote three oratorios: *St. Paul* (1837), *Elijah* (1846), and *Christus* (unfinished at the time of his death). In addition, he wrote some choral lieder, motets, and psalm settings. His fame as a choral composer is based primarily on his oratorios, of which *Elijah* is the most frequently performed. Mendelssohn's *Lobegesang (Hymn of Praise)* is a choral orchestral piece including chorus, tenor, and two soprano soloists in the last and longest movement.

Franz Liszt (1811–1886) wrote three masses (one for men's voices and organ, one for mixed choir and orchestra, and one for mixed choir with organ), two oratorios, a psalm setting, and two choral symphonies. In addition to his Requiem setting, mentioned earlier, Hector Berlioz (1803–1869) wrote a Te Deum, an oratorio, and a choral symphony. Robert Schumann (1810–1856) wrote an oratorio entitled *Paradise and the Peri,* which is still occasionally performed, and several sets of part songs, many of which are performable by a well-established high school choir (an excellent example is *Zigeunerleben—Gypsy Life*). The choral legacy of Gustav Mahler (1860–1911) consists of his three choral symphonies.

Brahms, in addition to the *German Requiem,* wrote choral settings of folksongs, other choral lieder, and several choral/orchestral works, including a cantata. The Brahms settings of folk songs are feasible repertoire for a high school or even a well-established junior high choir (or any choir interested in some delightful pieces).

Anton Bruckner (1824–1896) composed three masses, a Te Deum, and a setting of Psalm 150, as well as several shorter sacred and secular choral works. Bruckner was a devout Catholic and his sacred music reflects his profound faith. Some of his shorter works are approachable by a high school choir (an excellent example is the motet *Locus Iste),* but others are too demanding for young singers in terms of pitch and dynamic range. All are notably beautiful in their depth of emotion, harmonic ingenuity, and dynamic contrast.

The general characteristics of Romantic style were discussed earlier. With regard to the performance of choral music, a few points should be noted. The Romantic composers tended to write out exactly what they wanted in the way of dynamics, tempo, and expression. A problem in performance practice related to the Romantic period is found in Romantic *editions* of earlier music. Such editions tend to include many expressive markings that were never intended by the composer. Any edition of music written before 1750 that contains dynamic, tempo, and expressive markings not clearly identified as editorial is suspect.

In performing music of the Romantic period, the tempo should be elastic, reflecting the expressive nuances of text. The idea of *rubato* (mentioned earlier) wherein the tempo varies is an important aspect of Romantic style.

The tone to be used for Romantic music should be full and rich. Singers should never push the tone or make it strident, and great care must be exercised in selecting music from this era for performance by a school choir. To perform many of the great choral/orchestral masterworks effectively requires mature voices, capable of producing a wide range of pitch, dynamics, and expression.

The Romantic era was a period in which individual expression was of critical importance in the interpretation of music. Romantic composers used standard notation and indicated in relatively specific terms the way they wished for their music to be performed. In performing the choral music of the period, study the text and the markings of the composer in the score. These indications provide the basis for an effective performance.

✣ TWENTIETH-CENTURY MUSIC ✣

For the choral music educator wishing to study and perform music of the twentieth century with his or her ensemble, the problems to be solved in terms of style and performance practice are different than those related to earlier periods in music history. Although its chronological proximity makes information concerning twentieth-century style accessible (in the case of contemporary composers, it may even be possible to speak with them directly if there are questions), there are certain genres of twentieth-century music that present unique challenges for the choral music educator and for the singer.

One important characteristic of the comprehensive choral music education program is the inclusion of a wide range of high-quality repertoire, yet some choral music educators avoid the use of much of the music of our own time because they are not comfortable with the style, techniques, or notation employed. We encourage you to more fully explore high-quality contemporary music (even the seemingly esoteric) and suggest ways every secondary school choral ensemble can begin to experience some of the interesting and aesthetically pleasing genres of twentieth-century music.

The use of extreme dissonance, melodic lines divided between various voice parts, polytonality, polymeter, and the use of avant-garde notation and performance procedures are examples of some of the special technical problems to be surmounted in studying and performing certain styles of twentieth-century music. Conversely, the music of many twentieth-century composers is crafted in a style reminiscent of the Romantic period and is relatively straightforward melodically, harmonically, and rhythmically. As choral music educators, it is our responsibility to introduce students to the entire range of musical creativity evidenced by contemporary composers.

The most important single characteristic of twentieth-century choral music is its diversity. Since 1900, a variety of trends have had an impact on musical composition. Moreover, since the twentieth century is still in progress, it is impossible to view it with the same perspective we apply to earlier periods in music history. Often, the music of a single composer will exhibit features of various styles. For example, Igor Stravinsky (1882–1971) wrote music during various periods in his long life that has been referred to as primitivist, neoclassical, expressionist, and serial.

The Romantic infatuation with tone color has continued into the twentieth century. Avant-garde choral composers have experimented with a variety of techniques intended to exploit the variety of timbres possible for the human voice. To communicate effectively and to accommodate the variety of innovative choral techniques found in twentieth-century choral compositions, new notational systems have been devised.

During the nineteenth century, the tonal system of harmony was fully exploited, and, in the view of some composers, its potential for conveying new ideas was completely exhausted. Throughout that century, chromaticism played an increasingly prominent role, leading to the emotional and highly chromatic music of Richard Wagner. Harmonic developments in the twentieth century have been dramatic. Composers have experimented with a variety of alternatives to traditional tonality, including serial (twelve tone) technique, atonality, polytonality, and quartal harmony.

Likewise, revolutionary rhythmic ideas have been adopted by twentieth-century composers. Asymmetrical rhythms, nonmetered chantlike singing, polymeters, and other forms of rhythmic innovation have influenced musical style.

During the twentieth century there has been unprecedented growth in school music programs in the United States. There are hundreds of composers who write music specifically intended for use by school and church choral ensembles, with careful consideration of the range, tessitura, and dynamic limitations of singers of varying levels of vocal technique and maturity. Many of the choral pieces published each year for use in the schools are of high quality.

Twentieth-Century Stylistic Trends

Some important twentieth-century stylistic trends are listed here, with a brief explanation of important characteristics of each.

Impressionism. Impressionism represented an important transition from nineteenth-century romanticism to the twentieth century. The originator of impressionism was Claude Debussy (1862–1918), and the style was continued by his contemporary, Maurice Ravel (1875–1937). Both Debussy and Ravel were French, and were inspired by French symbolist poets (e.g., Mallarmé and Verlaine), and Impressionist painters such as Monet and Renoir. A technique employed by the Impressionist painters used primary colors applied in small patches or dots, which were blended in the eye of the observer when viewed from a distance. The result was a misty, shimmering effect—an impression of an object.

Impressionist music creates a similar dreamy, shimmering feeling (quite different from the emotionalism found in the music of the late Romantic period). Musically, this effect was created in several different ways. In Debussy's orchestral music, a wide variety of tone colors is employed, featuring many brief solos by woodwinds, strings (most notably the harp) or muted brass instruments, creating splashes of tone color analogous to the visual use of color by the Impressionist painters. Harmonically, the tonal center is obscured through the use of whole-tone and pentatonic scales, church modes, and the exploitation of individual chords and their colors (as opposed to their function within a tonality). Rhythmically, the music avoids strong metrical accentuation.

Although the Impressionist composers are noted primarily for their orchestral and keyboard music, as well as art songs, both Debussy and Ravel wrote impressionistic choral music, exemplified by Debussy's *Trois Chansons de Charles d'Orléans* and Ravel's *Trois Chansons.*

Expressionism/Serialism. Expressionism was a musical style that developed in Germany and Austria during the first quarter of the twentieth century. It was a reaction against not only late nineteenth-century romanticism, but against impressionism as well. As was the case with impressionism, Expressionist composers were inspired by writers and visual artists.

Expressionists were concerned with inner feelings and the unconscious mind, and presented distorted and fragmented images of insanity and death. Musical Expressionists included Arnold Schoenberg (1874–1951), Alban Berg (1885–1935), and Anton Webern (1883–1945).

Schoenberg's early music, such as his string sextet *Verklärte Nacht (Transfigured Night,* 1899), was actually Romantic in style. His cantata *Gurrelieder (Songs of Gurre,* 1901) utilized an expanded orchestra, narrator, five soloists, and four choirs. During the first decade of the twentieth century, Schoenberg completely abandoned tonality and began to write atonal music, characterized by the extensive use of dissonance and complete absence of tonal center.

In the early 1920s Schoenberg developed his twelve tone, or serial compositional technique. In serial music, both melody and harmony are derived from the twelve tones of the chromatic scale, arranged in a particular order called a tone row. Each of the twelve tones is equal in importance to every other (in contrast to the tonal system, which centers on the relationship of notes and chords to the tonic). The tone row provides the basis for an entire composition. The notes of the tone row may be inverted, reversed, or inverted *and* reversed, or it may be transposed to begin on any of the twelve notes of the chromatic scale.

Excellent examples of twelve tone choral music are found in Webern's two cantatas (which are entitled simply *Cantata No. 1* and *Cantata No. 2).* Serial music challenges even advanced choirs with its unique harmonic organization, but it is worthy of investigation by the choral conductor. Opportunities to listen to serial music and to study its organization should be provided for students, even if technical difficulties prevent its inclusion in the repertoire scheduled for performance. Serial compositions, even the Webern cantatas, have been performed successfully by a few fine high school ensembles.

Neoclassicism. After the First World War, a style of musical composition known as neoclassicism became popular. As the name implies, the inspiration for this style was found in earlier music. There is no mistaking a twentieth-century Neoclassical composition for a mass by Mozart or Haydn; the twentieth-century Neoclassical composers emulate the eighteenth-century emphasis on form, objectivity, and restraint, but employ new harmonic and rhythmic techniques. Intellect takes precedence over emotion, and absolute music, without extramusical associations, is favored. Old forms, such as fugues and dance suites, provide an interesting framework for startlingly innovative music.

Many composers have written music in the Neoclassical style, including Benjamin Britten (1913–1977) Stravinsky, Francis Poulenc (1899–1963), and William Schuman (1910–1992). An excellent example of Neoclassical choral music is Stravinsky's *Symphony of Psalms,* written in 1930.

Avant-Garde Music. Avant-garde choral music utilizes nontraditional techniques and symbols to convey the composer's musical ideas. It often allows for much greater individual decision making on the part of choir members, and thus takes some control away from the conductor. This can be an exciting opportunity for individual musical growth, but it can also be somewhat intimidating for the choral teacher and students.

Introducing Your Choir to Twentieth-Century Music

As we mentioned previously, certain twentieth-century music is written in a NeoRomantic style, and may not present the technical challenges found in the more esoteric styles. Because of its accessibility, most choirs have the opportunity to perform this style of music. For a more complete picture of the kinds of pieces being composed in the twentieth century, it is necessary to provide choirs with opportunities to study and perform music that is more unconventional.

In teaching any subject, it is educationally sound to start with the familiar and to proceed to the unfamiliar. Therefore, if you and your choir lack experience with avant-garde music, it is probably a good idea to begin with a selection that contains strong traditional writing, but which also introduces a new, contemporary stylistic element to the choir.

An example of such a selection is a piece entitled "Bach Again" by Edwin London and Rhonda Sandberg.[1] It is based on the Bach chorale "Come Sweet Death." The chorale is notated in traditional style and is presented initially in that style. The performance notes that accompany the piece provide the information needed for the presentation of the piece in avant-garde style. In addition to the performance notes, *choralography* is also suggested. Choralography is a subtle movement, facial expression, or gesture that is added to a choral performance to enhance the text or mood.

The relatively simple and straightforward technique of having each member of the choir sing his or her own vocal line at their own tempo and with their own expression simultaneously creates a constantly changing blend of sound and is extremely effective. I have heard several choirs perform this piece and have conducted it, and it often attracts more comment than any other selection on the program. Such a composition provides a choir with an initial taste of avant-garde choral sound and is not technically demanding.

A piece that has become a classic and contains elements of the traditional and the avant garde is Knut Nystedt's "Praise to God." It contains several avant-garde techniques, including *sprechstimme* (speech rhythm or, literally, "speaking voice"), tone clusters, and strong dissonances:

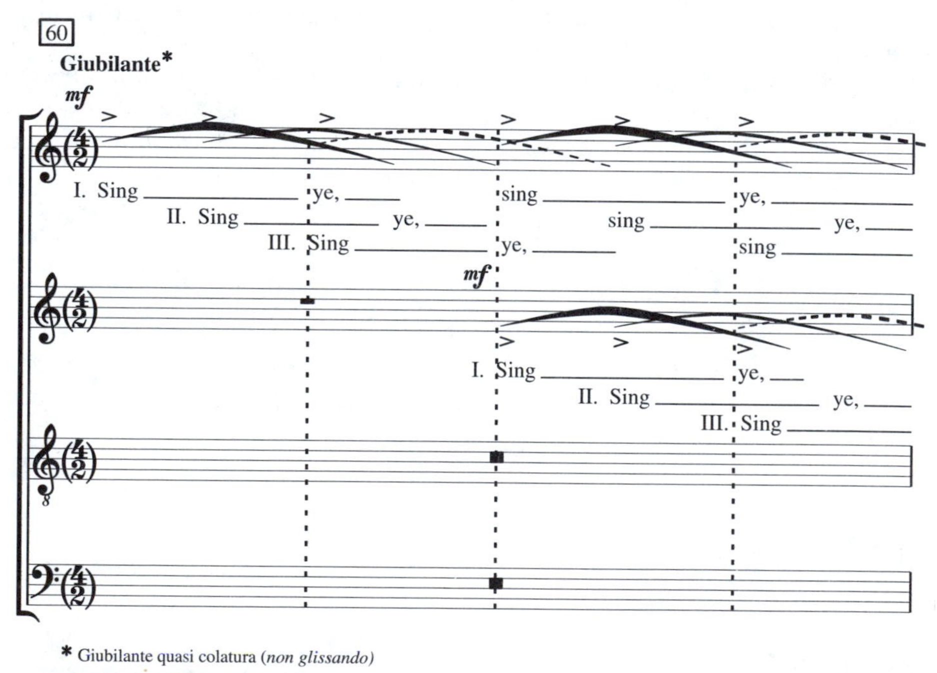

* Giubilante quasi colatura (*non glissando*)

EXAMPLE 6.8

A piece that can be enjoyed by both high school and middle school choirs is Ernst Toch's "Geographical Fugue," which consists entirely of *sprechstimme.* Another piece that is challenging but approachable by an established ensemble is Slögedal's "Antiphona de Morte" ("Antiphon of Death"). It also contains a variety of avant-garde techniques. The opening of the composition features the choir whispering the text, creating an eerie effect.

EXAMPLE 6.9

One of the twentieth century's most innovative and creative choral composers was Charles Ives (1874–1954). His music presents a variety of challenges and rewards for the performer and listener. A piece that presents challenges but has become a staple of the choral repertoire is Ives's *Psalm 67.* Examine the following excerpt:

EXAMPLE 6.10

This piece is written in two keys (bitonality). The women's parts are written in C major, while the men's section is centered in G minor. In teaching this piece to your choir, rehearse the men and women separately until they are secure with their line and tonality. Then combine the men and women. The combination of the two keys is remarkably expressive of the emotion inherent in the text.

A final example of an often performed twentieth-century work is Egil Hovland's *Saul,* which relates the dramatic story of the conversion of Saul of Tarsus: This interesting composition uses avant-garde techniques and is within the capabilities of an experienced high-school choir.

Saul

(For Narrator, Mixed Chorus, and Organ)

Acts 8:1-4, 7 and 9:1-4
Adapted, F. P.

Egil Hovland

NARRATOR: And on that day a great persecution arose against the church in Jerusalem; and they were all scattered throughout the region of Judea and Samaria, except the apostles. Devout men buried Stephen, and made great lamentation over him.

4-5" ← But Saul laid waste the church, and entering house after house, he dragged off men and women and committed them to

Canon I. T.*) *Women: Enter independently approximately one-half second apart.*

NAR. prison. Now those who were scattered went about preaching the word. Unclean spirits came out of many who were possessed, crying with a loud voice; and many who wer paralyzed or lame were healed.

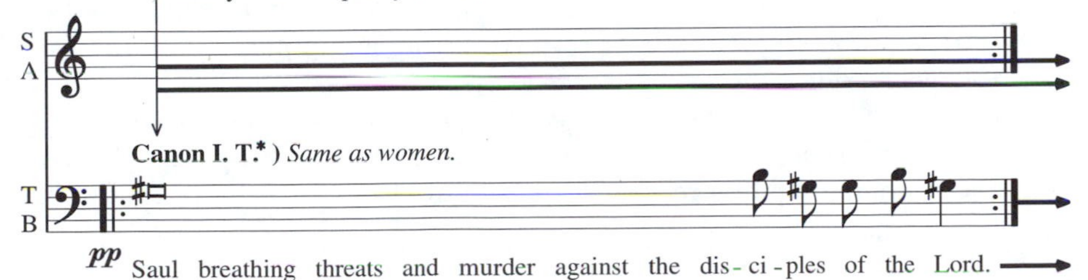

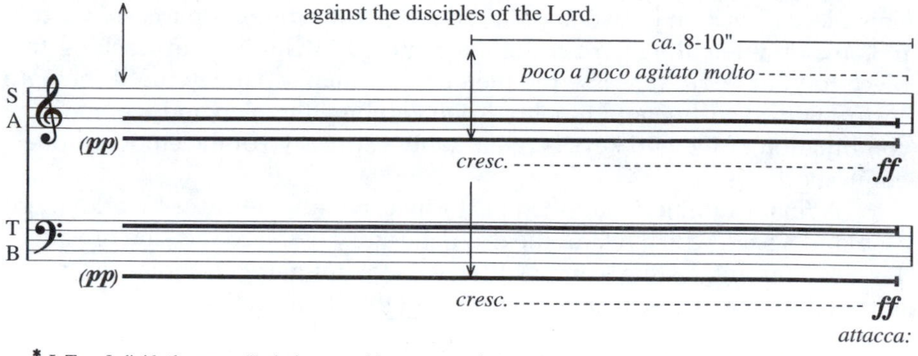

* **I. T.** = Individual tempos. Each singer sets his own tempo independent of others. All stop at director's signal.

EXAMPLE 6.11

African American Spirituals

The spiritual has been an important part of American choral music throughout this century. In fact, during the twentieth century the spiritual has been the best known and most often performed type of American folk music. The great spiritual composers and arrangers of the first half of the century, including William Dawson, Jester Hairston, Harry Burleigh, and Hall Johnson, have been succeeded by a talented group of contemporary composers and conductors including Roland Carter, Andre Thomas, Marvin Curtis, Wendell Whalum, Brazeal Dennard, and others.

When Africans were brought to the United States as slaves in the eighteenth century, they brought with them their religious beliefs and social customs, which were viewed with suspicion by their owners. As succeeding generations of African Americans adapted to plantation life, the spirituals they sang represented a blend of African, European, and American religious, social, and musical elements.

Spirituals may be divided into two categories: sorrow songs and jubilees. Sorrow songs are notable for their slow tempos, melancholy emotional content, and intensity of feeling. Examples of sorrow songs include such pieces as "Sometimes I Feel Like a Motherless Child," "Nobody Knows the Trouble I've Seen," and "Deep River." Jubilees, in contrast, feature fast tempos, rhythmic drive and syncopation, and a joyful message. Some examples of jubilees include "In That Great Gittin' Up Morning." "Ain'a That Good News," and "I Got Shoes." The texts of spirituals are often based on scripture, and the plight of the African American is compared with the people of Israel held in bondage by Pharaoh.

In addition to biblical messages, the texts of spirituals often convey double meanings and a message of protest. A text concerning crossing over the river Jordan or getting ready for Judgment Day could be interpreted not only in terms of its strictly biblical meaning, but in terms of crossing a river to freedom (perhaps via the underground railroad) or getting ready for a day of earthly emancipation from bondage.

As mentioned earlier, spirituals were a folk tradition, passed from one generation to the next by word of mouth. They became widely known in the last quarter of the nineteenth century. The first singing group to popularize the spiritual was the Jubilee Singers of Fisk University, Nashville, Tennessee, which began to tour in 1871. The Fiske Jubilee Singers were followed by other ensembles, both collegiate and professional, which disseminated spirituals around the world.

Collections of spirituals were published, assuring that this important musical heritage would be preserved. Spirituals were performed by concert artists both black and white, by choirs of all descriptions, and even by instrumental ensembles. With the popularization of this music it became increasingly remote from its folk origins. As a result, there have been some inappropriate stylistic accretions to the singing of spirituals that have done a disservice to the African American musical tradition. A few suggestions concerning the performance of spirituals may help facilitate authentic performances of this important, vital, and musically interesting genre.

Perhaps the most important point in performing spirituals is sincerity. Although the jubilee tradition is characterized by its rhythmic interest and liveliness, it is religious music. Spirituals were not intended to be entertainment and should not be presented as such. Certainly they are exciting for singers to sing and for an audience to hear, but they are not minstrel songs and should not be presented in that spirit. The snapping of fingers is associated with the minstrel tradition and is to be avoided in the performance of spirituals. Hand clapping and foot tapping are acceptable expressions of the joy to be found in the texts of many spirituals, but it is interesting that among the African American slaves care was taken in performing "ring spirituals" that the feet did not cross, as in dancing, as the singers moved around the circle.

Another issue to be considered in the performance of spirituals is the use of dialect. When Africans were brought to this country to be slaves against their will they sought to adapt to the English language. Certain English sounds, however, were completely unknown in many African dialects. An example was the "th" sound. Thus, in some arrangements of spirituals, "with" is indicated as "wid" and "the" is "duh." When a word ends in "ing" the ending is changed to "in," such as "comin'" for "coming." Another example of African American dialect that actually is simply good diction for any choral piece is to minimize the consonant "r" so that "brother" becomes "brothuh" and "more" becomes "moh." If students and conductor are aware that the sounds of the dialect represent efforts of African American slaves to adapt to an alien culture it can enhance their understanding of the music as well as their performance of it.

✣ SUMMARY ✣

This chapter has focused on style in choral singing. Choral style emerges through the manipulation of the basic elements of music, such as tempo, dynamic range, and vocal quality. Comprehensive choral music education seeks to inform students about all aspects of the compositions being rehearsed and performed. Knowledge of style in choral singing requires a synthesis of diverse information related not only to various musical elements but also to the historical context of a choral composition. When students help to make musical decisions and are knowledgeable of the stylistic reasons for changes in tempo, tone quality, dynamics, and other musical elements, they grow not only as choral performers but as musicians.

To begin to understand choral style it is necessary to comprehend the flow of music history. Our discussion of the topic has been presented in historical context, beginning with the Renaissance through the present day. Important composers, forms, and stylistic trends have been presented.

Only in the last thirty years has the importance of style and performance practice been recognized by choral music educators. With this recognition has come increased research, generating new knowledge and enabling choral conductors to recreate with greater accuracy the sounds intended by composers who lived centuries ago.

Questions

1. Why has the matter of style and performance practice received increased attention from choral musicians in recent years?
2. What is meant by style? How can the style of a musical selection be changed?
3. What were some important centers of musical activity during the Renaissance?
4. How should the accentuation of Renaissance music be approached by the comprehensive choral music educator?
5. What is the role of the editor in the performing editions of Renaissance music available today?
6. How can you tell when a musical selection is well edited?
7. How does the Baroque approach to rhythm and accentuation differ from that of the high Renaissance? How does this relate to harmonic changes that occurred in the music?
8. When did instrumental music begin to overshadow choral music in its importance to stylistic development?

9. What is there about Romantic music that requires careful examination and consideration before programming it for a high school choir?
10. How can a high school choir be introduced to avant-garde music in an educationally sound fashion?
11. How did the spiritual develop in the United States? Name two important aspects of performance practice as it relates to the spiritual.

Note

1. J. S. Bach, Edwin London, and Rhonda Sandberg, "Bach (again)/ Come Sweet Death" (Fort Lauderdale: Aberdeen Music, 1986, "Performance Notes").

Suggested Reading

ARTZ, FREDERICK. *From the Renaissance to Romanticism.* Chicago: University of Chicago Press, 1962.

BARZUN, JACQUES. *Berlioz and His Century: An Introduction to the Age of Romanticism.* Chicago: University of Chicago Press, 1982.

———. *Classic, Romantic, and Modern.* Garden City, NY: Anchor Books, 1961.

BROOKS, TILFORD. *America's Black Musical Heritage.* Englewood Cliffs, NJ: Prentice-Hall, 1984.

BROWN, HOWARD MAYER, and STANLEY SADIE, eds. *Performance Practice: Music After 1600.* New York: Norton, 1989.

BUKOFZER, MANFRED F. *Music in the Baroque Era: From Monteverdi to Bach.* New York: Norton, 1947.

DART, THURSTON. *The Interpretation of Music.* New York: Harper Row, 1963.

DONINGTON, ROBERT. *Baroque Music: Style and Performance.* New York: Norton, 1982.

———. *The Interpretation of Early Music* (2nd ed.). London: Faber and Faber, 1965.

DORIAN, FREDERICK. *The History of Music in Performance.* New York: Norton, 1966.

EINSTEIN, ALFRED. *The Italian Madrigal.* Princeton, NJ: Princeton University Press, 1971.

———. *Music in the Romantic Era.* New York: Norton, 1947.

FISHER, MILES. *Negro Slave Songs in the United States.* New York: Russell and Russell, 1968.

HAIRSTON, JESTER. *Negro Spirituals and Folk Songs.* New York: Bourne, 1960.

HARMON, R. ALEC, and ANTHONY MILNER. *Late Renaissance and Baroque Music.* London: Barrie and Rockliff, 1959.

HASKELL, HARRY. *The Early Music Revival.* London: Thames and Hudson, 1988.

JEPPESON, KNUD. *The Style of Palestrina and the Dissonance* (2nd ed.) New York: Oxford University Press, 1946.

JOHNSON, JAMES W., and J. ROSAMOND. *The Book of Negro Spirituals.* New York: Viking Press, 1969.

KENYON, NICHOLAS, ed. *Authenticity and Early Music: A Symposium.* New York: Oxford University Press, 1988.

KITE-POWELL, JEFFREY T., ed. *A Practical Guide to Historical Performance: The Renaissance.* New York: Early Music Press, 1989.

LONGYEAR, REY M. *Nineteenth-Century Romanticism in Music* (3rd ed.). Englewood Cliffs, NJ: Prentice Hall, 1988.

MACCLINTOCK, CAROL. *Readings in the History of Music in Performance.* Bloomington: Indiana University Press, 1979.

MAY, JAMES D. *Avant Garde Choral Music.* Metuchen, NJ: Scarecrow Press, 1977.

NEUMANN, FREDERICK. *New Essays on Performance Practice.* Ann Arbor, MI: UMI Research Press, 1989.

PAINE, GORDON, ed. *Five Centuries of Choral Music: Essays in Honor of Howard Swan.* Stuyvesant, NY: Pendragon Press, 1988.

PALISCA, CLAUDE V. *Humanism in Italian Renaissance Musical Thought.* New Haven: Yale University Press, 1986.

PLANTINGA, LEON. *Romantic Music.* New York: Norton, 1984.

POOLER, FRANK, and BRENT PIERCE. *New Choral Notation.* New York: Walton, 1971.

RANGEL-RIBEIRA, VICTOR. *Baroque Music: A Practical Guide.* New York: Schirmer, 1981.

RATNER, LEONARD G. *Classic Music: Expression, Form, and Style.* New York: Schirmer, 1980.

RINGER, ALEXANDER. *The Early Romantic Period.* Englewood Cliffs, NJ: Prentice Hall, 1990.

ROSEN, CHARLES. *Classic Style.* New York: Viking Press, 1971.

SACHS, KURT. *Rhythm and Tempo: A Study in Music History.* New York: Norton, 1953.

SOUTHERN, EILEEN. *The Music of Black Americans: A History* (2nd ed.). New York: Norton, 1983.

STRUNK, OLIVER. *Source Readings in Music History.* New York: Norton, 1950.

TOMLINSON, GARY. *Monteverdi and the End of the Renaissance.* Berkeley: University of California Press, 1987.

ULRICH, DONALD. *A Survey of Choral Music.* New York: Harcourt, Brace, Jovanovich, 1973.

WHITE, J. PERRY. *Twentieth-Century Choral Music: An Annotated Bibliography of Music Suitable for Use by High School Choirs.* Metuchen, NJ: Scarecrow Press, 1982.

ZASLAW, NEAL. *The Classic Era: From the 1740's to the End of the Eighteenth Century.* Englewood Cliffs, NJ: Prentice Hall, 1990.

Chapter Seven

Administration of the Choral Music Education Program

❖❖❖

❖ INTRODUCTION ❖

To a greater degree than most other teachers, the choral music teacher must be a competent administrator. Although the primary purpose of a choral music education program is the musical education of the participants, choral directors are usually involved in public relations and recruitment; budgeting; fund-raising; scheduling; maintenance of music and equipment; the selection, purchase, and maintenance of appropriate apparel for the school's ensembles; and numerous other administrative areas.

In order to administer programs effectively, you must be well organized. There are many demands on the time of the choral music teacher. The ability to organize your schedule for maximum ease and efficiency is a skill worth developing. Applying good organizational skills to your total schedule facilitates the accomplishment of goals and objectives specifically related to choral music education. It also reduces the likelihood of burnout and unhealthy stress.

❖ ORGANIZATIONAL PRINCIPLES[1] ❖

Choral music education is a stressful profession. Dealing with students, parents, administrators, and colleagues in a variety of contexts is draining. The pressure of public performance is demanding (choral directors have always been accountable to the public for the results of their programs because they are regularly on public display). One key to the appropriate handling of stress is the effective management of time. The ability to use time wisely will exert a marked influence on your professional success. More importantly, managing time effectively will enhance the quality of your life, both personal and professional.

Instructional planning requires careful budgeting of time. In many choral music education contexts time may be perceived as fleeting: Will there be sufficient time for rehearsal before the upcoming concert? Will there be enough time to introduce the students to the desired musical concepts? The organization of time can provide the key to your staying power, that is, the length of your professional career. A step-by-step approach is needed to gain better control of time and deal with the stressful business of choral music education. The need for effective time management extends beyond the classroom.

The first step involves assessing your priorities. What are your personal, professional, financial, social, and spiritual goals? Set aside a block of time to establish objectives for each of these important aspects of your life. Take time to consider what things are most important to you. A *balance* is needed among the various components. Overemphasis on the professional sector of life, at the expense of other areas, will inevitably lead to burnout. Make a written list of your objectives in all areas and review it periodically.

When you arrive at a list that reflects your priorities, evaluate how well your current activities match your objectives. Choral music teaching can be such a consuming activity that it is possible to let years slip by without stopping to consider how well your current activities reflect the priorities you have established for your life. Also, some activities may remain in your schedule when you no longer contribute meaningfully to them or derive satisfaction from their accomplishment.

It is easy to be drawn into activities that may not be a part of your plan. Evaluate every project or activity in which you are involved, and eliminate those that do not fit your objectives. Consider whether the sheer number of activities is too great to allow a significant and fulfilling role in any of them. Committing to a wide variety of projects that are not related to your goals is potentially a devastating source of stress and frustration.

Just as comprehensive choral music education requires careful organization, the other areas of life also benefit from planning and scheduling priorities. If you want to spend time with your family (or alone), to study, or to relax, plan it far ahead. Put it into your schedule. To be effective, this kind of planning needs to be done months in advance. Then, as other commitments with students and colleagues begin to fill your days and evenings, you will be able to schedule your professional commitments around the blocks of family time, leisure time, and thinking time you have already committed. A common problem in this area occurs when a music educator fails to honor the commitments made to the nonprofessional areas of life. Once the schedule is made and it reflects your priorities, adhere to it. When asked whether you can assist with the service club's annual sing-along, you can honestly respond that you have a previous commitment in your schedule. Do not allow seemingly urgent but unimportant requests to cause the cancellation of important (though not immediately urgent) commitments made to yourself and your family.

If your schedule is overloaded, return to the first strategy and reevaluate your objectives. A lack of balance between personal and professional pursuits creates stress that will negatively affect every aspect of your life and might shorten your professional career. A balanced way of life can prolong a career in choral music education to thirty, forty, or more satisfying years.

When scheduling time, plan ahead for the increased professional demands that will be made on you at certain times of the year. It is likely that December will be a particularly busy month, filled with holiday concerts, caroling for shut-ins, grading, and a variety of other seasonal obligations (particularly if you are also a church musician). It is likely that the beginning and the end of any semester will require extra time and energy. Plan some time for recuperation after these periods.

How many things can you do well? How many different activities can you pursue before an overload occurs and the quality of your work suffers? Music educators are required to perform a variety of tasks: They are called on to act as administrators, salespersons, and fund-raisers as well as teachers and musicians. Therefore, you must set priorities, and delegate some activities to others.

Nonmusical tasks should be passed on to capable students, parents, or other volunteers. Some activities that might be effectively delegated could include something as complex as organizing a fund-raising campaign or as simple as making phone calls or delivering an announcement of an upcoming concert to the local newspaper. For delegation to be effective, both the task and the person to whom it is assigned must be chosen carefully. If you match individuals and tasks carefully, (1) you are relieved of time-consuming responsibilities that do not necessarily require your expertise, (2) others are given responsibilities that will facilitate their personal or musical growth, and (3) the tasks may be accomplished more efficiently than if you had attempted them under impossible time pressures.

Do you set priorities among your activities? The key to successful time management is setting priorities *in advance*. Perhaps a different structuring of your schedule would make you a more effective teacher and facilitate your students' musical growth. Is there some element of rehearsal planning that is inefficient? Change it. Are there other activities in which you would like to become involved? Start to adjust your schedule so your use of time reflects the priorities of your life.

Check with your physician and start slowly, but budget some time for physical activity. Walk, jog, bicycle, swim, or do any other kind of aerobic exercise that appeals to you. It must be something you enjoy and that fits into your schedule.

Eat sensibly. A person who is inactive or overweight is much more susceptible to stress, fatigue, and depression as well as many physical problems ranging from headaches to heart disease. You need not run marathons or subsist on nuts and berries to attain the degree of fitness necessary to combat stress and fatigue. A thirty-minute exercise session three or four times per week and a reasonably healthy diet will provide the necessary level of fitness for a successful and satisfying life.

Adequate rest, relaxation, and sleep are essential to a balanced life. Budget time each week for rest and relaxation. Do not use this time for professional activity; instead, relax and pursue totally different activities from those in your everyday routine. In addition to regular time for relaxation (at least weekly), set aside a longer period once or twice each year for a real vacation. These vacations need not be extravagant trips to exotic destinations; such expeditions are often exhausting rather than invigorating. The key to a successful and restful vacation is to change your regular routine and to indulge in relaxing activities.

As people mature, there is often the tendency to stick to familiar foods, people, music, and routines. Force yourself to read diverse materials and to learn about the unfamiliar. Your choral music teaching will have greater depth if you bring to your classes a range of knowledge that encompasses nonmusical areas. Current events, history, the visual arts, and many other subject areas will sharpen your perspective on your musical activities. Take a course on a topic that is new to you at a local college or university. Not only will you stretch yourself intellectually, but it is enlightening to sit on the other side of the desk from time to time.

The potential rewards of implementing these strategies are too important to ignore. They can help you focus on areas that are crucial to you and that match your talents, interests, and training. They can prolong your career, enhance your effectiveness as a music educator, and improve the quality of your life. Your professional life must coexist in a balanced relationship with your personal life. Failure to budget time for all aspects of your life may result in lack of success in *any* aspect and in greater stress and frustration. Employing the strategies outlined here will bring better balance, stability, and satisfaction to your career and life.

The strategies described in this section should facilitate control of your total schedule. With your personal schedule organized, you will be able to deal effectively with the various areas of administration required to organize the choral music education program.

✣ PUBLIC RELATIONS ✣

Public relations is a highly important aspect of the administration of your program. To obtain the support necessary to maintain a high-quality program, you must relate well to various constituencies at the school and in the community. This is accomplished in a variety of ways, including the development of quality, visibility, and communication.

Quality. The idea of quality is self-explanatory. People appreciate good quality in items they purchase, in the lifestyle they pursue, and in the activities in which they participate. At all times, the choral music education program's high quality should be evident to those who come in contact with it. Communicating the importance of this idea of quality to potential students and supporters requires the development and implementation of certain strategies.

The most obvious area where high quality will be evident is in the performance level of the ensembles. However, as you begin to develop a program, the *musical* quality of the choirs may not be at the level you wish it were or where it will be after five years of development. Most of the people with whom you will come in contact, however, will not be aware of the nature of a fine choral performance until they are educated. Therefore, it is likely their sensitivity to the performance level of the group will initially be relatively low, but will grow as the performance level of the ensemble increases.

These same people, however, will immediately appreciate quality in other aspects of the choral performance. Is the auditorium clean and attractive? Has anything been done to enhance the appearance of the stage? Are there printed programs? Are they of good quality? Does the choir *look* good? Do the singers convey a sense of professionalism as they walk on stage and onto the risers? Have the pieces included in the program been selected with sensitivity to the audience? All of these areas will contribute to the public's impression of the quality of your efforts, regardless of the actual performance level of the ensemble.

This idea of quality should permeate every aspect of your choral work. Letters, flyers, press releases, and all publications issued by the choral program should be of the highest quality possible. Use the personal computer to facilitate time management and efficiency. Word processing, graphics, and page layout programs can greatly enhance both the quality and the efficiency of your work. In the current era of desktop publishing, with the availability of a variety of excellent software programs, it is relatively easy to maintain control of the quality of publications, and there is little reason for sloppy, unprofessional, or unattractive written or printed communication.

The students involved in choir should be taught about the importance of quality. They are representatives of the program, both when they are performing and at all other times. If this idea can be instilled in all those associated with the choral music education program, you will have taken a major step toward the projection of a positive image in the school and the community.

Visibility. The choral music education program should be promoted at every opportunity. If you are by nature modest and unassuming about your activities and accomplishments, set these reservations aside in dealing with the promotion of the choral music education program.

If there is an individual in your school or school district responsible for public relations, develop a good working relationship with that person and indicate your desire to develop an ongoing program of good relations with the rest of the school and the community. If there is no public relations director, work with the choir parents to develop the necessary strategies and materials to enhance the visibility of the choral program in the community. Some ways to develop public awareness and heighten the visibility of the choral program could include any of the following:

1. A newspaper article in the school or local newspaper concerning *you,* the new choral director (remember, this is not a time for modesty), highlighting both your background and accomplishments and your plans for the program.
2. Publicize a concert to benefit a local charity. Some high school choirs have accepted cans of food to be donated to a local food pantry as the price for admission. Enlist the aid of the charity to be helped in terms of publicizing the event. Some choirs have even woven an entire concert theme around a particular community concern (e.g., hunger). The charity receives needed donations and publicity and the choir performs a needed service.
3. Newspaper articles should be written about choral students who have achieved special distinction (selected for district or all-state choir, made a high rating at solo and ensemble contest, etc.). Highlight the activities of an "unsung hero" who works behind the scenes for the choir—a student, parent, or other volunteer.
4. Organize a music honor society (for example, organize a chapter of Modern Music Masters, a national music honor society affiliated with the Music Educators National Conference). The activities of the society can be limited to a yearly induction ceremony perhaps accompanied by a recital, or can be as involved as weekly meetings and other activities. Be sure to send out a press release concerning any such events and to invite the administration and families of student members. Such an event could be an excellent opportunity to have a member of the administration speak to parents concerning the value of music in the schools or some other topic of interest.
5. Send invitations to your concerts or other special events to individuals with whom you are particularly interested in establishing relationships (the superintendent, local civic officials, other music educators, etc.)
6. Invite a prominent local personality to participate in a concert through the narration of a selection or a dramatic reading.
7. Utilize local talent or alumni as guest soloists.
8. Invite talented musical artists from the community into the school to make presentations to your choral students concerning their musical experiences, careers, and aspirations.

9. Combine your choir with an ensemble from another school or schools and present a joint concert.

Encourage choir members and parents to suggest new ways to enhance the visibility of the choral program in the community.

Communication. Communication is vital to the successful choral program. Accurate communication is important both within the choral program, with the school as a whole, and with the public.

Within the program, be sure the students involved have a clear understanding of your objectives, requirements, and scheduling obligations. To the extent possible, determine the year's schedule as the year begins. Discuss the schedule with the students so all have a clear understanding of their mandatory attendance at any scheduled chorus event. Some directors assemble a choir handbook that lays out the policies, procedures, and schedule for the year.

Be sure such information is also conveyed to the choir parents. Parental cooperation is necessary in order for students to be present at choir events. Schedule a demonstration concert early in the year, with special invitations to parents, so they can see what is involved in the choir program and the objectives their children are accomplishing through choral music. Appendix D is a sample of an informational packet distributed to choir parents in the fall at St. Charles West High School, St. Charles, Missouri (Doris Hylton, choral director).

Communicate within the school. Be certain all choir plans have the approval of the principal. After consulting with the administration, check the school calendar and be sure there are no conflicts and then add the choir events. If you have something scheduled that involves students being excused from other classes (a trip to festival, a concert by a visiting choir, etc.), be sure to send a note to the teachers concerned in advance. Also, be mindful of such occasions when other teachers need to have students pulled from your rehearsals. Such disruptions should be minimized to the extent possible.

Use posters, press releases for radio and television, newspaper articles, and any other means you can think of to communicate to the public what is being accomplished by you and your students. In creating and circulating press releases and other publicity, ascertain what the deadlines are for each of the periodicals where they are submitted. The material should be submitted sufficiently in advance so that it can appear one to four weeks ahead of the event it publicizes, for maximum impact.

Here is a sample press release:

PRESS RELEASE

University Singers Present Concert

The University Singers of the University of Missouri-St. Louis will present a concert at St. Mark's United Methodist Church, 315 Graham Road, Florissant, Missouri, on Sunday evening, March 28, 1993, at 7:30 P.M. The program will include choral music from a wide range of composers, styles, and periods, ranging from Renaissance composer Jacobus Gallus to selections from "Phantom of the Opera," by Andrew Lloyd Webber. Works by Bach, Mendelssohn, Fauré, and Brahms will also be presented, along with twentieth-century compositions by Cecil Effinger, Andre Thomas, George Gershwin, Edwin London, and David Maddux.

The University Singers have appeared in concert halls and on community, church, and university artists series throughout the country. The choir has been heard on classical music radio stations and has released four stereo recordings. They have performed in the Kennedy Center for the Performing Arts in Washington, D.C., and the Kentucky Center in Louisville.

Admission is $5.00. Tickets are available from the UM-St. Louis Music Department office, from members of the University Singers, or at St. Mark's United Methodist Church. For further information call 553–5992.

✣ RECRUITMENT ✣

A thriving choral program requires the active and successful recruitment of student participants. No matter how fine your conducting technique or how perceptive your ear for intonation and blend, these skills will be of little use if students are not attracted into your program and retained.

Work closely with the guidance department. Let them know of your expectations and goals for the choral program. Advertise in the school newspaper when it is time for students to sign up for classes for the next semester or academic year. Have a membership drive. Make it no longer than a week in duration, but encourage current choir members to make a particular effort to recruit new members for the ensemble. Make the present members of the choir aware of the need to tell their friends about the good experiences they are enjoying in the choir. Take the opportunity to visit with students in the cafeteria or other locations where they gather before or after school.

Maintain a good relationship with colleagues who teach at the schools that feed your school. Take the choir to the feeder school for a concert presentation each year. Organize other opportunities for the students who will be coming to your school the following year to hear and interact with your choir. Include them in a concert at your school—this will benefit the programs at both schools.

The public relations strategies mentioned in the previous section will help attract students to the program; in addition, a few other ideas may help facilitate recruitment, including an emphasis on respect for each choral participant, the development of pride and tradition, and the provision of an enjoyable experience for each student participant.

Developing Pride and Tradition

Many things can be done to promote pride and tradition within a choral program. Establish a system of awards for choir members, and present them publicly at the final concert of the year or at an end-of-the-year awards banquet.

A comprehensive choral music education program helps student participants explore their personal strengths and limitations and become more fully aware of their personal identity. This happens most readily in an atmosphere of mutual respect, where each individual is valued—for his or her personality, voice, attitude, and skills. Regard for each individual is at the core of comprehensive choral music education. Students will be attracted to a program where they know they will be secure and each individual is valued for his or her unique attributes. They should be encouraged to have respect for themselves, their peers, the teacher, and the school.

Encourage excellence by recognizing the outstanding choir student each year. A plaque on the wall of the choir room listing the names of recipients over the years will do much to stimulate pride in students and motivate them to try to win the award.

Recognize years of membership in the choirs with appropriate awards, such as choir letters, sweaters, or pins. There are a variety of companies that specialize in providing such awards.

Welcome back alumni to visit rehearsals, to talk with students about their experiences since high school. Also, invite alumni back to participate in a concert each year. Select a song that is popular with the students, and sing that each year as the alumni return for their special recognition.

Events and programs that are worthwhile should be repeated. Find out what works and what does not, and develop the things that are successful into choir traditions.

Enjoyment

As choral music educators, we have many musical, social, and educational objectives for our students. Students want to have an enjoyable time. These are not mutually exclusive goals. Be sure there is an opportunity for students to have fun as they participate in the choral program.

In the chapter on rehearsal techniques we discussed the matter of humor in choral rehearsal. Each rehearsal, in fact each interaction with students, should be as pleasant and enjoyable as possible. In addition, however, there should be opportunities specifically designed for students to enjoy themselves. Schedule choir picnics, softball games, after-concert parties, and any other kind of event where students can have the opportunity to enjoy each other's company.

As the choral director, enjoy the students! Secondary school students are fun to be with. Of course, students need a choral music teacher they can respect and admire, but this does not mean you can never relax and allow yourself to observe and enjoy the students as they act like typical teenagers at a choir party or picnic. These kinds of experiences will enhance the choral experiences you provide and help build enthusiasm for the program.

✣ BUDGET ✣

Choral music education programs, like most other endeavors, require financial support: Money must be allocated and expended in order for a program to function. The financial resources available are limited; it can safely be assumed there will be more demands for funds than funds available to meet those demands, particularly in the present era of budgetary and personnel cutbacks in the public schools. A basic understanding of budget and finances will enhance your chances of competing successfully for financial support. Once funding is obtained, the employment of sound fiscal practices will help ensure that the money is wisely spent. Therefore, some consideration of budgetary matters is an important factor in planning and implementing your program.

Musicians have a negative reputation in this area of finances and budgeting. This reputation has been earned over the years by music educators who fail to understand or who ignore budgetary policies and procedures. If you can avoid being stereotyped as a "flaky musician," a major step will have been made toward establishing a solid program.

To start with, learn about the budgetary procedures at your school. Determine how much money is currently budgeted for the choral program, how the budget is organized, and what the financial procedures are for making purchases.

Find out who is responsible for record keeping and make friends with that individual. Once you have determined what the correct procedures are in terms of purchase orders, requisitions, and other kinds of paperwork, be sure to follow them. Do not go to the local music store and order a thousand dollars worth of music and then try to figure out whether the funds are available and the correct procedure for placing an order.

Once you have established your budget, make a complete survey of the choral music facilities and equipment and determine what is presently available at the school. Then ascertain what is needed, both in terms of ongoing expenses (music, books, pencils, chalk, paper, etc.) and capital items (one-time expenditures for equipment such as choral risers, choir apparel, acoustical shell, sound equipment, computer hardware, etc). Compile a complete list of your needs in terms of equipment and supplies (see Table 7.1 for an illustration of such an inventory and wish list).

TABLE 7.1 Current Inventory

Books, Music, and Recordings
Octavo music: 630 selections
Collections: 34
Solo literature: 62 books
Texts and reference books: 96
Record albums: 73
Audio cassettes: 51
Compact discs: 42
Computer software: Integrated application program and page layout program

TABLE 7.1, cont'd.

Pianos and Benches	
6′ grand (stage)	
Upright (rehearsal room)	
Console pianos (3) (practice rooms)	
1 artist's bench	
4 piano benches	
Office Equipment	
Desk (1)	
Chair (1)	
Filing cabinets (14) (office and choral library)	
Shelving (in storage room)	
Racks for choral costumes	
Typewriter	
Personal computer	
Music sorting rack	
Choral Room	
Portable choral risers (8 sections)	
75 chairs	
Six full-length mirrors	
Choral folio cabinet	
Director's chair	
Director's stand	
Podium	
150 choral folders	
Audiovisual Equipment and Supplies	
Sound system in choral room:	
turntable	
compact disc player	
dual cassette deck	
speakers (2)	
receiver	
Portable sound system:	
microphones (6), microphone stands (6), and cords (6)	
Synthesizer	
Sequencer	
Choral Attire and Props	
100 tuxedo jackets and trousers, plus accessories	
150 dresses	
25 show choir outfits	
Miscellaneous costumes	
Miscellaneous props	
Needs	
Macintosh Computer	$1,200
Stylewriter printer	300
Midi Box and cables	30

TABLE 7.1, cont'd.

Acoustical shell (six sections)	1,500
Higher quality portable P.A. system	300
Camcorder	1,200
Tripod	100

Keep your inventory list available and update it as necessary. As various needs are filled, or as some items are no longer high-priority needs, make the necessary adjustments. In this way, you will be prepared if funds suddenly become available or you are asked what you need. This will happen from time to time, and the person who is well prepared with a carefully thought out and prioritized list will stand the best chance of having some needs met.

In addition to onetime equipment requests, such as the list in Table 7.1, there also needs to be a yearly request for ongoing needs in terms of music, transportation expenses, supplies, and any other items required to operate the choral program (see Table 7.2).

The list and budget presented in Tables 7.1 and 7.2 are quite realistic. A choral music educator is responsible for thousands of dollars worth of equipment and supplies. Each choral music educator and each school district have unique characteristics that will help determine an appropriate list of equipment and supplies and level of expenditures.

Initially, the most important aspect of dealing with the budget is to work within the constraints of the current system—follow the rules. As you become more familiar with the organization of the school and your own needs as the choral director there are certain things to work for in order to get maximum financial support for the program:

1. Generally, it is better to have several smaller budget categories rather than one big one. It is easier to justify several small categories.
2. Get anything possible out of the music budget and into a general account (things like chalk, paper, textbooks, etc.). As with number 1, the objective is to delimit the money requested specifically for music items, maximizing the effect of the money budgeted in that area. If your budget is set up with an item for textbooks, multiple copies of choral music could be placed in that category.
3. Work for as much autonomy as possible in determining how you spend the money allocated for the choral music program.

TABLE 7.2 Budget for Supplies: Current Academic Year

Choral music purchase:	$2,000
Books, tapes:	350
Transportation expense:	2,000
Software purchase:	500
Equipment maintenance and repair:	1,000
Piano tuning:	500

Administrators tend to be more receptive to budgetary concerns if you have been businesslike in your dealings with them and if they have been educated about the value of music for students. Understandably, a program that is successful in the eyes of the principal and superintendent will receive more favorable consideration than one that is not. Educate administrators about the educational and aesthetic value of the experiences provided in music class and the need for financial support in order to make those experiences possible.

Purchasing Choral Music

The purchase of music is a big expenditure and the price has risen steeply in recent years. A few points regarding the purchase of music may be helpful.

Music may be purchased from a variety of sources. If the local sheet music dealer maintains a stock of choral music, this can be a very helpful resource for browsing as well as for purchase. Such music dealers also support choral music education through their participation in state, regional, and national conventions of the Music Educators National Conference and the American Choral Directors Association and by advertising in organizational publications. They often provide music for use in reading sessions and clinics and display recent publications and products at in-service meetings. Music may also be purchased through mail-order outlets, which may provide a discounted price for multiple copies of selections. Remember that the mail-order distributor often does not have the expense of maintaining a stock of music nor does such a company support the professional organizations in the same way as the local dealer. Each choral music educator needs to decide where to spend the money allocated for the purchase of music.

In ordering music, be sure to provide as much information as possible to the supplier. Most important is the octavo number of the selection. A publisher may have a variety of editions of a particular title available in various voicings. The potential for confusion is greatly lessened if the octavo number is included along with the title, composer, voicing, and publisher.

Illegal Photocopying

The illegal photocopying of copyrighted music has become a major problem for the profession in recent years. The easy availability of high-quality photocopying machines in churches and schools, combined with scarce resources for the purchase of music, exacerbate the situation.

Aside from the issue of illegal photocopying, a variety of areas of copyright regulations have an impact on choral music educators. These include the right to perform copyrighted music under certain circumstances, to sell recordings of concerts for profit, and to broadcast performances on radio or television. Jay Althouse has written an excellent booklet outlining the various aspects of copyright as they pertain to music educators (see Suggested Reading).

The copyright issue is both a moral and a legal concern. Part of the problem occurs when a music educator takes the short-term versus the long-term view of the consequences of photocopying. In the short term, it may appear advantageous to purchase one copy of a selection and make sixty photocopies for use with a choir. However, there are a variety of negative consequences. First, it is illegal to photocopy under the circumstances given. Second, it deprives the composer and publisher of the financial reward of making such music available. Also, the practice of illegal photocopying diminishes any financial incentive for future creative activity on the part of composers and discourages publishers from producing a variety of music of good quality. The illegal photocopying of music also drives up the cost of choral music, penalizing the majority of directors who obey the law. Finally, if you examine the actual cost of photocopying, it is significant and may even exceed the cost of purchasing the necessary number of copies.

Under certain circumstances it is legal to photocopy copyrighted music. If music has been ordered for a particular occasion and has not arrived, it may be photocopied for the occasion and then replaced with the purchased copies. Limited sections of music may be copied for classroom use, provided they are *not intended for performance* and the section copied *does not constitute a performable whole* (e.g., a complete section or selection).

Both the Music Educators National Conference and the American Choral Directors Association have issued statements and publications outlining their position on the matter. Recently, the ACDA added to their membership application the following statement:

> As an ACDA member, I will comply with the copyright laws of the United States of America. (Compliance with these laws is also a condition of participation by clinicians and performing ensembles that appear on any ACDA-sponsored event or convention.)

Obviously, this matter is of considerable importance to the professional organizations. The violation of copyright regulations is detrimental to the choral music education profession.

✣ FUND-RAISING ✣

The increased importance of fund-raising to music education activities can be discerned by a visit to the exhibit area at a state music conference. Pizza, candy, citrus fruit, candles, and other items are displayed by a variety of fund-raising companies specializing in school programs.

A choral program that receives adequate fiscal support without having to fund-raise represents an optimal situation. A career in choral music education should not mean having to raise the money to fund basic instructional activities. If you find yourself in a position where there is a tradition of fund-raising to support the basic educational activities of the choral program, you should work to change the system. Music and the other arts are an integral part of the complete public school curriculum and should be funded in the same way as other academic subjects.

Conversely, there may be things that would be beneficial to the development of the choral program that are not funded through the regular budget—a trip to a festival, a concert tour, or an expensive piece of equipment. In these cases, fund-raising may be necessary and justified to accomplish your objectives.

If you undertake a fund-raising project, follow these few basic principles:

1. Communicate with the administration. Secure your principal's approval prior to initiating any fund-raising activity.
2. Select a fund-raising project in which you are selling a useful product or service, of good quality, and through which you provide consumers with good value for their money.
3. Do not select a fund-raising project that requires the purchase of a large inventory of product without having the money, or at least the orders for the product, in hand.
4. Compare projects and select one that will assure you maximum profits for the effort expended by both you, the parents, and the students.
5. Delegate fund-raising projects to parents who can be given the responsibility for implementation, relieving you of some of the work.
6. Communicate. Be sure another school organization is not selling pizza (or candy or citrus fruit) at the same time as your students.
7. Be sure potential customers are aware of the project through newspaper publicity, posters, and word of mouth advertising.
8. Try to find a project that can be repeated for several years. This has several important advantages. Potential customers will become accustomed to purchasing the product from your organization. Your parents and students will require less preparation if they are familiar with the product and the sales process. Repeating a project also saves the effort and time expended in evaluating potential projects and selecting a new one each year.

A convenient way to raise money for a choral program is to include a page of patrons or pages of advertising in the printed program for the concerts of the ensemble. A flyer from St. Charles West High School, St. Charles, Missouri, and a letter to patrons form the University of Missouri-St. Louis are found in Figures 7.1 and 7.2.

✣ SCHEDULING ✣

If you can work with the administration and the guidance department to secure an advantageous schedule for your choral ensembles, this is an excellent step toward making your program available for and accessible to students.

St. Charles West Choirs

present

Let Me Entertain You

featuring the music of

Jule Styne
Cole Porter
Irving Berlin
George and Ira Gershwin

Patron Information

Proceeds from this show will help provide equipment and uniforms for the choirs at St. Charles West High School. Thank you for your support.

Name:
Message: (Total of 8 to 10 words — 40 to 50 spaces)

Donation: $15.00

- -

Let Me Entertain You

February 25, 26, 27, 1993
7:30 p.m.
St. Charles West High School

Please present this at the ticket booth
for two complimentary tickets.

FIGURE 7.1 St. Charles West Patron Request

In recent years, there has been a trend toward making choral music an extracurricular offering rather than a part of the core curriculum in the school. To combat this way of thinking, parents, administrators, and school boards must be constantly reminded of the importance of music to the curriculum and the philosophical and aesthetic bases of music in the curriculum (see Chapter 9 for a detailed discussion of the importance of a philosophy of music education and the place of music in the curriculum). If music's curricular position is threatened, it may be necessary to mobilize parental support and to clearly articulate the importance of choral music education to all interested parties.

November 1992

Dear friend:

The Madrigal Ensemble of the University of Missouri-St. Louis will be taking their third international concert tour to London, England, from December 26, 1992 to January 2, 1993. The UM-St. Louis Madrigal Ensemble will be performing at Westminister Cathedral, the Kingston Vale Church, and a variety of other sites. The funds for the air fare and housing have been raised by the student members of the Ensemble.

We are seeking to defray some of the additional costs currently being borne by individual students for their meals and other expenses while in London. For this reason, we are seeking patrons from among our friends and area businesses.

Donations of any size would be appreciated, and a contribution of $25.00 or more would be recognized through the inclusion of the donor's name in a listing of Patrons, to be included in the printed programs for our Holiday Madrigal Feasts at UM-St. Louis, as well as in the programs for our British tour.

Thank you for considering this worthwhile request.

Sincerely,

John Hylton
Associate Professor of Music

- -

Your name, or your company's name as you would like it to appear in the programs:

____

Contribution amount: __________________________

THANK YOU FOR YOUR HELP!

FIGURE 7.2 UM–St. Louis Patron Letter

From the standpoint of the music educator, the more periods there are in the school day, the better. More periods in the day increases scheduling flexibility. Currently, a six- or seven-period day seems to be the most popular scheduling option. Teachers in certain disciplines, such as English, mathematics, and science, tend to favor the six-period day because it requires fewer preparations and each class is somewhat longer, which they find advantageous. The music teacher must initiate and defend the idea of greater scheduling flexibility for students. Talented students feel pressure to take increasing numbers of courses to prepare for college. Obviously, the more classes students are required (or at least strongly encouraged) to take and the fewer periods they have in which to take them, the less flexible the schedule becomes. The notion of taking choir for all four years of high school is very difficult in the context of a six-period day. The potential for students to take a variety of classes that interest them is severely limited.

In districts where a six-period day has been adopted, there are sometimes efforts made to increase flexibility by incorporating a "zero hour" class before school. During this period, students may take a required class, such as physical education or English, freeing up time during the regular school day. Similarly, there may be such offerings at the end of the regular school day. Although this system is better than nothing, it still places an extra burden on academically gifted students who are interested in scheduling classes in a variety of subject areas.

Individual teachers should determine what kind of schedule works best for them, but we can make some generalizations concerning *when* to schedule choral ensembles during the school day. There are some distinct advantages to scheduling a select ensemble during first period. This will allow the scheduling of meetings or rehearsals from time to time before school, which can run into the regular rehearsal period. During the first period, both the teacher and the students are fresh (although some individuals may not yet be fully awake).

The last period in the school day similarly provides the opportunity to occasionally extend the rehearsal, depending, of course, on students' individual schedules. But by the last period, students and teacher tend to be tired out. Students may be distracted thinking of their after-school job, social activity, or athletic practice.

My experience has been that it is best to avoid, where possible, the periods immediately before and after lunch. Before lunch, students are hungry, and immediately after lunch, they may be lethargic. Having made these comments, it should be noted that highly successful choirs have met during any period of the school day. The most important variable in determining whether a choir will be successful is the choral music educator who leads it. It is advantageous to spread your rehearsals out during the school day. If you have a planning period or two, they are most effective when interspersed among the other periods in the day. Alternate nonperformance and performance classes if possible.

✣ THE CHORAL LIBRARY ✣

The development and maintenance of a varied library of significant choral music is critical to the growth of a successful choral music education program (see Chapter 5). Here we discuss the organization, storage, and maintenance of the choral library.

The choir librarian(s) must be a person who is responsible, reliable, and who enjoys organizational details. Carefully consider the individual who will have this responsibility, since the right person can potentially be of enormous help. Conversely, an unsatisfactory choice will create significant stress and inconvenience.

Once the right person has been chosen for this important assignment, give them careful instruction concerning how to accomplish the work at hand efficiently. Devise a system for the distribution and collection of choral music from choir members. The system should provide for ease of distribution and collection and accountability for the music on the part of each choir member. If music is missing or is damaged beyond normal wear and tear, there must be a way to collect money for repair and replacement. Music should be numbered, and each choir folder assigned a corresponding number. A folder cabinet in the choral room is a convenient means of storage. Such a cabinet is pictured in Figure 7.3.

A sign-out sheet should be used by students who wish to take music home for practice. The choir librarian can work with the folders when the choir is not present, distributing, collecting, and inspecting music.

The centerpiece of the organization of the choral library is a card file. A sample format for such a filing system is indicated in Figure 7.4.

The information to be included may be modified according to your individual needs, but certain basic information is essential. The card file can then be a convenient reference as you consider your programming needs. Rather than shuffling through hundreds of folders or boxes full of music to determine what titles are available and in what quantities, refer to the file. To

FIGURE 7.3 Folder Cabinet from Wenger

TITLE: ______________________________

COMPOSER: ________________________

ARRANGER: ________________________

VOICING: __________________________

PUBLISHER: ________________________

OCTAVO #: _________________________

OF COPIES: ______________________

DATES PERFORMED: ________________

FIGURE 7.4 Format for Choral Library Card File

complement the card file, maintain a folder or folders of single copies of all of the titles, so that once you select a title you can study it easily.

Many choral music educators have computerized their file systems, using one of the many databases available today. As with most computer systems, there is a significant investment of time required initially to learn how to use the software and then to enter all of the data. Once that is accomplished, the time investment is recouped, as cards may be modified and additions made to the file with a minimum of effort.

In addition to organizing the card file, devise a system for storing the actual choral scores. A variety of storage systems have been used, including file folders in cabinets, cardboard folders on shelves, or filing boxes arranged on open shelves.

The optimal system for storing music is probably cardboard boxes arranged on open shelves. This kind of storage system allows for maximum flexibility. When new music is purchased, you can easily add it to the library without having to rearrange envelopes or folders of music in cabinets. A disadvantage of this system of filing is that is requires a relatively large amount of storage space. Figure 7.5 illustrates this filing system.

With the cost of choral music averaging $1.50 to $2.00 per copy (and rising), the maintenance of the choral library is very important. Scissors, tape, marking pens, storage containers, and an adequate work space must be made available for the choir librarian(s). As music is collected, it should immediately be sorted, inspected, and repaired. In the normal course of events music will require taping and other forms of minor repair. If this is done on an ongoing basis, the job will not be overwhelming.

FIGURE 7.5 Filing System

Another strategy for reducing the cost of music for choral ensembles is to borrow copies of the pieces to be performed. Borrowing works best if an ongoing arrangement is established with another choral director of similar tastes. This makes the arrangement mutually beneficial. It may also be helpful to offer to rent the necessary music from a colleague at another school to compensate for the wear and tear on the music and the effort necessary to pull it from the file, count it, and check it back in upon its return.

✣ WEARING APPAREL ✣

What to wear? This is a question that confronts the choral director as soon as a performance is planned. There are a variety of choices and each has advantages and disadvantages. The primary factors to keep in mind while considering this decision are appearance, cost, and appropriateness for the kinds of performances presented by the ensemble.

As a starting point, some sort of uniform wearing apparel is highly desirable for any ensemble. Choral ensembles are judged immediately by an audience or by adjudicators on their appearance. This judgment occurs before a sound is heard, and it predisposes the listener to either a positive or negative view of the performance. Of course, appearance is based on more than the outfits the ensemble wears, but uniform attire is extremely important in creating the correct impression.

A variety of companies currently supply performance attire for choral ensembles. Some popular choices of wearing apparel include the following:

1. Some type of uniform dress, assembled from students' current wardrobes (for ensembles with limited financial resources)
2. Choir robes
3. Tuxedos and gowns
4. Blazers and dresses

A choral ensemble can look quite presentable and uniform without a major outlay of funds. Shirts or blouses of a uniform color with dark blue or black pants or skirts creates a somewhat formal and uniform look for a choir. Most students own, or can easily acquire these items. Other appropriate outfits can be devised with minimal costs—a sweater of a particular color with slacks or skirts, for example. Even if students need to purchase a sweater or pair of trousers, these are items that can be kept by the student and worn again and again as part of their regular wardrobe.

Choir robes have traditionally been a popular choice of apparel. Choir robes look uniform and hide the differences in height and weight among choir members very effectively, eliminating visual distractions from the choral sound. Choir robes are very appropriate in church settings and for the performance of sacred repertoire. They are less satisfactory when the repertoire is secular, popular, or lighter in nature. A variety of companies manufacture robes for choirs. The price can vary greatly, depending on the quality and durability of the garment.

A type of apparel that has gained great popularity in recent years is tuxedos and gowns. Used tuxedos may be available from a rental outlet at a reasonable price, particularly if the merchant routinely supplies tuxedos for students from your school to wear to the prom and other formal occasions. Formal outfits for men can be purchased for under $100 per person. Some companies are producing inexpensive performance apparel that is not as durable as that designed for many years of use. This type of outfit is fine if it is intended for one year's use. Gowns may be constructed by seamstresses among the choir parents or by hiring someone, or they may be purchased. Gowns and tuxedos look formal, but adapt better to the performance of both sacred and secular repertoire than choir robes. Careful consideration should be given to the design of the gowns to be sure students of varying heights, weights, and body shapes can wear them comfortably, and that the gowns tend to minimize, rather than emphasize, the physical differences between students. Blazers and dresses are another type of outfit that is appropriate for many types of repertoire and a bit less formal than tuxes and gowns. We discuss the outfitting of specialized ensembles, such as madrigal ensembles, vocal jazz groups, and show choirs in Chapter 8. With all choir apparel, insist on uniformity in shoes, socks, and hose. The effect created by thousands of dollars worth of wearing apparel and many hours of effort can be ruined by one pair of high-top athletic shoes or one pair of red socks.

✣ PARENTS' ORGANIZATIONS ✣

Parents' organizations can be a tremendous help to the choral music educator. They can help foster accurate, rapid communication between school and home. They can provide needed expertise and labor for choir projects of all kinds, from chaperoning to fund-raising. But organizations can also develop into an obstacle to sound choral music education if they are not monitored closely or if their function is unclear.

A basic organizational principle to keep in mind in dealing with parents' groups is that musical decisions (repertoire, programming, etc.) should be the exclusive province of the professional music educator. Nonmusical concerns (e.g., should we attend this particular festival next year and how shall we raise the money for the trip) and political advocacy for the choral music program are the appropriate focus for parents' organizations.

If a parents' organization for choral music students does not exist at your school, it is desirable to initiate one. Be certain to thoroughly discuss the matter with your principal, and lay out clear guidelines concerning the responsibilities and limitations of the parents' group.

Even more desirable than a "Choir Parents" organization is a "Music Parents" organization. Such an organization reinforces the notion that all of the music organizations in a school are working together toward common goals. In practice, it is difficult to change a preexisting successful organization associated with one ensemble into an inclusive music parents' group; understandably, parents are reluctant to convert something successful, to which they have already contributed and worked for, to a new organization. Nevertheless, it is philosophically and educationally justifiable to work toward such a unified organization.

✣ SUMMARY ✣

Although you can be a fine musician, educator, and an excellent conductor without being an effective and well-organized administrator, your job as choral music educator is much easier and less stressful if you develop administrative and organizational skills. This chapter presented some basic issues that will make the choral music educator's task easier and less frustrating and help facilitate a longer and more productive career in choral music education.

We began by discussing a few general organizational principles to facilitate time management and control of stress. The importance of goal-setting, balance, and careful monitoring of priorities was discussed. This was followed by discussion of some specific administrative areas that are part of the choral music educator's responsibility, including public relations, recruitment, budget, scheduling, maintaining the choral library, performance apparel, and parents' organizations.

Questions

1. Why is it undesirable to "give 100 percent" to your professional effort?
2. How should you prioritize your various activities and set up a schedule for the year?
3. How can a choral music educator who is rebuilding a program convey the idea of high quality to the public?
4. What kinds of things should be publicized in the school newspaper concerning a choral program?
5. Why is it important to maintain a "wish list" of desired equipment, even when there is no immediate prospect it will be funded?
6. Why is it important to refrain from the illegal photocopying of choral music?
7. Is fund-raising an acceptable use of the choral music educator's time? What kinds of expenses justify the planning and implementation of choral fund-raising projects?
8. From the choral music educator's standpoint, which is more desirable: a six-period or seven-period school day? Why?
9. What criteria should be used in selecting a choir librarian? What kinds of systems are available for the storage of music?
10. List the advantages and disadvantages of choir robes versus tuxedos and gowns for a concert choir.
11. What are some potential problems inherent in choir parents' organizations? How can they be avoided?

Note

1. Material in this section is derived from John Hylton, "Ways to Manage Stress and Avoid Teacher Burnout," *Music Educators Journal* (February 1989), pp. 29–31.

Suggested Reading

ALTHOUSE, JAY. *Copyright: The Complete Guide for Music Educators.* East Stroudsburg, PA: Music in Action, 1984.

GARRETSON, ROBERT L. "Music Curricula," *International Encyclopedia of Education*, vol. 6, pp. 3457–3463, Oxford, England: Pergamon Press, 1985.

GEERDES, HAROLD P. *Planning and Equipping Educational Music Facilities*. Reston, VA: Music Educators National Conference, 1975.

HERTZ, WAYNE S. "Physical Facilities and Equipment," in Kenneth L. Neidig and John W. Jennings (eds.), *Choral Director's Guide*. West Nyack, NY: Parker, 1967.

HOFFER, CHARLES R. *Teaching Music in the Secondary School*. Belmont, CA: Wadsworth, 1983.

KLOTMAN, ROBERT H. *Scheduling Music Classes*. Reston, VA: Music Educators National Conference, 1968.

———. *The School Music Administrator and Supervisor: Catalysts for Change in Music Education*. Englewood Cliffs, NJ: Prentice-Hall, 1973.

MENC COMMITTEE ON STANDARDS. *The School Music Program: Description and Standards*. Reston, VA: Music Educators National Conference, 1986.

Chapter Eight

Planning for Special Events and Specialized Ensembles

✣ ✣ ✣

✣ INTRODUCTION ✣

We first discuss a variety of special choral events in this chapter including contests, festivals, clinics, exchange concerts, choir retreats, concerts by visiting choirs, and tours. These kinds of occasions can do a great deal to help motivate students and to add interest to the comprehensive choral music education program. Plan such events in the context of the overall program, based on the educational and motivational implications for each of the students participating.

Specialized ensembles can also play an important part in the comprehensive choral music education program. Whether it is a vocal jazz group, a madrigal ensemble, a show choir, or any other kind of specialized singing group, it should be carefully planned to fit into the overall choral curriculum. We present some basic guidelines for teaching some of the most common specialized ensembles.

✣ CONTESTS AND COMPETITION ✣

A choral contest can involve competing directly against the other ensembles participating for trophies or other awards, with the choir deemed the best winning a "Sweepstakes Trophy" or some other similar-sounding award.

Alternatively, a contest can involve adjudication and evaluation according to some preestablished absolute criteria, against which each choir is judged.

Samples of adjudication sheets used for a choral competition are provided in Figure 8.1.

UNIVERSITY OF MISSOURI–ST. LOUIS
GATEWAY MUSIC FESTIVAL
CONCERT CHOIR ADJUDICATION SHEET

School: ____________________

Director: ____________________ Rating: ________

Selections	Composer
1. ____________	____________
2. ____________	____________
3. ____________	____________

Tone quality: 15 points. . . . . Total ________
(freedom and resonance of tone
at all dynamics, quality of tone
of chorus, sections, and soloists)

Intonation: 15 points. . . . . .Total ________

Diction: 15 points. . . . . .Total ________
(clarity of consonants, purity of
vowels, intelligibility of text)

Rhythmic accuracy: 10 points. . . . . Total ________

Balance/Blend: 15 points. . . . . Total ________
(of ensemble, within sections,
between sections)

General musicianship
and interpretation: 25 points. . . . . Total ________
(tempo, dynamics, style, phrasing.)

Quality and suitability of literature
for the ensemble: 5 points . . . . Total ________

FINAL SCORE ________

Judge's Signature ____________________

UNIVERSITY OF MISSOURI–ST. LOUIS
GATEWAY MUSIC FESTIVAL
SHOW CHOIR/VOCAL JAZZ ADJUDICATION SHEET

School: ______________________________

Director: ______________________________ Rating: ________

Selections	Composer
1. ______________________	______________________
2. ______________________	______________________
3. ______________________	______________________

Tone quality: 15 points. . . . . Total ____________
(freedom and resonance of tone
at all dynamics, quality of ensemble,
sections, and soloists)

Intonation: 15 points. . . . . Total ____________

Balance/Blend: 15 points. . . . . Total ____________
(of ensemble, solo and tutti ensemble,
within sections, between sections)

General musicianship
and interpretation: 25 points . . . . .Total ____________
(tempo, dynamics, style, phrasing,
diction)

Visual elements: 15 points. . . . . .Total ____________
(choreography, staging,
costumes, vitality)

Show elements: 15 points. . . . . .Total ____________
(programming, transitions,
accompaniment)

FINAL SCORE ____________

Judge's Signature ______________________

FIGURE 8.1 Gateway Festival Adjudication Sheets

The question of the role of competition in the choral program has been debated for many years. Listed here are some of the arguments for and against competition. After thoughtful consideration, you must make your own decision on the value of competition and its place in your particular program.

Arguments for Competition

Students enjoy competition. Given a choice of attending a festival or other competition and receiving "comments only" versus a numerical rating in which the ensemble is judged and evaluated relative to some absolute standard or to other groups, students prefer to be rated. It does not seem to make a great deal of difference whether the individual or group is likely to receive a high or low rating. Students want to find out how they compare to their peers.

Competition is motivational for students and directors. The knowledge that the results of one's efforts will be on the line shortly is a powerful incentive for students to work diligently to learn the music and to assimilate the information given them in rehearsal to help them improve.

Competition is educational for students and broadens their perspectives. Finding out how a performance is objectively rated by a panel of impartial adjudicators provides students with accurate information concerning their performance level and accomplishments. This helps to positively reinforce good work or to verify the need for more preparation.

Competition is educational and motivational for the choral music educator. It provides an opportunity to receive constructive criticism and an objective evaluation of the results of the choral music teachers' musicianship and rehearsal techniques.

Competition helps prepare students for the future. In business, in sports, in the military, and in later academic pursuits, there will always be competition, and we, as educators, must prepare students for it.

Competition provides one means of accountability for a choral music education program. It provides evidence for administrators, school boards, and parents when a program is successful (or when it is not).

Arguments Against Competition

Choral music provides a way for students to enjoy a powerful group experience without the added pressure of competing. Students who may not have the intellectual or athletic prowess to make straight "A's" or to play varsity sports can be successful in music and feel the pride of accomplishment in a noncompetitive situation. Participation in a contest introduces needless stress into an otherwise noncompetitive activity.

Competition produces winners and losers. While winning is gratifying, losing can be quite the opposite. In a contest using a numerical rating system, whether right or wrong, the recipients of a I are viewed as winners: the recipients of a rating of II or lower are often viewed (at least by themselves) as losers.

Competitive ratings do not necessarily reflect improvement that may have been made in a choral program. A choral music educator may have taken a choir that was in poor condition and improved it greatly in the course of a year. When the vastly improved choir goes to contest, the judges don't consider progress in the program relative to the previous year.

Competitive ratings can give the wrong message to school board members, administrators, and parents. Is the objective of choral music education to produce the most polished performance of the limited number of selections (usually two or three) to be performed at contest, or is it to provide students with a representative variety of quality choral literature?

How should a program where three months of the year are devoted almost exclusively to preparation of pieces for contest (and where top ratings result) be compared to one where a balanced approach to choral literature is maintained and the selections to be performed for contest are part of a carefully planned choral curriculum? You should view competition, along with every other matter, in light of its impact on the personal and musical growth of the student participants.

Competing Effectively

After weighing the arguments for and against competition, you may decide it has a place in your choral music education program and you will take your choir to contest. Moreover, you may find when you move into a new position that there is a tradition of competition at the school, and it is expected the choir will participate in contests. If, for any reason, you find yourself preparing an ensemble for competition, then Lamb has presented the situation succinctly and well:[1]

1. You and your students are entered in a contest against other high school students.
2. Contests involve winners and losers.
3. If you are going to compete in contests, compete to win.

Preparing a choir to successfully compete in a contest is somewhat different than preparing for a concert presentation. The following list provides some basic ideas to keep in mind in preparing a choir for competition:

- Select repertoire the choir can perform comfortably. While it is admirable and educationally sound to challenge a choir with new pieces that will force them to grow musically, when preparing for contest the objective is to receive the best possible rating. Therefore, be conservative in selecting music. It is far better to perform a relatively straightforward piece with security, enthusiasm, and expression than it is to present a more complex selection that has not been completely mastered.
- Pick music that will show off your choir's capabilities and accomplishments, rather than reveal the choir's weaknesses. If you have a particularly strong tenor section, select a piece that displays their beautiful tone and flexibility to good advantage. Conversely, if your tenors (or altos, sopranos, or basses) are inexperienced, don't choose a selection for contest that requires them to sing a high exposed passage for eight measures.

- At the risk of stating the obvious, select music representing a variety of styles, composers, and periods. On many occasions a choir has brought three pieces to contest, all from the same period and in the same style. Judges will be impressed if your choir performs a variety of music confidently and with a good sense of style.
- Include some music in a foreign language. Having said that, it is also critical to use correct pronunciation. Ask a foreign language teacher to listen to and critique the group on their diction at some point prior to the contest. It is also probably most prudent to use a selection in Latin. There seems to be more general agreement among adjudicators on how to pronounce Latin correctly than there is concerning French, Italian, German, or other languages. Again, the intent here is to compete successfully.
- It may not be so obvious, but it is prudent to select pieces that are not often performed. Even if your choir's rendition of "Elijah Rock" by Jester Hairston is definitive, most adjudicators have developed certain preconceived notions of how "Elijah Rock," "The Last Words of David" by Thompson, and other often performed repertoire should sound. If your interpretation differs from that of the adjudicator, the choir's rating may suffer. It seems that each year there is a particular newly composed selection or arrangement that is performed by choir after choir in concert and at contest. Avoid using such pieces for contest—after several repetitions, the judge may be tired of it, and it probably will not be to your advantage to be the fourteenth choir to perform the piece on a given day. Constantly be on the alert for repertoire that is solid literature, but which has not been performed frequently at competitions and concerts in your area.
- Pay close attention to the appearance, attire, and attitude of the ensemble as they enter and leave the stage. As with a regular concert audience, adjudicators form an opinion of a choral ensemble before a note is sung, based on the appearance of the choir and the manner in which they walk onto the stage and onto the risers. This procedure should be practiced and observed until it flows smoothly.
- Prepare students for the unexpected and for singing in less than optimal conditions. Many things tend to happen at contests that can cause disruption of the schedule and interfere with the students' concentration. Prepare them for the fact that the acoustics, the piano, the audience (which is usually comprised of the students and parents with whom they are competing), the adjudicators, and the pressure of a competitive situation can all be disconcerting. There may be unexpected delays before the choir sings, or they may need to wait onstage, on the risers, as an adjudicator finishes his or her comments on the previous ensemble. Try to foresee any such situation and prepare the choir for it.
- If your choir's performance will deviate from the printed score, it is probably a good idea to include a note to this effect for the adjudicator. This would include transposing into a different key, adding or deleting

music, or altering a selection in any way. It is often highly desirable to make such alterations. Simply be sure the adjudicator knows about them and is aware that you, the conductor, are aware of the changes being made.

- After the contest, follow up on the experience with your students. If the judges have made written comments, share them with the choir—the good, the bad, and the ugly. If the comments were recorded, play the tapes for the students. Ask the students what *they* thought of their performance. Do the students agree or disagree with the evaluations and comments of the adjudicators? How do the students rate other performances they heard at contest? Use the experience of competition in a positive and educational way to enhance your students' musicianship.

Before, during, and after the competition, stress to the students the importance of doing their best. Whether a I, II, or whatever rating is assigned, make it clear that if they have done the best job they are capable of, they will have succeeded in your eyes.

✣ CLINICS AND FESTIVALS ✣

For the purposes of this discussion, clinics and festivals are defined as follows:

Clinic: An event where an outside expert comes to your school and works with your choir. The length of such an event may vary from one period to a full day or longer, and may or may not culminate in public performance.

Festival: An event that involves several choirs (or representatives from several choirs) who come together to work with an outside expert, usually culminating in a public performance.

These are operational definitions. One often hears the word *festival* applied to a contest, in which choirs come to a location to be rated. Such festivals sometimes also include a *clinic* in which one of the adjudicators comes to the stage at the conclusion of each ensemble's performance and works with the students for ten to twenty minutes, pointing out positive and negative aspects of their performance and offering suggestions for improvement.

This discussion concerns the planning and organization of clinics and festivals. Seriously consider hosting such events, for they can benefit both you and all of the students in the choir.

Planning Choral Clinics

A choral clinic at your school can have a huge positive impact on your program:

1. The students get another perspective on the music they are preparing.
2. A visiting clinician will usually offer a mix of rehearsal stategies and interpretive ideas, some of which may be new to the students and some of which will reinforce and amplify what you have been saying for months. When the clinician offers suggestions and strategies that are compatible with the things you have been saying all along, it reinforces your work. New ideas also help to make the music come alive for students and may offer you new insights.
3. It is helpful for you to see how someone else works with the choir and to have the opportunity to sit at the back of the room and quietly observe both the clinician and the students and the way they interact.
4. Students feel their efforts are important when an expert takes the time to work with them and helps them improve their music making.

The first step in planning such an event is to discuss the idea with your principal and to determine where it fits best into the school calendar and at what point in the year it will be most beneficial for the choir. Plan the clinic several months ahead. Clinics are most effective when they are scheduled on a regular school day. If this is not feasible, they also can be held outside the regular school day; with sufficient advanced notice and planning, students can adjust their schedules accordingly.

Perhaps the most important point in preparing for a successful clinic is to select the right clinician for your choir. There are some very fine choral conductors and music educators with excellent programs who do not work well with secondary school students. The best way to determine whether a clinician is right for your students is to observe him or her at work in a similar setting. It also helps to get recommendations from other choral directors you trust. Do not assume from attending a fine concert presented by the clinician's own ensemble that he or she will be effective in working with your students. Sometimes a director is highly effective in working with students over the course of a semester or a year, but unable to communicate effectively in the context of one or two hours or days.

If you are in your first or second year in a particular position, you may wish to bring in a person who is particularly strong in basic vocal technique. After a few years, you may wish to have an expert on style or performance practice work with your students on a particular piece of music. Different clinicians have different strengths. Consider the personality of the clinician as he or she works with choirs. Some clinicians are able to teach concepts of choral music in a very entertaining and lively fashion; others are more restrained and academic in approach. You will need to determine whether a particular clinician's methods are the right ones for your choir.

When you contact the prospective clinician, negotiate the fee. Give the clinician an idea of your choir, its performance level, and what you are hoping to gain from the clinic. Ask the clinician for a photo and some biographical information to use in preparing your students for the clinic and in publicizing it.

It is important to prepare the students for the visit of the clinician. They should have the music well learned in advance of the clinician's visit. If the students know at least the basic pitches and rhythms, then the clinician can focus on more sophisticated concerns. It is pointless to go to the extra effort and expense of bringing in a clinician and then have them spend their time (and your money) teaching the choir the correct notes. In addition, students should be aware the clinician may do things differently than their regular director, and that this is all right. Tempos, dynamics, and the expressive content of the music may be approached differently by the clinician. Students should be open to trying new things with the guest conductor.

Be sure to leave time in the schedule at the end of the event for you to meet with the clinician. This is an opportunity to ask any questions you may have about the clinician's approach, and a time when the clinician may make candid observations or suggestions to you concerning the choir.

After the clinic, solicit your students' reactions to the clinician. Undoubtedly there will be ideas the clinician used in rehearsal or suggestions made to you that will be helpful as you continue to rehearse the music.

Concerts and Clinics by Visiting Choirs

A very beneficial experience for your high school choir can be a visit from a choir on tour in the area. College and university choirs often are available to visit a school, to present a concert, and to listen to the host high school choir. The visiting director may be available for a brief clinic with your choir. Such experiences provide a variety of positive effects for all involved, and when a collegiate choral ensemble is touring in an area the cost for your school can be little or nothing. Seek out such opportunities for your students to hear the work of other choirs and to see the kinds of choral experiences that are available after high school.

Alert your students to choral concerts being presented in your area. Every time they have an opportunity to hear other ensembles sing, it broadens their perspective on choral music in general and on their own efforts in particular. It can be worthwhile to organize a trip for the entire choir to hear an evening concert by a fine choral ensemble. Perhaps the choir could provide the transportation and each student would purchase their own ticket as a means of controlling costs yet at the same time subsidizing the students' experience.

Festivals

A festival, as defined earlier, involves multiple choirs, or selected students from multiple choirs, combining forces for the preparation and presentation of a public concert under the direction of a guest conductor. Festivals are often sponsored by the music educators or choral directors' association in a given state, region, or district, or they may be presented by a particular school. Festivals can involve entire ensembles or quartets from ensembles, combining for rehearsal and performance.

As was the case with clinics, a key aspect of preparation for a festival is to be sure the student participants have the music learned when they arrive at the event. In this way, all participants will derive maximum benefit from the experience and from the clinician's expertise. If your students attend a festival, it is your responsibility to be certain they are well prepared. Sometimes, prefestival rehearsals are held to facilitate preparation. In any case, the better prepared your students are for a festival, the more benefit they will derive from participation.

If you decide to host a festival, then the preparation involves many of the same areas as in preparing for a clinic. In addition, you must decide on the format for the festival. Will it involve entire choirs or selected students? How many participants will be included? How will they be selected? If the festival involves entire choirs, will the clinician work with each choir individually, or will the entire time be devoted to the combined group? Will there be prefestival rehearsals to facilitate the learning of the music?

Depending on how it is organized, a festival can provide an opportunity for students who might not be included in a highly select ensemble like district, regional, or all-state chorus to have the experience of singing with a large choral ensemble under the direction of a notable choral conductor. Conversely, it can be made highly selective with competitive auditions or with each participating school sending a mixed quartet of their top singers. In planning the event, a decision must be made as to its nature and the population of student singers who will be included.

When you host a festival, there are many advantages for your students. Even if the festival is highly select, all of the students at the host school can be given the opportunity to observe rehearsals and to assist with the hosting duties. If your program is still in its early stages of growth, it is highly stimulating for students to observe how a more advanced choral ensemble rehearses and performs, and it can help motivate them to work toward such an experience for themselves.

Choir Retreats

It can be very useful at or near the beginning of the school year to have an opportunity for extended rehearsal, socialization, and time to get acquainted with the choir. A choir retreat can provide an opportunity for such activities.

A Saturday works best for this purpose. As with any event, secure administrative approval, clear a date in the school calendar, and plan a format. Such a retreat can be an excellent opportunity for parental involvement in food preparation, recreation, and general supervision.

It is desirable to plan such a retreat in a location with recreational facilities for swimming, softball, or volleyball, and with the necessary facilities for food preparation and service. The schedule for the day could be as follows:

9:00–9:30 A.M.	Get-acquainted activity
9:30–11:00 A.M.	Rehearsal
11:00–11:20 A.M.	Snack
11:20 A.M.–12:30 P.M.	Recreational Activities
12:30–1:30 P.M.	Lunch
1:30–3:00 P.M.	Rehearsal
3:00–5:00 P.M.	Recreational Activities
5:00	Supper

The balance between rehearsal and recreation can be altered as necessary, but there should be some of each. Pay special attention to structuring rehearsals to give students a feeling of success and accomplishment. The recreational periods should be designed to provide opportunities for students to become better acquainted.

✣ TOURS AND TRAVEL ✣

Unquestionably, travel is a very effective motivator and aid to choir recruitment. The fact that a choir travels to a festival in another city, takes a trip to perform at Disney World or somewhere similar, or presents a concert tour in a variety of interesting locations can be a major inducement for new members to become part of the program and can help motivate the students already involved. Literally the entire world is available to the choir that has sufficient interest in and financial support for travel. The question is how the travel fits into the framework of the comprehensive choral music education program.

Travel can be a highly educational, broadening, and entertaining experience for students. An exchange concert with another school can be an inexpensive and enjoyable travel possibility. A concert tour to Europe, in which a choir can perform pieces in the same concert venues where the pieces were performed originally under the direction of the composer, can be an unforgettable experience.

The first decision you need to make concerning choir travel is how the travel fits into the educational program of the ensemble. As with so many activities (e.g., concerts, fund-raising activities, contests) it is important to keep the travel plans in the proper perspective so an upcoming tour or trip to a festival does not become the entire focus of the program. With that cautionary note in mind, if you, the students, and the parents wish to raise the necessary funds and the administration approves, then planning can proceed.

An important consideration of a specific trip will be the cost. Of course, the further the group travels and the longer the time on the road, the more expensive the trip will be. Many variables can make a trip more or less expensive, however. What kind of accommodations will be required? How many students can stay in a room? Are overnight stays in private homes with host families acceptable and available? Are student accommodations at a university available? How will the group travel? By air? By bus?

You may have sufficient contacts and experience to organize a tour or trip yourself. A weekend trip to an area with which you are familiar might be relatively easy to organize. If you have the necessary contacts in churches or schools to organize the concerts, it is relatively straightforward to select a motorcoach company and proceed.

Figures 8.2 and 8.3 show two itineraries for concert choir trips. The first is for a one-day trip to Washington, D.C. Does this sound like an enjoyable day for the students and director? Not really: three concerts in one day, along with a two-hour coach trip in the morning and again in the evening. Insufficient time to look at even a small section of the Smithsonian Institution. No real time for lunch. This is an endurance contest rather than a choir trip. I speak with conviction, since this was an actual trip taken by my high school choir. A more reasonable schedule is illustrated in Figure 8.3.

WILLIAM PENN HIGH SCHOOL CHOIR
Trip Schedule

Washington Cathedral
U.S. Soldier's and Airman's Home
Gettysburg United Methodist Church

6:15 A.M.	Depart William Penn
8:30 A.M.	Arrive Washington Cathedral
9:00–10:00 A.M.	Rehearsal at Cathedral
10:30–11:00 A.M.	Program Time
11:00–12:00 A.M.	Service at Cathedral
12:15–12:45 P.M.	Tour of the Cathedral
12:45 P.M.	Depart Washington Cathedral
1:15 P.M.	Arrive at Soldier's and Airman's Home
1:30 P.M.	Concert
2:15 P.M.	Depart Soldier's and Airman's Home
2:30 P.M.	Arrive Smithsonian Institute
2:30–4:15 P.M.	Free Time
4:15 P.M.	Depart Smithsonian Institute
6:00 P.M.	Arrive Gettysburg United Methodist Church
6:00–7:00 P.M.	Dinner at Gettysburg United Methodist Church
7:00–7:30 P.M.	Rehearsal at Church
8:00–9:30 P.M.	Concert at Church
9:45 P.M.	Depart Gettysburg United Methodist Church
10:45 P.M.	Arrive at William Penn

Get up early enough to eat a good breakfast before we leave. Chorus members should bring a bag lunch if they want to eat on the bus as we travel from the cathedral to the Soldier's Home. There will be time for Chorus members to purchase something to eat at 2:30 at the Smithsonian Institute. There will be dinner provided at Gettysburg United Methodist Church at 6:00 P.M.

FIGURE 8.2 William Penn Washington Trip

Hampton, Virginia, Trip: William Penn H.S. Choir
Schedule for Trip

Friday, April 29

William Penn H.S. Choir departs from Pershing Ave. Lobby	6:00 A.M.
William Penn Choir arrives at Phoebus H.S.	12:00 noon
Lunch at Phoebus H.S.	12:30–1:00 P.M.
William Penn H.S. Choir rehearsal in auditorium	1:15–2:30 P.M.
Combined Choir rehearsal	2:30–4:00 P.M.
William Penn Choir members and chaperones meet hosts	4:00–4:30 P.M.
Unpack and dinner with host	4:30–7:30 P.M.
?? Social event ?? ???	8:00–10:30 P.M.

Saturday, April 30

William Penn Choir reports to Phoebus H.S. for departure to Busch Gardens	9:00 A.M.
William Penn Choir arrives at Busch Gardens	10:30 A.M.
Free time for choir at Busch Gardens	10:30–5:15 P.M.
Board buses for return to Hampton	5:15 P.M.
William Penn Choir departs Busch Gardens	5:30 P.M.
William Penn Choir arrives at Phoebus H.S.	6:30 P.M.
Concert at Phoebus H.S.	8:00 P.M.

Sunday, May 1

William Penn H.S. Choir departs Hampton	1:00 P.M.
William Penn Choir arrives at William Penn High School	7:00 P.M.

FIGURE 8.3 Hampton, Virginia, Trip

A more extended tour, or a visit to a distant city, may require the services of a company who can assist with the travel, accommodations, and concert arrangements. In the last few years, there has been a proliferation of companies who sponsor music festivals, make tour arrangements (both national and international), or provide interesting concert venues in attractive concert halls. The quality and cost of such services vary widely, so carefully investigate any company you are considering.

If you work with a travel company, what services do they provide? Will they set up concerts for your ensemble? If so, what will they do to promote the events? How will the revenue from the concerts be used? Ask for references. Ascertain how well the company has done in working with groups previously. Has anyone attended the concerts they arrange? How long has the company been in business? If the company does not have an established record in working with musical organizations, avoid using their services. They may prove to be excellent, but let someone else provide them with their initial experience in setting up musical events and take the risk involved in working with an unknown company.

If you are traveling to a commercial music festival (a contest, actually, according to our definition), determine how many choral ensembles will be participating at the particular site. Will you have the opportunity to see and hear the other choirs? Who are the adjudicators? Is there the opportunity for a clinic with an adjudicator? Based on previous years, are the comments from the adjudicators constructive and educationally sound? Does the emphasis seem to be on education as well as competition? What is included in the package provided by the festival organizer? How much additional expense will need to be borne by students? There is a wide range of quality represented in the many commercial festivals available today.

✣ SPECIALIZED ENSEMBLES ✣

It is not within the scope of this text to include an exhaustive discussion of the various kinds of specialized ensembles that can be included in a comprehensive choral music education program. Our intent here is to present some basic ideas concerning specialized ensembles and some guidelines for developing some of the more common varieties.

The choral curriculum is discussed in more detail in Chapter 9. Every choral program should include a select and a nonselect ensemble. In this way the basic musical needs of every student in the school will be met. Students who wish to participate in the choral program should be required to participate in the primary ensemble before they are allowed to audition for one of the specialized groups. In this way, the program retains the correct educational priority and emphasis on the primary choir. Beyond this basic requirement, the kind of ensembles to include in a program should be based on your expertise and the interests of your students.

Both students and teacher must have interest in an ensemble in order for it to be a success, but as a practical matter if you are competent and interested in a particular kind of ensemble, it is likely student interest will be aroused and a tradition of success established. If there is high student interest in a particular type of ensemble, it may be worthwhile for you to seek out additional training to become proficient in the area in question.

Show Choirs

Show choirs are popular in some areas of the country and can be a means of building great student interest in the choral program. Show choirs are also controversial. An important issue is related to the proportion of "show" versus "choir" in the show choir. Proponents argue show choirs provide students with opportunities to perform music in a style that can provide gainful employment for them, movement and music are natural partners, and the choreography involved in show choirs enhances the music. Critics contend show choirs are not legitimate choral ensembles, they detract from the success of other choral ensembles in the program, student participants are often exploited to provide good school public relations, the music performed by show choirs is not of acceptable quality, and their popularity cheapens the choral art.

My position is that there are good and bad show choirs as well as good and bad show choir music. In some situations show choirs are an appropriate part of the choral curriculum and in other instances they receive undue emphasis. In some school settings students are exploited through a heavy schedule of performances, but in others they are not. Show choirs perform one style of choral music, some of which is of high quality and some of which is poor. The same things could be said of most kinds of specialized choral ensembles.

If you wish to have a show choir, or you find yourself in a situation where it is expected that a show choir will be part of the curriculum, the following are a few basic suggestions.

1. Be sure to create a choir that is choreographed, rather than a group of dancers who also try to sing. In teaching material to the group, teach the singing first, and be certain the choir members are comfortable with the music *before* working on the choreography.
2. Unless you have strong talent in the area of choreography, engage the services of someone to design and teach the movement. It is important to find a person who understands that the movement should enhance the singing rather than detract from it. People who teach dance for a living often have difficulty with this concept. Perhaps there is an alumnus of the group who is available to assist with the choreography. Initially, it is possible that someone or some group of individuals in the choir may have the interest and experience to do the choreography.
3. Costumes for the show choir should be dramatic and showy, but they should be designed so students can accomplish the necessary movements comfortably and without embarrassment; this is not the place for outfits that are too tight, translucent, or feature plunging necklines for the women.
4. Suit the choreography to the music. It is permissible and desirable to have some elaborate and energetic movements, but place them in the interludes when the choir is not singing. When the choir, or a section of the choir is singing, be sure they are facing the audience. It is disconcerting to the listener to have a group of singers suddenly do an about-face and march upstage—the sound disappears. For a ballad, place the group in a pose, and focus entirely on the sound.
5. Smaller is better. The larger the group, the harder it is to choreograph. The more choreography included in the show, the more difficult it will be to make the music sound good.
6. To make this style of music work, particularly in a large room, requires a sound system. The better the quality of the sound system, the better the ensemble will sound (assuming the music is well prepared). Give the choir ample time to rehearse with the sound system so they are ac-

customed to holding the microphone, picking it up and replacing it on the stand as needed, and other matters specifically related to the sound equipment.

7. Many good video resources are available that can aid in teaching movements to a show choir. Many choral publications also include an instructional video in which choreography designed for the selection is demonstrated. There are also some books and videos that deal with show choir choreography in general.
8. A good show choir can be in great demand. The public enjoys the entertainment provided at the concerts, and school administrators appreciate the good public relations that can result from appearances by the show choir. Keep the goals and objectives of the total choral music curriculum in mind, and do not overschedule the show choir. Remember that performance is a part of the choral music education process; it is not the ultimate goal.

Madrigal Ensembles

Madrigal ensembles and madrigal feasts have achieved great popularity over the past few years. Madrigal singing is an excellent way to build student musicianship, since it is a kind of vocal chamber music. As is the case with show choirs, if a madrigal ensemble is part of your choral program, it should be available for students as a supplement to their primary choral experience. A few points concerning madrigal ensembles may help prevent problems.

1. The madrigal ensemble should be limited to anywhere from ten to twenty-four singers. Madrigals were designed to be sung in intimate surroundings by a small group of singers, probably one per part. To present them with some authenticity, the group should be limited in size.
2. Elizabethan costumes help create the proper character and period for the madrigal singers (see Figure 8.4). Perhaps the drama department has costumes from a Shakespearian production that can be borrowed. Alternatively, costumes could be constructed by parent volunteers if there is sufficient interest and expertise.
3. A variety of resources are available today, with information concerning all aspects of madrigal ensembles, including the presentation of madrigal feasts. Some are listed at the end of the chapter.
4. Presenting a madrigal feast is a multifaceted event, which can involve both choral and instrumental music, dance, drama, and food service. This is advantageous in the sense that you can determine what resources are available and build a madrigal feast around them, maximizing areas of strength and minimizing areas of weakness.
5. To have a successful madrigal feast requires good food service. Do what you can to assure the food tastes good, is served at the appropri-

ate temperature, and at the correct time. Carefully review with the food service personnel how the food should be served and the sequence of music, drama, and food service involved. If it is the first time a feast has been presented, or if the food service personnel are new, it would be worthwhile to have a sample meal prepared in advance of the performance so any problems can be corrected. Although the quality of every aspect of the feast should be as high as possible, most people notice problems with food service, whereas musical flaws may escape their attention.

6. If the madrigal feast becomes an annual event, determine which elements should be retained each year and what should be varied. If everything is changed, then guests will have no idea what to expect. Some elements should be retained and made a tradition. Conversely, if every detail remains unchanged from year to year, the event can quickly become stale for both the director, the performers, and the guests.
7. Madrigal singers must be able to sing with great expression and to interact comfortably with the audience. In this style of singing, there will be times when each voice must carefully blend with others in the section and other instances where the tone quality should be more soloistic. Although madrigal ensembles tend to focus on music from a particular style and period, there is a great variety of music represented.
8. There are materials available (music, scripts, etc.) with information concerning madrigal feasts with a non-Elizabethan focus, such as dinner in the colonial United States or in the period of Dickens. There are many thematic possibilities.

FIGURE 8.4 University of Missouri–St. Louis Madrigal Ensemble

Vocal Jazz

Vocal jazz ensembles require strong musicians to be successful. Some of the vocal jazz arrangements available today are among the most technically demanding choral music on the market. There are others that have been written for school choirs or have been modified (simplified).

If you are interested in establishing a vocal jazz ensemble and you have some background in it, by all means do so, because it is an excellent means of developing musicianship. If you are personally lacking in experience, find a successful vocal jazz program to observe, and talk with the director. There are excellent recordings of many vocal jazz arrangements by currently popular groups. Listening to ensembles like The Manhattan Transfer, Take 6, Rare Silk, and others will provide some idea of vocal jazz style.

A good quality sound system is required to perform vocal jazz effectively. Another requirement is an excellent instrumental rhythm section.

Barbershop

Barbershop quartet singing continues to enjoy great popularity among people of all ages. As with every other kind of specialized vocal ensemble, it requires specialized knowledge and strong musicianship to create a fine quartet.

The Society for the Preservation and Encouragement of Barbershop Quartet Singing in America has many resources available for choral music educators at low cost. If there is a chapter near you, invite a quartet to come to your school for a demonstration. A particular advantage of barbershop singing is that it can help to stimulate male interest in the choral program and help combat the idea that singing is somehow sissy or something more appropriate for women.

In the past, there was a tendency on the part of barbershop ensembles (both male and female) to sing with an unnaturally pushed straight tone. Currently, this does not seem to be the case, but barbershoppers should always employ the same kind of natural free sound as other choral singers.

Men's and Women's Choirs

Although the palette of timbres available in a men's or women's choir is more limited than in a mixed ensemble, there is a large and ever-increasing body of men's and women's choral repertoire available today. The importance of these kinds of ensembles has been recognized by the ACDA, which has established national repertoire and standards committees (with regional and local committees as well) related to each of the two areas.

In American public schools in the 1990s, women's choirs are much more prevalent than men's ensembles. Often, nearly all interested male singers in a school are needed in the select choir, but because of the larger number of women interested in singing, a treble choir is established to accommodate those who do not participate in the mixed ensemble.

Whether or not your choral curriculum includes an ongoing men's or women's choir, the addition of an SSA or TTB selection to a program presented by the mixed choir can add pleasing variety to a concert. In either case, seating/standing arrangements for women's and men's ensembles are found in Figures 8.5 a through d.

Figures 8.5a and 8.5b illustrate two possible configurations for four-part men's ensembles. Figure 8.5a is an arrangement that works well when the choir is numerically unbalanced with a shortage of tenors. Figure 8.5b is the optimal arrangement for a well-balanced men's ensemble.

Figures 8.5c and 8.5d illustrate sitting/standing arrangements for women's ensembles. Figure 8.5c is for a three-part women's group. The placing of the S1 part in the middle allows the two voices that typically harmonize (S2 and A) to tune easily to the melody. Another popular configuration that has worked successfully for four-part women's choirs is illustrated in Figure 8.5d.

FIGURE 8.5 Seating Charts for Men's and Women's Choirs

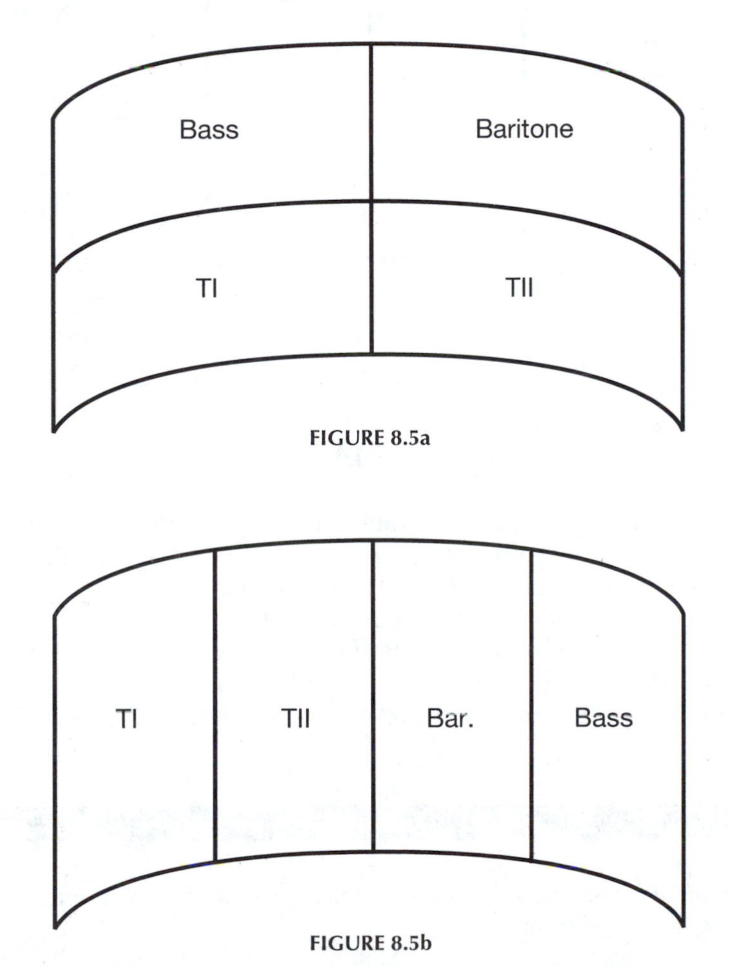

FIGURE 8.5a

FIGURE 8.5b

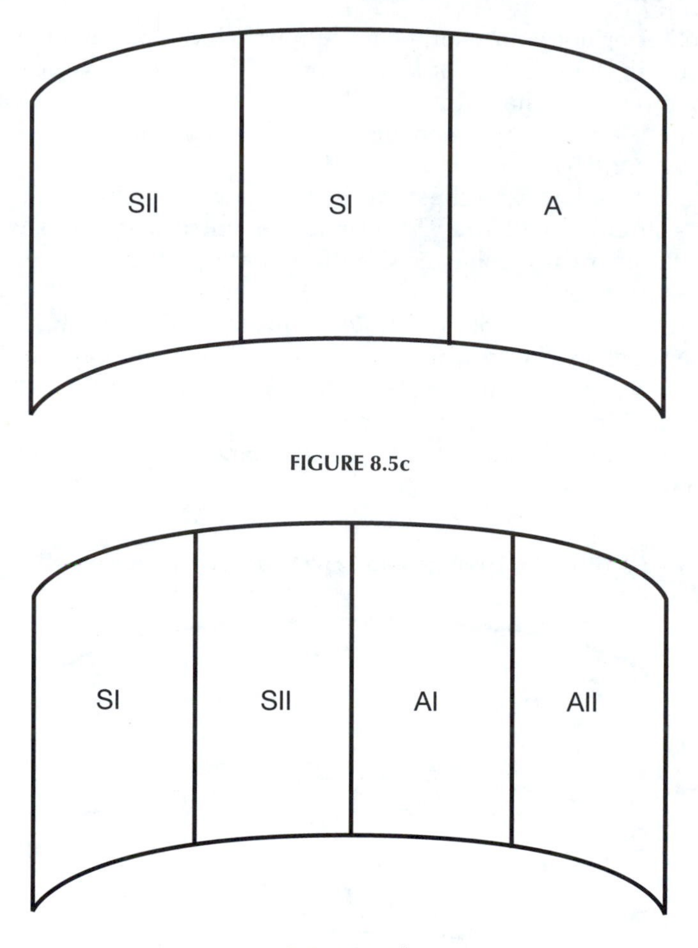

FIGURE 8.5c

FIGURE 8.5d

✣ SUMMARY ✣

Special events and specialized ensembles have a place in the comprehensive choral music education program. They can enrich and deepen the personal and musical development of each student. The primary basis for their inclusion in the program should be their educational value.

Specialized ensembles should be a part of a balanced program and not overshadow the primary choir. Such ensembles should draw on the interests of students and the expertise and background of the choral music educator.

Questions

1. On what basis should special events be included in the activities of your choral program?

2. What kinds of specialized ensembles do you believe would work well in your choral program? Why?
3. What are some arguments for and against choral competitions? What is your personal position on this issue?
4. Are there any differences in selecting literature for a choir to perform at competition versus a concert?
5. Distinguish between a clinic and a festival, as defined in this chapter.
6. What criteria should be used in selecting a clinician to work with your choir?
7. How would you evaluate a travel company's ability to arrange a tour for a choral ensemble?
8. What are some factors in selecting a choreographer and creating choreography for a show choir?

Note

1. Gordon H. Lamb, *Choral Techniques*, 3rd ed. (Dubuque, IA: William C. Brown, 1988, p. 234).

Suggested Reading

ALBRECHT, SALLY. *Choral Music in Motion*. East Stroudsburg, PA: Music in Action, 1984.

ANDERSON, DOUG. *Jazz and Show Choir Handbook*. Chapel Hill, NC: Hinshaw, 1978.

BRANDVIK, PAUL. *The Complete Madrigal Dinner Booke*. San Diego: Curtis Music, 1984.

FISSINGER, EDWIN. *The Madrigal Concert: Choral Music for the Madrigal Dinner, Renaissance Fest, and Madrigal Concert*. Milwaukee: Jenson, 1981.

GARRETSON, ROBERT L. *Conducing Choral Music*. Englewood Cliffs, NJ: Prentice Hall, 1988.

HABERLEN, JOHN, and STEPHEN ROSOLACK. *Elizabethan Madrigal Dinners*. Champaign, IL: Mark Foster, 1978.

LAMB, GORDON H. *Choral Techniques, (*3rd ed.) Dubuque, IA: William C. Brown, 1988.

MILLER, KENNETH E. *Vocal Music Education*. Englewood Cliffs, NJ: Prentice Hall, 1988.

ROE, PAUL F. *Choral Music Education*. Englewood Cliffs, NJ: Prentice-Hall, 1983.

Chapter Nine

Comprehensive Choral Music Education[1]

✣✣✣

✣ INTRODUCTION ✣

Throughout this text we have used the term *comprehensive choral music education.* A brief explanation of it was presented in the Introduction and each chapter has focused on a particular and specific area of skill or knowledge important to the comprehensive choral music educator.

This chapter expands on the basic premise we presented in the Introduction. We first discuss the development of a carefully conceived philosophy of music education. Then we place comprehensive choral music education in historical perspective, alluding to the work of some music educators and aestheticians. Finally, we present the basic principles of comprehensive choral music education. We synthesize the many seemingly disparate areas discussed throughout the book and clarify their relationship to the overall approach.

✣ DEVELOPING A PERSONAL PHILOSOPHY OF CHORAL MUSIC EDUCATION ✣

Every music educator has a philosophy that helps determine his or her approach to any situation in the classroom and in life. Even if you have never articulated that philosophy or even consciously thought of it, it will be apparent in your actions.

Consider the following choral music educators:

Director A: Director A has an award-winning concert choir. Each spring the group participates in district choral festival where they consistently receive the highest rating. They also travel to a commercial festival in some other city each year. The students have an enjoyable time, the choir again receives high ratings, and even has won the "sweepstakes trophy" awarded to the best choir at the festival. In addition to the concert choir, the rest of Director A's teaching load consists of a women's chorus, a men's group, a theory class, and a music appreciation class. The only class Director A is truly interested in, however, is the concert choir, and he has found the most efficient way to produce high-quality performances from the choir is to drill the music into them by rote. The rest of the teaching schedule is given little attention and preparation. The principal, the parents, and the school board all seem to be pleased with Mr. A's efforts, since his concert choir has earned a reputation for choral excellence throughout the state.

Director B: Director B has been teaching for twenty-three years in the same school. Her program is well established. Director B is known as a fun individual. The literature selected for the choral ensembles is often superficial, but it is easily learned, there is a lot of humor in the classroom, and a good time is had by all. As Ms. B's principal has been heard to say on more than one occasion, "All I'm concerned with is that the kids have a great time and learn to love music. Ms. B really does a bang-up job! Students leave her class enthusiastic and eager for more music classes." As was the case with Mr. A, Ms. B is quite well regarded by parents, students, and administrators because she makes her classroom fun.

Director C: Director C receives satisfaction from watching her students grow musically and personally. She spends a large amount of time selecting music that is varied in style, composer, and period and carefully monitors student growth. Performance opportunities are carefully selected and are a part of the ongoing music education process that occurs in her classroom. The students who have participated in the program for a year or more have become more independent in their musical decision making, sometimes astonishing Mrs. C. with their perception and knowledge. However, of the three fictitious choral educators described here, Mrs. C is the least popular with her parents and administrators. In fact, a parent of one of Mrs. C's students whose niece sings in the concert choir at Mr. A's school has talked with the principal about the need for a more competitive choir that travels extensively and enters more contests and festivals.

Each of the choral music educators just described has a philosophy of choral music education. They may not have thought about it much recently (or perhaps ever), but it is obvious from the way they run their programs. Director A has obviously made performance the primary objective of his program. According to his philosophy, a high rating is the measure of success, and those he works with and for seem to be pleased. Director B believes having a good time and entertaining both the students in the program and those who come to the concerts is of critical importance. Success, for Ms. B, is measured in terms of her own fun-loving personal and educational philosophy and it is a good match with the attitude of her principal toward students and music. Mrs. C is the hardest of the three teachers for administrators, parents, and teaching colleagues to understand. Her emphasis is on the students and their personal and musical growth. This growth is not always obvious to casual observers.

Each of these three teachers feels successful personally. Obviously, Mrs. C. has taken the comprehensive approach to instruction, and her accomplishments are of the most lasting value for the people the program is intended to serve—the students. Does this mean performance level is unimportant? No. Does it mean music instruction should not be fun? Definitely not. Performance standards, enjoyment, and student growth are all commendable and should all be a part of the successful choral music education program. The emphasis they are each given in a particular program depends on the choral music educator's philosophy.

Each of you who intends to have a career in choral music education or may already be pursuing one must develop a cogent, logical philosophy of music. Why is a philosophy important?

1. It provides inspiration to the music educator.
2. It provides justification for the inclusion of choral music education in the curriculum.
3. It provides a basis for the selection of goals, objectives, and activities to be included in the program.

Let us examine each of these three factors in the importance of philosophy in a bit more detail.

1. It provides inspiration to the music educator. On a day-to-day basis, choral work is not uniformly exciting, affirming, and immediately rewarding. There will be days when you may feel overwhelmed with the negative aspects of the position (e.g., a student's behavior is disappointing, an administrator expresses dissatisfaction—rightly or wrongly—with some aspect of the program, or parents call to express the opinion their child was treated unfairly in the selection of soloists for the upcoming concert). At times like these, your philosophy serves as an anchor. When it seems the things you are trying to accomplish are unappreciated and successes are few and far between, the choral music educator who has carefully thought through *why* he or she is doing the job has a secure and consistent internal source of inspiration and encouragement no matter what external pressures occur.

2. It provides justification for the inclusion of choral music education in the curriculum. School programs in music and the other arts are currently under attack. Recent years have seen federal aid for education sharply decreased. At the same time, local and state economies have been unable to replace these losses. Thus there is a limited amount of funding available for education. This has resulted in increased scrutiny of current educational offerings.

The temptation for administrators and school boards seeking to balance the budget is to view music as an extracurricular frill. Only if we have thought through our philosophy of music education, have a clear understanding of the importance of music in the school curriculum, and can demonstrate the way in which our philosophy is implemented through our program will we be able to mount an effective defense against those who seek to eliminate or relegate to extracurricular status programs in choral music education.

3. It provides a basis for the selection of goals, objectives, and activities to be included in the program. Probably the most important reason for having a carefully developed philosophy of choral music education is that it provides guidance in establishing activities, goals, and objectives. Without a philosophy to undergird and lend cohesion to a program, it will lack direction. Certainly our students, parents, administrators, members of the media, and a variety of other constituencies will provide an agenda for our program (or for its elimination) if we do not have a philosophical justification for it ourselves. Our philosophical viewpoint will guide the activities we select for our students.

To develop a cogent personal philosophy of choral music education, the question needs to be asked, "Why is it important to have choral music in the schools?" Here are some answers to this question:

1. Music is basic to every society and provides a vehicle for the transmission of cultural values.
2. Music is a basic expression of our humanity.
3. Music stimulates affective and aesthetic experiences.
4. Twentieth-century Americans are avid consumers of music and should be educated so as to become informed consumers.

No society has ever been discovered that did not have a musical tradition. Music and the other arts provide a vital link to the past. The history of a culture is transmitted from one generation to another through works of art. Therefore, the arts in general, and music specifically, must be studied in order to gain an understanding of our society. The study of music of other societies and cultures facilitates an understanding of life in other times and places. The study of music of the various ethnic groups comprising contemporary American society encourages an understanding of the diversity of our culture.

In addition to providing a means for discovering our collective cultural identity and traditions, music also is a way to discover personal strengths, limitations, and identity. Through experiences in music, we become more fully human.

Music is an excellent vehicle for affective and aesthetic experiences. The affective domain focuses on feelings or emotions. Perhaps to a greater degree than any other subject, music facilitates the education of feelings as students respond to the qualities of great choral music in rehearsal and performance. The feelingful response of students to the choral music they experience, based on a heightened understanding of the content of the music studied, brings us to the realm of aesthetic education, which we discuss later in the chapter.

Americans purchase millions of dollars worth of compact discs, tapes, records, and videos, along with the tape decks, CD players, videocassette recorders, and other equipment on which to play them. Radio stations present music of all descriptions, and their presence is pervasive as people work, drive their automobiles, and relax. An entire industry has sprung up whose purpose is to manipulate people's feelings through music. Audiotapes are marketed that have been designed to make us eat faster in a restaurant, be more productive in the workplace, or more relaxed when visiting the dentist. Although these seem to be relatively benign uses of music, they can be utilized for less salutary reasons. Indeed, demagogues have used music to foment negative emotions (for example, at Nazi party rallies of the 1930s). The lyrics of some contemporary music have generated debate about their influence on young listeners. So it is incumbent on the American educational system to educate musical consumers, enabling them to make informed choices of the music they listen to and adding to their understanding of the potential of music to manipulate emotions.

There are many nonmusical reasons for including music in the school curriculum, such as the development of citizenship, learning about pride in the group, promoting good health through teaching about correct posture and breathing, developing leadership and human relations skills. Also, many of the things we teach and learn in music class transfer to other academic areas and facilitate the learning of English, mathematics, and social studies.

But music, because of its unique qualities, requires no nonmusical justification for inclusion in the curriculum. Music is intrinsically worthy of study. In fact, choral music educators who attempt to base their philosophical positions on nonmusical justifications for music programs are in dangerous territory. If, for example, music is justified strictly on the basis of the way it facilitates the learning of math or English, then the obvious question is "Why not simply do the more efficient thing and simply teach math and English?"

Take time to consider why you have decided on a career in choral music education, the value of music in the schools, and your personal ideas concerning the broad goals of instruction. Obviously, the philosophical basis of this book is a comprehensive approach to choral music education. It is up to you to take the ideas presented here and the results of your own thinking and to create a personal philosophical statement concerning your work in the schools.

Once you have created your personal philosophical statement, compare it to the philosophy of any district where you are considering employment. The two statements should be compatible. Also, from time to time, review what you have written. As you gain experience in choral music education, you will undoubtedly find that your ideas and priorities evolve. Changes in your thinking should be reflected in your philosophy and implemented in your teaching.

✣ CHORAL MUSIC IN THE UNITED STATES ✣

Singing has been an important part of U.S. music education from its inception. The colonial singing schools, the establishment of vocal music classes in the Boston public schools, the development of nineteenth-century singing societies, and the choral innovations of the 1920s and 1930s, leading to the present day, have all focused on vocal performance.

The Eighteenth and Nineteenth Centuries

In colonial America, the need for improved singing at church services led to the establishment of singing schools. Taught by a traveling singing master, the singing school was typically located in a church, tavern, or other public building with adequate space, providing instruction in both music reading and the rote singing of hymns. It lasted for a period of weeks, after which the singing master received compensation for his services from the clientele served and moved on to a new location. The singing school provided an early example of an accountable music program that filled a need for enhanced musical skills. Singing schools flourished from around the second decade of the eighteenth century until the emergence of public school music, beginning with the establishment of the first American public school music program in Boston in 1838.

Another institution that helped foster the composition and performance of choral music as well as encourage public awareness and appreciation of choral singing was the singing society. Singing societies became popular in the first half of the nineteenth century, both in Europe and the United States. The Handel and Haydn Society of Boston, which became one of the most prestigious musical organizations in the country, was established in 1815. Other singing societies were created, primarily in the eastern states, including well-regarded ensembles in New York, Chicago, Philadelphia, and Cincinnati. These societies, along with similar organizations in Europe, provided a receptive audience for the choral-orchestral works of the European Romantic composers.

The singing schools and the singing societies were important to the development of choral music in the United States. Both institutions sought to improve the caliber of vocal music. The singing schools, established in the eighteenth century, were utilitarian in that they were established to enhance worship in colonial churches by improving the singing of the congregations. The singing societies, developed in the nineteenth century, were intended to foster the singing of high-quality choral music for its own sake and were therefore motivated by the intrinsic merit of choral singing. The intrinsic importance of choral music must be an important component of our own justifications for music programs in the schools even today, as the twentieth century nears its end.

In 1838, Lowell Mason established the first public school music program in the United States in Boston, Massachusetts. During the second half of the nineteenth century, increasing numbers of school systems included vocal or choral music education in their programs (though not necessarily in their curricula). The kinds of singing experiences provided for students ranged from oratorio performances, sometimes involving the entire student population, to group recreational and assembly singing, to glee clubs that performed lighter popular musical selections. Some of these choral experiences were a required part of the curriculum, and others were extracurricular.

At the turn of the century, the nation was primarily rural, and communications were still relatively primitive. Although the gramophone record was introduced in England in 1901, it would be another fifteen years before recordings became popular in the United States, and it was not until the 1920s that regular radio broadcasts were firmly established. Choral music in the schools was stimulated and delimited by the individual vision and creativity of the local music teacher, administration, and school board.

While it is clear that there was significant musical activity in the United States during the nineteenth century, the situation did not encourage the development of a consensus on the kinds of choral experiences that should be provided for students. There was no national organization to provide a forum for discussions among music educators.

In 1907, the Music Supervisors National Conference was created, at a meeting of music teachers in Keokuk, Iowa. Twenty-six teachers had gathered to learn a new teaching technique developed by Philip Hayden, a music teacher in the Keokuk public schools. It was decided they should meet regularly to discuss issues related to music in the schools. The organization changed its name to the Music Educators National Conference (MENC) in 1934, and it is presently the primary professional organization for music teachers in U.S. public schools. Today, the *Music Educators Journal,* its flagship publication, along with a variety of other books, journals, pamphlets, promotional materials, and videotapes, as well as regular national, regional, and state conferences and political advocacy activities, foster professional growth and development for the profession.

During the first half of the twentieth century, several other events, personalities, and trends influenced the development of choral music education in the United States. The first of these was the a cappella choral tradition.

The A Cappella Tradition

The a cappella tradition began at St. Olaf College in Northfield, Minnesota, when F. Melius Christiansen founded the St. Olaf Lutheran Choir in 1912. Although there were certain antecedents to this development (the first choir actually termed an a cappella choir was established at Northwestern University by Peter Lutkin in 1892, and there were several well-known and well-regarded African American choral ensembles which predated that), it was the touring program of the St. Olaf Choir and the resultant national acclaim it received that moved collegiate, high school, and church choirs around the country in the direction of a cappella singing.

The term *a cappella* literally means "in the chapel" and originally simply referred to music that was intended to be sung in that setting without instruments, or at least without an independent instrumental part. The a cappella style of choral singing that developed at St. Olaf College in the early twentieth century, although it did involve unaccompanied choral singing, included several other distinctive elements. The starting pitch for each selection was provided by a member of the choir using a pitch pipe, in as subtle a manner as possible. The tonal ideal was a perfectly blended sound, in which the characteristics of individual voices were merged into polished choral unity. Another hallmark of the St. Olaf Choir was secure intonation, and much of the choir's rehearsal time was devoted to the refinement of these two elements of blend and intonation. The range of literature performed tended toward Christiansen's own quasi-Romantic compositions and arrangements and other unaccompanied repertoire. Music was memorized and ten hours of weekly rehearsal time was devoted to the preparation of a relatively small number of selections for performance on tour.

The acclaim given to the St. Olaf Choir, particularly in the 1920s and 1930s, attracted the attention of choral directors around the country. Numerous other colleges and universities formed a cappella ensembles. For the first time, a variety of fine collegiate choral ensembles were heard by large numbers of people in locations throughout the United States.

High schools around the country also began to assimilate a cappella techniques, and by the middle of the 1930s the tradition had reached its peak of popularity. Even in schools that did not include an a cappella ensemble, the influence of the style was evident in higher standards of performance, a new emphasis on unaccompanied singing, and the programming of compositions written in the a cappella style, exemplified by the works of F. Melius Christiansen. Christiansen presented annual choral workshops during the summer months that were attended by thousands of choral conductors over the years, at which he described and demonstrated his techniques.

As the a cappella style of singing gained prominence, a reaction against some of its characteristics occurred. Some aspects of the style that were found objectionable included the narrow range of literature performed, the vocal demands made on singers as their voices were assimilated into the characteristic a cappella blend, and the aesthetic desirability of the distinctive, unitary tone quality resulting from a cappella choral techniques. Some echoes of this debate linger to the present day.

A Change in Direction

Beginning in the 1940s, the mainstream of American choral music began to change course, away from the a cappella ideal toward a new emphasis on the integrity of the musical score, a varied concept of choral tone, and a higher level of formal training for choral music educators. Several diverse factors contributed to this change in direction.

The choral philosophy and techniques of Robert Shaw began to attract national attention in the 1940s. He was hired by Fred Waring in 1938 to conduct the Waring Glee Club. In 1945, Shaw left the Waring organization to develop his own ensemble, and it was his work with the Collegiate Chorale and the Robert Shaw Chorale over the next two decades that best exemplifies his approach to choral music. There are many aspects of Shaw's personality and choral techniques that have had an impact on American choral conductors (these are well described by Swan, 1988),[2] but the most important for our discussion are his emphasis on the integrity of the musical score and on the performance of choral/orchestral masterworks, and the varied tone quality he elicited from his singers.

Shaw's feelings regarding the integrity of the musical score crystallized during a year of intensive study (1943–1944) with Julius Herford, which led to a collaboration between the two that continued until Herford's death in 1981. Shaw assimilated Herford's uniquely personal and intensive approach to the structural and contextual score analysis of choral masterworks. The idea that the music of Palestrina, Brahms, and Beethoven could each require a distinctly different choral concept was antithetical to the a cappella notion that a single beautifully blended sound was appropriate for all types of literature. Shaw's emphasis on the performance of extended choral/orchestral compositions ran counter to the prevailing custom of programming relatively short, unaccompanied sacred pieces performed in a cappella style.

These changes in philosophy and choral technique were reinforced by other developments in the 1950s and 1960s. The expansion of opportunities for graduate study in music, including the initiation of doctoral programs in choral conducting, affected American choral music education in several ways. Large universities, which could grant specialized advanced degrees in choral conducting, began to supplant small liberal arts colleges as the primary preparers of American choral conductors and to focus the attention of the profession on score study, musicological issues, and the performance of major choral/orchestral works. The advent of doctoral programs in choral conducting also encouraged the notion of choral conducting and choral music education as two distinct fields for advanced study.

The founding of the American Choral Directors Association (ACDA), in 1959 has also influenced the mainstream of American choral music over the past thirty-five years. Initially, the ACDA met in conjunction with meetings of the MENC, convening its first independent national convention in 1971, in Kansas City, Missouri. Currently, the ACDA includes over 15,000 members, and provides an important state, regional, and national forum for the discussion of choral music concerns. Through its program of conferences and publications, it has encouraged communication among choral directors, high performance standards, and the recognition of excellence in choral music. Currently, the organization is assuming a larger role as a political advocate of choral music in the United States.

The Advent of Comprehensive Musicianship

The events and trends we have described to this point focused mainly on the *product* of experiences in choral music. Rehearsal techniques and ideals of choral sound were considered in relation to their impact on performance. The effect of the music on choral singers was secondary, with the primary importance attached to the music. Singers were considered servants of the choral art insofar as they contributed to a fine performance. In the 1950s, an era of curricular reform in American education began that started in the areas of science and mathematics, but which provided the impetus for a new discussion in choral music education—discussion of the curricular value of music, the impact of choral music on students, and consideration of the outcomes of various philosophies and methodologies of choral music education.

The event that inaugurated the era of curricular reform in the United States was the launching of the Sputnik satellite by the Soviet Union in 1957. From the end of World War II until the launching of Sputnik, the prevailing attitude in the United States was one of complacency regarding our technological achievements and confidence in our military superiority over other nations. With the launching of Sputnik, this attitude was replaced with one of alarm over Soviet technological advances.

The American educational system was closely scrutinized, and a variety of efforts at curricular reform were undertaken. Initially, these efforts at curricular reform were primarily concerned with the areas of science and mathematics, but music educators also began to examine the efficacy of their work in U.S. public schools.

Of course, since the early days of U.S. public school music education, its proponents have expressed their views concerning the impact of musical experiences on individuals. Within the profession, during the late nineteenth and early twentieth centuries, such issues were discussed as the merits of rote versus note methods of teaching music reading, the use of choral music experiences as a means of developing music appreciation, and the need to musically educate the entire school population versus a select few ("Music for every child, every child for music"). During this period, choral and instrumental ensembles became a fixture at most American high schools. The events of the 1950s, however, lent a new urgency to the consideration of the place of choral music in the school curriculum, and this discussion has continued literally to the present day.

In music education, beginning with the Young Composers Project, and continuing through the Yale Seminar, the Contemporary Music Project, the Tanglewood Symposium, and numerous other symposia, publications, papers, and curriculum projects, the profession examined a variety of issues related to the musical education of American children. One result was the articulation of the idea of comprehensive musicianship and its implementation in several curriculum projects. Comprehensive musicianship is a multifaceted concept, which manifested itself in a variety of ways in U.S. music education during the 1960s and 1970s. Its influence is still felt today, and it is an important underlying principle of comprehensive choral music education.

The roots of comprehensive musicianship may be traced to the Young Composers Project, which began in 1959. A purpose of this project, which was funded by the Ford Foundation, was to encourage close interaction and understanding among composers, music educators, and students. This was accomplished by placing young composers in American communities, where they created music specifically designed for the individuals and ensembles in that particular setting.

The Young Composers Project continued until 1968 and the MENC became involved in its administration. Out of the Young Composers Project developed the Contemporary Music Project, which continued until 1973. Expanding far beyond the notion of placing young composers in the schools, the Contemporary Music Project issued a variety of publications, held conferences, and sought to promote and explain the idea of comprehensive musicianship.

To refer to "the idea of comprehensive musicianship" is actually somewhat misleading, since comprehensive musicianship evolved and developed to the point where it included a variety of related but distinct ideas. Other curriculum projects that advocated a comprehensive approach to music instruction included the Manhattanville Music Curriculum Project and the Hawaii Curriculum Project. Gatherings such as the Tanglewood Symposium in 1967 were concerned with aspects of comprehensive musicianship as well as other issues.

The underlying principle of comprehensive musicianship was that the study of music should be approached in an integrated, rather than a fragmented manner. Many of the ideas of comprehensive musicianship were most readily applied in the general music class and in collegiate music history and theory course sequences. However, the basic ideas espoused by the Contemporary Music Project also have relevance for teachers and students in choral and instrumental ensembles. Three of the basic tenets of comprehensive musicianship are described here.

1. *Students should be given the opportunity to learn about music through a variety of experiences with a particular musical context.* In working with a particular musical selection, the best way for students to learn about it is for them to study its historical context, its theoretical basis, its expressive implications, and issues related to style and performance practice. Students develop concepts related to these areas not through the rote teaching of a vocal line or through simply memorizing facts, but through singing, playing, questioning, analyzing, and *experiencing* the music. The rehearsal becomes a setting in which students are encouraged to think, to analyze, and thereby to grow musically.

History, style, theory, expression, and all aspects of music were to be approached *together,* in an integrated fashion. This idea had profound implications for teachers and students at all levels of music education and in all areas of specialization. Programs were instituted at colleges and universities wherein classes in theory and history were integrated, so the commonalities between the areas could be fully explored. For studio teachers employing the principles of comprehensive musicianship, it was no longer satisfactory simply to tell a student to articulate a passage of keyboard music in a particular manner. Instead, the comprehensive approach was to guide the student to understand *why* that articulation was appropriate, based on an understanding of the various aspects of musical structure. For choral directors, the notion of simply rote teaching the line to be sung by each part was not educationally valid.

2. *As its name implies, the Contemporary Music Project sought to impress on music teachers the importance of giving students a wide variety of musical experiences with a rich and varied repertoire of musical literature, including a wide range of contemporary music.* The need for greater variety in the repertoire used in music class was not limited to the promotion of contemporary music, but also included older music and the music of many cultural traditions and styles.

At the time the Contemporary Music Project began, it was felt that music teachers were insecure in their own knowledge of repertoire from outside the western European eighteenth- and nineteenth-century traditions. To alleviate this problem, seminars and publications focused on strategies for teaching music that did not follow the rules of eighteenth-century counterpoint, did not employ symmetrical meters, and that lacked the other traditional structural elements with which music teachers were most comfortable. Music educators were made aware of a vast range of music that was largely being ignored in American music classrooms at all levels.

The Young Composers Project, which initiated this thought process, was designed to encourage the interaction of the composers of contemporary music with those who performed it. In the process, greater understanding was created on the part of both. As the Young Composers Project evolved into the Contemporary Music Project, students were encouraged to investigate the historical and cultural milieu in which music was created.

3. *Through a wide variety of musical experiences with a rich and varied repertoire of musical literature, students develop an understanding of the basic structure and properties of music.* Music has a structure based on certain commonalities found in every composition. Through the teaching of comprehensive musicianship, these commonalities are understood by the student. The basic indivisible building blocks of music are pitch, intensity, duration, and timbre. Through experiences in music class, students should be helped to discover the way in which each of these elements is manipulated by a composer, the manner in which they are combined in a musical composition, and the relative importance of each element to a particular composition.

Although the concepts of comprehensive musicianship were formulated, refined, and disseminated in the 1960s and early 1970s, their influence on American music education is still strong in the 1990s. Elementary general music series books reflect the notion of music's common elements and the need to acquaint students with the conceptual structure of music. There have been a variety of research studies (mostly related to instrumental music education) examining a comprehensive approach to rehearsal. Articles in the *Music Educators Journal* and other publications by the MENC have encouraged a multicultural approach to various aspects of music education. A recent MENC publication, *Teaching Choral Music,*[3] is published along with a packet of choral pieces and includes a study and rehearsal guide for each selection based on the composition's historical and stylistic context and musical structure. *Something to Sing About* and *Something New to Sing About*, two publications developed by G. Schirmer,[4] include teaching suggestions based on the structure and context of the music included. In the 1970s, the Hawaii Music Project produced several volumes whose explicit purpose was to facilitate the development of comprehensive musicianship through choral performance.[5] Each of these publications, as well as several others, is an outgrowth of principles of comprehensive musicianship.

The Current Scene

As indicated earlier, the United States entered a period of unprecedented questioning and critiquing of the educational establishment in the late 1950s. This era has continued to the present day. Following the first wave of curricular reform came additional periods of intensive scrutiny. In 1983, the release of *A Nation at Risk*,[6] an educational critique produced by the Carnegie Foundation, once again prompted widespread questioning of the theory and practice of U.S. education. As was the case in the earlier reform effort, public attention was focused primarily on science and mathematics, along with English and foreign languages.

The social climate in the United States has changed dramatically in the last three decades. America has moved from a nation of traditional families, with one wage earner and a mother who stayed at home to raise the children, to one where two incomes are viewed as necessary for economic comfort by a majority of young couples. Mothers who stay at home with their children are a minority today. Divorce, one-parent families, and blended families have become much more common. Drug abuse is a nationally recognized problem of huge proportions. Teenage suicide is increasingly common. The AIDS (Acquired Immune Deficiency Syndrome) epidemic has become a leading cause of death among young people. Violence in the schools has attracted major attention from the media as metal detectors, police guards, and other protective strategies are used to keep guns and other weapons out of schools.

These social problems have a direct impact on the public schools, since the schools reflect the society they serve. Music teachers, along with other educators, routinely receive inservice training on suicide prevention, on dealing with students who abuse drugs, and on coping with the variety of other societal problems brought into the classroom.

As the social fabric of the United States has been disrupted, the economic climate of the schools has also changed. When the first wave of curriculum reform occurred in the 1960s, the federal government played a major role in funding educational programs. During the 1980s federal funding for educational programs was dramatically cut back. The theory was that with the curtailment of federal funding for education, state and local support would increase, and the control of education would reside more fully and appropriately at those levels. In fact, at the same time federal funding was decreasing, state and local governments also experienced decreasing revenues and were unable to maintain their previous levels of support, let alone make up for lower levels of federal aid to education.

As a result of all of these changes, the position of music in the schools has been questioned, and there has been increasing emphasis on the political advocacy of music education by the MENC, the ACDA, and other musical organizations. An annual event that began as "Music in Our Schools Day" in the 1970s has expanded into "Music in Our Schools Month," sponsored by MENC and featuring "The World's Largest Concert" each year. The purpose of the event is to enlighten the public about the importance and the results of U.S. music education. At the same time, individual music educators have begun to recognize the need for asserting the importance of music in the schools for America's students. Materials to promote music in the schools (packets of information for music teachers, as well as pamphlets, buttons, T-shirts, bumper stickers, and the like for distribution to the public) have been developed by MENC.

In the midst of this turmoil, American choral directors have continued to produce choral organizations at all levels that present concerts of astonishing virtuosity. The fact that choral music educators have continued to strive for excellence in the face of increasingly difficult working conditions is a noteworthy accomplishment.

In today's political, social, and economic climate, it is critically important that choral music educators understand why choral music in the public schools is so vital to the education of American students, and why our programs must be both musically and educationally sound. Comprehensive choral music education aims to provide the kinds of experiences for students they cannot receive from other areas of the curriculum, which are essential in order to live life to the fullest at the end of the twentieth century.

✣ BASIC PRINCIPLES ✣

The basic principles of comprehensive choral music education are as follows:

Principle 1: Comprehensive choral music education focuses on the student.

Principle 2: Comprehensive choral music education involves examples of the finest in choral literature, whose salient characteristics are understood by each member of the ensemble, presented at the highest level of excellence attainable.

Principle 3: Comprehensive choral music education is aesthetic.

Principle 4: The results of comprehensive choral music education can be evaluated, and such evaluation is an important component of the process.

Let's examine each principle in more detail.

1. *Comprehensive choral music education focuses on the student.* Throughout the twentieth century there have been excellent choral performing groups in many American secondary schools. Today, one only needs to attend a national convention of the ACDA to hear dazzling displays of choral virtuosity produced by ensembles from around the country.

Technical excellence and the highest musical standards are critically important to comprehensive choral music education, but the primary purpose for music in the schools is to nurture the student participants. This goal must be kept in the forefront of your thinking; otherwise, it is very easy for misplaced priorities and educationally indefensible practices to become part of the program. These undesirable priorities and practices can appear to be quite positive unless they are viewed in the context of comprehensive choral music education, which focuses on the child.

Over the years numerous debates have centered on the seeming dichotomy between process and product. In reality, such debates are useless and the notion of a dichotomy is specious. *Both* process and product are important in comprehensive choral music education. Through the process of rehearsals and concert presentations (not to mention trips to contests or festivals, social events, and a variety of other interactions), students are guided to increasingly complex levels of musical understanding and appreciation as well as enhanced understanding of themselves and their peers. Some would consider the presentation of a fine concert the ultimate product of a choral program, but in comprehensive choral music education the presentation of concerts represents one aspect of a continuum.

Some music educators and other choral conductors tend to view their work in a linear fashion (see Figure 9.1). In this model, the result of a period of rehearsal is a performance, which constitutes the final goal of the choral music education process. For professional choral conductors this is probably an accurate and valid representation of their work. A work or a set of works is selected, rehearsed, and performed. The process is driven by the goal of performance. Once the goal is achieved, the process stops until a new goal is defined (the next performance) and then it is repeated. For a choral conductor adopting this model of the choral music education process, the goal is to produce the finest choral perform-ance possible within the constraints of rehearsal time available. Once the performance has occurred, the process ends and then starts anew with each new performance goal. Ensemble members may acquire some knowledge from the process that can be generalized to other pieces of music, but the primary purpose of the whole endeavor is the achievement of the performance goal.

Rehearsals (Process) → Performance (Product)

FIGURE 9.1 A Linear View of Choral Music Education

——Rehearsals———Performance———Rehearsals———Performance———→

Process

FIGURE 9.2 Another Linear View

Other conductors view performance as a part of the process of choral music education (see Figure 9.2). In this model, the performances have become a part of the process rather than an end point to a linear progression. The process of choral music education is conceptualized as a succession of rehearsals interspersed with performances. This is preferable to the first model in that it removes some of the emphasis on performance by making it a part of the ongoing process.

The model for comprehensive choral music education may also be conceptualized in circular fashion (see Figure 9.3).

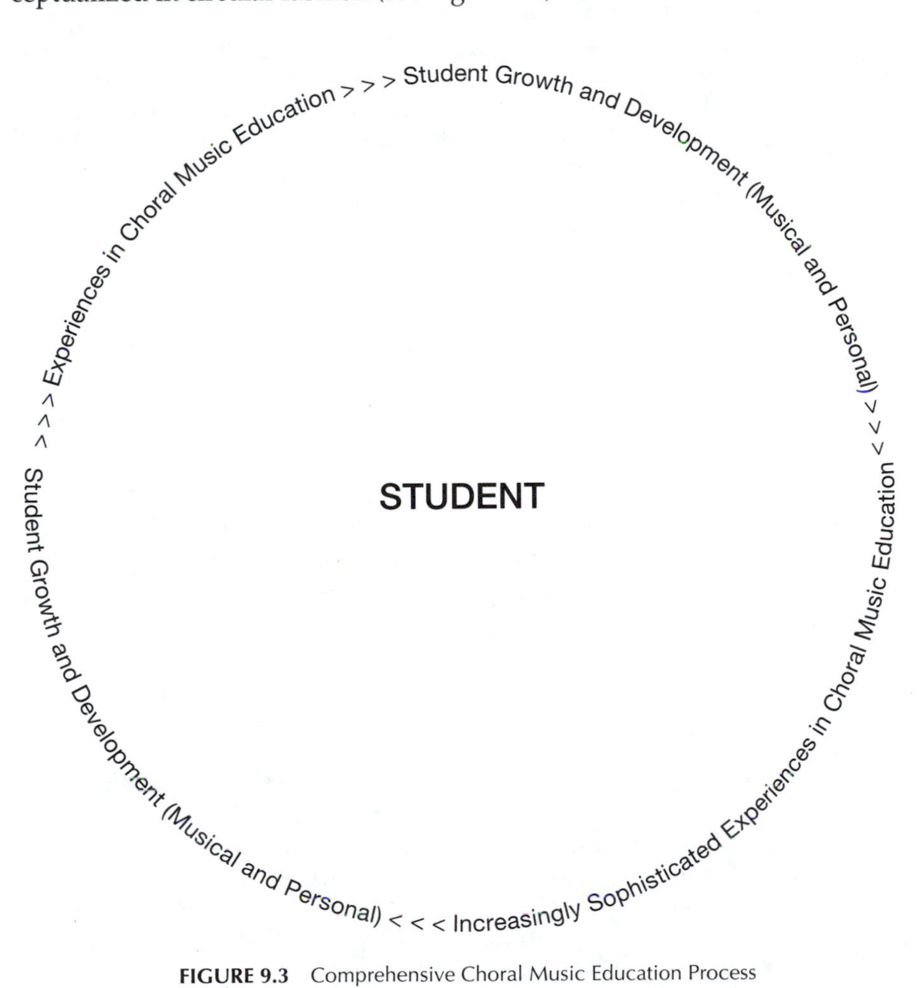

FIGURE 9.3 Comprehensive Choral Music Education Process

In this model, the student is the central focus of the process, and increasingly sophisticated experiences are provided as the student's personal and musical development progresses. In the comprehensive music program each individual's value and uniqueness are appreciated and enhanced.

It is not enough for students to be able to sing their part with accuracy. Comprehensive choral music education should provide a vehicle for students to learn about all aspects of music, including styles, periods, and the melodic, harmonic, rhythmic, and expressive aspects of the pieces under consideration. This requires an additional layer of preparation and planning for the comprehensive choral music educator.

Each person's voice is as unique as his or her fingerprints, and as students learn about their individual vocal characteristics they are learning more about one of their most distinctive personal characteristics. As students participate in rehearsals and concerts they gain an increasing understanding of their own strengths and weaknesses and insights into their interactions with individuals in the choral ensemble.

Abraham Maslow, the celebrated humanistic psychologist, posited a hierarchy of human needs. According to Maslow's thinking, after fulfilling certain basic needs such as food, shelter, and safety, humans seek aesthetic fulfillment in order to meet higher-level psychological and aesthetic needs and to become fully "self-actualized."[7] Maslow indicated that music provides an important vehicle for self-actualization.

There are many dimensions to the meaningfulness of choral music experience for participants. Research has shown that choral music education experiences meet student needs in terms of knowledge of self, knowledge of others, need for achievement, spiritual growth, communication skill, and musical knowledge. Since the comprehensive choral music educator continuously monitors the impact of the experiences the group is having on the individuals in it, and the focus is on the participants rather than on the next concert, opportunities for individual growth in a variety of areas is facilitated.

A final point concerning the importance of the individual in the ensemble to the comprehensive choral music education program: By placing the emphasis on the individual, some of the pressure of public performance on the choral music educator is removed. Of course, the presentation of high-quality performances is still critically important. Only by challenging students to strive for excellence can a program be truly successful. We want our programs to be successful. However, there is a potential problem with placing our entire emphasis on the attainment of exemplary choral singing.

There are a few choral ensembles around the country which help to set the standard for choral excellence. For example, in the 1950s and 1960s the Robert Shaw Chorale (along with a few other excellent professional and collegiate ensembles) toured, made recordings, and in all respects provided an enviable model of fine choral sound, repertoire selection, and stylistic distinctiveness. Currently, at any national convention of the ACDA, one hears a variety of choirs that have been selected through careful, objective audition procedures and represent the finest in choral music making.

When these fine ensembles sing, they are listened to and applauded by an audience of several thousand enthusiastic choral directors whose groups were *not* selected to appear. Most choral conductors will never conduct a choral ensemble that is of the caliber of those appearing at a national convention. Are they all failures because their ensembles have not attained the degree of choral technique displayed at such events? Certainly not! Yet if our objective is simply to produce an excellent concert, and we are judging ourselves against the high choral standards displayed by the finest ensembles, then we will certainly fail.

Is the director who goes into a choral situation that has deteriorated and begins to rebuild it, and who receives a rating of II at contest a failure or a less successful music educator than the conductor who inherited a top-flight program and received a I? Is the director who focuses entirely on the rote teaching of three selections for contest and receives the top rating a success?

The answer to these questions must be determined based on what the choral music educator is trying to accomplish. If we seek to emulate the finest ensemble and that is our sole criterion for success, most of us will be failures. If our focus is on the students and their development as musicians and as persons, all of us can be a success.

Does this mean we should simply "let the kids have fun with the music" or that the comprehensive choral music educator's standards for performance should be any lower than the next person's? Does it mean we need not worry about evaluating each student's progress toward the attainment of the musical goals we have established? Of course not. It does mean, however, that we are looking beyond performance level and technique to the people with whom we are working—the students. Once we do this, then we can happily set the very highest standards for our performances, do our very best to attain those standards, work to develop our own musicianship and that of our students, and not feel we or they are unsuccessful.

Choral music is an area of the curriculum in which every student in the ensemble can and should feel successful. Unlike the basketball team or the football team where there are five individuals or eleven individuals who make up the starting team and everyone else is "second string," success in choral music requires every single member of the choir to contribute his or her very best effort, and every single member has the opportunity to be an important, valued, and contributing part of a successful musical team.

2. *Comprehensive choral music education involves the finest in choral literature, understood by each member of the ensemble, presented at the highest level of excellence attainable.* Recall the material from Chapter 2 concerning long-range rehearsal planning. The starting point for the planning process for a year of successful choral music education was the selection of worthwhile musical literature. Students were then guided to discover the important structural, aesthetic, and contextual characteristics of the pieces during the rehearsal process.

The question of just what constitutes fine choral literature has been the basis for heated debate among choral music educators. In Chapter 5, we established and discussed criteria for the selection of music. If those criteria are conscientiously and consistently applied to every music purchase, a library of fine literature will result. The problem occurs when choral directors fail to use the criteria in making music selections. The whole process of rehearsal planning is initiated with the choosing of repertoire. If this initial step is not carefully made, the rest of the process cannot succeed.

For some choral directors, fine choral literature seems to be what is newly available and recommended by the music dealer at a reading session each year. Of course, there are fine choral pieces published each year, but each choral director must use the criteria suggested earlier in order to separate the selections that are good choices for a given choir in a particular year from the far greater number that are not suitable.

Some choral directors seek to emulate previous choral experiences. They purchase selections that were successful for the high school or collegiate choral ensemble in which they participated. Of course, there may be selections from such groups that will work well with your choir, but the criteria listed in Chapter 5 should be applied as you choose the music.

Another problem for directors who have been in the field for several years is the repetition of a limited group of pieces over and over. As you work with a choir, you will find certain pieces work well and bear repetition (after the students who sang the piece have graduated, of course). This is an advantage for choral conductors who have been in the field for a few years. The problem occurs when directors become too dependent on a particular piece, set of pieces, or style of music and simply keep recycling them year after year.

People change. A piece that worked well with one choir may not be satisfactory with another. Also, you as the conductor need to be stimulated to grow as a musician and a person. One of the best ways to do this is to keep abreast of developments in the field and to be aware of new, challenging, and appropriate repertoire.

Initially, for the beginning choral conductor, the challenge is to become conversant with the choral repertoire that has already become widely accepted and valued. This experience began in your college or university classes as you studied music history and literature and developed knowledge of the music from the past several hundred years that is available for choral performance. This knowledge can be expanded by making a thorough survey of the choral library at your school, by visiting with other choral music educators who have successful programs, and by spending time at a music dealer browsing through choral files.

Another excellent way to get a feel for the kinds of choral pieces being performed on the cutting edge of the profession is to attend professional meetings of the ACDA and the MENC and their state organizations. At such events, there are numerous opportunities to hear fine choral music as well as to attend reading sessions, clinics, and special interest sessions.

In the end, after acquiring as much information as possible, the decision as to what constitutes the finest choral literature for you and your ensemble is a personal one. If it is based on logical and consistent criteria and if the objective is the musical growth of the student participants through their experiences with the repertoire, then your decision will be the best one possible.

The rehearsal procedures we suggest in Chapter 2 are intended to make rehearsals efficient, enjoyable, and educational. This kind of rehearsal and performance will result in students who are comprehensively chorally educated. For students to understand a piece of music requires a mode of rehearsal leadership that focuses on the development of such understanding.

An expression that has been around for many years, but which has recently enjoyed renewed popularity in educational circles is the *teaching of critical thinking*. Hilary Apfelstadt has written a chapter in a collection of readings edited by Eunice Boardman (1989) devoted to this topic.[8] In it she describes various ways in which singers learn music. Sometimes, a low-level, stimulus-response technique is the most efficient and most appropriate way to teach a particular aspect of a choral selection. For example, in considering the pronunciation of a foreign text, you might pronounce the text (stimulus) and the class would immediately respond (response). If, however, you apply this same teaching strategy to every aspect of the music, it is not the most educationally sound approach.

We want to engage our students in musical decision making as we rehearse. Does this mean we give up the responsibility for making determinations about the way the music should sound? Of course not. However, it is sometimes astonishing how much knowledge and insight students already possess concerning aspects of choral music, *if they are asked*. It is important for choral music educators to ask questions of students. When rehearsing the basses, ask the rest of the choir, "Which way was better? The first or second time through? Why?" In considering a particular musical phrase, ask the choir, "Where is the peak of this phrase? How should we vary our dynamics in order to make the phrase drive toward that point?" It is also informative to occasionally ask, "What can we do to improve our singing of that piece?" As students gain experience, they become very astute concerning choral singing. They know the answers to our questions.

Asking questions of students has several excellent effects. It keeps the entire class engaged in the rehearsal process, even if the focus is on a particular section and its problems at a given moment. It helps you maintain an interesting and varied rehearsal routine. It prods students to think about what they are doing, rather than mindlessly merging their voices into a collective sound that is developed exclusively by rote learning.

By encouraging students to think about what they are doing, questioning technique will facilitate their individual musical and personal growth. In Chapter 2 we said one of our most important goals as music educators is to get our students to buy into what we are doing. By asking questions, students are drawn into a collaborative effort to make music, rather than being used as "choral cannon fodder" or cogs in a music-making machine. Through questioning techniques we facilitate student musical growth.

The final part of principle 2 indicates that the choral music selected for the ensemble will be presented at the highest level of excellence attainable. This is an important point. For the comprehensive choral music educator, there are many more concerns than simply a high performance level or a successful concert presentation. This does not mean, however, that high choral standards are unimportant. On the contrary, they are critical to a comprehensive choral music education program.

The question is, how do we establish and maintain high standards? A few points in this regard may be helpful. Actually, it is probably impossible to *maintain* high standards. The standards you establish for a choral program and for your own personal musicianship can either improve or weaken. They do not remain static. So the question really is, how can I continue to improve myself and my program?

Part of the answer to this question lies in the choral music educator's intellectual curiosity. There must be consistent growth in musical knowledge and in general knowledge of history, current events, visual art, and any other areas that strike your fancy. In earlier chapters, we presented some ideas concerning how a student conductor could prepare for a career in choral music education. As a student, you are forced to grow as a potential choral music educator as you move through the curriculum. Once you have completed an undergraduate degree and are in the field, the temptation is to fail to seek out opportunities for continued growth. Continue to study. Read widely, attend classes, seminars, clinics, and take advantage of other opportunities for personal, intellectual, and musical development.

Take every opportunity to listen to fine choral ensembles, both in live concerts and through recordings. Do not be afraid to have your choral work evaluated. Have outside friends, choral experts who may be visiting your school with a choir, and anyone who is willing to do so watch you rehearse and listen to your singers perform. Be open to new ideas.

3. Comprehensive choral music education is aesthetic. The term *aesthetics* has been used for centuries. It relates to the question of what constitutes beauty and how we perceive the expressive qualities of an object. Discussions of aesthetics and the publication of books and articles concerning the power of music to provide an "aesthetic experience" for students are quite common during the latter half of the twentieth century.

When we speak of aesthetics and education,we are most significantly involved in an aspect of learning termed the affective domain. Bloom (1956) described three learning domains: cognitive, affective, and psychomotor. The cognitive domain relates to the education of the intellect, the affective domain is concerned with the education of feelings, and the psychomotor domain involves training in physical movement. Most experiences in choral music involve some aspects of all three domains, but it is helpful to consider which domain is dominant in a given activity or experience.

In comprehensive choral music education, we provide students with experiences that facilitate their development in all three areas. For example, the ability to understand musical notation (at whatever level of musical refinement) is primarily a cognitive skill. When we teach students the correct posture for singing, this is psychomotor learning. However, it is in the affective area, the education of feeling, that music has special efficacy. When a student's aesthetic awareness is developed through choral music, this is affective education.

Successful choral music education has always heightened students' aesthetic sensitivity. However, the publication of Bennett Reimer's *A Philosophy of Music Education* in 1970 (followed by a second edition in 1989), has helped focus the attention of music educators on the importance of providing students with an aesthetic education. Although there has been a tendency to focus on the general music class when aesthetic education is discussed, it has important implications for the performing ensemble and is an important aspect of comprehensive choral music education.

A basic premise of aesthetic education is that the meanings that music produces reside in its intrinsic expressive qualities. The musical experiences provided for students through our programs should enhance their perception of musical events and evoke a resultant feelingful reaction to those events.

In general music class, aesthetic education is extensive and comprehensive. Student participants in choral ensembles actualize musical materials that have previously been created. As this occurs, students are aesthetically educated if they participate in artistic decisions concerning music's intrinsic expressive qualities. According to Reimer, "performance is intensive and selective in its approach to the art of music."[9]

The intensive nature of the choral singer's interactions with the music under consideration is an important part of what makes choral music education such an important setting for aesthetic education. Students can participate in musical decisions and place the results of their decisions in front of the public as they perform the music.

To accomplish this objective in choral ensembles requires a rethinking of the purposes, methods, and desired results of choral music education. For optimal aesthetic music education to occur through choral performance, music literature must be selected and sequenced in such a way that it promotes intensive, refined, and focused interactions with the expressive qualities of a choral composition. Rehearsal experiences should be structured so students are encouraged to make musical decisions as an ongoing part of the rehearsal process. Recall the earlier discussion of the work of Hilary Apfelstadt concerning the teaching of critical thinking skills to choral students. Both in terms of aesthetic education and in order to teach students how to think critically, they must be engaged in the rehearsal process at a higher level than rote learning of a vocal line.

Reimer highlights the distinction between music educators and "skill drillers." While recognizing that the development of skill in singing is critically important to effective choral music education, the central idea is that students should develop general musical knowledge and independence in musical expression through their choral music education experiences. This requires the relinquishing of some of the instructor's autonomy in the interest of encouraging student creativity and independence.

Aesthetic choral music education also requires a rethinking of the ways in which students and programs are evaluated. Of course, a primary means of evaluating the success of a choral program remains the level of musicality displayed in public performance. This is not conclusive evidence, however, that students are growing in personal awareness of the aesthetic qualities in a piece of music. Other efforts must be made to determine the students' growth in perception and feelingful reaction to music, through discussions of their valuing of music and through consideration of their ability to make independent musical judgments.

Comprehensive choral music education is intentionally focused on the aesthetic development of the student singers in the program. Aesthetic education through choral music is part of the student-centered approach that distinguishes it from noncomprehensive programs.

4. The results of comprehensive choral music education can be evaluated, and such evaluation is an important component of the process. In a sense, choral music educators have always been accountable for the results of their work. Unlike teachers of English, history, mathematics, or science, the work of the choral conductor is immediately on display at a public concert. Likewise, if the choir goes to a festival or contest and is rated by a panel of adjudicators there is immediate feedback and a numerical rating assigned.

We have been less successful, however, in identifying goals for our instruction and creating strategies and techniques for evaluating whether the individual students in our ensembles are accomplishing them. Too often, the evaluation of students is based on their attendance at rehearsals and concerts, or perhaps their attitude toward the class as noted by the instructor. For the comprehensive choral music educator, an accurate evaluation of student progress toward the goals we have established is an important component of the program.

We have already described some aspects of evaluation in other chapters. A few ideas will help stimulate your thinking about ways to evaluate the accomplishment of the goals you have established for instruction. For the comprehensive choral music educator it does not suffice to base a student's grade simply on his or her participation in a choral ensemble.

Evaluation of choral programs implies we know what we are trying to accomplish in chorus class. Traditionally, we have done an excellent job of evaluating the product of our efforts, the choral performance. This sort of evaluation will certainly continue, and is valid and crucial for success. A problem occurs when this kind of evaluation is the sole basis for determining the success or failure of a program. This can lead to a situation where three pieces learned by rote, earning a "I" at contest, constitute the choral curriculum.

A goal for evaluation must be to evaluate more comprehensively. If music is to continue as a full-fledged part of the curriculum, we must know what kind of learnings are resulting from choral participation and make efforts to evaluate not only performance, but also to examine the choral music education process objectively to determine the musical and aesthetic development of the students.

Evaluation should be part of the day-to-day rehearsal routine in the comprehensive choral program. Through questioning the students concerning the musical characteristics of the literature under consideration and discussing with them the desirability of one approach to a particular expressive or stylistic issue versus another, it will be easy to get a sense of how well the class comprehends the structure of the music and its expressive qualities.

Take the opportunity to listen to students sing individually, or at least in quartets. See how well they can sing their part. If it will facilitate matters, have the students sing their part with a tape of the accompaniment. Record the students as they sing, and maintain a cumulative record on tape of their vocal progress. It can be rewarding for student and teacher to listen to a recording made by a student in the first semester in the choral program and compare it to his or her eventual level of achievement.

Prod students to evaluate performances, their own and those of other ensembles. Discuss the performances with them. Musical and expressive characteristics, vocal strengths and weaknesses, likes and dislikes concerning the music selected for performance—any such area can provide a fruitful topic for discussion.

Part of this ongoing evaluative effort should measure the affective results of choral music education. The use of questionnaires, portfolios, journals, and other indicators of student affective development can provide additional bases for evaluation.

✣ THE COMPREHENSIVE CHORAL CURRICULUM ✣

The most effective and beneficial music program is fully integrated and sequentially organized throughout the curriculum, from kindergarten through high school. The framework on which such a program is constructed is the structure of music itself, considered in combination with characteristics of the students we instruct. The structure of music and student interaction with its elements (melody, harmony, rhythm, form, style, and expression) produce the expressive impact of the choral music we rehearse and perform. These elements are embodied in the literature to be considered with our students. In an integrated choral curriculum, the literature selected should help individuals develop increasingly sophisticated concepts of the music they perform and enjoy aesthetic experiences of increasing depth as they move through the grades.

To create and maintain an integrated choral music program requires communication between choral music teachers at the elementary, middle school/junior high, and high school levels. Curricular decisions should be made through collaborative effort, resulting in a curriculum that draws on the full resources of the district's choral music personnel. A choral curriculum is more likely to be effectively implemented if it is designed by the choral teachers. As students move through the various grade levels, the integrated choral curriculum will build on their previous experiences. It will mean the students who arrive at the high school will have a common body of musical knowledge and experience.

Students' first choral music experiences occur in the context of their elementary general music classes. Elementary general music classes tend to be the most carefully planned musical experiences that are provided for students. This sequential, carefully organized approach must be continued as students experience increasingly intensive musical experiences in choral ensembles at the middle school and high school levels.

This kind of comprehensive approach will have a variety of excellent practical results. In particular, two important areas will improve. First, there is the matter of literature selection. If the choral curriculum has been designed so elementary students study music from several different stylistic periods, in English and Latin, then the middle school teacher can make a better informed decision about the music to be performed at that level. If the high school director knows that incoming students from the junior high school have experienced music in English, German, Latin, and Italian, representing a variety of styles, composers, and periods, this will enable the high school teacher to be more effective. Secondly, in a comprehensive program, the transition from elementary to junior high school is not a leap into the unknown, but a smooth and continuing process, in which the positive experiences of the elementary school continue into the middle school years. Literature is carefully selected, and instructional techniques are designed to build on elementary experiences and to prepare students for high school and adult choral singing. Of course, an important residual effect of such organization is the encouragement and retention of the young male singer through his vocal change. Although few might argue against the need for comprehensive, carefully sequenced programs, in which the structure of music provides the organizational framework, currently the full implementation of such programs is relatively rare.

Individualization

Educators in the visual arts have a much easier task than choral directors, when it comes to individualizing instruction. The creation of a painting or a sculpture is, by its very nature, an individual task. In choral music, in order for a successful performance to happen, individuals must conform to a unified concept of choral sound, musical style, and other aspects of good choral singing. How is it possible to individualize instruction in such a regimented discipline?

Individualized programs are accessible. Scheduling practices are such that student participation is facilitated. Choral classes are provided that meet the needs of students with varying degrees of musical talent. Within the choral ensemble, opportunities should be provided for independent musical decision making.

A variety of teaching methods should be used, including questioning techniques aimed at developing students' independent musical thinking. Although the end result may be a unified concept of choral sound, rehearsal time may be profitably invested in discussion of various kinds of choral tone, experiments with various kinds of choral sound for a given piece of music, discussion of the composer, the period, or the style of the piece of music, and the presentation to the class of various musical problems encountered in the selection. The questions and other activities should be suited to the individual abilities of the various students in the room.

A third way choral music may be individualized is through provision for the special needs of students in your classroom. This can range from recognizing physical handicaps and adapting the environment to accommodate them to a sensitivity to individual student needs and situations.

There is an understandable tendency on the part of music teachers to focus attention on the talented students in choral ensembles as well as those who are problematic. Generally speaking, music educators have done a good job of nurturing students with musical talent. Nevertheless, those students constitute a very small percentage of the individuals with whom we come in contact. If we believe in the old rallying cry, "Music for every child, and every child for music," then we need to give attention to the needs of the average students. This is philosophically and pragmatically sound, since they constitute the overwhelming majority of the school population. These individuals will become taxpayers, school administrators, and parents.

The Multicultural Imperative

In the last twenty-five years, choral music educators have become increasingly cognizant of the richness of the musical traditions of a variety of cultures. The importance of this topic for the comprehensive choral music educator rests on two ideas. First, in a world that continues to be more and more closely interconnected, students need to be aware of the diversity of cultures and traditions found in other locations. Secondly, even in the last fifteen years, the United States has become increasingly culturally diverse, and there has been a corresponding heightening of interest in celebrating that diversity. The notion of the United States as a melting pot has been replaced, in the minds of many, with the idea of a salad bowl, in which the individual components retain their identity, contributing to an interesting and colorful combination.

Throughout the twentieth century, music educators have increasingly recognized the importance of folk music of a variety of traditions to the musical education of children. In recent years there has been a strong movement toward the inclusion of music from a wide variety of the world's cultures in our music classes. Probably the first area in which this was accomplished with some success was in the general music class. For the last quarter of a century, elementary music texts have included increasing amounts of music from traditions outside the stream of traditional western European music composition.

In 1967, the MENC convened the Tanglewood Symposium, which sought to examine the status of music education and to establish some new directions for American music education. Among the conclusions reached by the symposium participants was a need for the inclusion of a wide variety of culturally diverse music in U.S. classrooms.

Since the Tanglewood Symposium the MENC has published many articles and other publications describing music from a variety of cultures, strategies for teaching the music of these cultures, and reaffirming the importance of multicultural education. Three special issues of the *Music Educators Journal* have been devoted exclusively to multicultural music education. For a discussion of the development of multicultural education in the United States, see Terese Volk's excellent article.[10]

Fortunately, greatly increased resources for the choral musician in terms of performable and exciting music from a variety of cultures have recently become available. At recent national meetings of the ACDA, a wide diversity of music from a variety of cultural traditions has been included in the programs of various participating ensembles as well as in the interest sessions.

To stimulate your thinking regarding the music of a variety of traditions, see Appendix C for a listing of some representative choral publications.

✣ SUMMARY ✣

This chapter examined the historical and philosophical bases for comprehensive choral music education. Principles of comprehensive choral music education were articulated along with a description of a sequentially organized choral curriculum. Chapter 10 describes the choral profession on the verge of the twenty-first century and provides some guidelines on student teaching, securing a position, and professional development.

Questions

1. What is meant by comprehensive choral music education? How is it related to the idea of comprehensive musicianship?
2. How did choral music develop in the United States prior to 1900?
3. What is meant by the "a cappella tradition"?
4. What developments in the 1950s and 1960s led to a greater emphasis on the integrity of the musical score?

5. What event provided the impetus for educational reform in the 1960s, including the development of comprehensive musicianship?
6. Define aesthetic education. How is it related to comprehensive choral music education?
7. What impact will the implementation of comprehensive choral music education have on the performance level of an ensemble?
8. How can experiences in choral music education stimulate students' critical thinking?
9. Is the development and articulation of a personal philosophy of music education of any practical benefit to the comprehensive choral music educator?
10. Why does choral music merit inclusion in the school curriculum?

Notes

1. Portions of the chapter were adapted from John Hylton, "Choral Curriculum: Twentieth-Century Trends and Twenty-First Century Issues," presented at the Suncoast Music Education Forum on Curriculum, University of South Florida, Tampa, March 5, 1991. Used by permission.
2. Howard Swan, "The Development of a Choral Instrument," in Harold A. Decker and Julius Herford, *Choral Conducting Symposium* (2nd ed.) (Englewood Cliffs, NJ: Prentice Hall, 1988), pp. 7–68.
3. *Teaching Choral Music: A Course of Study* (Reston, VA: Music Educators National Conference, 1991).
4. *Something to Sing About* (New York: G. Schirmer, 1982). *Something New to Sing About* (New York. G. Schirmer, 1989).
5. Lee Kjelson, *Comprehensive Musicianship Through Choral Performance* (Honolulu: University of Hawaii, 1976).
6. National Commission on Excellence in Education, *A Nation at Risk: The Imperative for Educational Reform* (Washington: U.S. Government Printing Office, 1983).
7. Robert A. Choate, *Documentary Report of the Tanglewood Symposium* (Washington: Music Educators National Conference, 1968), p. 73.
8. Hilary Apfelstadt, *"Musical Thinking in the Choral Rehearsal,"* in Eunice Boardman, ed., *Dimensions of Musical Thinking*. (Reston, VA: Music Educators National Conference, 1989).
9. Bennett Reimer, *A Philosophy of Music Education* (2nd ed.) (Englewood Cliffs, NJ: Prentice Hall, 1989), p. 186.
10. Terese Volk, "The History and Development of Multicultural Music Education as Evidenced in the *Music Educators Journal*, 1967–1992," *Journal of Research in Music Education*, 41, (2), (Summer 1993), pp. 137–155.

Suggested Reading

ABELES, HAROLD, ROBERT KLOTMAN, AND CHARLES HOFFER. *Foundations of Music Education.* New York: Schirmer, 1984.

BLOOM, BENJAMIN S., M. D. ENGELHART, E. J. FURST, W. H. HILL, AND D. R. KRATHWOHL, *Taxonomy of Educational Objectives.* Handbook I, *Cognitive Domain.* New York: David McKay Company, 1956.

BOARDMAN, EUNICE. *Dimensions of Musical Thinking.* Vienna, VA: Music Educators National Conference, 1990.

CENTER FOR RESEARCH IN MUSIC TEACHING AND LEARNING. "Focus: The Contemporary Music Project," *The Quarterly, 1,* Greeley, Colorado: University of Northern Colorado, 1990.

DECKER, HAROLD, AND JULIUS HERFORD. *Choral Conducting Symposium* (2nd ed.). Englewood Cliffs, NJ: Prentice Hall, 1988.

GARDNER, HOWARD. *Frames of Mind.* New York: Basic Books, 1983.

HYLTON, JOHN. "Dimensionality in High School Students' Perceptions of the Meaningfulness of Choral Singing Experience," *Journal of Research in Music Education, 29,* pp. 287–303.

KEENE, JAMES. *A History of Music Education in the United States.* Hanover, NH: University Press of New England, 1982.

KRATHWOHL, D. R., B. S. BLOOM, AND B. B. MASIA. *Taxonomy of Educational Objectives.* Handbook II, *Affective Domain.* New York: David McKay Company, 1964.

KNUTSON, BRIAN. *Interviews with Selected Choral Conductors Concerning Rationale and Practices Regarding Choral Blend,* Unpublished doctoral dissertation, Florida State University, 1987.

MOODY, WILLIAM (ed.). *Artistic Intelligences: Implications for Education.* New York: Teachers College Press, 1990.

MUSSULMAN, JOSEPH. *Dear People . . . Robert Shaw.* Bloomington: Indiana University Press, 1979.

NATIONAL COMMISSION ON EXCELLENCE IN EDUCATION. *A Nation at Risk: The Imperative for Educational Reform.* Washington, DC: U.S. Government Printing Office, 1983.

PIERCE, EDWARD E. *Julius Herford: His Life, Teaching, and Influence on the Choral Art in the United States,* Unpublished doctoral dissertation, University of Northern Colorado, 1988.

REIMER, BENNETT. *A Philosophy of Music Education* (2nd ed.). Englewood Cliffs, NJ: Prentice Hall, 1989.

WHITE, PERRY. "Significant Developments in Choral Music Education in Higher Education: 1950–1980." *Journal of Research in Music Education, 30,* pp. 121–128.

Chapter Ten

The Choral Profession

✣ ✣ ✣

✣ INTRODUCTION ✣

Comprehensive choral music education is an exciting process. The choral music profession is interesting, rewarding, and challenging. It also tends to be consuming, requiring the choral music educator to establish priorities in life so as to grow professionally and yet maintain adequate recreation, rest, and time for a personal life.

A career in choral music education provides an opportunity to have a dramatic positive impact on the lives of students. It is very rewarding to be shopping at the local mall or attending a musical or athletic event and be approached by a former student who participated in choral music and who graduated some years earlier and thanked for your efforts on his or her behalf. Often the graduate who is most appreciative was not one of the stars of the program, and may even have been a problem child.

Although the diversity of its demands is both a blessing and a curse, the professional life of a choral music educator is interesting and varied, since he or she must be a fine musician, a vocal technician, a skillful communicator, an organized administrator, and a motivational and enthusiastic leader. To remain competent and qualified as a choral music educator requires both formal and informal continuing education.

While there have been some modest improvements in teachers' salaries in recent years, if excellent compensation is your primary professional goal, it would be wise to reconsider a career in this field. The financial rewards are relatively modest, particularly in relation to other professions requiring similar preparation, training, and dedication. Careful planning is essential to minimize financial stresses and should be done early in your career.

Working conditions vary greatly from one position and from one school district to the next. Success in a choral position is certainly facilitated by a supportive administration, talented students, interested parents, adequate financial support, and good facilities. However, the biggest factor in the success or failure of any choral music education program is the teacher. There have been highly successful programs in situations where any or all of the working conditions have been woefully inadequate; when an enthusiastic and skillful music educator arrived on the scene, the program began to thrive. Often, when this kind of improvement occurs, some of the other nonmusical aspects also begin to improve as the program becomes more widely known and appreciated by parents and administrators.

Many of you are probably in the final stages of preparing for a career in choral music education. To begin with, we discuss student teaching. The student teaching experience is an important milestone in the preservice training of the choral music educator, and we present some specific guidelines to help you derive maximum benefit from it. Of course, following the student teaching semester usually comes a search for employment. This chapter also discusses strategies for a successful search for a position, ideas concerning ongoing professional growth and responsibility, and future trends in choral music education.

✣ STUDENT TEACHING ✣

Most prospective teachers begin to become involved in the profession as undergraduates. Through prestudent teaching experiences in the schools, student memberships in professional organizations, and other similar activities, the preservice choral music educator begins to gain an appreciation of what is involved in the profession.

The final step in the undergraduate preparation of the choral music educator is the student teaching experience. The notion of student teaching may seem to be a contradiction in terms. How can you be a student and a teacher at the same time? It is an interesting time in your professional development, for you must relate to the cooperating teacher(s) and the university supervisor as a learner and to the students you interact with as a professional educator.

The term *student teacher* may appear to be an oxymoron, but in reality, following student teaching and for the rest of your professional life, you must seek out new information (be a student) while at the same time imparting information to others (teaching). During the student teaching semester, you are placed in a situation to learn and grow. This involves maintaining an openness to the cooperating teacher's philosophy, methods, and procedures as well as a willingness to accept constructive criticism.

It is advantageous when an undergraduate music education curriculum affords multiple opportunities to observe and assist in the elementary and secondary schools at various times in your development prior to the student teaching experience. This allows you to get a carefully controlled and delimited taste of life in the real world of teaching prior to the intensive experience provided in student teaching.

Such clinical experiences should help reinforce or modify your decision concerning a choral music education career relatively early in the undergraduate years, lessening the likelihood your student teaching experience will become a final barrier or discouragement. If, however, your student teaching experience seems to indicate you should explore another career path, it is still better to make that discovery prior to entering the field than to do so one, three, or more years later.

Open, full communication is critical during the student teaching semester. If any aspect of the university supervisor's expectations, suggestions, or other information is not clearly understood, ask quickly for clarification. If you feel a need for more feedback or further explanation of a constructive criticism from the cooperating teacher, discuss this as soon as feasible. Misunderstandings are most easily avoided in an atmosphere of open communication.

Although as a student teacher you are still learning, and your personality, style, teaching techniques, and musical abilities will be under intense ongoing scrutiny (probably for the last time during your career), you should relate to the students and other colleagues at the school in a fully professional manner. This involves punctuality, appropriate style of dress, the competent and timely handling of noninstructional responsibilities, and other similar matters.

Arrive at school on time. This does not mean at the same time as the students, but at a time mutually agreed on by you and your cooperating teacher, which will probably be well in advance of the students' arrival. Concerning attire, initially it is probably wise to overdress. Then, as you observe the style of dress of other faculty at the school, your dress can be modified to conform to the norm for the faculty.

Remember that you are now a professional in the eyes of the students. It is wise to relate to them in a consciously formal way, particularly at first, to help make the differentiation between student and student teacher completely clear. This is particularly important for student teachers who are twenty-one or twenty-two years old and youthful in appearance.

A cooperating teacher may assign you various administrative tasks such as attendance taking, grading, and the like. Take such assignments seriously and conscientiously. The manner in which you assume responsibilities will impress not only your cooperating teacher but others who come in contact with your work.

Take the opportunity to learn as much as possible about every aspect of the school setting in which you student teach. Check with your cooperating teacher to determine the feasibility of observing other classes in the school or other schools in the district so you gain an understanding of the working of the total music curriculum.

It would be highly unusual for you to be placed in a situation where every aspect of the cooperating teacher's mode of operation is congruent with your expectations or previous experiences. Each teacher develops a uniquely personal approach to instruction. Observe with a critical eye everything at the student teaching site, but generally it is most beneficial to use the methodologies employed by the cooperating teacher, since those have proven successful in that particular situation.

It is quite appropriate to ask why something is done a particular way or how the cooperating teacher came to use a particular technique. You might have a new method or technique to try out in which the cooperating teacher might be interested. Remember, however, that you are a guest at the school and should not criticize aspects of the operation that do not conform to your expectations. The faculty lounge is not the right forum to express opinions concerning the operation of the school or the methods of the cooperating teacher. Discuss such observations or concerns with your college/university supervisor.

Become acquainted with school administrators. Occasionally a position will become vacant in the school or district where an individual student teaches. When this occurs, the wider the network of acquaintances you have cultivated, the better the chances of being seriously considered to fill the vacancy.

✣ SECURING YOUR FIRST POSITION ✣

A bachelor's degree at the end of your undergraduate studies marks the end of that phase of your formal education. It is an exciting and positive time for the recognition of an academic accomplishment. For most graduates, it is also a time of some anxiety, since the impending conclusion of your undergraduate career also signifies the beginning of the search for a professional position. A variety of strategies will help you in your search for gainful employment in the field of choral music education.

Actually, the process of finding a position in choral music education and making yourself the best possible candidate for that position begins long before the awarding of the undergraduate degree. Even before the end of your undergraduate studies, you should cultivate a network of associations, not only among fellow students, but including university faculty members and music educators in the public schools. Take advantage of any opportunity to visit in the public schools, to observe classes, and to ask questions of the teacher. Some such opportunities should be provided as part of your college or university curriculum. Seek out additional opportunities to get into the public schools and to observe what is happening there. On such occasions, take care to present yourself in the most positive fashion. Dress neatly, speak clearly, and act professionally. Take advantage of opportunities to attend professional meetings, inservice workshops, and conventions. Such events afford not only opportunities for learning, but for establishing relationships with others in the profession.

Develop a résumé of your professional life that maximizes your strengths and pertinent experiences. With the widespread availability of excellent software packages designed to create appealing résumés, there is no reason not to have a visually impressive document. Use the spell checker if it is part of the program, and carefully proofread to correct errors in punctuation and word usage (it works best to have a third party proofread your work). Modify it as needed to adapt the résumé for particular positions, accentuating those portions of your background most pertinent to the position under consideration.

Most colleges and universities have a career planning and placement office to assist in your search for a professional position. Typically, they assemble a placement file for the prospective teacher containing transcripts, letters of reference, and résumé. It is convenient to be able to have such a package sent to prospective employers as needed. Check regularly with your placement office to ascertain what positions are available. Work closely with university music faculty to be aware of positions that may become open.

Limit your search for an initial position as little as possible, maximizing your opportunities for possible interviews and employment. For example, if you begin your search by limiting it to senior high school choral positions, you greatly restrict your chances of securing a position. Senior high school choral positions tend to be filled by experienced teachers, often from within the district where the opening occurs. Be as flexible as possible in your initial job search.

If you hear of a position, secure an application for employment in that district. It is also acceptable and desirable to secure applications from school districts in which you have an interest, even if there is no position presently available. Often, a position for the fall semester will suddenly open up late in the summer, and it is advantageous to have an application on file. Fill it out neatly and completely; remember that an impression of you will be conveyed by your résumé before a prospective employer has an opportunity to meet you in person. Some applicants are typically eliminated from consideration simply because of a poorly prepared or sloppy cover letter or résumé. A sample format for a cover letter to a prospective employer is provided in Appendix G.

When you send a cover letter and résumé, ask the placement office to send a copy of your placement file as well. Follow up with a phone call or letter a week or two later to confirm the materials have been received.

The next step in the process is the interview. Prior to your appointment, learn as much as possible about the position, the school district, and the population it serves. What is the reputation of the music program of the district? How well is it supported by the administration? Prepare a list of a few questions. Review your own record, philosophy of music education, and general background in order to be prepared for questions from the interviewer.

Dress neatly and conservatively. Arrive five to ten minutes ahead of the appointed time. The interview may be conducted by a music supervisor, a personnel director, a principal, or by another administrator. Shake hands firmly, establish eye contact, smile pleasantly, and be prepared to listen carefully and to respond thoughtfully to questions from the interviewer.

Allow the interviewer to control the direction of the interview. Answer questions completely but succinctly. Try to ascertain the attitudes of the interviewer on the topics discussed. When given the opportunity, ask a few well-chosen questions that will convey to the interviewer you have prepared for the interview and will give you the opportunity to get a feel for the administrative attitude toward music education.

Always keep in mind the principal objective of the interview: to gain employment in the district. Do not take up too much of the interviewer's time with your questions and frame them in positive terms. Refrain from making lengthy answers to the interviewer's questions. Keep your answers clearly focused on the questions asked and do not digress. At the conclusion of the interview, thank the administrator for the opportunity to meet him or her, and leave.

Following the interview, you will either be offered a position or not, depending on the decision of the interviewer. There is little to be done to influence the decision at that point. Should an offer be extended, it should be accepted or declined within a few days (no more than a week), although it is reasonable to expect a brief period for consideration. If you are in the enviable position of considering two or more positions, consider the factors that will influence your professional growth and satisfaction in a particular position.

One consideration of course, is salary. All other things being equal, a higher salary certainly could be the deciding factor in choosing between two job possibilities. However, other factors may be considerably more important to your happiness and success in a particular position than the salary. The degree of administrative support, schedule, facilities and equipment available, and budget should all be considered.

Often the first position you obtain requires a rebuilding job in terms of the number of students participating and the kinds of musical experiences being provided. There are many advantages associated with beginning a career in such a position rather than in a well-developed program. If you are hired to lead a thriving and successful program there will be considerable pressure to maintain that level of success, preferably by following the same procedures as your predecessor. In a program that requires rebuilding, any success will clearly be to your credit, and you will be able to refine your own musical and leadership skills as the program develops.

Once you have a few months of teaching experience in a particular position, the advantages and disadvantages of the situation will become much clearer. Although it is undesirable to move from one position to another several times in quick succession, carefully consider your options at all times. If a change in jobs, particularly early in a career, seems advantageous due to negative circumstances associated with a particular position, you should explore this possibility.

✣ PROFESSIONAL GROWTH AND DEVELOPMENT ✣

In choral music education, as in many other areas of endeavor, you either improve or diminish in effectiveness. It is virtually impossible simply to maintain a particular level of proficiency. Without continued study and the absorption of new ideas and techniques, you will gradually lose effectiveness.

For continued success in choral music education, seek professional growth and development at every opportunity. Continue to attend concerts by choral ensembles of all levels and abilities. Seek the advice of fellow directors when confronting a problem, whether it concerns musical style, dealing with parents, or solving a discipline problem.

Read the professional journals. The latest scholarship tends to be reflected in the pages of periodical literature. It may mean throwing the journals into a box until summer and then catching up, but reading *The Choral Journal, Music Educators Journal,* or any of the many publications devoted to education, music, or both, will keep you abreast of current developments in the field. The journals contain reviews of the latest books. If something stimulates your interest, purchase a personal copy or order it for your school library.

Attend the meetings of your professional organizations. Seminars, interest sessions, reading sessions, and informal conversation with colleagues from around the state, the country, or the world will provide a fresh perspective on your daily effort to provide appropriate experiences for your students.

Pursue graduate study in whatever area of music best suits your needs and interests. Choral conducting, music education, voice, musicology, or any other related field are possible choices. Graduate study can be taken in large or small doses, ranging from a one-day workshop to three or more years in residence at a university pursuing a doctoral degree. The most important thing, in the words of a current advertising slogan, is to "Just do it!" Whatever the specific area of study you select, you will build on and expand your present foundation of skills, attitudes, and understandings.

At a minimum, every choral music educator should maintain a membership in the Music Educators National Conference and the American Choral Directors Association. It benefits the profession, since you will financially support the activities of the organization, and it will benefit you, since you will be receiving the publications, invitations to inservice meetings, conventions, and other information from the organization. Many other excellent musical and educational organizations are worthwhile, but association with the two mentioned here are essential.

Communicate with and be supportive of your fellow choral music educators. Initially, it will be helpful to call on your peers for advice and assistance. As you gain experience, be prepared to assist others with their problems and concerns. Your school district may have a formal mentoring program that matches newly graduated teachers with more experienced colleagues for the purposes of feedback, counsel, and encouragement. Even if such a formal program does not exist in your district, seek opportunities to be supportive of colleagues at all levels of experience. Your own teaching proficiency will grow as you work with others to help them improve.

✣ ETHICS ✣

As with aesthetics, when we speak of *ethics,* we use a term that has been a topic of discussion for philosophers for centuries. When we talk about ethics as applied to the field of choral music education, we are referring to standards of conduct in the profession. When you hear the comment concerning a fellow choral educator, "He [or she] is a very ethical person," it is a high compliment.

Ethics has become an increasing concern in a variety of fields during the last decade of the twentieth century. Multiple scandals in the world of finance have focused public attention on the need for high ethical standards in that field. In medicine, advances in forms of treatment, the debate on the efficacy of high-cost, high-technology treatments for the terminally ill, the question of who will receive medicines and therapies which are limited in availability, and a variety of other complex issues in medical ethics have been widely discussed in the general press. The ethical standards of a variety of notable political figures are debated.

The establishment of standards of ethical conduct in the field of choral music education helps maintain its claim to an important place in the school curriculum. If the profession did not have such standards, it would be much more easily relegated to extracurricular or cocurricular status.

What specific qualities are we referring to when we talk about an ethical choral music educator? Perhaps the most important area of ethics is that of relationships. The nature of the relationships we develop with students, colleagues, administrators, and the public will reveal our ethical standards.

Students want to respect their teachers. In relating to students it is desirable to be friendly, but they are not interested in acquiring another peer. This idea is particularly important for the new teacher, who may be relatively close in age to the students. Students will respond positively to an individual who is honest, who makes the welfare of the students a high priority, who maintains a classroom environment that is secure and facilitates learning, and who is fair and consistent in student-teacher interactions.

Relationships with teaching colleagues should also be governed by certain standards. Avoid criticizing colleagues. Make a conscious effort to be courteous, friendly, and supportive of others' professional efforts. Try to look at situations from the perspective of your fellow teachers.

If a problem should develop in a relationship with another faculty member, make an effort to resolve the matter with the individual involved. In working in a school, you relate to a large number of colleagues, some of whom may be negative in their views concerning the school, the administrators, and education in general. Do not be unduly influenced by such negativism, and avoid participation in faculty room discussions that focus on the negative. Do not disparage the efforts of other choral directors. Keep in mind that everyone develops his or her own style of teaching, and that there will be differences in approach among competent educators. Remember that everyone is working to educate students and to help them reach their full potential. If this goal is kept in mind, differences among colleagues can be minimized.

If there is a matter of concern, discuss it with the appropriate person. This brings us to the matter of relationships with administrators. Communicate with and consult with administrators. Feel free to discuss areas of concern, but make an effort to frame such discussions in a positive manner. If you are attempting to secure permission for a particular project or purchase, clearly explain its benefits and attempt to accept any decision as gracefully as possible. This mode of operation will be of benefit in the long run.

In relating to parents and to the general public, it is important to communicate frequently, keeping people informed of the activities of the choral program. Provide sufficient advance notice of choir events so they can be accommodated in parents' calendars.

✣ DISCIPLINE ✣

The area of discipline is a matter of concern to everyone involved in the field of education. If discipline in the classroom cannot be maintained so students feel safe and secure, then learning is significantly inhibited. Numerous books have been devoted exclusively to the topics of classroom management and discipline (see Suggested Readings). The intent of our discussion is to present some basic ideas concerning the maintenance of discipline and classroom management.

Discipline is a particularly important and complex concern for the choral music educator. Students must not only be made to behave in a way that does not impede the learning of their peers, they must also be capable of expressing the emotional content of the music under consideration. Balancing the need for classroom decorum with the necessity for relatively uninhibited expression of emotion requires careful guidance of student enthusiasm and excitement.

Here are some basic ideas concerning discipline:

1. The maintenance of good discipline results from effective rehearsal techniques.
2. Establish guidelines based on mutual respect and common aspirations.
3. Be positive.
4. Be consistent (and objective).
5. Be persistent.
6. Do not reward unacceptable behavior.
7. Communicate with and seek the cooperation of parents.

Effective rehearsal technique and the maintenance of good discipline are interdependent and closely related. The notion that students must be convinced to buy into the choral music making process is critical to the establishment of appropriate classroom behaviors. The maintenance of a neat and orderly rehearsal space, careful sequencing of pieces to be rehearsed, the pace of activity, and your ability to identify areas for musical improvement and to make the appropriate correction will all contribute to a smoothly flowing rehearsal and a well-disciplined ensemble. All of the components of rehearsal technique we discussed in Chapter 2 influence the discipline of the class.

Assuming that effective rehearsal techniques are employed, there are still some basic principles to consider in dealing with the behavioral issues that will inevitably occur from time to time. Even if you have a very effective teaching and rehearsal style, there will be occasions when students may bring to the classroom a problem from their home environment or when they may be feeling the effects of a problem that occurred in another class.

Establish guidelines at the beginning of the school year regarding appropriate behavior in the choral music class and discuss them with choir members. One basis for these guidelines must be respect: self-respect on the part of all concerned, respect of students for the authority of the teacher, and respect from the teacher for each student in the class. The other basis for classroom guidelines must be a shared aspiration for a positive educational experience with choral music. If the guidelines are presented on the basis of these two areas, students will tend to accept and appreciate them. Only adopt those guidelines mandated by the school administration, along with those you deem essential. Keep the number of rules to the minimum necessary for a safe, organized, and respectful environment for music making.

All of our interactions with students must be as positive as possible. Actively seek opportunities to reinforce behaviors, attributes, and anything else about a student that is meritorious. People need positive reinforcement. Even as adults, we thrive on sincere praise. For an adolescent, this need is even greater, particularly when a home environment is less than positive. The most effective positive reinforcement is emphatic, specific, and clear. This is actually an extension of effective rehearsal technique, where in the choral music educator positively reinforces desired musical progress.

Even in dealing with an infraction of the rules, the correction should clearly focus on the inappropriate behavior and not on the perpetrator of it. It is important to avoid attacking the person of any individual in your choral ensembles. This is related to the idea of respect for each individual with whom you interact. In dealing with unacceptable behavior, be unemotional. A display of emotion may actually *reinforce* the undesirable behavior. The deterrent will be the sanction that is applied. Clearly state to the offender that the behavior is unacceptable and must stop.

Have a clear understanding of the sanctions available in dealing with inappropriate behavior. Do not threaten students, but be certain of your ability to keep any promise with regard to the consequences of inappropriate behavior.

Avoid unnecessarily escalating a situation. Sometimes it is sufficient to simply notice the behavior in order to stop it. If Jane is whispering to her neighbor, simply interject her name into a statement you are making or direct a question to her, indicating you are noticing her behavior. Another response might be to make a shift in seating assignments. If an inappropriate behavior is more serious, then some time out of the situation may be necessary for the student. The length of the time out and the setting (the hall? the principal's office? at home?) should be related to the seriousness of the offense, the age of the student, and whether this is a chronic problem.

Reserve discussion of a disciplinary situation with the perpetrator for a private setting, not in front of the class. There are two important reasons for this: It deprives the offender of an audience (which may be a reinforcer of problematic behavior) and it allows the individual to save face. The objective of the interaction is to prevent future problems, not to humiliate or punish (in the negative sense) the offender.

Interactions with students should be consistent. It is not easy to be consistent in one's interactions from one day of the week to the next and from one student to the next. Be on guard for the "halo" or "pitchfork" effects, in which we prejudge a student based on his or her past positive or negative behavior. Treat all students in the same manner, whatever your personal feelings toward them, their talent, their behavior, or their role in the ensemble.

Closely related to the idea of consistency in our actions toward students is the notion of persistence. It may be necessary to make several interventions with a particular student in order to change a behavioral pattern.

We have already stressed the importance of communication with parents as part of an ongoing program of public relations. If efforts have been made to communicate all of the positive things that are happening with the choral program, discussion of specific concerns related to a child's behavior should be much easier. In any case, keep parents informed if a child is creating a problem in chorus class. In speaking with parents, suggest things they can do at home that will help improve the child's behaviors in school.

In all of our dealings with students, the objective is to model appropriate behaviors. Viewed in this light, even a discipline problem requiring teacher intervention is an opportunity for students to learn about how to cope with interpersonal situations.

✣ RESEARCH IN CHORAL MUSIC EDUCATION ✣

All who are involved in choral music education are involved in research. It could be as basic as checking the dates of the composer of a choral piece or as complex as the writing of a doctoral dissertation of several hundred pages on the madrigals of Monteverdi. The demands on your time in starting and maintaining an excellent choral program can make it appear that research is not a high priority topic. Nevertheless, even if you do not have the time or the inclination to pursue a formal research project, a basic means of professional development is to maintain knowledge of current research in the field.

Stay abreast of current research by reading the professional journals and by attending the conventions and other meetings of the MENC, the ACDA, and other professional organizations. Start a personal library of issues of the professional journals to which you subscribe. After a short time you will have an increasingly valuable research resource for your personal use.

A research membership in MENC entitles the member to receive quarterly issues of the *Journal of Research in Music Education,* the primary source for new research in choral music education. In recent years, an additional research publication has been added to the list of publications produced by MENC. Called *Update: Applications of Research in Music Education,* it provides practical applications of recent research in a variety of areas of the profession, presented in a clear and concise manner, intelligible to any music educator.

The techniques and terminology of quantitative research in music education can seem formidable to the reader without a background in the area. When in doubt, check with a college or university music educator for help in interpretation.

As you gain experience in the field of choral music, the need for more information will become evident. To present an intellectually honest and stylistically accurate performance of a selection may require research into music history, performance practice, and style. Reading, checking with authorities who may be available to you, and consulting with other choral music educators may lead to more formal research in the context of a graduate program.

As we mentioned in Chapter 9, the last thirty years have produced a proliferation of research into style and performance practice as it relates to choral music. To be an effective choral music educator requires an ongoing commitment to learn as much as possible about the music we explore with students and about the ways students learn about music most effectively.

✣ THE FUTURE OF THE PROFESSION ✣

The current status of choral music education in the United States is an eclectic mixture of the positive and negative. Many exemplary music programs around the country offer students excellent opportunities for personal and musical growth through carefully planned, sequentially developed experiences. Too often, however, the musical experiences offered lack cohesion, communication, and articulation from grade level to grade level and from subject to subject. We are losing a large number of young men from our programs at the junior high level. An unprecedented variety of well-edited choral music is currently available, yet large numbers of trite and trivial choral pieces are currently being published, purchased, and performed.

A popular cliché states there are no problems, only opportunities. The American educational scene in the 1990s and beyond offers many such opportunities for the choral music educator. As related in Chapter 9, in the current era of educational retrenchment, the place of music and the other arts in the curriculum has been questioned. In some instances, music programs have been eliminated from school district budgets, relegated to extracurricular status, or curtailed. Under these circumstances, choral music educators must be prepared to articulate in an accurate and compelling fashion the reasons why music and the other arts merit inclusion in the curriculum.

The development of high-quality comprehensive choral music education programs is certainly an important component of this issue. Unfortunately, however, choral music educators can no longer afford the luxury of being apolitical and depending on the quality of their work in the schools to assure continued support by administrators and taxpayers.

One important part of maintaining a proactive position is for the choral music educator to stay informed of developments that could have an impact on the choral music program. These developments could be local; for example, the school district where you are employed could experience a shortfall in tax revenues requiring the curtailment of expenditures. Such developments could be national; the impact of developments in Washington concerning funding for the arts and for education exerts an impact around the country. They could be international; concern over the effectiveness of U.S. schools versus those in Europe or Japan has created a renewed preoccupation with the teaching of science and technology.

In addition to being informed, the choral music educator should be involved. Involvement could mean attending school board meetings or actively participating with your students in activities related to Music in Our Schools Month. Certainly, involvement means supporting the efforts of the professional organizations to publicize and strengthen the position of music in the schools.

Partnerships between the school and the community have the potential to enhance choral music education and to promote music as a lifelong activity. In the last thirty years, the idea of enhancing interaction with the community has been urged by such panels as the Yale Seminar and the Tanglewood Symposium. The results of choral music education have always been more prominently displayed to the community than the results of other subjects in the school curriculum.

This is a potentially powerful means of developing community support. Occasionally, this support is realized (usually when a crisis erupts and the curricular position of some aspect of the music program is challenged). Much potential community support is unrealized, however. Bringing community musical resources into the classroom will enrich students' musical experiences. Professional musicians, representatives from the music industry, and alumni of the choral program can provide new insights into music making for students if they are given the opportunity to do so.

Choral students should be made aware of the opportunities available to them for continuing their participation in music activities after graduation. Students should be informed about community ensembles in which they may participate, and encouraged to attend performances by local community groups.

As choral music educators, we need to consider our role in continuing education in music. Changing demographic data reveal an increasing proportion of older adults in the United States. The popularity of programs such as Elderhostel, which returns senior citizens to college campuses for a variety of classes and programs, offers evidence of the need for further similar experiences. Older Americans are only one segment of the population whose needs have not been adequately considered by music educators. Consideration should be given to the role of choral music in the continuing education of a changing American population.

The United States is increasingly diverse in its ethnic mix, and the populations of various national backgrounds are increasingly proud and eager to maintain their cultural identity. Therefore, multicultural music educators not only provide students with a knowledge of foreign cultures, but they also enhance our understanding of ourselves as a nation. The world is shrinking. The capability for instantaneous communication and increasingly rapid transportation around the globe has dramatically heightened the need for better understanding of our fellow residents of the planet.

Difficult challenges and an unprecedented variety of demands confront the choral music educator of the 1990s and beyond. Despite its problems and perplexities, the profession of choral music education also holds the opportunity for a fulfilling career.

✣ SUMMARY ✣

The choral music profession is a demanding yet fulfilling one. This chapter presented some guidelines for a successful student teaching experience and strategies for securing a professional position in choral music education. Continuing education and professional growth are important to the successful choral music educator; opportunities for both formal and informal professional growth were discussed.

Ethical standards of conduct help establish the validity of the choral music education profession, and guidelines in this important area were presented. Discipline and classroom management often cause apprehension, particularly for preservice choral music educators. A variety of principles for maintaining a safe and orderly environment for learning have been discussed. Finally, current and future trends and a discussion of strategies for developing community support for choral music were presented.

Questions

1. Although the term *student teacher* may seem to be a contradiction in terms, why does it apply to teachers at every stage of professional growth?

2. When questions arise concerning teaching strategies or other aspects of the cooperating teacher's procedures, how and when should this be discussed?
3. What can you do as an undergraduate to prepare for the process of securing a position in choral music education?
4. What is the role of the placement office in the search for a teaching position?
5. Name two or three things to keep in mind in preparing for an interview with a prospective employer.
6. Is it possible to maintain a particular level of teaching proficiency over a number of years in the profession?
7. What are three ways to grow professionally after the completion of undergraduate studies?
8. What is meant by professional ethics in the field of choral music education?
9. List three strategies for maintaining effective discipline in the choral classroom.
10. Name an issue you believe will be important to the choral music education profession as the twenty-first century begins.

Suggested Reading

ALBERT, LINDA. *A Teacher's Guide to Cooperative Discipline.* Circle Pines, MN: American Guidance Service, 1989.

CANTER, LEE, with MARLENE CANTER. *Assertive Discipline: A Take-Charge Approach for Today's Educator.* Los Angeles: Canter and Associates, 1976.

COLLINS, IRMA. *Why Teach? Why Music? Why Me?* Reston, VA: Music Educators National Conference, 1992.

COLWELL, RICHARD (ed.). *Handbook of Research on Music Teaching and Learning.* New York: Macmillan, 1992.

COWDEN, ROBERT (ed.). *Careers in Music.* Reston, VA: Music Educators National Conference, 1989.

LAMB, GORDON. *Choral Techniques.* Dubuque, IA: Wm. C. Brown, 1988.

MILLER, KENNETH. *Vocal Music Education.* Englewood Cliffs, NJ: Prentice Hall, 1988.

ROBINSON, RUSSELL. *Preparing to Teach Music in Today's Schools: The Best of MEJ.* Reston, VA: Music Educators National Conference, 1993.

Appendix A

The Music Code of Ethics*

❖❖❖

Music educators and professional musicians alike are committed to the general acceptance of music as an essential factor in the social and cultural growth of our country. Music educators contribute to this end by fostering the study of music among children and by developing a greater interest in music.

This unanimity of purpose is further exemplified by the fact that a great many professional musicians are music educators and the fact that a great many music educators are, or have been, actively engaged in the field of professional performance.

The members of high school instrumental groups—orchestras and bands of all types, including stage bands—look to the professional organization for example and inspiration. The standards of quality acquired during the education of these students are of great importance when they become active patrons of music in later life. Through their influence on sponsors, employers, and program makers in demanding adequate musical performances, they have a beneficial effect upon the prestige and economic status of the professional musicians.

---

*Published by the American Federation of Musicians, Music Educators National Conference, American Association of School Administrators, National Association of Elementary School Principals, and National Association of Secondary School Principals. Used by permission.

Since it is in the interest of the music educator to attract public attention to his attainments, not only for the main purpose of promoting the values of music education but also to enhance his position and subsequently his income, and since it is in the interest of the professional musician to create more opportunities for employment at increased remuneration, it is only natural that some incidents might occur in which the interests of the members of one or the other group might be infringed upon, either from lack of forethought or lack of ethical standards among individuals.

In order to establish a clear understanding as to the limitations of the fields of professional music and music education in the United States, the following statement of policy, adopted by the Music Educators National Conference and the American Federation of Musicians and approved by the American Association of School Administrators, the National Association of Elementary School Principals, and the National Association of Secondary School Principals, is recommended to those serving in their respective fields:

✣ I. MUSIC EDUCATION ✣

The field of music education, including the teaching of music and such demonstrations of music education as do not directly conflict with the interests of the professional musician, is the province of the music educator. It is the primary purpose of this document and the desire of all the parties signatory hereto that the professional musician shall have the fullest protection in his efforts to earn his living from the playing and rendition of music; to that end it is recognized and accepted that all music to be performed under this section of the "Code of Ethics" herein set forth is and shall be performed in connection with nonprofit, noncommercial, and noncompetitive enterprises. Under the heading of "Music Education" the following are included:

1. School functions initiated by the schools as a part of a school program, whether in a school building or other site.

2. Community functions organized in the interest of the schools strictly for educational purposes, such as those that might be originated by the parent and teachers association.

3. School exhibits prepared as a courtesy on the part of a school district for educational organizations or educational conventions being entertained in the district.

4. Educational broadcasts that have the purpose of demonstrating or illustrating pupils' achievements in music study or that represent the culmination of a period of study and rehearsal. Included in this category are local, state, regional, and national school music festivals and competitions held under the auspices of schools, colleges, and/or educational organizations on a nonprofit basis and broadcast to acquaint the public with the results of music instruction in the schools.

5. Civic occasions of local, state, or national patriotic interest, of sufficient breadth to enlist the sympathies and cooperation of all persons, such as those held by the American Legion and Veterans of Foreign Wars in connection with their Memorial Day services in the cemeteries. It is understood that affairs of this kind may be participated in only when such participation does not in the least usurp the rights and privileges of local professional musicians.

6. Benefit performances for local charities, such as the Red Cross and hospitals, when and where local professional musicians would likewise donate their services.

7. Educational or civic services that might be mutually agreed upon beforehand by the school authorities and official representative of the local professional musicians.

8. Student or amateur recordings for study purposes made in the classroom or in connection with contest, festival, or conference performances by students. Such recordings shall be limited to exclusive use by the students and their teachers and shall not be offered for general sale to the public through commercial outlets. This definition pertains only to the purpose and utilization of student or amateur recordings and not to matters concerned with copyright regulations. Compliance with copyright requirements applying to recordings of compositions not in the public domain is the responsibility of the school, college, or educational organization under whose auspices the recording is made.

✣ II. ENTERTAINMENT ✣

The field of entertainment is the province of the professional musician. Under this heading the following are included:

1. Civic parades (where professional marching bands exist), ceremonies, expositions, community concerts, and community-center activities; regattas; nonscholastic contests, festivals, athletic games, activities, or celebrations, and the like; and national, state, and county fairs (see section I, paragraphs 2 and 5 of this document for further definition).

2. Functions for the furtherance, directly or indirectly, of any public or private enterprise; functions by chambers of commerce, boards of trade, and commercial clubs or associations.

3. Any occasion that is partisan or sectarian in character or purpose.

4. Functions of clubs, societies, and civic or fraternal organizations.

Statements that funds are not available for the employment of professional musicians; or that if the talents of amateur musical organizations cannot be had, other musicians cannot or will not be employed; or that the amateur musicians are to play without remuneration of any kind, are all immaterial.

This code is a continuing agreement that shall be reviewed regularly to make it responsive to changing conditions.

Appendix B

Latin Texts: Ordinary of Mass and Requiem Mass

✣ ✣ ✣

✣ THE ORDINARY OF THE MASS ✣

Kyrie

Kyrie eleison, Christe eleison. Kyrie eleison.

Lord, have mercy. Christ, have mercy. Lord, have mercy.

Gloria

Gloria in excelsis Deo. Et in terra pax hominibus bonae voluntatis. Laudamus te. Benedicimus te. Adoramus te. Glorificamus te. Gratias agimus tibi propter magnam gloriam tuam. Domine Deus, Rex coelestis, Deus Pater omnipotens. Domine Fili unigenite, Jesu Christe. Domine Deus, Agnus Dei, Filius Patris. Qui tollis peccata mundi, miserere nobis. Qui tollis peccata mundi, suscipe deprecationem nostram. Qui sedes ad dexteram Patris, miserere nobis. Quoniam tu solus sanctus. Tu solus Dominus. Tu solus Altissimus, Jesu Christe. Cum Sancto Spiritu, in gloria Dei Patris. Amen.

Glory to God in the highest. And on earth peace to men of good will. We praise Thee. We bless Thee. We worship Thee. We glorify Thee. We give thanks to Thee for Thy great glory. O Lord God, heavenly King, God the Father almighty. Lord Jesus Christ, the only-begotten Son. Lord God, Lamb of God, Son of the Father. Who taketh away the sins of the world, have mercy upon us. Who taketh away the sins of the world, receive our prayer. Thou who sitteth at the right hand of the Father, have mercy upon us. For Thou alone art holy. Thou alone art Lord. Thou alone, O Jesus Christ, art most high. With the Holy Spirit, in the glory of God the Father. Amen.

Credo

Credo in unum Deum, Patrem omnipotentem, factorem coeli et terrae, visibilium omnium, et invisibilium. Et in unum Dominum Jesum Christum, Filium Dei unigenitum. Et ex Patre natum ante omnia saecula. Deum de Deo, lumen de lumine, Deum verum de Deo vero. Genitum, non factum, consubstantialem Patri: per quem omnia facta sunt. Qui propter nos homines, et propter nostram salutem descendit de coelis. Et incarnatus est de Spiritu Sancto ex Maria Virgine; et homo factus est. Crucifixus etiam pro nobis; sub Pontio Pilato passus, et sepultus est. Et resurrexit tertia die, secundum Scripturas. Et ascendit in coelum: sedet ad dexteram Patris. Et iterum venturus est cum gloria, judicare vivos et mortuos: cujus regni non erit finis. Et in Spiritum Sanctum, Dominum et vivificantem: qui ex Patre Filioque procedit. Qui cum Patre et Filio simul adoratur, et conglorificatur; qui locutus est per prophetas. Et unam sanctam catholicam et apostolicam Ecclesiam. Confiteor unum baptisma in remissionem peccatorum. Et expecto resurrectionem mortuorum. Et vitam venturi saeculi. Amen.

I believe in one God, the Father almighty, maker of heaven and earth, and of all things visible and invisible. And in one Lord Jesus Christ, the only-begotten Son of God. Born of the Father before all ages. God of God, light of light, true God of true God. Begotten, not made; of one substance with the Father: by whom all things were made. Who for us, and for our salvation, came down from heaven. And was made flesh by the Holy Ghost of the Virgin Mary: and was made man. He was also crucified for us, suffered under Pontius Pilate, and was buried. And on the third day He rose again, according to the Scriptures. He ascended into heaven: He sitteth at the right hand of the Father. And He shall come again with glory to judge the living and the dead; and of His Kingdom there shall be no end. I believe in the Holy Spirit, the Lord and Giver of life, who proceedeth from the Father and the Son. Who together with the Father and the Son is adored and glorified: who spoke to us through the prophets. And in one holy, catholic and apostolic Church. I confess one baptism for the remission of sins. And I expect the resurrection of the dead. And the life of the world to come. Amen.

Sanctus

Sanctus, Sanctus, Sanctus Dominus Deus Sabaoth. Pleni sunt coeli et terra gloria tua. Osanna in excelsis.

Holy, Holy, Holy Lord God of hosts. Heaven and earth are full of Thy glory. Hosanna in the highest.

Benedictus

Benedictus qui venit in nomine Domini. Osanna in excelsis.

Blessed is He who comes in the name of the Lord. Hosanna in the highest.

Agnus Dei

Agnus Dei, qui tollis peccata mundi, miserere nobis. Agnus Dei, qui tollis peccata mundi, miserere nobis. Agnus Dei, qui tollis peccata mundi, dona nobis pacem.

Lamb of God, who takest away the sins of the world, have mercy upon us. Lamb of God, who takest away the sins of the world, have mercy upon us. Lamb of God, who taketh away the sins of the world, grant us peace.

✣ MISSA PRO DEFUNCTIS (REQUIEM MASS) ✣

Introit

Requiem aeternam dona eis, Domine: et lux perpetua luceat eis. Te decet hymnus Deus in Sion, et tibi reddetur votum in Jerusalem: exaudi orationem meam: ad te omnis caro veniet. Requiem.

Eternal rest grant to them, O Lord: and let perpetual light shine upon them. A hymn, O God, becometh Thee in Sion; and a vow shall be paid to Thee in Jerusalem. O hear my prayer: all flesh shall come to Thee. Eternal rest.

Kyrie eleison

Kyrie eleison. Christe eleison. Kyrie eleison.

Lord, have mercy. Christ, have mercy. Lord, have mercy.

Gradual

Requiem aeternam dona eis, Domine: et lux perpetua luceat eis. In memoria aeterna erit justus: ab auditione mala non timebit.

Eternal rest give to them, O Lord: and let perpetual light shine upon them. The just shall be in everlasting remembrance: he shall not fear the evil hearing.

Sequence

1. Dies irae, dies illa, Solvet saeclum in favilla: Teste David cum Sibylla.	Day of wrath, that day of warning, Shall dissolve the world into ashes, As David prophesied with Sybil.
2. Quantus tremor est futurus, Quando judex est venturus, Cuncta stricte discussurus!	What great trembling there will be, When the judge shall come To investigate all things.
3. Tuba mirum spargens sonum Per sepulcra regionum, Coget omnes ante thronum.	Wondrous sound the trumpet flingeth, Through earth's sepulchers, All before the throne it bringeth.
4. Mors stupebit et natura, Cum resurget creatura, Judicanti responsura.	Death is struck, and nature also, All creation is awaking, To answer the Judge.
5. Liber scriptus proferetur, In quo totum continetur, Unde mundus judicetur.	A written book will be made known, Containing all, from which The world will be judged.
6. Judex ergo cum sedebit, Quidquid latet apparebit: Nil inultum remanebit.	When the Judge is seated, Whatever is hidden will be revealed, And no wrong shall be unpunished.
7. Quid sum miser tunc dicturus? Quem patronum rogaturus, Cum vix justus sit securus?	What shall I, frail man, say? Which protector shall I ask for, When the just are scarcely secure?
8. Rex tremendae majestatis, Qui salvandos salvas gratis, Salva me, fons pietatis.	King of terrifying majesty, Who dost free salvation send us, Fount of pity, save me.
9. Recordare, Jesu pie, Quod sum causa tuae viae: Ne me perdas illa die.	Remember, merciful Jesus, That I am the cause of your journey; Do not cast me out on that day.

10. Quarens me, sedisti lassus:
Redemisti crucem passus:
Tantus labor non sit cassus.

Faint and weary you sought me,
On the cross of suffering you redeemed me.
Such great labor shall not be in vain.

11. Juste judex ultionis,
Donum fac remissionis,
Ante diem rationis.

Just Judge of vengeance
Grant Thy gift of absolution,
Before that day of reckoning.

12. Ingemisco, tamquam reus:
Culpa rubet vultus meus:
Supplicanti parce, Deus.

Guilty, now I groan;
My face is red with shame.
Spare, O God, Thy supplicant.

13. Qui Mariam absolvisti,
Et latronem exaudisti,
Mihi quoque spem dedisti.

You who absolved Mary
And heeded the thief
Have also given me hope.

14. Preces meae non sunt dignae:
Sed tu bonus fac benigne,
Ne perenni cremer igne.

My prayers are not worthy;
Yet, good Lord, kindly grant
That I not burn in everlasting fire.

15. Inter oves locum praesta,
Et ab haedis me sequestra,
Statuens in parte dextra.

With Thy favored sheep O place me,
Separate me from the goats
Stationing me on Thy right hand.

16. Confutatis maledictis,
Flammis acribus addictis,
Voca me cum benedictis.

When the wicked are confounded,
Doomed to fierce flames,
Call me with Thy saints.

17. Oro supplex et acclinis,
Cor contritum quasi cinis:
Gere curam mei finis.

I pray, kneeling and suppliant,
My heart contrite, as ashes;
Care for me at my end.

18. Lacrimosa dies illa,
Qua resurget ex favilla

Ah, that day of tears on which the guilty shall rise

19. Judicandus homo reus:
Huic ergo parce Deus.

From the embers for judgment.
Spare them then, O God.

20. Pie Jesu Domine,
dona eis. Amen.

Merciful Lord Jesus, grant them rest.
Amen.

Offertory

Domine Jesu Christe, Rex gloriae, libera animas omnium fidelium defunctorum de poenis inferni, et de profundo lacu: libera eas de ore leonis, ne absorbeat eas tartarus, ne cadant in obscurum: sed signifer sanctus Michael, repraesentet eas in lucem sanctam: Quam olim Abrahae promisisti, et semini ejus.

Hostias et preces tibi, Domine, laudis offerimus: tu suscipe pro animabus illis, quarum hodie memoriam facimus: fac eas, Domine, de morte transire ad vitam: Quam olim Abrahae promisisti, et semini ejus.

Lord, Jesus Christ, King of Glory, deliver the souls of all the faithful departed from the pains of hell and from the deep pit: deliver them from the lion's mouth, that hell may not swallow them up, and may they not fall into darkness; but may Thy holy standard-bearer, Michael, lead them into the holy light; which Thou didst promise to Abraham and to his seed.

We offer to Thee, O Lord, sacrifices and prayers: do Thou receive them in behalf of those souls whom we commemorate this day. Grant them, O Lord, to pass from death unto life; which Thou didst promise to Abraham and to his seed.

Sanctus

Sanctus, Sanctus, Sanctus Dominus Deus Sabaoth. Pleni sunt coeli et terra gloria tua. Osanna in excelsis.

Holy, Holy, Holy Lord God of Sabaoth. Heaven and earth are full of Thy glory. Hosanna in the highest.

Benedictus

Benedictus qui venit in nomine Domini. Osanna in excelsis.

Blessed is He who comes in the name of the Lord. Hosanna in the highest.

Agnus Dei

Agnus Dei, qui tollis peccata mundi, dona eis requiem. Agnus Dei, qui tollis peccata mundi, dona eis requiem. Agnus Dei, qui tollis peccata mundi, dona eis requiem aeternam.

Lamb of God, who takest away the sins of the world, grant them rest. Lamb of God, who takest away the sins of the world, grant them rest. Lamb of God, who takest away the sins of the world, grant them eternal rest.

Communion

Lux aeterna luceat eis, Domine: cum sanctis tuis in aeternum, quia pius es. Requiem aeternam dona eis, Domine, et lux perpetua luceat eis. Cum sanctis tuis in aeternum, quia pius es.

May light eternal shine on them, O Lord. With Thy saints forever, for Thou art merciful. Eternal rest give to them, O Lord: and let perpetual light shine upon them. With Thy saints forever, for Thou art merciful.

Responsory After Absolution

Libera me, Domine, de morte aeterna, in die illa tremenda: quando coeli movendi sunt et terra: Dum veneris judicare saeculum per ignem. Tremens factus sum ego, et timeo, dum discussio venerit, atque venture ira. Quando coeli movendi sunt et terra.

Dies illa, dies irae, calamitatis et miseriae, dies magna et amara valde. Dum veneris judicare saeculum per ignem. Requiem aeternam dona eis Domine: et lux perpetua luceat eis. (The Responsory is then repeated up to "Tremens.")

Deliver me, O Lord, from eternal death in that awful day: when the heavens and the earth shall be moved: when Thou shalt come to judge the world by fire. Dread and trembling have laid hold on me, and I fear exceedingly because of the judgment and the wrath to come. When the heavens and the earth shall be shaken.

O that day, that day of wrath, of sore distress and of all wretchedness, that great and exceeding bitter day. When Thou shalt come to judge the world by fire. Eternal rest grant to them, O Lord, and let perpetual light shine upon them. (The Responsory is then repeated up to "Dread.")

Appendix C

Multicultural Choral Examples

❖❖❖

The following listing contains representative examples of choral music from a variety of national, cultural, and ethnic traditions. Consult with music dealers and publishers for additional repertoire. In the case of African American spirituals, there is a wide variety available from many publishers.

African and African American

Bagley, Peter. "Live a Humble," SATB, Alfred, 6606.

Dennard, Brazeal. "Hush! Hush! Somebody's Callin' My Name," Various voicings available, Shawnee Press.

Leck, Henry. "South African Suite," SAB or SSA, Plymouth, HL-400.

Maddux, David. "O Sifune Mungu," SSATTB, Word, 3010467168.

Ray, Robert. "Gospel Mass," SATB, Hal Leonard, HL 4470714.

Still, William Grant. "The Blind Man," SAB, Theodore Presser, GP309.

Thomas, Andre. "Keep Your Lamps," SATB, Hinshaw, HMC-577.

Tucker, Judith Cook. "Yonder Come Day," AA Cambiata, World Music.

Whalem, Wendell. "Betelehemu," TTBB, Lawson-Gould, 52647.

Asian

DeCormier, Robert. "Ahrirang" (Korean), SATB, Lawson-Gould, 51540.

DeCormier, Robert. "Suliram" (Indonesian), SATB, Lawson-Gould, 51755.

Jergenson, Dale. "Prairie Love Song" (Chinese), SATB, Laurendale Associates, CH-1038.

Ogura, Ro. "Hotaru Koi" (Japanese), SSA, Theodore Presser, 312-41520.

Schafer, R. Murray. "Gamelan" (Southeast Asian), Four-part Arcana Editions.

Terri, Sally. "Chi-Chi Pap-pa" (Japanese), SATB, Lawson-Gould, 51201.

Hispanic

De Cormier, Robert. "La Virgen Lava Panales" (Spanish), SATB, Lawson-Gould, 552227.

Goetze, Mary. "A Zing-A-Za" (Brazilian), SSAA, Boosey and Hawkes, OCTB6276.

Jimenez, A. "La Paloma Se Fue" (Puerto Rican), SA, World Music.

Jimenez, A. "Si Me Dan Pastales" (Puerto Rican), SATB, World Music.

Roberts, H. A. "Tumbando Cana" (Cuban), SATB, Lawson-Gould, 51685.

Rose, Gregory. "Five Spanish Carols," Various voicings, World Music.

Middle Eastern

Adler, H. "By the Waters of Babylon," SATB, Transcontinental, 990241.

Eddleman, D. "Nes Gadol Haya Sham" (Yiddish), SSA, Kjos, GC150.

Hunter, R. Horah: "Chanitah" ("Three Palestinian Dances"), Lawson-Gould, 569.

Rao, Doreen. "Hashivenu, Unison," Boosey and Hawkes, OCTB6430.

Tucker, J. C. "Hag Shavuot," SSA or SAB, World Music.

North American

Archer, Violet. "Three French-Canadian Folk Songs," SATB, Berandol, 917A7AJ.

Dalglish, Malcolm. "Reel a' Bouche" (French-Canadian), SSA, Plymouth, HL-215.

Henderson, Watson. "La Chasse L'Eté" (French-Canadian), Unison, Gordon Thompson.

Ramish, Imant. "Song of the Stars" (Native American), SSA, Boosey and Hawkes.

Smith, Gregg. "Now I Walk in Beauty" (Native American), SATB, G. Schirmer, 12374.

Somers, Harry. "Feller From Fortune" (Canadian), SATB, Gordon Thompson.

Swift, Robert. "I'se the B'y" (Newfoundland), SATB, C.P.P. Belwin, DMC8194.

Appendix D

Sample Choral Policies*

❖❖❖

Vocal Music Course Objectives

- To provide the student with an opportunity to develop proper vocal technique through correct posture, breath control, basic diction principles, and a pleasant singing tone.
- To provide the student with an opportunity to develop perceptual, cognitive, affective, and psychomotor skills through choral experiences.
- To provide the student with an atmosphere of acceptance within the group and positive reinforcement of the student's individual voice resulting in a growing lifetime activity that gives personal enrichment to life.

Music Department Philosophy

The importance music holds in the life of our society cannot be overestimated. We believe, therefore, that every student should have the opportunity to create and respond to singing and listening to music. The sharing of

*St. Charles West High School, St. Charles, MO., Doris Hylton, choral director. Used by permission.

these experiences with others, develops perceptual, cognitive, affective and psychomotor learning. The study of music accelerates self-development, task completion ability and group effort, and provides a growing lifetime activity which gives personal enrichment to life.

High School Vocal Music Philosophy

We believe the high school vocal music program should be comprehensive in nature with the goal of developing both musical concepts and skills that will enable the student to become a better musician and to make decisions about music. Building on a foundation of musical concepts that deal with elements such as rhythm, melody, harmony, dynamics, texture, tonality, and form, musical experiences should be developed sequentially following sound educational practices. Vocal skills involve an understanding of these elements of music as well as a knowledge of the fundamentals of good vocal production and a knowledge of the various styles and periods of choral literature.

Singing should be a satisfying activity both physically and mentally. It should provide the student with a natural avenue of self-expression and emotional release, and fulfill the need for group participation and self-esteem. While performance is an important part of the choral program, rehearsals should include the study of the music literature being performed. Both elective and selective ensembles should provide an opportunity for students at various levels of musical ability to participate in both the learning and performing experience.

Participation in the high school choral program should allow the student to develop a positive attitude toward music, to make value judgments about the many styles of music in today's society and to feel comfortable using music as a vehicle of personal expression in both performance and recreation.

Grading Criteria

1. Attendance at performances—see attendance policy
2. Attitude toward daily rehearsal—a positive attitude toward the music and a courteous attitude toward other people
3. Activity—participation in daily rehearsals—includes being on time, having your music, following directions, etc.
4. Ability—based on singing tests performed with one voice on a part and/or written tests

Each area is worth 20% to 30% of the total grade each quarter. Extra credit may be given for participation in nonrequired events such as All District Choir at the discretion of the director, providing there have been no unexcused absences from any required performances during the quarter.

Attendance Policy

1. Attendance at all performances is required and only two excuses will be accepted:
   a. student illness
   b. death in the immediate family
2. A note must be given to the teacher with the signature and telephone number of a parent or legal guardian so that the excuse may be verified. Upon verification, the student will receive a C for that performance.
3. Work is not an acceptable excuse. Advance notice of performance dates will allow time to rearrange work schedules.
4. Unexcused absences receive an F.
5. Because of the interaction of the individuals as a group, no work can be given to make up lost performance time.

1992-93 Choir Calendar

October 1	Student Recital, Choir Room
October 5, 6	All District Choir Auditions, Pattonville HS
October 29	*FALL CHOIR CONCERT*
October 31	All District Choir Festival, Pattonville HS
December 17	*WINTER CHOIR CONCERT*
January 9	Suburban 9-10 Honors Choir, Lafayette HS
March 11	Spring Vocal Recital, Auditorium
March 13	District Solo/Solo Ensemble Festival, Pattonville HS
March	Spring Musical, Auditorium
March 25	Concert: SCW & SCHS Choirs & Orchestra, SCHS Auditorium
April 27, 28	District Large Ensemble
April 30	State Solo/Small Ensemble Festival, Columbia UMC
May	Voice Lab Recital, Choir Room
May 8, 9	Worlds of Fun Festival, Kansas City
May 20	*SPRING CHOIR CONCERT AND AWARDS*

The above does not include fundraising events or additional performances by Entertainment West.

Your assistance is needed in the following areas. Please let me know if you can help with these activities:

1. Costumes: Fitting present costumes, repairs, new costumes, and checking in costumes at the end of the year. Students and parents are responsible for their child's costume once it is checked out of school.
2. Chaperones for trips, festivals, performances, and the musical.
3. Programs: Typing and ad layout
4. Fundraising: Collect money, check items, distribute items, head events.

5. Handyman: Shelves in closet, musical sets, repairs.
6. Transportation: Drive students to event when a bus is not needed. Students are not allowed to drive to performance events.
7. All Parents: Check with student to determine if choral music needs extra rehearsal.
8. All Parents: Be responsible for student attending required performances.
9. All Parents: Check to see that the choir costume is complete and clean for all performances.

Vocal Music Schedule

Period 1	Conference Period
Period 2	Men's Choir
Period 3	Concert Choir
Period 4	Voice Lab
Period 5	Treble Choir
Period 6	Madrigal Choir

The students and I would be very pleased to have you visit one of our rehearsals. Please do not hesitate to call me with any questions or concerns.

Doris Hylton, Director
555-5121 ext. 140 School
555-1916 Home

Appendix E

Music Publishers and Distributors

❖ ❖ ❖

This listing is accurate as of January 1, 1994. Check with your music dealer if more current information is required.

Aberdeen Music, Inc. (order from Plymouth Music Co.)
Agape (order from Hope Publishing Co.)
Alexandria House, 468 McNally Dr., Nashville, TN 37211.
Alfred Publishing Co., P.O. Box 10003, 16380 Roscoe Blvd., Van Nuys, CA 91410.
Antara Music Group, P.O. Box 210, Alexandria, IN 46001.
Art Masters Studios, Inc., 2710 Nicollet Ave., Minneapolis, MN 55408-1630.
Associated Music Publishers, Inc., 24 E. 22nd St., New York, NY 10010 (order from Hal Leonard Publishing Corp.)
Augsburg Fortress Publishing House, 426 S. Fifth St., Box 1209, Minneapolis, MN 55440.
AVI Music Publishing Group, 10116 Riverside Dr., Suite 200, Toluca Lake, CA 91602
Bärenreiter Music Publishers (order from Foreign Music Distributors)
Beckenhorst Press, P.O. Box 14273, Columbus, OH 43214.
Belmont Music Publishers, P.O. Box 231, Pacific Palisades, CA 90272.
Belwin-Mills Music (see CPP/Belwin Music)
Irving Berlin Music Corp., 29 W. 46th Street, New York, NY 10019
Big 3 Music Corp. (order from CPP/Belwin Music)
Birch Tree Group, Ltd., 180 Alexander St., Princeton, NJ 08540
Fred Bock Music Company, P.O. Box 570567, Tarzana, CA 91357
Boelke-Bomart, Inc., and Mobart Music Publications (order from Jerona Music Corp.)
Boosey & Hawkes, Inc., 24 E. 21st St., New York, NY 10010-7200
Bote & Bock Musikverlag (order from Hal Leonard Publishing Corp.)
Bourne Company, 5 W. 37th St., New York, NY 10018

Breitkopf & Härtel (order from Broude Bros, Ltd.)
Broadman Press, 127 Ninth Ave. N., Nashville, TN 37234
Broude Brothers, Ltd., 141 White Oaks Rd., Williamstown, MA 01267
Cambiata Press, P.O. Box 1151, Conway, AR 72032
Carus-Verlag, Stuttgart (order from Mark Foster Music Co.)
Chantry Music Press, 32 N. Center St., Springfield, OH 45502
Chappell Music Co. (order from Hal Leonard Publishing Corp.)
Charter Publications (order from J.W. Pepper & Son, Inc.)
Cherry Lane Music Co., Inc., 10 Midland Ave., Port Chester, NY (order from Alfred Publishing Co.)
John Church Company (order from Theodore Presser Co.)
Franco Columbo Publications (order from CPP/Belwin Music)
Concordia Publishing House, 3558 S. Jefferson Ave., St. Louis, MO 63118
Consolidated Music Publishers, Inc. (order from Music Sales Corp.)
Coronet Press (order from Theodore Presser Co.)
CPP/Belwin Music, 15800 N.W. 48th Ave., P.O. Box 4340, Miami, FL 33014-9969
Creative World Music Publications (order from Sierra Music Publications)
Curtis Music Press (order from Neil A. Kjos Music Co.)
J. Curwen & Sons (order from Hal Leonard Publishing Corp.)
Dartmouth Collegium Musicum (order from Shawnee Press, Inc.)
Roger Dean Publishing Company (order from The Lorenz Corporation)
Oliver Ditson (order from Theodore Presser Co.)
ECS Publishing, 138 Ipswich St., Boston, MA 02215
Edition Musica, Budapest, Hungary (order from Boosey & Hawkes, Inc.)
Edition Musicus, P.O. Box 1341, Stamford, CT 06904
Editions Salabert (order from Hal Leonard Publishing Corp.)
Elkan-Vogel, Inc. (order from Theodore Presser Co.)
European American Music Distributors Corp., 2480 Industrial Rd., Paoli, PA 19301
The Evangel Press (order from Art Masters Studios, Inc.)
Faber Music, Inc. 50 Cross St., Winchester, MA 01890
Carl Fischer, Inc., 62 Cooper Sq., New York, NY 10003
J. Fischer & Bros. (order from CPP/Belwin Music)
H.T. Fitzsimons Co., (order from Antara Music Group)
Harold Flammer, Inc. (order from Shawnee Press, Inc.)
Foreign Music Distributors, 13 Elkay Drive, Chester, NY 10918
Mark Foster Music Company, Box 4012, Champaign, IL 61820
Sam Fox Music Sales Corp. (order from Plymouth Music Corp., Inc.)
Frank Music Corp (order from Hal Leonard Publishing Corp.)
Galaxy Music Corporation (order from E.C. Schirmer Music Co.)
Galleria Press (order from Plymouth Music Co.)
Genesis III Music Corp. (order from Plymouth Music Co.)
Gentry Publications, (order from Intrada Music Group)
G.I.A. Publications, 7404 S. Mason Ave., Chicago, IL 60638
Glory-Sound (order from Shawnee Press, Inc.)
H. W. Gray Company, Inc. (order from CPP/Belwin Music)
Greystone Press (order from Plymouth Music Co.)
Hansen House, 1804 West Ave., Miami Beach, FL 33139
Harmonia (order from Foreign Music Distributors)
T.B. Harms Co. (order from Warner Brothers Publications)
The Frederick Harris Music Co., Ltd., 340 Nagel Dr., Buffalo, NY 14225-4731
Heritage Music Press (order from The Lorenz Corporation)
Heugel and Cie (order from Theodore Presser Co.)
Hinrichsen Edition (order from C. F. Peters Corp.)
Hinshaw Music, Inc., P.O. Box 470, Chapel Hill, NC 27514-0470
The Raymond A. Hoffman Co. (order from Intrada Music Group)

Charles W. Homeyer & Co. (order from Carl Fischer, Inc.)
Hope Publishing Co., 380 S. Main Place, Carol Stream, IL 60188
Intrada Music Group, P.O. Box 1240, Anderson, IN 46012
Ione Press (order from ECS Publishing)
Jenson Publications, Inc., 7777 W. Bluemound Rd., Milwaukee, WI 53213
Jerona Music Corp., P.O. Box 5010, Hackensack, NJ 07606-4210
Joclem Music Publishing (order from Boosey & Hawkes, Inc.)
Edwin F. Kalmus & Company, Inc., P.O. Box 5011, Boca Raton, FL 33433-8011
Kendor Music, Inc., P.O. Box 278, Delevan, NY 14042
E. C. Kerby, Ltd. (order from Hal Leonard Publishing Co.)
Neil A. Kjos Music Co., 4382 Jutland Dr., P.O. Box 178270, San Diego, CA 92117-0894
Laurel Press (order from The Lorenz Corp.)
Lawson-Gould Music Publishers, Inc., 250 W. 57th St., Suite 932, New York, NY 10107
Hal Leonard Publishing Corp., 7777 W. Bluemound Rd., Milwaukee, WI 53213
The Lorenz Corporation, 501 E. Third, St., Dayton, OH 45401
Malecki Music, Inc., 4500 Broadmoor, P.O. Box 150, Grand Rapids, MI 49501-0150
Manna Music, Inc., P.O. Box 218, Pacific City, OR 97135
Margun/Gunmar Music, Inc., 167 Dudley Rd., Newton Centre, MA 02159
Edward B. Marks Music Company (order from Hal Leonard Publishing Co.)
MCA Music Publishing, 1755 Broadway, 8th Floor, New York, NY 10019 (order from Hal Leonard Publishing Co.)
McLaughlin & Reilly Company (order from Warner Brothers Publications)
Mercury Music Corp. (order from Theodore Presser Co.)
Merion Music Corp. (order from Theodore Presser Co.)
Edwin H. Morris & Co., Inc. (order from Hal Leonard Publishing Corp.)
Music Press (order from Theodore Presser Co.)
Music Sales Corp., 225 Park Ave. South, New York, NY 10003
Music 70 Publishers, 170 N.E. 33rd St., Ft. Lauderdale, FL 33334
National Music Publishers, 1326 Santa Ana, P.O. Box 8279, Anaheim, CA 92802
Novello Publications (order from Theodore Presser Co.)
Orbiting Clef Productions, Inc., 108 Woodland Ave., Summit, NJ 07901
Orpheus Music Co. (order from Plymouth Music Co., Inc.)
Oxford University Press, 200 Madison Ave., New York, NY 10016
Paterson's Publications, Ltd., London (order from Carl Fischer, Inc.)
Paull Pioneer Publications (order from Shawnee Press, Inc.)
J. W. Pepper & Son, Inc., 2480 Industrial Blvd., Paoli, PA 19301
Performers' Editions (order from Broude Brothers, Ltd.)
C. F. Peters Corp., 373 Park Ave. South, New York, NY 10016
Plymouth Music Co., Inc., 170 NE 33rd St., P.O. Box 24330, Ft. Lauderdale, FL 33334
Theodore Presser Co., Presser Place, Bryn Mawr, PA 19010
Pro-Art Publications (order from CPP/Belwin Music)
Providence Press (order from Hope Publishing Co.)
G. Ricordi & Co. (order from Hal Leonard Publishing Corp.)
R. D. Row Music Co. (order from Carl Fischer, Inc.)
Sacred Music Press (order from The Lorenz Corp.)
Santa Barbara Music Publishing, 260 Loma Media, Santa Barbara, CA 93103
G. Schirmer, Inc., 225 Park Ave. South, New York, NY 10003
Arthur P. Schmidt Co. (order from Warner Brothers Publications)
Schmitt, Hall & McCreary (order from CPP/Belwin Music)
Schott & Company (order from European American Music Distributors Corp.)
The Shapiro, Bernstein Organization (order from Plymouth Music Co., Inc.)
Shawnee Press, Inc., Waring Drive, Delaware Water Gap, PA 18327-1099
Somerset Press (order from Hope Publishing Co.)
Southern Music Co., 1100 Broadway, P.O. Box 329, San Antonio, TX 78292-0300

Spratt Music Publishers (order from Plymouth Music Co., Inc.)
Staff Music Publishing Co., Inc. (order from Plymouth Music Co., Inc.)
Stainer & Bell, Ltd. (order from ECS Publishing)
Studio 4 (order from Alfred Publishing Co.)
Studio P/R, Inc. (order from CPP/Belwin Music)
Summa Productions (order from Art Masters Studio, Inc.)
Summy-Birchard Co. (order from Warner Brothers Publications, Inc.)
Tabernacle Publishing Co. (order from Shawnee Press, Inc.)
Templeton Publications (order from Shawnee Press, Inc.)
Tetra/Continuo Music Group (order from Plymouth Music Co., Inc.)
Gordon V. Thompson Music, 29 Birch Ave., Toronto, Ontario, Canada M4V IE2 (order from Oxford University Press)
Transcontinental Music Publications, 838 Fifth Ave., New York, NY 10021-7046
Triune Music, Inc. (order from The Lorenz Corp.)
TRO, 11 W. 19th St., New York, NY 10011
Tuskegee Music Press (order from Neil A. Kjos Music Co.)
UNC Jazz Press, College of Performing and Visual Arts, School of Music, Jazz Studies Division, University of Northern Colorado, Greeley, CO 80639
Universal Edition (order from European American Music Distributors Corp.)
Walton Music Corp. (order from Plymouth Music Co., Inc.)
Warner Bros. Publications, 265 Secaucus Rd., Secaucus, NJ 07096-2037
Joseph Weinberger, Ltd., London (order from Boosey & Hawkes, Inc.)
Williamson Music Co., 598 Madison Ave., New York, NY 10019
Willis Music Co., 7380 Industrial Rd., Florence, KY 41042
Word Music, Inc., 5221 No. O'Conner Blvd., Suite 1000, Irving, TX 75039
The Zondervan Music Group, 365 Great Circle Rd., Nashville, TN 37228

Appendix F

Cover Letter to Prospective Employer

300 Elm Street
Smithville, N.Y.
January 4, 1995

Dr. Jerry Roland
Assistant Superintendent for Personnel
Jonesburg School District
Jonesburg, N.Y.

Dear Dr. Roland:

I am writing to you concerning employment in your district as a choral/vocal music teacher. I will receive my bachelor of music education degree from the University of Smithville in May 1995, and will be certified by the state of New York to teach choral/vocal music, grades K-12.

While a student at the University, I have been active in the University Singers, the Madrigal Ensemble, and served as treasurer of our student chapter of the Music Educators National Conference. I have enclosed a copy of my professional résumé outlining my background, experience, and interests.

Please send me an application for employment in your district. I have requested that my credentials file, including transcripts and letter of reference, be sent to you from the University, and I would be happy to supply any additional information you require. I would welcome the opportunity to speak to you concerning choral music education positions available in your district for the fall semester.

Thank you for your consideration of this request.

Sincerely,

Susan E. Burke

Acknowledgments

"Every Valley" by John Ness Beck: Copyright 1976 by Beckenhorst Press. Used by permission.

"No. 7 Lacrymosa" from Mozart's *Requiem:* Used by kind permission of C. F. Peters Corporation.

Opening measures and "Credo" from Beethoven's *Mass in C Major;* "Jesus, I Will Ponder Now" by J. S. Bach; "O Sacred Head, Now Wounded" by J. S. Bach; "All Glory Be to God on High" by J. S. Bach: Reprinted by permission of CPP/BELWIN, INC., Miami, FL. All Rights Reserved. Used by Permission.

"All I Ask of You" from *The Phantom of the Opera:* Music by Andrew Lloyd Webber. Lyrics by Charles Hart and Richard Stilgoe. Copyright © 1986 The Really Useful Group Ltd. All Rights for the United States and Canada administrered by PolyGram International Publishing, Inc. International Copyright Secured. All Rights Reserved.

"Four Chorales from 'Saint Paul'" by F. Mendelssohn: Adapted by Dale W. Barker. Copyright © 1962 (Renewed) G. Schirmer, Inc. (ASCAP). International Copyright Secured. All Rights Reserved. Reprinted by Permission.

"Zigueunerleben" by R. Schumann: Copyright 1968 by Lawson-Gould Music Publishers, Inc. Used by permission.

"Crawdad Hole," arranged by Mary Goetze: © Copyright 1985 by Boosey & Hawkes, Inc. Used by permission.

"Still, Still, Still," arranged by Norman Luboff: Copyright 1958–1960, Walton Music Corporation. Used by permission.

"No Mark" from FOUR PASTORALES by Cecil Effinger: Copyright © 1964 (Renewed). G. Schirmer, Inc. (ASCAP). International Copyright Secured. All Rights Reserved. Reprinted by Permission.

"O Magnum Mysterium" by Tomás Luis de Victoria, edited by Alice Parker and Robert Shaw: Copyright © 1953 (Renewed) G. Schirmer, Inc. (ASCAP). International Copyright Secured. All Rights Reserved. Reprinted by Permission.

"Two Chorales from the Christmas Oratorio, 'Break Forth O Beauteous Heavenly Light,'" arranged by J. S. Bach, edited by Carl Deir: Copyright © 1935 (Renewed) G. Schirmer, Inc. (ASCAP). International Copyright Secured. All Rights Reserved. Reprinted by Permission.

"It Is Good to Give Thanks" by Kirke Mechem: Used by permission of Carl Fischer, Inc.

"O Eyes of My Beloved" by Orlando Di Lasso: Copyright 1936, renewed 1958, E. C. Schirmer Music Company. Used by permission.

Gloria by Vivaldi: Copyright 1961 by Walton Music Corporation. Used by permission.

"Praise to God" by Knut Nystedt: Copyright © 1968 by Associated Music Publishers, Inc. (BMI). International copyright secured. All rights reserved. Reprinted by permission.

"Antiphora de Morte" by Barne Slögedal: Copyright 1969, Walton Music Corporation. Used by permission.

"The Sixty-Seventh Psalm" by Charles E. Ives: Copyright © 1939 (renewed) by Associated Music Publishers, Inc. (BMI). International copyright secured.

Saul by Egil Hovland: Copyright 1972, Walton Music Corporation. Used by permission.

Index

T